Artificial Intelligence and Internet of Things in Smart Farming

This book provides a broad overview of the areas of artificial intelligence (AI) that can be used for smart farming applications, through either successful engineering or ground-breaking research. Among them, the highlighted tactics are soil management, water management, crop management, livestock management, harvesting, and the integration of Internet of Things (IoT) in smart farming.

Artificial Intelligence and Internet of Things in Smart Farming explores different types of smart farming systems for achieving sustainability goals in the real environment. The authors discuss the benefits of smart harvesting systems over traditional harvesting methods, including decreased labor requirements, increased crop yields, increased probabilities of successful harvests, enhanced visibility into crop health, and lower overall harvest and production costs. It explains and describes big data in terms of its potential five dimensions—volume, velocity, variety, veracity, and valuation—within the framework of smart farming. The authors also discuss the recent IoT technologies, such as fifth-generation networks, blockchain, and digital twining, to improve the sustainability and productivity of smart farming systems. The book identifies numerous issues that call for conceptual innovation and has the potential to progress machine learning (ML), resulting in significant impacts. As an illustration, the authors point out how smart farming offers an intriguing field for interpretable ML. The book then delves into the function of AI techniques, such as AI in accelerating the development of nano-enabled agriculture, thereby facilitating safe-by-design nanomaterials for various consumer products and medical applications.

This book is for undergraduate students, graduate students, researchers, and AI engineers who pursue a strong understanding of the practical methods of machine learning in the agriculture domain. Practitioners and stakeholders would be able to follow this book to understand the potential of ML in their farming projects and agricultural solutions.

Features:

- Explores different types of smart farming systems for achieving sustainability goals in the real environment
- Explores ML-based analytics such as generative adversarial networks (GAN), autoencoders, computational imaging, and quantum computing
- Examines the development of intelligent machines to provide solutions to real-world problems, emphasizing smart farming applications, which are not modeled or are extremely difficult to model mathematically
- Emphasizes methods for better managing crops, soils, water, and livestock, urging investors and businesspeople to occupy the existing vacant market area
- Discusses AI-empowered nanotechnology for smart farming

Artificial Intelligence and Internet of Things in Smart Farming

Mohamed Abdel-Basset, Hossam Hawash, and Laila Abdel-Fatah

CRC Press
Taylor & Francis Group
Boca Raton London New York

CRC Press is an imprint of the
Taylor & Francis Group, an **informa** business

Designed cover image: Shutterstock

First edition published 2024
by CRC Press
2385 NW Executive Center Drive, Suite 320, Boca Raton FL 33431

and by CRC Press
4 Park Square, Milton Park, Abingdon, Oxon, OX14 4RN

CRC Press is an imprint of Taylor & Francis Group, LLC

© 2024 Taylor & Francis Group, LLC

ISBN: 9781032502557 (hbk)
ISBN: 9781032508764 (pbk)
ISBN: 9781003400103 (ebk)

DOI: 10.1201/9781003400103

Typeset in Times New Roman
by Apex CoVantage, LLC

Contents

About the Authors

Dr. Mohamed Abdel-Basset is an IEEE Senior Member. He received his B.Sc., M.Sc., and Ph.D. degrees in operations research from the Faculty of Computers and Informatics, Zagazig University, Egypt. He is currently an associate professor, Head of Department of Computer Science with the Faculty of Computers and Informatics, Zagazig University. He has published more than 400 articles in international journals and conference proceedings. He is working on the application of multi-objective and robust metaheuristic optimization techniques. His current research interests include optimization, machine learning, deep learning, artificial intelligence, operations research, data mining, computational intelligence, applied statistics, decision support systems, robust optimization, engineering optimization, multi-objective optimization, swarm intelligence, evolutionary algorithms, and artificial neural networks.

Dr. Hossam Hawash is a senior researcher with the Faculty of Computers and Informatics, Department of Computer Science, Zagazig University, Egypt. He obtained his B.Sc., M.Sc., and Ph.D. degrees in computer science in 2016, 2020, and 2023, respectively, from the Faculty of Computers and Informatics, Department of Computer Science, Zagazig University. His area of interest includes computation intelligence, optimization, machine learning, deep learning, artificial intelligence, fuzzy learning, explainable artificial intelligence, and the Internet of Things.

Dr. Laila Abdel-Fatah received her B.S., M.Sc., and Ph.D. degrees in information systems and decision support from the Faculty of Computers and Informatics, Zagazig University, Egypt. She is currently a lecturer with the Faculty of Computers and Informatics, Department of Computer Science, Zagazig University. Her research interests include computation intelligence, fuzzy logic, artificial intelligence, the Internet of Things, metaheuristic algorithms, geographic information systems, and spatial optimization.

Preface

Welcome to the world of smart farming! This book is an inclusive exploration of the revolutionary concept of smart farming, which involves the convergence of cutting-edge technologies and agricultural practices to transform traditional farming into a more efficient, sustainable, and data-driven approach. With the global population steadily increasing and environmental challenges becoming more pronounced, smart farming offers a promising solution to meet the growing demand for food while minimizing resource consumption and environmental impact.

Chapter by chapter, we will go aboard on a journey of exploration, uncovering the challenges faced by traditional farming practices and the transformative solutions that smart farming offers. From the introduction to the concept of smart farming and its related technologies to the integration of artificial intelligence, machine learning, and the Internet of Things in agriculture, we will navigate through the diverse landscape of modern agricultural innovation.

In Chapter 1, "Introduction to Smart Farming," we lay the foundation by discussing the limitations of traditional farming, from resource-intensive practices to economic pressures and climate vulnerability. We then define smart farming and explore the technologies that make it possible, such as artificial intelligence, big data, and blockchain.

Chapter 2, "Big Data in Smart Farming," takes a closer look at how big data is transforming agriculture. We explore different types of smart farming data, the dimensions of big data, and its applications across various farming practices.

Moving forward, Chapter 3, "Conceptualization of Machine Learning for Smart Farming," introduces machine learning (ML) as a critical tool in modern agriculture. We classify different types of ML algorithms and discuss their applications in optimizing crop yield, detecting diseases, and automating various farming processes.

Chapter 4, "From Field to Database: Sensors, Data Collection, and Efficient Management in Smart Farming," delves into the world of agricultural sensors. We explore the wide array of sensor types and their applications in monitoring soil health, plant conditions, water quality, and livestock behavior. Additionally, we discuss how data from these sensors are collected, managed, and processed to drive informed decisions in smart farming.

In Chapter 5, "Maximizing Yield, Minimizing Water: Machine Intelligence for Precision Irrigation and Water Management," we focus on the crucial aspect of water management in agriculture. We explore how evapotranspiration modeling, precision irrigation systems, and AI analytics help optimize water usage and increase crop yield.

Chapter 6, "Innovations in Livestock Monitoring: A Machine Learning Journey," highlights the advancements in livestock monitoring using ML techniques. We discuss how data collection and predictive analytics enhance livestock health, productivity, and welfare.

Chapter 7, "Enhancing Crop Health with Machine Learning: Disease and Weed Identification Strategies," showcases the potential of machine learning in disease and weed detection, leading to better crop management and increased agricultural productivity.

Chapter 8, "Automated Harvesting and Robotics in Agriculture," explores the exciting world of automated harvesting and robotics in agriculture. We discuss how machine learning and robotics play an essential role in revolutionizing harvesting processes.

In Chapter 9, "The Convergence of AI and IoT in Smart Farming," we explore the powerful synergy between artificial intelligence and the Internet of Things in agriculture. The chapter discusses how this convergence enhances automation, data analytics, and decision-making in farming.

Lastly, Chapter 10, "Toward Agriculture 5.0: The Convergence of Machine Learning and Nanotechnology for Next-Generation Farming," ventures into the realm of nanotechnology in smart farming. We explore the applications of nanomaterials, nanosensors, and nanobots, along with the integration of machine learning to improve agricultural practices.

This book aims to serve as a comprehensive resource for agricultural enthusiasts, researchers, students, and professionals eager to explore the limitless possibilities of smart farming. Through its comprehensive content, real-world case studies, and futuristic visions, readers will gain valuable insights into the transformative power of technology in shaping the future of agriculture.

As you journey through the pages of this book, we hope you'll be captivated by the possibilities that smart farming holds and encouraged to join the movement toward a more sustainable, productive, and technology-driven agricultural future. Happy reading and welcome to the era of smart farming!

1 Introduction to Smart Farming

1.1 INTRODUCTION

Since ancient times, agriculture has played a crucial role in human history and continues to do so today. Domesticating animals and plants a few thousand years ago and implementing crop rotations and other advances in farming practices just a few hundred years ago are just two examples of the many changes that have occurred there during this time. Human-made fertilizers and pesticides were the last innovation a few decades ago. These days, a new paradigm in farming has emerged thanks to information communication technology (ICT) services; it's called "smart farming," and it's transforming the agricultural industry. Smart farming aims to maximize output while simultaneously enhancing quality and decreasing production costs. To this end, this chapter introduces smart farming as a field of agriculture that promises to bring revolution in food management and production. The discussion describes how smart farming evolved from precision agriculture. It explores different types of smart farming systems for achieving sustainability goals in the real environment.

1.2 TRADITIONAL FARMING PRELIMINARIES

The agricultural landscape has undergone a profound evolution over centuries, rooted in the practices of traditional farming that have sustained humanity for generations. However, in recent times, a paradigmatic shift has emerged—a transition from conventional methodologies toward a dynamic and technology-infused approach known as smart farming. This shift signifies a pivotal moment in agricultural history, where the fusion of advanced technologies, particularly Artificial Intelligence (AI) and the Internet of Things (IoT), has redefined the possibilities within the agricultural sector. Traditional farming methods, characterized by manual labor, limited data-driven decision-making, and conventional resource-intensive practices, face unprecedented challenges due to climate variability, diminishing resources, and growing global food demand. In response, the integration of AI and IoT has ushered in an era of smart farming, offering innovative solutions that optimize resource usage, enhance productivity, and promote sustainability. This transformative journey from traditional farming to smart farming marks not just a technological advancement but a fundamental revolution in how we cultivate the land and feed the world.

The term "farming" system can be defined as follows (Groot et al., 2012; Behera and France, 2016; Dignac et al., 2017):

Definition I: *The act or practice of cultivating food plants, sowing seeds, and working the soil.*

DOI: 10.1201/9781003400103-1

1

Definition II: *An interconnected system involving soil, plants, animals, tools, energy, labor, capital, and other inputs, partly under the control of farming families, is subject to diverse influences, including political, economic, institutional, and social factors operating on multiple levels.*
Definition III: *A group of agro-economic activities that take place in a specific agrarian area and are linked to one another.*

Farming is done to enhance soil physical conditions, allow for better root development and hence tree anchoring, increase root access to soil nutrients and moisture, and improve planting quality. In addition, it eliminates competing weeds, enhancing moisture and nutrient availability to planted seedlings, and creates a surface over which pesticides may be sprayed efficiently. It is critical to find the best approach for ground preparation in each given field condition. A cost-effectiveness balance must be established; on some sites, such as those with extensive weed infestation, it will be economically impossible to create plantations due to the high expenses of eradicating these types of weeds. Furthermore, improper cultivation may contribute to erosion (Bogale, 2020). Farmers should be aware that if heavy labor is necessary, preparatory equipment might be extremely particular; in such cases, great attention must be paid to limit erosion. Farming might not be suitable for areas experiencing extremely high rainfall, especially for soils that are moderately to highly eroded and have a slope exceeding 15%. Also, it is necessary to cultivate the soil when it is friable, which is when it is dry enough to crumble from cultivation but not so dry that it pulverizes. Without inverting the soil profile, the dirt should only be elevated high enough to induce fracture and then quickly lowered again. The usual method of soil cultivation is disking.

Moreover, farming and plant care methods vary according to the type of crop to be produced. In other words, from germination through seed production, each plant passes through a succession of phases. The entire time of all of these phases, referred to as the life cycle, differs among plants (Fedele et al., 2014; Perronne et al., 2017; Prasad et al., 2020). So, what are these varieties of crops based on their life cycles? There are three kinds: annuals, biennials, and perennials (see Figure 1.1). Plants that are annual or seasonal have a year-long life cycle. Crops of the annual variety must be transplanted every season since only dormant seeds may transfer from one generation to the next such as tomatoes, eggplant, peas, beans, sunflowers, and cereals. Flowering plants known as biennials have a two-year biological life cycle (two growing seasons). The plant develops vegetative organs like leaves, stems, and roots throughout the first year. The plant then goes into a resting phase and spends the cold season overwintering underground. During the second growth season, the plant extends its stem, develops flowers and seeds, and ripens them before it dies. Carrots, onions, cabbage, and parsley are examples of biennial crops. Plants known as perennials can survive for more than two growth seasons. Every season, this variety typically produces new herbaceous parts from the same root system. Trees and bushes including pears, apples, peaches, and nuts (such as walnuts, almonds, and hazelnuts) are examples of perennials. Some ground coverings and herbaceous blooming plants fall within the perennial category as well.

FIGURE 1.1   Example of Crops with Different Life Cycles.

As previously mentioned, farming is a complicated process that includes interoperability between different ecosystems. Therefore, using traditional farming methods can lead to enormous losses. Moreover, Climate changes are amplifying the necessity for more sophisticated farming methods capable of effectively managing and adapting to rapid and successive changes in weather patterns. This necessity has given rise to the term "Smart Farming." Traditional farming suffers from numerous challenges that are subject to ongoing debate and discussion. These challenges encompass a wide range of issues, including environmental concerns such as land degradation, loss of biodiversity, and water scarcity. Additionally, economic pressures, market volatility, and labor shortages pose significant obstacles for farmers striving to maintain profitability and sustainability. The reliance on conventional practices without data-driven insights limits the optimization of resources and reduces the resilience of agricultural systems in the face of changing climates and evolving market dynamics. Moreover, the social dimension of traditional farming raises questions about food security, rural livelihoods, and the equitable distribution of resources and opportunities. As agriculture remains a critical component of global food production, the exploration of these challenges sparks essential conversations about the need for innovative solutions, such as smart farming with machine learning (ML) applications, to ensure a more efficient, sustainable, and resilient agricultural future.

1.2.1   Resource-Intensive Practices

Conventional farming often relies heavily on resource-intensive practices that can lead to significant environmental impacts. Large-scale monoculture, where a single crop is cultivated over extensive areas, can deplete soil nutrients and increase vulnerability to pests and diseases. Excessive water usage, often through inefficient irrigation methods, can strain local water sources, leading to water scarcity and environmental degradation. Moreover, the reliance on chemical fertilizers and pesticides can result in soil degradation, water pollution, and harm to nontarget organisms.

1.2.2 Climate Vulnerability and Uncertainty

Conventional farming practices are susceptible to the unpredictable effects of climate change. Farmers face increasingly erratic weather patterns, extreme events like droughts and floods, and shifts in growing seasons. These climate uncertainties make it challenging to plan and optimize crop production. Crop losses due to unexpected weather events can have severe economic repercussions for farmers, impacting food availability and pricing for consumers.

1.2.3 High Labor Dependency

Traditional farming often demands substantial manual labor for activities such as planting, weeding, and harvesting. As rural populations migrate to urban areas, finding a sufficient workforce for labor-intensive tasks becomes increasingly difficult. Labor shortages can lead to delayed operations and, in some cases, crop losses. Moreover, the physical demands of traditional farming can discourage young people from pursuing agriculture as a career, further exacerbating the labor shortage issue.

1.2.4 Limited Data-Driven Decision-Making

Conventional farming practices traditionally rely on intuition, experience, and local knowledge for decision-making. While this expertise is valuable, the lack of access to real-time data and analytics limits the potential for optimizing farming practices. Farmers may not have sufficient information on soil health, weather patterns, or pest occurrences, which hampers their ability to implement precision agriculture techniques. Without data-driven insights, it becomes challenging to identify areas for improvement and make informed choices to enhance productivity and sustainability.

1.2.5 Economic Pressures and Market Volatility

Conventional farmers face economic pressures driven by factors such as fluctuating market prices, rising input costs, and international trade dynamics. Global market volatility can lead to unpredictable revenues, making it challenging for farmers to plan and invest in their operations effectively. Additionally, subsidies and government policies can influence market conditions, affecting the profitability and sustainability of conventional farming practices. The lack of economic stability can discourage farmers from adopting innovative and sustainable farming methods.

1.2.6 Land Degradation and Loss of Biodiversity

Conventional farming practices often contribute to land degradation and a loss of biodiversity. The expansion of agricultural land to meet growing food demands has led to deforestation and habitat destruction. Clearing natural ecosystems for cultivation disrupts ecological balance, resulting in the loss of plant and animal species. Moreover, continuous monoculture and intensive farming can deplete soil nutrients, leading to soil erosion and reduced fertility. This degradation reduces the land's long-term productivity and resilience, posing a significant challenge to sustainable agricultural practice.

As biodiversity declines, natural pest control mechanisms weaken, leading to increased reliance on chemical pesticides. This dependency further contributes to environmental harm and poses health risks to farmers and consumers. To address these challenges, smart farming practices aim to promote agroecological approaches that incorporate biodiversity conservation, crop diversification, and regenerative farming techniques. By restoring ecological balance, farmers can enhance ecosystem services, improve soil health, and reduce their ecological footprint.

1.2.7 Lack of Access to Modern Agricultural Knowledge and Technology

In many regions, conventional farmers face limited access to modern agricultural knowledge, technology, and resources. This lack of access hampers their ability to adopt innovative practices and make informed decisions. Traditional farming communities often lack infrastructure for data collection and dissemination, limiting their exposure to weather forecasts, market information, and agronomic insights. Additionally, financial constraints can hinder farmers' capacity to invest in technology and tools that could optimize their operations. Bridging the digital divide and providing training and resources to farmers is crucial to overcome this challenge. Initiatives such as agricultural extension programs, knowledge-sharing platforms, and government support can empower farmers with the necessary information and tools to improve productivity and resilience. Moreover, partnerships between private companies and local communities can facilitate the introduction of affordable and accessible technologies, empowering farmers to transition toward smarter and more sustainable farming practices.

1.2.8 Long-Term Sustainability and Climate Resilience

Conventional farming practices often prioritize short-term gains over long-term sustainability and climate resilience. Overreliance on chemical inputs and intensive farming may generate higher yields initially, but it can lead to soil degradation and reduced ecosystem health over time. Unsustainable water usage practices can deplete groundwater reserves and exacerbate water scarcity in the long run. Additionally, the carbon footprint of conventional agriculture contributes to climate change, as greenhouse gas emissions from agricultural activities continue to rise.

To ensure long-term sustainability and climate resilience, there is a pressing need to adopt climate-smart agricultural practices. These practices encompass a range of strategies, including sustainable water management, agroforestry, conservation agriculture, and renewable energy integration. By embracing sustainable and climate-resilient approaches, farmers can mitigate the impacts of climate change, reduce resource depletion, and contribute to global efforts to combat environmental challenges.

1.3   PRINCIPLES OF SMART FARMING

The history of agriculture dates back thousands of years, with early human societies engaging in primitive farming practices to cultivate crops and domesticate animals. In the Neolithic period around 10,000 BCE, the Agrarian Revolution marked a significant turning point as communities transitioned from a nomadic, hunter-gatherer lifestyle to settled agricultural societies. During this period, humans began cultivating crops such as wheat, barley, rice, and maize, which led to the development of permanent settlements. Simple tools like wooden plows and handheld sickles were used to till the soil and harvest crops, laying the foundation for subsistence farming.

Throughout history, technological innovations played a crucial role in transforming farming practices and increasing agricultural productivity. In ancient civilizations like Egypt, the introduction of irrigation systems, such as the shaduf and qanats, facilitated controlled water supply for agriculture. The use of animal-drawn plows and the harnessing of draft animals improved efficiency in planting and cultivation during the Middle Ages. However, one of the most significant advancements came in the mid-twentieth century with the Green Revolution. Innovations in plant breeding, fertilizers, and pesticides, along with the adoption of high-yield crop varieties, dramatically increased crop production and averted widespread famine in developing countries.

The late nineteenth and early twentieth centuries witnessed the mechanization and industrialization of agriculture. The development of steam-powered and later gasoline-powered tractors revolutionized land preparation, reducing the labor required and increasing the scale of farming operations. Other agricultural machinery, such as combined harvesters and threshers, further mechanized harvesting and postharvest processes. The advent of refrigeration and transportation systems allowed for long-distance distribution of perishable goods, enabling the emergence of commercial agriculture and global trade in food products. These advancements led to substantial increases in agricultural efficiency but also raised concerns about environmental impact, such as soil degradation and water pollution from increased chemical use.

In the latter part of the twentieth century and into the twenty-first century, the Digital Age brought forth a new era in agriculture: precision farming. The convergence of computer technology, data analytics, and GPS technology revolutionized farming practices once again. Precision agriculture, also known as smart farming, utilizes a network of sensors, drones, and satellite imagery to monitor and manage crops with unprecedented accuracy. Farmers can collect real-time data on soil moisture, temperature, and nutrient levels, allowing for precise application of water and fertilizers. ML algorithms analyze vast datasets to optimize planting, detect diseases early, and forecast yields more accurately. By reducing resource wastage and environmental impact, precision agriculture aims to address the challenges of sustainable food production and adapt to the changing climate. As technology continues to evolve, the integration of artificial intelligence (AI), robotics, and automated systems is paving the way for even more efficient and sustainable farming practices in the future.

Technological advancements are altering the farming industry. Precision farming, digital farming, and smart farming have emerged because of agricultural modernization and the use of digital technologies. Despite the fact that these terms are frequently used interchangeably, they have a small distinction in connotation. Precision farming can be seen as an agricultural management strategy that uses technology to monitor, gauge, and assess the requirements of specific fields and crops. The cornerstone of digital farming is derived from the creation of value from data. Digital farming entails going beyond the availability of data to get actionable insight and substantial added value from it. It is possible to think of smart farming as the development of precision and digital agriculture. All farm processes are included in smart farming, not just specific machinery. In contrast to precision farming, the emphasis in smart farming is not on exact measurement or identifying variations within a field or between specific crops. The prominence is more on data application and access, specifically how to make wise use of the information that has been gathered.

As mentioned before, smart farming could be a new lever to promote other common or rising trends in agricultural exploitations, rather than only massive, traditional farming exploitations (Moysiadis et al., 2021). In other words, smart farming can be considered a strategy for transforming and reorienting agricultural systems to promote development and food security efficiently and sustainably in the face of climate change (also, it can be referred to as "climate-smart agriculture"). Moreover, it can determine which production systems and supporting institutions are best suited to address the challenges of climate change for particular locations, to maintain and improve agriculture's capacity to support food security in a sustainable manner. Besides handling various conditions in climate changes, smart farming is expected to boost productivity, cut costs by decreasing inputs such as fuel, fertilizer, and pesticides, reduce labor efforts, and eventually improve the quality of the completed goods. As a consequence, the term "smart farming" can be defined as follows (Mohamed, 2023; Said et al., 2021):

Definition I: *A new expression in the farming sector, trying to shift the existing approaches to creative solutions based on ICTs.*
   Definition II: *A new concept that refers to cultivation practices with the use of advanced technology.*
   Definition III: *The use of information and data technology to optimize complicated farming operations.*

In particular, crop rotation, the management of nutritional deficiencies in crops, the management of pests and diseases, recycling, and water harvesting are the fundamental achievements of smart farming in terms of sustainable agriculture, all of which contribute to a safer environment overall (Bacco et al., 2019). Living things rely on biodiversity, yet they are also polluted by waste emissions, pesticide and fertilizer use, decaying dead plants, and so on. Because the release of greenhouse gases has an impact on humans, animals, plants, and the ecosystem, it is necessary to improve the environment for life.

Regrettably, not all regions of the earth's surface are appropriate for agriculture due to a variety of constraints such as soil quality, topography, temperature, climate, and the fact that most significant cultivable areas are not homogeneous. Furthermore, current farmed land is divided due to political and budgetary factors, as well as rising urbanization, which continually puts a strain on arable land supply. Total agricultural acreage utilized for food production has recently decreased. Moreover, each agricultural field has various important properties, such as soil type, irrigation flow, nutrient presence, and insect resistance, which are all measured independently in terms of quality and quantity for a given crop. Crop rotation and an annual crop growth development cycle require both geographical and temporal changes to optimize crop yield in the same land. Most of the time, a single crop experiences changes in features, or the same crop is cultivated throughout the whole farm and necessitates site-specific analysis for optimal yield production (Kujawa et al., 2022). To overcome these many difficulties and produce more with less land, new smart techniques are required.

1.4   SMART FARMING TECHNOLOGIES

The term "smart farming" refers to a variety of techniques and mechanisms used to maximize agricultural activities. In other words, it is a revolutionary concept that refers to farm management that uses technology such as the Internet of Things (IoT), robots, drones, and AI to raise the number and quality of goods while optimizing the amount of human labor necessary for production (Lytos et al., 2020). The raising of these technologies is now available not only to major corporations but also to tiny home farms. It enables farms to maximize productivity and compete with larger agribusinesses. Because smart agriculture practices provide clear advantages for businesses over traditional ways, it is worth delving more into the elements of this strategy (Charania and Li, 2020). This is a management concept centered on providing the agricultural business with the infrastructure necessary to harness new technologies for tracking, monitoring, automating, and analyzing processes.

1.4.1   SMART FARMING CYCLE

The smart farming cycle represents a systematic and iterative approach to modern agriculture, where technology and data-driven insights converge to optimize farming practices. This cyclical process involves several interconnected steps, each contributing to the overall efficiency and sustainability of agricultural operations. Comprising our interconnected steps—observation, diagnostics, decisions, and action—the original cycle empowers farmers to make informed choices and take targeted actions to improve their agricultural operations (see Figure 1.2).

By embracing this innovative approach, farmers can improve crop yields, optimize resource usage, reduce waste, and enhance overall farm performance (Triantafyllou et al., 2019). The smart farming cycle holds immense importance in addressing the challenges of feeding a growing global population, promoting sustainable land management, and mitigating the impact of climate change on agriculture. As technology and data analytics continue to advance, the smart farming cycle evolves and remains at the forefront of agricultural innovation, fostering a future where smart, efficient, and sustainable farming practices play a central role in meeting the world's food demands. In the following sections, we provide detailed steps for a fine-grained smart farming cycle.

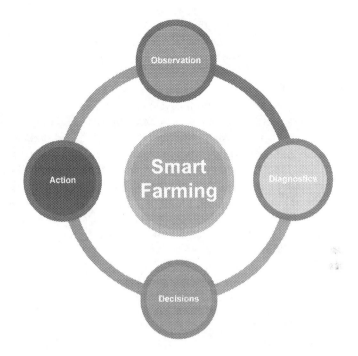

FIGURE 1.2 Cycle of Smart Farming.

1.4.1.1 Observation

The observation step is the foundation of the smart farming cycle, encompassing the systematic collection of data to gain insights into various aspects of the farm environment. This critical phase involves the deployment of cutting-edge sensing technologies and data-gathering techniques. Farmers employ a diverse array of tools, including IoT sensors, drones, satellites, weather stations, and on-field data collection devices, to monitor essential parameters such as soil moisture, temperature, humidity, weather conditions, crop health, and pest infestations. These sensing technologies offer real-time and granular data, enabling farmers to monitor the farm's conditions with unprecedented precision. Soil moisture sensors, for example, provide continuous readings of moisture levels, helping farmers make informed decisions about irrigation scheduling and water usage. Drones equipped with high-resolution cameras capture aerial images of the entire farm, facilitating crop health assessments and detecting early signs of disease or stress. Satellite imagery provides broader-scale data, allowing farmers to assess large agricultural areas and analyze crop performance on a regional scale (Bacco et al., 2018).

The observation step is not limited to physical data collection; it also includes data generated from digital sources, such as agricultural databases and historical records. Integrating this diverse dataset is vital for a comprehensive understanding of the farm's status and potential challenges. The observation step serves as the informational backbone that feeds into subsequent stages of the smart farming cycle, enabling precise diagnostics, data-driven decisions, and targeted actions for optimal farm management. By leveraging these advanced sensing technologies, farmers can enhance their knowledge of the farm environment, making informed choices to improve resource efficiency, crop productivity, and overall sustainability.

1.4.1.2 Diagnostics

The diagnostics step in the smart farming cycle is a critical phase that involves data analysis and insight generation based on the observations made during the data collection stage. In this step, the collected data, which includes information on soil health, crop conditions, weather patterns, and other relevant parameters, are processed and analyzed using advanced data analytics and ML techniques. Through data analysis, farmers gain a deeper understanding of the current state of their agricultural operations, enabling them to diagnose potential challenges and opportunities. Data analysis involves various statistical and computational methods to extract valuable insights from the large and diverse datasets collected from multiple sources. Descriptive analytics allows farmers to summarize and visualize the data, providing a clear overview of the farm's conditions and trends. For instance, farmers can create graphical representations of soil moisture levels over time, helping them observe variations and identify potential areas of concern. Diagnostic analytics delves deeper into the data to identify patterns, correlations, and potential causes for specific issues. ML algorithms come into play during diagnostic analytics, helping to uncover complex relationships between different variables and predict future outcomes.

Every smart agricultural system should include data analytics. If you can't make sense of the data you've acquired, it's useless. To acquire relevant insights from the obtained data, you must have sophisticated data analytics skills and use prediction algorithms and ML, that is, the sensor results are sent to customized software solutions for certain farm types or use case-independent platforms. The insight generation in the diagnostics step is crucial for identifying potential problems affecting the farm's productivity and sustainability. For example, data analysis might reveal instances of nutrient deficiencies, pest infestations, or adverse weather conditions that could negatively impact crop health. By understanding these factors, farmers can make informed decisions about the most appropriate measures to address the challenges identified. The diagnostics step, with its data-driven insights, serves as the basis for informed decision-making in subsequent stages of the smart farming cycle, enabling farmers to optimize their strategies and enhance overall farm performance. In the diagnostics step of the smart farming cycle, predictive and prescriptive analytics play key roles in guiding farmers toward data-driven decision-making. Predictive analytics leverages historical data and ML algorithms to forecast future outcomes and potential events. For instance, based on historical weather data and crop growth patterns, predictive analytics can forecast the expected yield for a specific crop during the current growing season. These predictions help farmers anticipate challenges and adjust their plans accordingly.

Prescriptive analytics takes the analysis one step further by providing actionable recommendations based on the insights generated. It goes beyond predicting what might happen and suggests the best course of action to achieve desired outcomes. For instance, prescriptive analytics might recommend precise irrigation schedules or customized fertilizer application rates based on soil nutrient levels and weather forecasts. By incorporating prescriptive insights, farmers can optimize their resource usage, reduce waste, and improve overall farm efficiency. The combination of predictive and prescriptive analytics in the diagnostics step empowers farmers with the knowledge to make proactive and data-driven decisions. Instead of relying on reactive measures when issues arise, farmers can adopt proactive strategies that prevent problems before they occur. These analytics-driven decisions are essential for smart and sustainable farming practices, as they enable farmers to adapt to changing conditions, mitigate risks, and optimize their agricultural processes for better outcomes. The diagnostics step serves as the bridge between data observation and informed decision-making, leading the way for the subsequent stages of the smart farming cycle, such as making precise decisions and taking targeted actions to optimize farming operations. Moreover, it can be sent to a cloud-hosted platform that has predefined decision rules and models, often known as "business logic," that determine the status of the studied device and highlight any inadequacies or needs.

1.4.1.3   Decisions

The decisions step in the smart farming cycle is a pivotal phase where farmers utilize the valuable insights generated during the diagnostics stage to make informed and data-driven decisions. Armed with data analysis and predictive/prescriptive insights, farmers can evaluate various options and strategies to optimize their agricultural practices. Data-driven decision-making enables farmers to move beyond traditional intuition-based approaches and consider precise and targeted actions that align with specific farm conditions and objectives. The user- and/or ML -driven components of the platform analyze issues to decide whether location-specific care is required and, if so, which type. During this step, farmers evaluate a range of factors, such as soil health, crop growth trends, weather forecasts, market conditions, and resource availability, to devise well-informed strategies. For example, based on predictive analytics, farmers can anticipate water stress periods and allocate irrigation resources efficiently to maintain optimal soil moisture levels. They can also optimize the timing and application of fertilizers based on the crop's nutrient requirements, reducing excess usage and potential environmental impacts. Additionally, data-driven decisions can aid in crop selection, allowing farmers to choose the most suitable varieties based on their performance in specific environmental conditions. Utilizing ML or self-learning technology, it is possible to anticipate the climate, features of the soil and water, carbon content, the spread of diseases and pests, and other variables.

The decisions step involves considering both short-term and long-term objectives. Farmers must strike a balance between maximizing current yields and preserving the long-term sustainability of their farming practices. Data-driven decision-making allows farmers to align their goals with environmental stewardship, resource conservation, and profitability, ensuring that their choices contribute to the overall resilience and success of their agricultural operations. The decisions phase often involves collaborative decision-making and knowledge sharing among stakeholders. Farmers may seek input from agronomists, agricultural experts, and data scientists to validate their insights and strategies. Collaborative platforms and knowledge-sharing networks enable farmers to access collective expertise and best practices, enhancing the quality of decisions made during this phase. Through collaborative decision-making, farmers can leverage the collective wisdom of their peers and domain experts to gain diverse perspectives on specific challenges and potential solutions. This open exchange of ideas fosters innovation and continuous improvement in farming practices. Moreover, it helps bridge knowledge gaps and facilitates the adoption of new technologies and techniques. Collaborative platforms also ease data sharing among farmers, enabling benchmarking against industry standards and regional performance metrics. By comparing their performance with others in similar environments, farmers can identify areas for improvement and adopt successful practices.

1.4.1.4 Action

The action step in the smart farming cycle is the culmination of the observation, diagnostics, and decision-making phases. Armed with data-driven insights and well-informed strategies, farmers now put their plans into action to optimize their agricultural operations. This step involves the practical implementation of precision farming practices and targeted actions based on the decisions made during the previous stages. Farmers use a range of technological tools and equipment to execute the planned actions effectively. Automated systems and robotics play a significant role in carrying out various tasks, such as precise planting, irrigation, and harvesting. For example, autonomous tractors equipped with GPS technology can accurately follow pre-defined routes, optimizing planting patterns and reducing overlap. Similarly, automated irrigation systems can adjust water application based on real-time data, ensuring optimal soil moisture levels and minimizing water wastage.

The implementation of data-driven strategies extends beyond field operations. In the context of livestock farming, smart farming technologies can monitor animal health and behavior using wearable sensors. These sensors can track vital signs, feeding patterns, and activity levels, enabling early detection of health issues and ensuring timely interventions. Farmers can use this information to provide personalized care and optimize animal welfare. Moreover, the action step involves monitoring and recording the outcomes of the implemented strategies. Farmers track the performance of their actions, comparing the actual results with the predicted outcomes from the diagnostics phase. This feedback loop allows farmers to evaluate the effectiveness of their decisions and make adjustments as needed. The action step is not the end of the smart farming cycle but rather a continuous loop that feeds back into the observation phase. Through continuous learning and adaptation, farmers use the outcomes of their actions to gain new insights and further optimize their farming practices. This iterative process enables farmers to refine their strategies, adapt to changing conditions, and continuously improve their agricultural operations.

Continuous learning is facilitated by the data collection and sensing technologies deployed on the farm. As more data is collected, farmers can gain a deeper understanding of the farm's performance over time. They can identify patterns and trends, enabling them to make more precise predictions and better-informed decisions in subsequent growing seasons. The adaptive nature of the action step is particularly valuable in addressing the dynamic challenges of agriculture, such as changing weather patterns, emerging pests, and market fluctuations. Farmers can adjust their strategies based on the evolving conditions, ensuring that their actions remain aligned with their goals and the changing environment.

Following end-user assessment and action, the cycle starts over at the beginning. In this phase, the maintenance check must be done. Maintenance of the smart farm's hardware is a major difficulty for smart solutions in agriculture, as sensors are often used in the field and can be easily destroyed. As a result, you must ensure that the embedded hardware is long-lasting and simple to maintain. Otherwise, you'll have to change your sensors more frequently than you'd want.

1.4.1.5 Data Integration and Communication

The data integration and communication step in the smart farming cycle is a crucial stage that involves collating and consolidating diverse data sources from various technologies and stakeholders. In this phase, farmers aim to create a unified and comprehensive view of their agricultural operations by integrating data collected from IoT sensors, drones, satellites, weather stations, and other devices. Additionally, data from external sources such as agricultural databases, market information, and historical records are also brought together for a holistic analysis. Data integration allows farmers to break down information silos and avoid redundancies by streamlining the data management process. Through integration, the collected data is organized and standardized, making it easier to process and analyze. Farmers use different data formats and protocols for various technologies, and data integration ensures seamless communication between these systems, allowing for interoperability and efficient data exchange. Moreover, data integration facilitates the correlation of data from different sources, enabling farmers to identify relationships and dependencies between various variables. For example, by combining soil moisture data from IoT sensors with weather data from weather stations, farmers can analyze the impact of rainfall on soil moisture levels. These integrated insights empower farmers to make well-informed decisions that consider a comprehensive set of factors affecting their farm's performance.

Data integration is closely linked to the communication aspect of the smart farming cycle. Efficient communication channels enable the real-time sharing of data and insights between stakeholders, including farmers, agronomists, data analysts, and agricultural experts. Collaborative platforms and knowledge-sharing networks serve as hubs for data exchange, facilitating discussions and interactions among diverse participants. Through real-time data sharing and collaboration, farmers can gain access to up-to-date information, market trends, and best practices. This timely exchange of information allows farmers to respond quickly to emerging challenges and make timely decisions based on the latest insights. For example, receiving early alerts about weather changes or pest outbreaks through communication channels enables farmers to take immediate action to protect their crops. Collaboration also encourages farmers to learn from each other's experiences and successes. By sharing data and best practices, farmers can gain valuable knowledge and expertise that can be applied to their own farming operations. Collaborative decision-making fosters innovation and continuous improvement, leading to more efficient and sustainable farming practices.

1.4.1.6 Risk Management

The risk management step in the smart farming cycle is a crucial phase where farmers proactively identify and address potential risks that could affect their agricultural operations. Smart farming technologies and data-driven insights play a pivotal role in this process, helping farmers assess and mitigate various risks to ensure the resilience and success of their farming endeavors. Here, farmers analyze a range of risks, including weather-related risks such as droughts, floods, extreme temperatures, and storms, as well as biological risks like pest and disease outbreaks. They also consider market risks, such as fluctuations in commodity prices and supply chain disruptions. By integrating data from weather stations, satellite imagery, pest monitoring systems, and market data, farmers gain a comprehensive understanding of the risk landscape and can make informed decisions to manage these challenges effectively. One of the key aspects of risk management is the early detection of potential threats. Smart farming technologies enable real-time monitoring and data analysis, allowing farmers to detect anomalies and emerging issues promptly. For instance, pest monitoring systems can identify pest populations at their early stages, prompting farmers to implement targeted interventions before the infestation becomes widespread. Similarly, weather forecasting helps farmers anticipate extreme weather events, enabling them to take preventive measures to protect crops and livestock.

Risk management in the smart farming cycle involves the formulation of adaptive strategies and contingency plans to address potential risks. Farmers develop flexible and resilient approaches to respond to changing conditions, ensuring they can adjust their operations when needed. For instance, if the weather forecast predicts a prolonged dry period, farmers may adopt drought-tolerant crop varieties or implement water-saving irrigation techniques. Contingency planning is another essential aspect of risk management, whereby farmers develop contingency plans to address potential worst-case scenarios and ensure preparedness for unexpected events. These plans outline the steps to be taken in the case of severe weather events, disease outbreaks, or market disruptions. By having well-defined contingency plans, farmers can act quickly and decisively during emergencies, minimizing potential losses and safeguarding their farm's productivity.

Furthermore, data-driven risk management allows farmers to optimize resource allocation and prioritize risk mitigation efforts. By assessing the severity and probability of various risks, farmers can allocate resources more efficiently to address the most critical challenges. For example, if a specific disease poses a significant threat to a crop, farmers may allocate more resources to implement targeted disease control measures to mitigate its impact.

1.4.1.7   Sustainability and Environmental Impact Assessment

The sustainability and environmental impact assessment step in the smart farming cycle is a critical phase where farmers systematically evaluate the ecological footprint of their agricultural practices. This step aims to assess the environmental implications of farming operations and identify opportunities for enhancing sustainability. Smart farming technologies play a vital role in collecting data on resource usage, greenhouse gas emissions, and other environmental indicators, providing valuable insights into the farm's ecological performance. In this context, farmers conduct a comprehensive assessment of their farming practices to determine their impact on the environment and natural resources. Data on water usage, energy consumption, fertilizer application, and pesticide usage are analyzed to understand the farm's resource efficiency and potential environmental risks. Farmers also consider the impact on soil health, biodiversity, and air and water quality, to ensure that their practices align with conservation and regenerative principles. The sustainability and environmental impact assessment step enables farmers to adopt a holistic approach to farming, where they strive to balance economic goals with environmental stewardship. By examining the ecological consequences of their actions, farmers can make informed decisions that promote sustainable land management, resource conservation, and reduced environmental pollution. This step is essential for enhancing the overall sustainability of agricultural operations and minimizing the environmental footprint of farming practices.

In this step, farmers identify opportunities to implement regenerative and climate-smart agricultural practices. Regenerative farming focuses on restoring and improving soil health, biodiversity, and ecosystem services. Practices such as cover cropping, crop rotation, and reduced tillage help to sequester carbon in the soil, enhance soil fertility, and reduce erosion. By integrating regenerative practices, farmers can contribute to carbon neutrality and combat climate change while promoting long-term sustainability. Climate-smart agriculture involves strategies that enhance the resilience of farming systems to climate variability and reduce greenhouse gas emissions. Farmers may adopt precision irrigation technologies to optimize water usage or implement climate-adaptive crop varieties that can withstand extreme weather events. Climate-smart practices enable farmers to adapt to changing environmental conditions, ensuring food security and sustainability even in the face of climate change challenges. The sustainability and environmental impact assessment step emphasizes the need for a balanced and integrated approach to agriculture, where economic prosperity goes hand in hand with environmental responsibility. By adopting regenerative and climate-smart practices, farmers contribute to environmental conservation, improve the efficiency of resource use, and create a more sustainable agricultural system.

As part of this step, farmers may seek certifications and recognition for their sustainable farming practices. Third-party certifications, such as organic farming certification or sustainability standards like Global good agricultural practices (GAP), provide validation of a farm's environmentally responsible practices. These certifications assure consumers that the food they consume is produced with a minimal environmental impact and aligns with sustainable agricultural principles. Certifications also open up access to niche markets that prioritize sustainable and eco-friendly products. Farmers who meet these standards can command premium prices for their produce, providing economic incentives for sustainable practices. Additionally, recognition for sustainable farming practices enhances the farm's reputation and strengthens its position in the agricultural industry.

1.4.1.8   Record-Keeping and Compliance

The record-keeping and compliance step in the smart farming cycle is a crucial phase where farmers maintain comprehensive and accurate records of their agricultural activities. This step involves recording data related to various aspects of farming operations, including crop planting and harvesting dates, input usage (e.g., fertilizers, pesticides, and water), weather conditions, and pest and disease management measures. Keeping detailed records is essential for tracking the farm's performance, evaluating the effectiveness of different strategies, and ensuring compliance with regulations and certifications. Maintaining thorough records enables farmers to con-duct historical analyses of past farming seasons, allowing them to identify trends, patterns, and areas for improvement. By comparing different approaches and prac-tices over time, farmers can refine their strategies and optimize resource allocation. Additionally, these records serve as valuable references for future decision-making and provide a historical context for understanding the farm's evolution. In the con-text of compliance, record-keeping plays a critical role in meeting regulatory require-ments and adhering to certification standards. Many agricultural certifications, such as organic farming or GAP, require detailed record-keeping to demonstrate adher-ence to specific guidelines. By maintaining accurate records, farmers can readily provide evidence of their compliance during inspections and audits, ensuring that their farming practices meet the necessary standards for sustainability, food safety, and environmental responsibility.

The adoption of smart farming technologies facilitates efficient record-keeping and compliance management. Digital tools, such as farm management software and mobile applications, streamline the data collection and record-keeping processes. Farmers can input data directly into digital platforms, minimizing the likelihood of errors and ensuring real-time updates. These digital tools also offer data visualization and analysis features, allowing farmers to gain insights from their records and make data-driven decisions. Moreover, digital record-keeping systems enable seamless integration with other aspects of the smart farming cycle, such as data integration and communication. Data collected from various sensors and devices can be auto-matically fed into the record-keeping software, simplifying the process of collating diverse data sources. This integration enhances the accuracy and completeness of the records, supporting informed decision-making and providing a comprehensive view of the farm's operations. Additionally, digital record-keeping systems offer data security and accessibility benefits. Farmers can back up their records in the cloud or secure databases, protecting valuable information from physical loss. Access controls can be implemented to ensure that only authorized personnel have access to sensitive data. This digitalization of record-keeping simplifies compliance management by providing quick access to necessary documents and data for certification purposes.

1.4.2 Other Auxiliary Smart Farming Technologies

From livestock tracking to sophisticated field mapping, IoT applications in smart agriculture vary by farm and market sector, climate, and geography. In many cases, off-the-shelf technologies will be ineffective, and you may want a customized smart agricultural additional solution (Sharma et al., 2022). In the following text, we dis-cuss several assistive technologies.

1.4.2.1 Connectivity

Smart agricultural software should be designed for field use. The information should be accessible on-site or remotely by a business owner or farm manager using a smartphone or desktop computer (Prajapati et al., 2023). Furthermore, each linked device should be self-contained and have sufficient wireless range to com-municate with other devices and relay data to the central server. The requirement to transfer data between various agricultural units remains a barrier to smart farming implementation. Needless to add, the link between these facilities must be stable enough to endure inclement weather and enable uninterrupted operations. Today, smart devices employ a variety of communication protocols. However, attempts to build universal standards in this field are ongoing. The arrival of 5G and technologies such as space-based Internet will, hopefully, aid in the resolution of this issue.

1.4.2.2 Satellite-Based Positioning and Monitoring

In smart farming, the most used positioning technology is global positioning system (GPS). GPS records precise latitude, longitude, and elevation data (Karthikeyan et al., 2021). Satellites of the GPS broadcast signals that allow GPS receivers to compute their location in real time and offer continuous locations while moving. Farmers may use precise location information to determine the specific location of field data such as insect incidence, soil type, weeds, and other impediments. The technique makes it easier to identify distinct field locations so that the essential inputs (seed, fertilizer, herbicide, insecticide, and water) may be applied to a specific field.

Satellite monitoring is particularly beneficial for large farmer cooperatives that must monitor the status of huge territories. Because of these highly scalable technologies, they may spread from a single field to a large region. Satellite-based crop monitoring feature makes it simple to follow vegetation across all locations in the same region.

1.4.2.3 Internet of Things

You have the option to integrate all the devices and solutions into a unified system thanks to IoT. All hardware and software have the ability to exchange data and carry out particular tasks depending on patterns. In particular, a vast network of sensors, drones, apps, and other hardware and software is difficult to manage. Smart farming IoT in agriculture tackles this challenge by combining all data sources that exist into a single functioning system via the Internet and wireless connectivity (Dagar et al., 2018; Boursianis et al., 2022). Farmers can now monitor and handle all data and devices in real time with a single smartphone without leaving the field.

This smart farming method increases total plant productivity, decreases waste, and optimizes the use of power, fuel, water, and fertilizer. Furthermore, based on the features of the company and sensor data, farmers may choose which procedures should be kept human and which jobs should be automated. The following are among the major solutions provided by IoT-based smart farming:

- Intelligent greenhouses with distinct microclimates
- Remote pasture and livestock management
- Drone surveillance of the land
- Financial analytics and long-term projections
- Precision irrigation
- Efficient control of pests and infection
- Crop and harvest monitoring
- Monitoring and making weather predictions

1.4.2.4   Artificial Intelligence

From tiny rice and tea growers to fruit orchards and even big agricultural holdings, AI (through computer vision, ML, and deep learning) enables the automation of formerly laborious procedures. Harvesting and agricultural sorting automation, for example, or precision irrigation to save water are examples (Chen et al., 2022). Furthermore, IoT devices such as Edge AI cameras may be put in the field, while drones produce aerial imagery. AI-based picture analysis and ML algorithms are then used to count fruit, monitor and anticipate fruit size, detect pests and plant illnesses, and even forecast production.

In particular, we need to find solutions to help farmers reduce or manage their risks. One of the most intriguing potentials is to use AI in agriculture on a worldwide scale. AI has the ability to revolutionize the way we think about agriculture by allowing farmers to obtain higher outcomes with less work while also providing several additional benefits. However, AI is not a self-contained technology (Nguyen Gia et al., 2019). AI can enhance currently established technology as the next stage in the transition from traditional to innovative farming. Agribusinesses must understand that AI is not a panacea. However, technology may provide concrete benefits to tiny routine tasks and ease farmers' lives in a variety of ways. So, how can we utilize artificial intelligence to promote sustainable agriculture? What are the potentials for AI in farming, and how might AI assist us in overcoming current challenges?

1.4.2.5   Big Data

It is inconceivable to envision the prospect of precise forecasting, activity planning, and developing more effective business models without big data. Smart farming and big data make it possible to make protracted decisions and take immediate action. Also, due to the wide range of data types in the agriculture business, determining the best data collection frequency can be difficult. Field-based, airborne, and environmental sensors, applications, gear, and equipment, as well as processed analytical data, can all be restricted and regulated (Wolfert et al., 2017). One of today's smart farming issues is the secure and timely transport and exchange of this data. In other words, a good internal infrastructure is required to guarantee that the smart farming application operates successfully (and that it can manage the data load). Additionally, the internal systems must be secure. Failure to adequately protect your system raises the likelihood of someone breaking into it, stealing your data, or even seizing control of your self-driving tractors.

1.5   CYBERSECURITY AND PRIVACY-RELATED ISSUES

Smart farming and its related technologies need the handling of vast amounts of data, which expands the range of security flaws that offenders might use for data theft and hacking assaults. However, data security in farming is still a relatively new notion. Drones, for example, are used on many farms to send data to farm machines. This equipment transmits information via the Internet but lacks security features such as user passwords and remote access authentication. Some fundamental security tips include monitoring data flow, utilizing encryption methods to secure critical data, leveraging AI-based security technologies to detect indications of suspicious behavior in real time, and storing data in the blockchain to maintain its integrity (Barreto and Amaral, 2018). To fully profit from smart farming, farmers must first become acquainted with the notion of data security, as well as develop and adhere to internal security regulations.

When you accept new technology, you have an excuse to explore a new field. In many circumstances, human actions cause misunderstandings and data loss. A skilled hacker with sufficient resources will always identify a flaw. Data collection is a treasure trove of information for cybercriminals. We must admit that cyberattacks continue to occur. We can take a huge step forward if we recognize that IoT devices might be susceptible. The application of smart farming in agriculture activates technology. Precision farming is a relatively new concept. Its major objective is to ensure proper cultivation. Farmers are well versed in risk management, crop development, seed production, climate, and planning cycles. The security issues, on the other hand, never concerned anyone. And in many situations, the acquired data was not protected. Smart farming faces a variety of concerns, including access to services, personal privacy fields, restricted information, and intellectual property. Even if the raw data is not strong on its own, it can be utilized to correlate information from other sources. It is possible to discover prospective volumes, influence accuracy expectations, or cause logistics disruption.

The farming business has begun the transition from paper to digital records. Farmers now incorporate sensors and gadgets into practically every activity, but IoT cybersecurity is not their major concern. Unfortunately, they are unconcerned that incorporating such technology might be dangerous and endanger people's lives. For every farmer, device cost and usefulness are the most important considerations. The farmer is happy as long as the machine works, and the manufacturer is happy as well. However, no one in this chain takes security seriously. Growers purchase monitors or thermostats with no IoT cybersecurity protection or update options. Communities often update these devices less regularly, generally after ten years or more. As a result, we can confidently state that these devices are susceptible. As a result, several cyberattacks have lately targeted the agriculture business.

1.6 EMERGING SMART FARMING TECHNIQUES

The future of agricultural productivity is smart farming. Its application enables producers to organize successful production management, satisfying the expanding population's demands while also establishing a compassionate and eco-friendly atmosphere. Farmers can benefit from significant control, monitoring, planning, and exploring possibilities provided by modern technology (Javaid et al., 2022). Without addressing global challenges, none of these smart technologies will be beneficial, of course. Here are several ways that smart farming will benefit the environment in the future.

1.6.1 HYDROPONICS

Hydroponics, a subset of hydroculture, is the practice of growing crops without soil to maximize the benefits of greenhouse farming. As a solution, hydroponic irrigation systems offer a regulated rate of administration of nutrients in water to crop roots. At the moment, mechanisms and devices detect a wide variety of factors and analyze data at specified intervals. Precise measurement and tracking of nutrient concentration in solution is critical for plant growth and taking into account its requirements. The IoT prototype has offered a solution for soilless agriculture and checks the concentration of multiple nutrients and water levels in real time.

An IoT-enabled automated smart hydroponics system is made up of three primary components: input data, a cloud server, and output data. These analyze characteristics such as pH level, water, nutrient-rich water-based solution, room temperature, and humidity in real-time and may be accessed from anywhere over the internet. The deep flow hydroponic system is a method of producing plants that involves planting roots in deep water layers and assuring continuous circulation of plant nutrition solution. Sensors built inside Raspberry Pi collect data on plant development variables such as pH, temperature, humidity, and water level in the hydroponic reservoir, and the data is processed and monitored automatically in real time to guarantee correct water circulation.

1.6.2 VERTICAL FARMING

Industrial agricultural farming techniques degrade soil quality quicker than nature can repair it. The alarming pace of erosion and usage of fresh water for agriculture has reduced arable land and increased the overburden on existing water reservoirs. Vertical farming (VF) allows plants to be kept in a perfectly regulated environment, considerably lowering resource consumption while boosting productivity at different periods. According to the number of stacks, just a percentage of the surface of the ground is required. VF is also incredibly successful at increasing yields while decreasing water usage when compared to traditional farming. The most important parameter is the carbon dioxide measurement. As a result, nondispersive infrared (NDIR) CO_2 sensors are essential for detecting and managing conditions in vertical farms.

1.6.3 PHENOTYPING

Phenotyping is a new crop engineering technology that connects plant genomes to ecophysiology and agronomy. Although the improvement of genetic and molecular tools is crucial for crop breeding, quantitative measurement of crop behaviors such as disease resistance, grain weight, and so on is insufficient owing to a lack of effective technology and efficient methodologies. Plant phenotyping is particularly valuable in researching the quantitative features responsible for development, resilience to various stressors, yield quality, and quantity under this situation. Sensing technologies and image-based phenotyping are used to screen bio-stimulants and understand their mode of action. IoT-based phenotyping is meant to observe crop and associated trait measures, as well as provide capabilities for crop breeding and digital agriculture. Trait analysis techniques and modeling assistance are used to determine the correlations between genotypes, phenotypes, and growth conditions.

1.6.4 AERIAL IMAGING AND DRONE TECHNOLOGY

Aerial imaging and drone technology have emerged as transformative tools for modern smart farming practices. Drones equipped with high-resolution cameras and multispectral sensors offer a bird's-eye view of agricultural fields, enabling farmers to gather crucial data on crop health, growth, and environmental conditions. These drones can fly at various altitudes, capturing detailed images and data that provide valuable insights into the farm's performance. The real-time and high-resolution aerial imagery obtained from drones allows farmers to identify issues such as nutrient deficiencies, irrigation problems, pest infestations, and weed encroachment much faster than traditional ground-based methods.

One of the significant advantages of using drones in smart farming is the efficiency and accuracy of data collection. Drones can cover large areas of farmland in a short amount of time, reducing the time and labor required for field inspections. This efficiency is especially valuable for large-scale commercial farms or farms with challenging terrains that may be difficult to access on foot. Moreover, drones can collect data at specific wavelengths using multispectral and thermal sensors, allowing farmers to monitor crop health beyond what the human eye can perceive. The data collected from these sensors enables farmers to make data-driven decisions about irrigation schedules, nutrient applications, and pest management, optimizing resource use and improving crop yields.

The integration of aerial imaging and drone technology with data analytics enhances the potential of smart farming. With advanced image processing and data analysis, farmers can create detailed crop health maps, detect stress factors, and predict yield estimates. ML algorithms can analyze the collected data and provide actionable insights for precise decision-making. For example, ML models can detect early signs of disease or nutrient deficiencies, enabling farmers to take targeted and timely actions to mitigate potential crop losses. These data-driven insights lead to more efficient resource management, reduced use of pesticides and fertilizers, and ultimately, improved sustainability of farming practices. As drone technology continues to evolve, the cost of drone systems and data analytics tools is becoming more accessible to farmers of all scales. The democratization of this technology allows even small-scale farmers to take advantage of aerial imaging and data analytics for their operations. The widespread adoption of drones in smart farming is expected to revolutionize agriculture, promoting more efficient and sustainable practices that support global food security and environmental conservation.

1.6.5 PRECISION LIVESTOCK FARMING

Precision livestock farming (PLF) is a cutting-edge approach that utilizes advanced technologies and data analytics to monitor and manage livestock with unprecedented precision. Through the use of wearable devices, sensors, and data analytics, PLF enables farmers to track vital information such as animal health, behavior, and performance in real time. By continuously collecting and analyzing data, farmers can make informed decisions to optimize feeding regimes, detect early signs of disease or stress, and improve overall animal welfare. PLF empowers farmers to provide personalized care to each animal, ensuring their well-being and enhancing productivity.

One of the significant benefits of PLF is its ability to improve animal health management. By monitoring individual animals closely, farmers can detect health issues at an early stage, allowing for prompt and targeted interventions. For example, wearable sensors can track an animal's body temperature, heart rate, and activity levels. Any abnormal patterns or deviations from the norm can trigger alerts, prompting farmers to investigate and address potential health problems immediately. This proactive approach not only improves animal health outcomes but also reduces the need for antibiotics and other medical treatments, contributing to more sustainable and environmentally friendly livestock farming. Furthermore, PLF helps optimize feeding strategies and resource utilization. The data collected from sensors and wearable devices can be used to assess an animal's feed intake, metabolism, and growth patterns. By analyzing this information, farmers can fine-tune their feeding regimes, ensuring that each animal receives the appropriate amount of nutrients and minimizing feed wastage. This precision in feeding leads to improved feed conversion rates, increased efficiency, and reduced environmental impact. By managing resources more efficiently, farmers can lower production costs while maintaining or even enhancing the quality of their livestock products.

The implementation of PLF also leads to enhanced data-driven decision-making. By aggregating and analyzing data from multiple sources, farmers can gain valuable insights into herd performance and behavior. These insights enable them to identify trends, patterns, and correlations that may not be apparent through traditional observation methods. With this knowledge, farmers can develop strategies to optimize breeding programs, improve breeding outcomes, and ensure that their livestock operations remain competitive and sustainable in a rapidly evolving agricultural landscape.

1.6.6 BLOCKCHAIN IN AGRICULTURE

Blockchain technology has emerged as a promising solution for various industries, including agriculture. In smart farming, blockchain offers numerous benefits by enhancing transparency, traceability, and efficiency throughout the agricultural supply chain. By creating an immutable and decentralized ledger, blockchain enables secure and transparent recording of every transaction and data exchange along the agricultural journey, from farm to table. One of the key advantages of blockchain in agriculture is its ability to improve traceability and food safety. By recording every step of the production process, including planting, harvesting, processing, and distribution, on the blockchain, consumers can easily trace the origin and journey of food products. This enhances food safety by quickly identifying the source of potential contamination or quality issues, allowing for more targeted recalls and reducing the risk of foodborne illnesses. With greater transparency and trust in the supply chain, consumers can make more informed choices about the products they purchase, leading to increased confidence in the food system. Blockchain also addresses the issue of food fraud and counterfeit products in the agriculture industry. By creating an unchangeable record of each transaction, blockchain ensures that the authenticity of food products can be verified at every step of the supply chain. This helps to prevent fraudulent practices such as mislabeling, adulteration, and false claims about product origin. Consumers can have confidence that the food they purchase is genuine and meets the quality standards they expect.

Moreover, blockchain enhances trust and fairness in agricultural trade and transactions. In traditional agricultural supply chains, there are often multiple intermediaries involved in buying and selling produce, which can lead to opacity and discrepancies in pricing and payments. By implementing blockchain, smart contracts can automate and execute agreements without the need for intermediaries, ensuring that all parties involved are held accountable and receive their fair share of profits. This decentralized approach to transactions streamlines processes, reduces administrative costs, and fosters trust and cooperation among stakeholders in the agricultural ecosystem.

Blockchain technology also has the potential to promote sustainability and support ethical practices in agriculture. With blockchain-enabled certifications, farmers can prove compliance with sustainability standards, fair trade practices, and organic farming methods. This transparency allows consumers to make more environmentally conscious choices, rewarding farmers who prioritize sustainable and ethical practices. Additionally, blockchain can be utilized to create carbon credits and trace carbon footprints in the supply chain, incentivizing emission reduction efforts and contributing to a more sustainable agriculture industry.

REFERENCES

Bacco, M., Barsocchi, P., Ferro, E., Gotta, A., & Ruggeri, M. (2019). The digitisation of agriculture: A survey of research activities on smart farming. *Array*, *3–4*, 100009. https://doi.org/10.1016/J.ARRAY.2019.100009

Bacco, M., Berton, A., Ferro, E., Gennaro, C., Gotta, A., Matteoli, S., Paonessa, F., Ruggeri, M., Virone, G., & Zanella, A. (2018). Smart farming: Opportunities, challenges and technology enablers. In *2018 IoT vertical and topical summit on agriculture—Tuscany, IOT Tuscany 2018* (pp. 1–6). https://doi.org/10.1109/IOT-TUSCANY.2018.8373043

Barreto, L., & Amaral, A. (2018). Smart farming: Cyber security challenges. In *9th International Conference on Intelligent Systems 2018: Theory, Research and Innovation in Applications, IS 2018 – Proceedings* (pp. 870–876). https://doi.org/10.1109/IS.2018.8710531

Behera, U. K., & France, J. (2016). Integrated farming systems and the livelihood security of small and marginal farmers in India and other developing countries. *Advances in Agronomy*, *138*, 235–282. https://doi.org/10.1016/BS.AGRON.2016.04.001

Bogale, A. (2020). Review, impact of land use/cover change on soil erosion in the Lake Tana Basin, Upper Blue Nile, Ethiopia. *Applied Water Science*, *10*(12), 1–6. https://doi.org/10.1007/S13201-020-01325-W/FIGURES/1

Boursianis, A. D., Papadopoulou, M. S., Diamantoulakis, P., Liopa-Tsakalidi, A., Barouchas, P., Salahas, G., Karagiannidis, G., Wan, S., & Goudos, S. K. (2022). Internet of Things (IoT) and agricultural unmanned aerial vehicles (UAVs) in smart farming: A comprehensive review. *Internet of Things*, *18*, 100187. https://doi.org/10.1016/J.IOT.2020.100187

Charania, I., & Li, X. (2020). Smart farming: Agriculture's shift from a labor intensive to technology native industry. *Internet of Things*, *9*, 100142. https://doi.org/10.1016/J.IOT.2019.100142

Chen, Q., Li, L., Chong, C., & Wang, X. (2022). AI-enhanced soil management and smart farming. *Soil Use and Management*, *38*(1), 7–13. https://doi.org/10.1111/SUM.12771

Dagar, R., Som, S., & Khatri, S. K. (2018). Smart farming—IoT in agriculture. In *Proceedings of the International Conference on Inventive Research in Computing Applications, ICIRCA 2018* (pp. 1052–1056). https://doi.org/10.1109/ICIRCA.2018.8597264

Dignac, M. F., Derrien, D., Barré, P., Barot, S., Cécillon, L., Chenu, C., Chevallier, T., Freschet, G. T., Garnier, P., Guenet, B., Hedde, M., Klumpp, K., Lashermes, G., Maron, P. A., Nunan, N., Roumet, C., & Basile-Doelsch, I. (2017). Increasing soil carbon storage: Mechanisms, effects of agricultural practices and proxies. A review. *Agronomy for Sustainable Development*, *37*(2), 1–27. https://doi.org/10.1007/S13593-017-0421-2

Fedele, A., Mazzi, A., Niero, M., Zuliani, F., & Scipioni, A. (2014). Can the life cycle assessment methodology be adopted to support a single farm on its environmental impacts forecast evaluation between conventional and organic production? An Italian case study. *Journal of Cleaner Production*, *69*, 49–59. https://doi.org/10.1016/J.JCLEPRO.2014.01.034

Groot, J. C. J., Oomen, G. J. M., & Rossing, W. A. H. (2012). Multi-objective optimization and design of farming systems. *Agricultural Systems*, *110*, 63–77. https://doi.org/10.1016/J.AGSY.2012.03.012

Javaid, M., Haleem, A., Singh, R. P., & Suman, R. (2022). Enhancing smart farming through the applications of Agriculture 4.0 technologies. *International Journal of Intelligent Networks*, *3*, 150–164. https://doi.org/10.1016/J.IJIN.2022.09.004

Karthikeyan, P. R., Chandrasekaran, G., Kumar, N. S., Sengottaiyan, E., Mani, P., Kalavathi, D. T., & Gowrishankar, V. (2021). IoT based moisture control and temperature monitoring in smart farming. *Journal of Physics: Conference Series*, *1964*(6), 062056. https://doi.org/10.1088/1742-6596/1964/6/062056

Kujawa, S., Dhanaraju, M., Chenniappan, P., Ramalingam, K., Pazhanivelan, S., & Kaliaperumal, R. (2022). Smart farming: Internet of Things (IoT)-based sustainable agriculture. *Agriculture*, *12*(10), 1745. https://doi.org/10.3390/AGRICULTURE12101745

Lytos, A., Lagkas, T., Sarigiannidis, P., Zervakis, M., & Livanos, G. (2020). Towards smart farming: Systems, frameworks and exploitation of multiple sources. *Computer Networks*, *172*, 107147. https://doi.org/10.1016/J.COMNET.2020.107147

Mohamed, M. (2023). Agricultural sustainability in the age of deep learning: Current trends, challenges, and future trajectories. *Sustainable Machine Intelligence Journal*, *4*(4), 1–20. https://doi.org/10.61185/SMIJ.2023.44102

Moysiadis, V., Sarigiannidis, P., Vitsas, V., & Khelifi, A. (2021). Smart farming in Europe. *Computer Science Review*, *39*, 100345. https://doi.org/10.1016/J.COSREV.2020.100345

Nguyen Gia, T., Qingqing, L., Pena Queralta, J., Zou, Z., Tenhunen, H., & Westerlund, T. (2019, September). Edge AI in smart farming IoT: CNNs at the edge and fog computing with LoRa. In *IEEE AFRICON Conference*. https://doi.org/10.1109/AFRICON46755.2019.9134049

Perronne, R., Diguet, S., de Vallavieille-Pope, C., Leconte, M., & Enjalbert, J. (2017). A framework to characterize the commercial life cycle of crop varieties: Application to the case study of the influence of yellow rust epidemics on French bread wheat varieties. *Field Crops Research*, *209*, 159–167. https://doi.org/10.1016/J.FCR.2017.05.008

Prajapati, J. B., Barad, R., Patel, M. B., Saini, K., Prajapati, D., & Engineer, P. (2023). *Smart farming ingredients: IoT sensors, software, connectivity, data analytics, robots, drones, GIS-GPS* (pp. 31–49). https://services.igi-global.com/resolvedoi/resolve.aspx?doi=10.4018/978-1-6684-6413-7.ch003. https://doi.org/10.4018/978-1-6684-6413-7.CH003

Prasad, S., Singh, A., Korres, N. E., Rathore, D., Sevda, S., & Pant, D. (2020). Sustainable utilization of crop residues for energy generation: A life cycle assessment (LCA) perspective. *Bioresource Technology*, *303*, 122964. https://doi.org/10.1016/J.BIORTECH.2020.122964

Said Mohamed, E., Belal, A. A., Kotb Abd-Elmabod, S., El-Shirbeny, M. A., Gad, A., & Zahran, M. B. (2021). Smart farming for improving agricultural management. *The Egyptian Journal of Remote Sensing and Space Science*, *24*(3), 971–981. https://doi.org/10.1016/J.EJRS.2021.08.007

Sharma, V., Tripathi, A. K., & Mittal, H. (2022). Technological revolutions in smart farming: Current trends, challenges & future directions. *Computers and Electronics in Agriculture, 201*, 107217. https://doi.org/10.1016/J.COMPAG.2022.107217

Triantafyllou, A., Tsouros, D. C., Sarigiannidis, P., & Bibi, S. (2019). An architecture model for smart farming. In *Proceedings—15th Annual International Conference on Distributed Computing in Sensor Systems, DCOSS 2019* (pp. 385–392). https://doi.org/10.1109/DCOSS.2019.00081

Wolfert, S., Ge, L., Verdouw, C., & Bogaardt, M. J. (2017). Big data in smart farming – A review. *Agricultural Systems, 153*, 69–80. https://doi.org/10.1016/J.AGSY.2017.01.023

2 Big Data in Smart Farming

2.1 INTRODUCTION

The widespread use of sensors to monitor conditions such as soil moisture, humidity, and temperature will be driven by "smart farming" over the coming years, with a correspondingly large amount of data predicted to be generated. Additional sources include information collected from weather stations, archives maintained by government agencies, and open-source datasets hosted in digital libraries. All of them involve massive amounts of disparate information that must be manipulated, transmitted in real time over wireless networks, and stored. The chapter explains and describes big data in terms of its potential five dimensions—volume, velocity, variety, veracity, and valorization—within the framework of smart farming. Current technical solutions, such as cloud computing, edge computing, and fog computing, are also discussed in this chapter. The chapter contributes to the body of knowledge by finalizing a standardized big data chain for smart farming systems, which builds on the earlier six-step chain consisting of data collecting, storage, transport, transformation, analytics, and marketing.

2.2 DIFFERENCES BETWEEN TRADITIONAL AND SMART FARMING

Smart farming focuses on increasing agricultural production via the use of technology—both hardware and software. Smart farming is concerned with the management of farms, plantations, and all associated farming operations via the use of IoT, drones, robots, technology, and artificial intelligence (AI) to find a path to predictable farm production.

Smart farming is concerned with the management of agricultural activities through the use of data obtained from multiple sources (historical, geographical, and instrumental). Technological advancement does not always imply that a system is intelligent. Smart agricultural technologies distinguish themselves by their capacity to collect and analyze data. Smart farming uses hardware (IoT) and software (software as a service, SaaS) to collect data and provide actionable insights to manage all agricultural activities, both pre- and postharvest. The data is well organized, always available, and full of information on every area of financial and field operations that can be accessed from anywhere in the globe.

Using automation in smart farming has various advantages over traditional agricultural methods, including better control over production operations, which improves cost management and lowers waste formation. Furthermore, smart farming facilitates the detection of abnormalities in crop growth and livestock health

DOI: 10.1201/9781003400103-2

TABLE 2.1

The Essential Differences between Traditional and Smart Farming.

No.	Traditional Farming	Smart Farming
1	Throughout the region, the same set of agricultural production procedures, often unscientific, are used.	Each farm is examined to determine the best crop kinds and input needs for maximum profitability.
2	Inadequate application of fertilizers and insecticides over the field.	All agricultural data is stored centrally on a digital platform.
3	Manually maintaining both field and financial data separately, resulting in inaccuracies and data loss.	Early identification and application of inputs solely in the afflicted area, resulting in cost savings.
4	Geotagging and zone determination are not supported.	It uses satellite photography to detect the various zones in crops.
5	There are no accurate weather forecasting systems.	Realistic meteorologists to enhance resource use and avoid losses.
6	Farmers' use of rudimentary tools makes the operation tedious and time-consuming.	Task automation boosts productivity and saves time and money.

through the use of innovative agricultural technologies. Table 2.1 shows the fundamental contrasts between traditional and smart farming approaches. Such a comprehensive innovative system needs consolidated management of enormous various data types. Next, we explore the different data types manipulated in the smart farming system.

2.3 TYPES OF SMART FARMING DATA

To offer ideal circumstances for plant development, smart farming makes use of sophisticated technologies such as IoT and AI. AI technology such as autonomous machinery, for example, may assist you in optimizing agricultural output, and Internet-enabled sensors can assist you in collecting, analyzing, and acting on crop data from anywhere. Because they give real-time data to plan and optimize resources and outputs, smart grow facilities may produce higher-quality crops with less waste. The ultimate objective of smart farming is to feed the world through food production that is sustainable, mechanized, linked, and environmentally benign.

Experts anticipate that we will need to raise food production by 70% by 2050 (Sleem, 2022; van Dijk et al., 2021). Smart farming technology can enable agriculture to scale to meet the needs of the future in the face of restricted resources, allowing it to satisfy the demands of a growing global population. To assure the greatest quality yields, several crops in various areas may be monitored and controlled remotely from anywhere. Manual operations can be automated to alleviate labor shortages, lower labor expenses, and boost output. Predictive analytics can guarantee that production and distribution are maximized to keep the globe fed in all locations and seasons. Before discussing how to manage this flood of data, let's explore the different types of data in smart farming. In particular, the gushing-out data can be classified according to the type of held information and the storage type.

2.3.1   Data Types According to Farming Practices

Farm data provides the cropping sector with several potentials for improved management and visibility into company performance. Equipment and software to monitor many farm-land characteristics will increase the utility of farm data when connected, but affordability (or lack thereof) will continue to be a major barrier to farmer adoption. Anyone acquainted with farming is aware that smart farming generates massive amounts of data, which can be utilized to influence management choices in a variety of ways. The following sections discuss the top three kinds of farm data that are commonly gathered.

2.3.1.1   Yield Projection Data

Yield mapping promises to improve farmers' visibility of land production by helping them to map, benchmark, and monitor variance. This is one of the major issues that countries are working together to tackle. One method is to boost the produce from existing farmlands. This sort of data offers farmers detailed information on rainfall patterns, water cycles, fertilizer requirements, and other topics. This helps businesses to make decisions such as what crops to grow and when to harvest for maximum revenue. The utility of this data grows over time as year-to-year variance in production distribution can be analyzed, providing a more detailed picture of farming performance. This data type's lower usefulness rating might be influenced by a variety of reasons. Adoption rates will always be affected by cost versus perceived advantage, but another area to investigate may be the relative utility of this data type in isolation versus in conjunction with soil and nutrient mapping data.

2.3.1.2   Soil Delineating Data

Soil health is heavily influenced by moisture and nutrient levels; therefore, changes in soil type combined with these features mean that various portions of a farm may result in greater crop production. It's no surprise that many crop farmers gather this sort of data, especially as their businesses grow and they strive to maximize production through efficient input and land usage. The capacity to map a property and its soil variability offers farmers valuable information on fertilizer use, application rate, and even the sort of plant to cultivate.

Pesticide administration has been a difficult topic because of the negative impacts on the environment. This data helps farmers manage this better by recommending which pesticides to apply, when to apply them, and how much to apply. Farmers may conform to regulatory laws and avoid abuse of chemicals in food production by regularly monitoring it. Furthermore, crops are more profitable since they are not harmed by weeds and insects. Soil mapping data might therefore enable farmers to invest in pesticides and fertilizers based on soil demands with a high level of knowledge and comprehension.

2.3.1.3   Supply Chain and Financial Data

One-third of the food produced for human consumption is wasted or squandered each year (Unkovich et al., 2023). This is a terrible truth given the industry's attempts to close the supply–demand imbalance. Food distribution cycles from the farmer to the market must be shortened to meet this. This kind of monitoring may be lifesaving for big farms, since it notifies users of tractor availability, service due dates, and fuel refill warnings. In essence, this optimizes utilization and ensures agricultural equipment's long-term health. This is unsurprising given that a farm is essentially a company that must account for its financial flow. Volatile commodity prices, weather, and growing input costs all raise the need for personal insight into farm finances in order to make educated business decisions, whether it's investing in a new tractor or purchasing seed for the following crop season.

2.3.2 DATA TYPES ACCORDING TO STRUCTURE

Agricultural data are variables and/or qualities that farmers need to carry out their commercial operations. Specific agricultural records or factors, such as crop types, yields, soils in use, and extensions, as well as business-related information, such as goods, suppliers, clients, and payments are included. Depending on the storage type in which the data is located, they are categorized as structured, semi-structured, or unstructured data (Parameswaran et al., 2022; Cravero et al., 2022; Ngo et al., 2023).

2.3.2.1 Structured Data Type

Structured data has a predefined format and hence a fixed length in memory; they are also simple to store because the database engine has already specified the logical structure. The data is structured in a recognizable format that allows individuals in an organization to easily access and retrieve it. Figure 2.1 shows an example of structured data that may be saved in a database using a date-type format. The day, on the other hand, is recorded as integer-type data. Because more accuracy is required, potential Evapotranspiration (ET0) is kept as float-type data as well as the mean of sunshine hours. This sort of information may be saved in a structured database since the data can be described as integer, date, time, float, char, varchar, or string data types, among others.

Relational databases are the most prevalent type of structured database because they employ the structure of data groups according to relational algebra as a storage basis. The data query language utilized is structured query language (SQL), a standard that enables the development and manipulation of data groups and associated data kinds (Yadav and Shekokar, 2022; Qin et al., 2023). SQL employs the SELECT statement to search for data, the INSERT statement to store data, the UPDATE statement to alter data, and the DELETE statement to delete data. Traditional analytics has concentrated on structured data since SQL queries can access it. MySQL, PostgreSQL, Oracle, and SQL Server are examples of relational databases.

2.3.2.2 Semi-structured Data Type

Semi-structured data is unstructured data that may be inadequate and has a structure that varies when new data is input; hence, their structures are unpredictable. This implies they are not table-oriented in a relational database architecture and are not ordered in object-oriented databases. Semi-structured databases allow for the storing of data from several sources that have similar qualities but differ in format. Emails, Extensible Markup Language (XML), JavaScript Object Notation (JSON), Comma-Separated Values (CSV) files, and Key-value are all examples of semi-structured

Evapo-Transpiration (ETo) Records for Irrigation Scheduling

Item	Unit	Jan	Feb	Mar	Apr	May	Jun	July	Aug	Sep	Oct	Nov	Dec
Temperature(mean)	°C	26	27	28	29	31	34	36	34	33	30	28	26
Temperature(max)	°C	29	29	31	32	34	38	41	39	36	33	31	28
Temperature(min)	°C	23	24	25	26	28	30	31	29	29	27	25	23
Wind speed (mean)	m/s	4.6	4.6	4.1	4.1	4.1	4.6	5.7	5.7	4.6	4.6	4.1	4.1
Relative humidity(mean)	%	69	71	73	74	70	53	43	44	60	65	67	71
Sunshine hours(mean)	hr	7.8	8.6	8.2	9.3	10.0	8.3	7.5	8.5	9.0	9.6	10.0	8.9
ETo	mm/day	5.0	5.3	5.4	5.9	6.6	8.3	10.4	10.1	7.7	6.6	5.7	4.7

FIGURE 2.1 Example of Structured Data Type in Smart Farming.

data. Figure 2.2 depicts semi-structured data in JSON format, indicating that the information is kept as a document rather than a data table. The data is extracted and then saved as needed at the moment, for example, the type of crop, emission information, update date, and so on.

Semi-structured databases, unlike relational databases, allow for the storing of current information without constructing a prior structure. On the contrary side, they enable the storage of specific information about a property, such as coordinate values. Semi-structured databases, in this sense, are scalable and adaptable to the analysis needs of decision-makers. Furthermore, these databases enable us to deal with and analyze clustered data volumes quickly. Semi-structured databases include MongoDB, CouchDB, Neo4J, and Redis, among others.

2.3.2.3 Unstructured Data Type

Unstructured data has no specified structure since it holds raw files such as bitmaps, photos, comments or text, email, and other non-database data types. Although emails are stored in a database, the message body comprises unstructured language that must be processed in order to retrieve the information. Files also including Motion Pictures Expert Group 3 (MP3), Portable Document Format (PDF), Joint Photographic Experts Group (JPG), Plain Text (TXT) documents, and Tag Image File Format (TIFF) are examples of unstructured data. Numeric data are the most basic since they may be saved in very few bytes. Each character of text is represented by one byte. Images and music, while on the other hand, need greater storage space. Remote

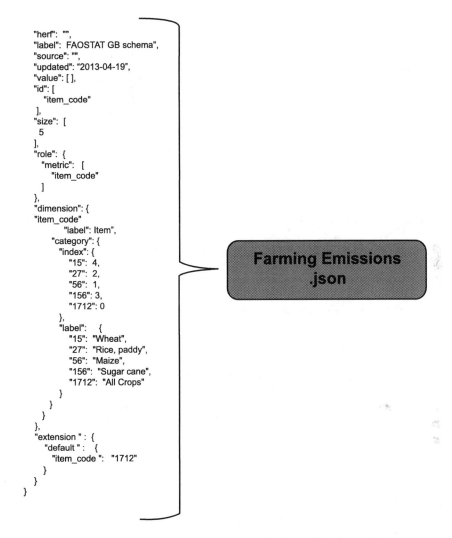

"herf": "",
"label": FAOSTAT GB schema",
"source": "",
"updated": "2013-04-19",
"value": [ ],
"id": [
    "item_code"
],
"size": [
  5
],
"role": {
  "metric": [
      "item_code"
  ]
},
"dimension": {
"item_code"
        "label": Item",
      "category": {
        "index": {
          "15": 4,
          "27": 2,
          "56": 1,
          "156": 3,
          "1712": 0
        },
        "label":   {
          "15": "Wheat",
          "27": "Rice, paddy",
          "56": "Maize",
          "156": "Sugar cane",
          "1712": "All Crops"
        }
      }
    }
},
"extension " : {
    "default " :   {
      "item_code ":   "1712"
    }
  }
}
}

Farming Emissions .json

FIGURE 2.2   Example of Semi-structured Data Type in Smart Farming.

sensing photographs, in particular, include a wealth of sensor data. Finally, movies require additional memory space since they utilize a sequence of stored pictures.

Unstructured data, unlike structured data, is difficult to browse, sort, or display, let alone analyze. To retrieve knowledge related to the enterprise, data transformation technologies and procedures are necessary. Unstructured data is captured by satellites surrounding the earth and capturing data from the earth via remote sensing. These photos depict the earth's character as viewed from space. Solar radiation reflected from the earth, infrared radiation, and backscattered radar intensity are some examples of data that may be acquired. These data are collected by sensors onboard satellites, which charge radiation of various wavelengths and provide multispectral raster data. Labeled multiband picture files (GeoTIFF), an extension of the TIFF format, are commonly

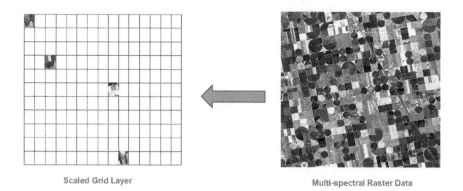

Scaled Grid Layer   Multi-spectral Raster Data

FIGURE 2.3   Example of Unstructured Data Type in Smart Farming.

used to store multispectral and multidimensional data. Because of the magnitude of the data, collecting this data type is a complex task since it must be processed swiftly using parallel and distributed systems. Because they contain data from several sensors about the geographic location, multiband pictures hold numerous values in a single pixel (see Figure 2.3). The bands for which information will be collected from the sensors are chosen based on the analysis required. Data from many bands may be utilized to create a more realistic depiction of Earth's surface phenomena.

Laser altimeters, radar, and Light Detection and Ranging (LiDAR) are the most frequently used active sensors in remote sensing. The visible, infrared, and thermal portions of the electromagnetic spectrum are used by passive sensors to detect the ambient radiation that is emitted or reflected by objects. RGB, hyperspectral, multispectral, and temperature sensors are a few examples of passive sensors. Through photogrammetric processing, LiDAR sensors in particular acquire 3D features in the form of point clouds. To estimate the biomass of the forest, statistics from LiDAR data are produced, including mean height, height percentiles, and other information. Amazon Web Services and Google Earth Engine (GEE) presently provide satellite images and analytical data. GEE employs Hadoop as a data storage, processing, and analytics platform. Researchers have used these high-performance computing platform methodologies to assess global trends, opening the door to large-scale geospatial analysis and monitoring.

2.4   BIG DATA BACKGROUND

As mentioned before, data are formless facts, or in other words, the lowest level of information and knowledge, taken from observations, direct recordings, and social activities. This data has become so huge in recent years that it is difficult to make use of it and analyze it using the traditional methods of obtaining information and knowledge from it. On the other hand, information is data that has undergone processing, analysis, and interpretation, and which can be used to derive different relationships between phenomena and make decisions.

Big data is a collection of datasets that are so large and complex that it becomes difficult to process them with just one database management tool or with traditional data processing applications. Challenges include capture, duration, storage, search, sharing, transfer, analysis, and visualization. The trend is due to large datasets because of the additional information derived from the analysis of one large set of related data, compared to separate, smaller sets with the same total data volume, allowing for correlations that reveal pivotal business trends, determine search quality, link legal citations, and combat corruption by guessing where corruption is likely to occur and determining interoperability conditions in real time. Various efforts have been proposed to describe big data challenges in terms of their potential dimensions. Next, the most popular classification will be discussed.

2.4.1 "Vs3" DIMENSION MODEL

In a research report and a number of related lectures in 2001, META analyst Doug Laney, now known as the Gartner Group, identifies challenges and opportunities for data growth as a 3D object, according to increasing volume (the amount of data), velocity (the speed of outgoing and incoming data), And variety (multiple data types and sources). Gartner and many companies in the industry now continue to use the "Vs3" model to describe big data. In 2012, Gartner updated its definition to read: "Big data is a high-volume, high-velocity or high-variety information asset that requires new forms of processing to enhance decision-making, deep understanding, and process improvement." (Gandomi and Haider, 2015; Veretekhina et al., 2022). To sum up, the three dimensions of big data according to Gartner are as follows:

- **Volume:** It is the number of terabytes of data that we release daily from the content and is also known as the size of the data extracted from a source, which determines the value and potential of the data to be classified as big data. It may be the most important feature in big data analysis.
- **Velocity:** This refers to how quickly data occurs. For example, the speed at which tweets are published differs from the speed at which remote sensors scan climate changes.
- **Variety:** It refers to the diversity of extracted data, which helps users, whether they are researchers or analysts, to choose the appropriate data for their field of research and includes structured data in databases and unstructured data that comes from its unstructured nature such as images, clips, audio recordings, videos, short messages and call logs, map data (GPS) and others. All of the previous data types require time and effort to prepare them in a suitable form for processing and analysis.

Note: To put it simply, big data is the huge amount of information that exceeds the capacity of traditional data processing methods and encompasses large, complex datasets characterized by their volume, variety, velocity, and other dimensions. For example, handle the daily transactions of a billion Facebook users daily or search (Exabyte) a million terabyte pages on the Internet. It is a relative matter that is constantly changing. What is currently huge will not be so in the near future, and data that is not huge now was huge a few years ago.

2.4.2 "Vs5" Dimension Model

Big data was only discussed in the early part of this century in terms of the "Vs3" model: volume, velocity, and variety. Two more Vs (value and veracity) have been developed throughout time to assist data scientists in better expressing and explaining the key qualities of big data. In particular, the five primary and intrinsic features of big data are the "Vs5" (velocity, volume, value, variety, and veracity). Knowing the "Vs5" enables data scientists to extract more value from their data while also enabling the scientists' company to become more customer-centric. The additional dimensions of "Vs5" can be listed as follows:

- **Veracity:** The fourth V among the "Vs5" of big data is veracity. It relates to the data's quality and correctness. Data collected may be incomplete, erroneous, or incapable of providing true, meaningful information. Overall, veracity refers to the amount of confidence in the obtained data.
- **Valorization:** The fifth and final V of big data is value. This refers to the value that big data may give, and it is closely related to what businesses can do with the data they collect. The ability to extract value from big data is required, since the value of big data rises considerably based on the insights that can be gleaned from it. Organizations can obtain and analyze data using the same big data techniques, but how they extract value from that data should be unique to them.

Note: Data might become jumbled and difficult to utilize at times. If the data is inadequate, it might produce more confusion than insights. In the medical profession, for example, if data on what medications a patient is taking are missing, the patient's life may be jeopardized. Both value and truthfulness contribute to the definition of data quality and insights.

2.4.3 General Framework of Big Data

Structure is provided through frameworks. The big data framework's primary goal is to create a structure for corporate organizations seeking to capitalize on the possibilities of big data. Big data demands more than simply experienced people and cutting-edge technology to achieve long-term success; it also necessitates structure and skills. The big data framework was created because, despite the obvious benefits and business reasons of big data, many businesses fail to incorporate a successful big data practice in their company.

2.4.3.1 Benefits of the Big Data Framework

For businesses, the big data framework provides a method that takes into consideration all organizational capabilities of a successful big data practice. From the definition of a big data strategy to the technological tools and skills that a business should have. The following are the primary advantages of implementing a big data framework:

- It provides a foundation for organizations that wish to get started with big data or expand their big data capabilities.
- It encompasses all organizational factors that must be considered in a big data company.
- It is provider agnostic. It is applicable to every organization, independent of technology, specialization, or tools.
- It offers a standardized reference model that can be applied across departments and countries.
- It establishes key and quantifiable skills in each of its categories, allowing the company to grow over time.

Big data is all about people. Even with the most modern computers and processors available, organizations will fail if they lack the necessary knowledge and skills. As a result, the big data framework strives to expand the expertise of anybody who is concerned with big data. The modular methodology and supporting certification scheme attempt to create big data expertise in a similarly organized manner. The big data framework provides a comprehensive structure for big data. It examines the key components that businesses should consider while establishing their big data organization. Every component of the framework is equally important, and organizations can only progress if they pay equal focus and effort to all components of the big data architecture.

2.4.3.2   The General Framework of Big Data

The big data framework is a systematic approach comprising six basic components, as summarized, that organizations must consider while establishing their big data structure. Figure 2.4 depicts the big data general framework.

The big data framework is composed of six major components that can be summarized as follows:

- **Big data strategy:** Enterprise organizations require a solid big data strategy in order to get meaningful outcomes from their big data investments. How can return on investment be realized, and where should efforts in big data research and analytics be concentrated? The options for analysis are virtually limitless, and organizations may rapidly become lost in zettabytes of data. The first step toward big data success is to develop a solid and well-structured big data strategy. Most organizations now view data as a strategic advantage. Organizations can get a competitive edge by being able to analyze massive datasets and detect patterns in the data. Netflix, for example, considers user behavior when selecting what movies or television shows to make. Alibaba, the Chinese sourcing platform, rose to prominence by determining which suppliers to lend money to and promote on their site. Big data has evolved into anrationess.

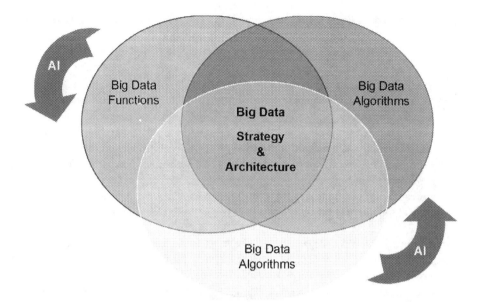

FIGURE 2.4   General Framework of Smart Farming.

- **Big data architecture:** This component of the big data framework evaluates big data environments' technological capabilities. It explores the many roles that exist inside a big data architecture and looks at the best design approaches. Organizations must be able to store and analyze vast amounts of data in order to operate with massive datasets. To do this, the company must have the necessary IT infrastructure in place to support big data. To assist big data analysis, enterprises should have a complete big data infrastructure. How should businesses build and configure their architecture to support big data? And what are the needs in terms of storage and processing?
- **Big data algorithms:** The framework's big data algorithms component focuses on the (technical) skills of everyone who wants to work with big data. It tries to lay a firm basis by introducing basic statistical operations and different types of algorithms. Understanding statistics and algorithms is a crucial competence for working with data. To get insights from data, big data specialists must have a strong foundation in statistics and algorithms. Algorithms are explicit instructions for solving a class of problems. Algorithms are capable of doing computations, data processing, and automated reasoning. Valuable knowledge and insights may be acquired by applying algorithms to massive amounts of data.
- **Big data processes:** To make big data effective in corporate organizations, more than simply skills and technology must be considered. Processes can assist businesses in focusing their efforts. Processes provide structure, quantifiable stages, and may be controlled efficiently on a daily basis. Furthermore, processes embed big data expertise into the business by following identical procedures and stages, making it "a practice" of the

organization. The analysis becomes less reliant on individuals, considerably increasing the odds of capturing value in the long run.

- **Big data functions:** Big data functions are focused on the organizational elements of big data management in businesses. This big data framework component examines roles and duties in big data organizations as well as how organizations might arrange themselves to build up big data roles. The effectiveness of big data efforts is heavily influenced by organizational culture, organizational structures, and job positions. As a result, we will go through several "best practices" for setting up corporate big data.
- **Artificial intelligence:** AI is one of the world's key topics of study today and holds a vast amount of promise. In this section of the framework, we briefly mention the relationship between big data and AI, which will be deeply discussed later in this book. Many organizations are eager to begin AI initiatives, but most are confused about where to begin. The big data framework approaches AI from the standpoint of offering commercial advantages to corporate organizations. This last component of the big data framework is a lifecycle of purposes. In order to give long-term value, AI may begin to continually learn from big data in the enterprise.

2.5 THE PRIMARY PRODUCTION FRAMEWORK OF BIG DATA IN SMART FARMING

Big data farming sensing technologies are frequently utilized to collect data and generate insights for building more effective farm operations. Although these technologies have grown more common in the previous decade, the use of sensors in agriculture is still in its infancy when compared to industries such as medical and transportation. These sensors may provide data such as soil moisture, temperature, and solar exposure, among others. Data acquired by IoT devices may be used to make key choices about the health and productivity of agricultural crops, which has a significant impact on farm revenue and food costs. To address the critical issue of feeding the world's rising population, agricultural technology businesses are employing IoT sensors to collect data in real time from crops and fields. Agribusinesses rely on analytics and technology to track numerous inputs and outputs in their operations. Therefore, big data farming is critical. When making strategic business decisions, big data farming should be taken into account. Big data farming may give insights into your company's profitability and assist in identifying patterns that may be harming the bottom line. It is no longer enough to analyze your data on its own; you must also compare it to other sources of pertinent information. When analyzing soil factors, for example, you may look at climate data or other publicly available information (Faroukhi et al., 2020).

In the context of employing big data techniques for atmospheric composition monitoring, our system design encompasses distinct layers, including the data source layer, ingestion, storage facilitated by Hadoop, the data management layer, infrastructure, and the security layer. This holistic approach ensures a comprehensive framework for acquiring, processing, and securing atmospheric data. The dataset is sourced from diverse channels, capturing pollutant gas emissions originating from agricultural, industrial, and transportation sources. This refined system architecture and data selection strategy aim to enhance the efficacy of our atmospheric monitoring framework, facilitating a more nuanced understanding of the sources and dynamics of pollutant emissions. Remote sensing was enabled to continually examine the atmospheric composition. A big data system can forecast whether fertilizers may trigger crop disease by making use of information like soil moisture, typical rainfall, and soil nutrients (Sleem, 2022). The big data process begins with data enrichment and continues with data clustering so that the data may be categorized and analyzed to provide suggestions. Finally, the Hadoop environment was employed to store and analyze ML data. Crops, weeds, food safety, biodiversity, remote sensing, farmer decision-making, insurance, funding, and climate change may all be better understood using big data. It also facilitates the establishment of supply chain platforms, giving agents access to high-quality goods, processes, and tools capable of boosting performance, forecasting demand, and addressing farmers based on crop needs, such as fertilizer application. By analyzing vast volumes of data from many sources, big data enables scientists and engineers to spot patterns and trends. Big data science has recently emerged as a crucial contemporary subject for data analysis. Big data encompasses a variety of traditional fields of AI, such as statistics, mathematics, and ML. Figure 2.5 shows the framework of big data in smart farming. Next, each phase of the framework will be discussed.

2.5.1　EDGE COMPUTING

Edge computing is a distributed computing platform that puts corporate applications closer to data sources like IoT devices or local edge servers. This closeness to data at its source can result in significant business benefits such as faster insights, faster reaction times, and increased bandwidth availability. It all comes down to location when it comes to edge computing. In conventional corporate computing, data is generated at a client endpoint, such as a user's PC. That data is sent through a wide area network, such as the Internet, and into the corporate local area network, where it is stored and processed by an enterprise application. The results of that task are subsequently communicated back to the client endpoint. Sending all of the device data to a centralized data center or the cloud generates bandwidth and latency difficulties. Edge computing is a more efficient option since data is processed and analyzed closer to the point of origin. Latency is considerably decreased since data does not travel over a network to a cloud or data center to be processed. Edge computing, and especially mobile edge computing on 5G networks, provides quicker and more complete data processing, allowing for deeper insights, faster reaction times, and better consumer experiences.

2.5.2　FOG COMPUTING

A computational layer between the cloud and the edge is known as fog computing. Whereas edge computing may deliver massive quantities of data straight to the cloud, fog computing may receive data from the edge layer before it reaches the cloud and determine what is and isn't important. Relevant data are saved in the cloud, while

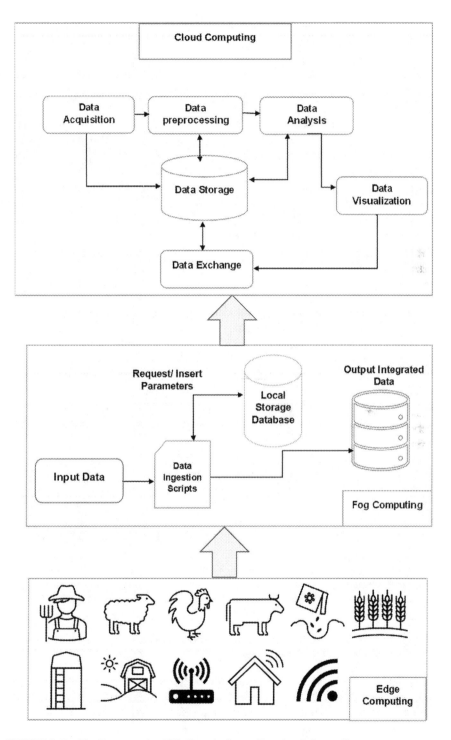

FIGURE 2.5   The Framework of Big Data in Smart Farming Primary Processes.

irrelevant data are destroyed or evaluated at the fog layer for distant access or to inform localized learning models.

The first step in the big data process is to specify the sources from which to extract the necessary data. The data must then be stored in one of the constructed representatives, which are built for unstructured, semi-structured, or structured data, respectively. Users aggregate bandwidth at access points like routers by positioning these closer to devices rather than building in-cloud channels for use and storage. As a result, less data may be transported away from data centers, over cloud channels and distances, reducing the total requirement for bandwidth. Another significant distinction between cloud computing and fog computing is data storage. Because less data requires immediate cloud storage in fog computing, users may instead subject data to strategic compilation and distribution rules meant to increase efficiency and save costs. It is simpler to capitalize on the current processing capacity in such devices by transferring real-time analytics into a cloud computing fog placed closer to those devices. This enhances user experience while reducing overall cloud loads.

2.5.3 CLOUD COMPUTING

Cloud computing is a massive, highly scalable deployment of computation and storage resources at one of numerous scattered worldwide sites (regions). Cloud providers also supply a variety of prepackaged services for IoT operations, making the cloud a popular centralized platform for IoT installations. Despite the fact that cloud computing provides far more than enough resources and services to tackle complex analytics, the nearest regional cloud facility can be hundreds of miles away from the point where data is collected, and connections rely on the same temperamental internet connectivity that supports traditional data centers. In reality, cloud computing is an alternative to—or often a supplement to—traditional data centers. The cloud may bring centralized processing considerably closer to a data source, but not at the network edge. In particular, the next stage is to use general data science, analytical tools, and algorithms (such as deep learning, ML, and online analytical processing (OLAP)) to examine the identified data. This enables decision-makers to visualize trends via data analysis. Farmers are empowered by data analytics because it provides them with useful insights about their agriculture business that allow them to predict market conditions, determine consumer behavior toward finished goods, account for inflation, and other variables that allow them to plan the entire process in advance, even before sowing the seeds. Farmers benefit from this because they may maximize their return on investment while eliminating avoidable losses.

2.6 THE SOCIOECONOMIC FRAMEWORK OF BIG DATA IN SMART FARMING

There has been a considerable tendency toward viewing the use of big data techniques and approaches to agriculture as a substantial potential for application of the technology stack, investment, and the creation of new value within the agri-food sector. As smart technologies and sensors proliferate on farms and farm data volumes and scope increase, agricultural operations will become more data-driven and data-enabled. Rapid advancements in the IoT and cloud computing are accelerating the phenomenon known as smart farming. Big data is playing an important, reciprocal part in this development: machines are outfitted with various sensors that measure data in their environment and utilize it to control the machines' behavior. This ranges from very simple feedback systems (such as a thermostat regulating temperature) to deep learning algorithms (e.g., to implement the right crop protection strategy). This is augmented by merging information with other, external big data sources such as weather or market data, or benchmarking with other farms. Because of the fast development of this field, it is impossible to provide a unified definition of big data, but in general, it is a phrase for datasets that are so massive or complicated that typical data processing applications are insufficient.

Figure 2.6 depicts the socioeconomic framework of big data in smart farming. As observed, the lowest layer of business processes focuses on the development and use of big data in the management of farming activities. As a result, this section was separated into three sections: the data chain, farm administration, and farm procedures. Through numerous decision-making processes in which information plays a vital role, the data chain interacts with agricultural activities and farm management processes. The stakeholder network (middle layer) includes all stakeholders participating in these activities, including not only big data consumers but also data management firms and regulatory and policy players. Finally, the network management layer represents the organizational and technological structures in the network that permit coordination and management of the processes done by the players in the stakeholder network layer. The higher layer of network management technology is concerned with the information architecture that supports the data chain.

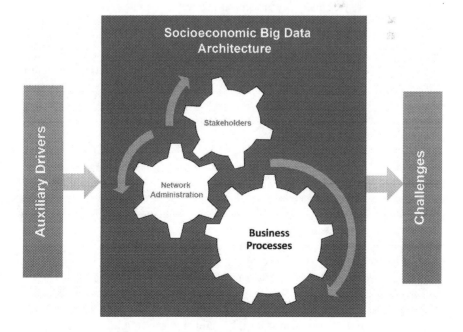

FIGURE 2.6   Illustration of Socioeconomic Big Data Architecture.

The organizational component is concerned with the data chain's governance and business model. Finally, various variables may be recognized as significant drivers for the growth of big data in smart farming, and as a result, problems can be deduced from this development. The subsections that follow give a more extensive description of each subcomponent of the framework's business processes layer and network management layer.

2.6.1 FARMING BUSINESS PROCESSES

Big data applications in farming are not strictly about primary production but play a major role in improving the efficiency of the entire supply chain and alleviating food security concerns. In other words, crop information is only profitable when it is effectively managed. Current developments in data management are causing smart farming to grow dramatically, as data has become a fundamental component in contemporary agriculture to assist farmers with critical decision-making. With objective information obtained by sensors, valuable advantages emerge with the goal of enhancing production and sustainability. This type of data-driven farm management is based on data that can boost efficiency by preventing resource waste and contamination of the environment. Data-driven agriculture, with the aid of robotic solutions using AI techniques, lays the groundwork for future sustainable agriculture.

2.6.1.1 Farm Procedures

A business process is a collection of logically connected operations carried out to accomplish a certain business objective. Business processes are classified as either primary or secondary. Primary business processes are those involved in the development of a product, its promotion, and delivery to the buyer. Secondary business processes enable the creation, implementation, and management of resources necessary in key processes. Farming business procedures vary greatly across different forms of production, such as cattle farming, arable farming, and greenhouse horticulture. A common trait is that agricultural productivity is dependent on natural circumstances such as climate (day length and temperature), soil, pests, diseases, and weather.

2.6.1.2 Farm Administration

Administration or management methods guarantee that business process objectives are met even when disruptions occur. The basic concept of control is the introduction of a controller that measures system behavior and corrects if measurements are not in accordance with system objectives. This means that they must have a feedback loop that includes a norm, sensor, discriminator, decision-maker, and effector. The main phases in this layer are as follows:

- **Sensing and observing:** The genuine performance of agricultural processes can be automatically measured using sensing devices, such as sensors or satellites. Furthermore, external data can be obtained to supplement direct observations.
- **Analysis and decision-making:** It compares measurements to norms that indicate expected performance (system objectives such as quantity,

quality, and lead time), detects deviations, and decides on the right action to eliminate the signaled disturbances.

- **Interoperability:** It prepares and executes the chosen interference to improve the performance of agricultural processes.

2.6.1.3 Data Manipulation

Data manipulation is a sequence of operations that occurs from data collection through decision-making and data commercialization. It encompasses all tasks required to handle data for agricultural management. As an essential component of business operations, data manipulation must include a technological layer that converts raw data into information, as well as a business layer that makes choices and extracts value from offered data services and business intelligence. The two layers may be interlaced at each level, and together they constitute the foundation of what has been known as the "value chain" of data. This chain consists of data collecting, storage, transport, transformation, analytics, and marketing.

2.6.2 STAKEHOLDERS

Stakeholder networks are very dynamic, with new actors adopting roles previously held by incumbents and incumbents assuming new responsibilities in connection to agricultural big data. Various accelerators, incubators, venture capital companies, and corporate venture funds are also involved. While corporations are heavily involved in big data and agriculture, start-ups are at the forefront of the action, delivering solutions across the value chain, from infrastructure and sensors to software that manages the multiple streams of data from across the farm. Furthermore, a rising number of tiny IT companies are releasing products that compete with their larger counterparts.

Venture capital firms are increasingly interested in investing in agricultural technology startups like Blue River Technology, which focuses on the application of computer vision and robots in agriculture. The newcomers to smart farming are technology businesses that have never been involved in agriculture. For example, Japanese technology companies like Fujitsu are assisting farmers with cloud-based farming solutions. Fujitsu gathers data (rainfall, humidity, soil temperatures) from a nationwide network of cameras and sensors to assist Japanese farmers in better managing their crops and expenditures. Data processing professionals are set to become producers' collaborators as big data delivers on its promise to radically improve producers' competitiveness.

Note: In light of the technological advances brought about by big data and smart farming, we want to comprehend the stakeholder network surrounding the farm. The research reveals significant alterations in roles and power relations among various participants in existing agri-food systems. We saw the shifting roles of old and new software providers in connection to big data and smart farming, as well as the rising landscape of data-driven initiatives with major roles for big tech and data corporations like Google and IBM.

2.6.3 NETWORK ADMINISTRATION

Network administration is concerned with stakeholder behavior and how it may be influenced to achieve the objectives of business processes. Two interrelated issues are deemed crucial for the adoption and continued expansion of big data applications: governance and business model. Governance refers to the legal and informal systems that regulate collaboration among stakeholders. Agreements on data availability, data quality, data access, security, accountability, liability, data ownership, privacy, and cost distribution are all important arrangements for big data management. There are three primary types of network governance: administrative discretion, standardization, and mutual adjustment. These forms correlate to the three types of network governance presented: lead organization-governed network, network administrative organization, and shared participant-governed network. The selection of a certain network governance structure tries to mitigate all types of contractual risks encountered between the various contracting parties in such a manner that transaction costs are reduced. When researching hybrid forms of organization, such as supply chain networks, two major dimensions should be identified: the allocation of decision rights, that is, who has the authority to make strategic decisions within the supply chain network, and the interorganizational mechanisms aimed at beneficial target behavior and trying to prevent unwanted behaviors (risk and rewarding mechanisms).

Besides, this layer comprises all hardware, software packages, communication standards, and so on that are used and required for adequate data management in the collaborative control of farming processes. The following elements will be mentioned:

- Data resources maintained in shared databases, as well as a common understanding of their contents.
- Information systems and services that enable these databases to be used and maintained. An information system processes information required to accomplish beneficial activities by utilizing activities, facilities, techniques, and procedures.
- The whole set of established technically and content-wise standards of coding and message, with accompanying usage processes, linked to common databases, required to provide seamless and error-free automated communication between business partners in a food supply chain network.
- The required technical infrastructure, that is, employees, as well as database, communication, software, and all related peripheral devices that will allow its use.

2.6.4 AUXILIARY DRIVERS

Innovations in smart farming are driven by push–pull forces, as with many technical advancements. Pull, because new technology is required to reach aims. Because new technology helps people or organizations to attain greater or new goals, there is a push. Farmers are searching for methods to enhance profitability and efficiency from a business standpoint by looking for ways to minimize expenses while also securing better pricing for their goods. As a result, they must make better, more optimum judgments and strengthen management control. Previously, advising services were based on generic knowledge acquired from research studies; now, there is a rising demand for information and expertise developed on-farm in its local-specific context. Big data technologies are expected to assist in attaining these aims more effectively. The effect of the weather, particularly its unpredictability, is a unique scenario for farming. Local weather and climatic data may greatly aid decision-making. A broad driver might be the reduction of paperwork due to various rules in agri-food production. From a public standpoint, global food security is frequently considered a major driver of future technical breakthroughs. Furthermore, customers are growing increasingly worried about food safety and nutritional components of food that affect health and well-being.

On the other hand, IoT is a broad future development in which all types of gadgets—smart items—are linked and interact with one another over local and global, frequently wireless network infrastructures. This is likely to result in drastic changes in farm management due to the availability of explicit information and decision-making skills that were previously unavailable, either technically or economically. As a result, there is an increase in the number of enterprises, which drives this data-driven development even further. Also, farmers may get their individual data from anywhere using wireless data transmission technology, allowing them to make educated decisions regarding crop production, harvesting, and the best way to bring their goods to market.

2.6.5 CHALLENGES OF SMART FARMING

Making solutions inexpensive for farmers, particularly those in developing nations, is a difficulty on the revenue side. The reciprocal value of big data is the idea that as more people utilize big data applications, more useful data will also increase. This is a crucial component that has to be thoughtfully included in business plans. The difficulty is in automating data collecting in a way that nearly eliminates expenditures. In order to transmit, integrate, and ultimately create applications out of on-farm data, investments are required in a common pool infrastructure. This is because on-farm data will typically stay in the hands of separate enterprises.

How to secure the privacy and security of big data is undoubtedly one of the largest concerns in governance. Because of this problem, data silos that are protected by individuals or businesses are sometimes preventing improvements. They worry that information will end up in the competitors' hands. Therefore, the first step in creating apps should be privileged access to big data and cultivating trust with farmers. Therefore, the agri-food chain has to establish new organizational links and forms of cooperation. In other words, it refers to having rapid access to the appropriate data sources for assessing core performance indicators, key performance indicators, and outcome indicators while developing effective growth plans.

REFERENCES

Cravero, A., Pardo, S., Galeas, P., López Fenner, J., & Caniupán, M. (2022). Data type and data sources for agricultural big data and machine learning. *Sustainability (Switzerland)*, *14*(23), 1–37. https://doi.org/10.3390/su142316131

Faroukhi, A. Z., Alaoui, I. E., Gahi, Y., & Amine, A. (2020). An adaptable big data value chain framework for end-to-end big data monetization. *Big Data and Cognitive Computing*, *4*(4), 34. https://doi.org/10.3390/BDCC4040034

Gandomi, A., & Haider, M. (2015). Beyond the hype: Big data concepts, methods, and analytics. *International Journal of Information Management*, *35*(2), 137–144. https://doi.org/10.1016/J.IJINFOMGT.2014.10.007

Ngo, V. M., Duong, T. V. T., Nguyen, T. B. T., Dang, C. N., & Conlan, O. (2023). A big data smart agricultural system: Recommending optimum fertilisers for crops. *International Journal of Information Technology (Singapore)*, 1–17. https://doi.org/10.1007/s41870-022-01150-1/tables/5

Parameswaran, T., Reddy, Y. C. A. P., Nagaveni, V., & Sathiyaraj, R. (2022). Era of computational big data analytics and IoT techniques in smart city applications. In *IoT and big data analytics for smart cities* (pp. 1–22). https://doi.org/10.1201/9781003217404-1

Qin, B., Hui, B., Wang, L., Yang, M., Li, B., Huang, F., Si, L., Jiang, Q., & Li, Y. (2023). Schema dependency-enhanced curriculum pre-training for table semantic parsing. *Knowledge-Based Systems*, *262*, 110264. https://doi.org/10.1016/J.KNOSYS.2023.110264

Sleem, A. (2022). Empowering smart farming with machine intelligence: An approach for plant leaf disease recognition. *Sustainable Machine Intelligence Journal*, *1*(1), 1–11. https://doi.org/10.61185/SMIJ.2022.1013

Unkovich, M., McKenzie, D., & Parker, W. (2023). New insights into high soil strength and crop plants; Implications for grain crop production in the Australian environment. *Plant and Soil*, *486*, 183–208. https://doi.org/10.1007/S11104-022-05862-Y

van Dijk, M., Morley, T., Rau, M. L., & Saghai, Y. (2021). A meta-analysis of projected global food demand and population at risk of hunger for the period 2010–2050. *Nature Food*, *2*(7), 494–501. https://doi.org/10.1038/s43016-021-00322-9

Veretekhina, S., Sergey, K., Pronkina, T., Khalyukin, V., Alla, M., Khudyakova, E., & Stepantsevich, M. (2022). Comparative analysis of big data acquisition technology from Landsat 8 and Sentinel-2 satellites. *Lecture Notes in Networks and Systems*, *503*, 41–53. https://doi.org/10.1007/978-3-031-09073-8_5/FIGURES/8

Yadav, N., & Shekokar, N. M. (2022). SQL injection attacks on Indian websites: A case study. In *Cyber security threats and challenges facing human life* (pp. 153–170). https://doi.org/10.1201/9781003218555-15

3 Conceptualization of Machine Learning for Smart Farming

3.1 INTRODUCTION

All applications of information and communication technology (ICT) are expected to benefit greatly from the use of machine learning (ML). Its ability to teach machines new skills without prior instruction holds great promise as a tool for a wide range of cutting-edge uses. ML, as one of the newest fields, promises to substantially impact the world in the next few decades in agriculture. Countless smart farming activities generate massive amounts of data from a variety of sources, which must be processed before any actionable insights can be drawn.

ML can be broadly categorized into several subfields based on the learning paradigm and the type of feedback or data available. The three primary categories are supervised learning, unsupervised learning, and reinforcement learning, each with its own unique characteristics and applications (see Table 3.1). Supervised learning is the most common and widely used form of ML. It involves training a model using labeled examples, where the input data is paired with corresponding target labels or desired outputs. The goal is for the model to learn a mapping function that can accurately predict labels for new, unseen data. Supervised learning can be further divided into classification or regression tasks. In classification tasks, the model learns to assign input data to predefined classes or categories. For instance, classifying crop diseases based on leaf images or predicting weather conditions (sunny, rainy, cloudy) based on atmospheric parameters. In regression tasks, the model learns to predict continuous numerical values. Examples include predicting crop yield based on environmental factors or estimating the market price of agricultural commodities.

Unsupervised learning involves training a model on unlabeled data, where the goal is to discover patterns, structures, or relationships in the data without any predefined labels or outputs. Unsupervised learning is particularly useful when the underlying structure or insights within the data are unknown. Unsupervised learning techniques can also be categorized into clustering or dimensionality reduction. Clustering algorithms group similar data points together based on their intrinsic characteristics or proximity. This can be used, for example, to identify different plant species within an agricultural dataset or segment customers into distinct groups based on their purchasing behavior. Dimensionality reduction techniques aim to reduce the complexity of high-dimensional data while preserving important information. They help visualize and understand data, identify key features, or facilitate downstream tasks. Examples include principal component analysis (PCA) or t-distributed stochastic neighbor embedding (t-SNE).

DOI: 10.1201/9781003400103-3

TABLE 3.1

Comparison of ML Types Based on Different Aspects.

Aspect	Supervised Learning	Unsupervised Learning	Reinforcement Learning
Data	Labeled data	Unlabeled data	Feedback in the form of rewards or penalties
Learning Goal	Predict or classify	Discover patterns or clusters	Maximize cumulative rewards
Training Process	Learn from labeled examples	Learn from unlabeled data	Learn from rewards and punishments
Examples	Crop disease detection	Crop clustering	Irrigation scheduling
Algorithm Types	Decision trees, support vector machines	K-means clustering, self-organizing maps	Q-learning, deep Q-networks
Input-Output	Environmental parameters, disease labels	Environmental data points	Environmental states, actions
Evaluation Metrics	Accuracy, F1 score, recall	Silhouette score, intra-cluster similarity	Cumulative reward, success rate
Application Areas	Crop yield prediction, pest detection	Anomaly detection, field segmentation	Autonomous robots, precision farming

Reinforcement learning involves an agent learning to make sequential decisions in an environment to maximize a reward signal. The agent interacts with the environment, takes actions, receives feedback in the form of rewards or penalties, and adjusts its behavior accordingly. Reinforcement learning is particularly applicable to dynamic and interactive scenarios, such as optimizing irrigation scheduling or autonomous crop management systems. Reinforcement learning consists of the following components:

- **Agent:** The learner or decision-maker that interacts with the environment.
- **Environment:** The external system or domain in which the agent operates.
- **Actions:** The decisions or choices made by the agent.
- **Rewards:** The feedback or evaluative signal that guides the agent toward desirable outcomes.
- **Policy:** The strategy or approach followed by the agent to select actions based on its current state.

It's important to note that within each category, there are numerous algorithms, techniques, and variations that cater to different learning scenarios and challenges. Understanding this taxonomy provides a foundation for selecting appropriate methods and algorithms based on the problem at hand and the available data.

3.2   DEFINITION OF MACHINE LEARNING

ML is a fascinating subfield of AI that is all around us. ML harnesses the power of data in novel ways. This incredible technology assists computer systems in learning and improving from experience by creating computer programs that can automatically access data and accomplish tasks through predictions and detections. In 1959, Arthur Samuel coined the phrase "Machine Learning." He described ML as "the branch of research that offers computers the ability to learn without being explicitly programmed." There is, however, no commonly recognized definition of ML. The word is defined variably by different sources (Boehmke and Greenwell, 2019; Hatzilygeroudis et al., 2023; Dong et al., 2023). Some of the prominent definitions include:

> *Definition I*: *ML is the process of programming computers to maximize a performance criterion based on example data or previous experience. We've defined a model up to some parameters, and learning is the execution of a computer program to optimize the model's parameters using training data or prior experience. The model may be predictive in order to make future forecasts, or descriptive in order to gather information from data.*
>
> *Definition II*: *ML is a topic of research dealing with the subject of how to build computer algorithms that automatically improve with experience.*
>
> *Definition III*: *ML is a data analysis technique that automates the creation of analytical models. It is a subfield of AI that is founded on the premise that systems can learn from data, recognize patterns, and make judgements with minimum human interaction.*

ML is significant because it provides organizations with insights into trends in consumer behavior and company operating patterns, as well as aids in the development of new products. Many of today's major organizations, like Facebook, Google, and Uber, have made ML a core aspect of their operations. ML has become a crucial competitive difference for many businesses. In other words, the need for ML is growing by the day. The necessity for ML stems from its ability to do tasks that are too complicated for a human to perform directly. As humans, we have some limits since we cannot access substantial amounts of data manually; therefore, we need computer systems, and this is where ML comes in to help us. We can train ML algorithms by feeding them massive amounts of data and allowing them to autonomously examine the data, build models, and anticipate the desired output. The cost function may determine the performance of the ML algorithm based on the amount of data. We can save both time and money with the aid of ML. The value of ML may be simply grasped by looking at its applications. ML is now employed in self-driving cars, cyber fraud detection, and facial recognition, among other applications. Several leading corporations, like Amazon, have built ML algorithms that monitor customer interest and propose products based on that data. The following are some major points that demonstrate the significance of ML:

- Increasing data production rapidly.
- Solving complicated issues that are tough for a person to solve.
- Making decisions in different sectors, including finance.
- Detecting hidden patterns in data and extracting usable information from them.

Therefore, ML is a critical component of the rapidly expanding discipline of data science. Algorithms are taught using statistical approaches to produce classifications or predictions and to find critical insights in data mining operations. These insights then influence decision-making within applications and enterprises, ideally influencing key growth indicators. As big data expands and grows, so will the market demand for data scientists. They will be expected to assist in identifying the most pertinent business questions and the data to address them. Following that, programmers select an ML model to employ, provide the data, and let the computer model train itself to detect patterns or make predictions. The human programmer may also change the model over time, including changing its parameters, to assist it in providing more accurate results. Some data from the training data is kept aside to be used as evaluation data, which assesses how accurate the ML model is when presented with fresh data. The result is a model that can be utilized with new sets of data in the future. The operational characteristics of a machine learning system may be categorized into two main types: descriptive and predictive. In the descriptive mode, the system utilizes available data to provide an explanation of past events or phenomena. On the other hand, in the predictive mode, the system leverages the available data to make informed forecasts or predictions about future events or outcomes. Alternatively, the system might be prescriptive in nature, wherein it utilizes the available data to provide recommendations for the appropriate course of action to be undertaken.

In general, the ML algorithm's learning system is divided into three key parts:

1. **Decision process:** ML algorithms are often used to create a prediction or classification. Your algorithm will provide an estimate of a pattern in the data based on some input data, which can be labeled or unlabeled.
2. **Fault function:** It examines the model's prediction. If there are known instances, a fault function can compare them to determine the model's correctness.
3. **Model optimization process:** If the model can fit the data points in the training set better, weights are modified to narrow the gap between the known example and the model prediction. The algorithm will repeat this "evaluate and optimize" procedure, updating weights automatically until an accuracy criterion is reached.

Standard ML is frequently classified by how an algorithm learns to improve its prediction accuracy. There are four fundamental techniques to learning: supervised learning, unsupervised learning, semi-supervised learning, and reinforcement learning. The algorithm that data scientists employ is determined by the sort of data they wish to forecast. Next, each ML type will be discussed.

The ML workflow provides a systematic approach to developing and deploying ML models. It consists of several key steps that guide the process from data collection to model evaluation and deployment. Understanding this workflow is crucial for effectively applying ML techniques in smart farming applications.

Data collection: The first step in the ML workflow is data collection. This involves gathering relevant and representative data from various sources, such as sensors, satellites, or databases. In smart farming, data can include environmental parameters (temperature, humidity), crop characteristics (growth stage, leaf color), or historical yield records. Ensuring the inclusivity of data collection involves considering diverse farming practices, crops, and regions to capture a comprehensive picture of the agricultural landscape.

Data preprocessing: Once the data is collected, it often requires preprocessing to prepare it for ML algorithms. This step involves cleaning the data by removing noise, handling missing values, and addressing outliers. Additionally, data normalization, standardization, or scaling techniques may be applied to ensure that features are on a similar scale. Inclusivity in data preprocessing involves considering potential biases, such as balancing the representation of different crops, regions, or farming practices within the dataset.

Feature engineering and selection: Feature engineering involves transforming the raw data into meaningful features that capture relevant information for the ML task. This may include extracting statistical features, creating new derived features, or applying domain-specific knowledge to enhance the predictive power of the model. Feature selection techniques can also be employed to identify the most informative features while reducing dimensionality and improving computational efficiency.

Model training: Model training is the core step in ML. It involves selecting an appropriate algorithm and training the model on the prepared dataset. In supervised learning, this step entails optimizing the model's parameters using labeled data to minimize the error between predicted and actual values. In unsupervised learning, the model learns patterns or structures in the data without explicit labels. Training algorithms can range from traditional techniques like linear regression or decision trees to more advanced approaches such as neural networks or support vector machines.

Model evaluation: After training, the model's performance needs to be evaluated to assess its effectiveness and generalizability. Evaluation metrics depend on the specific ML task and can include accuracy, precision, recall, F1 score, or mean squared error. Cross-validation techniques, such as K-fold cross-validation, help estimate the model's performance on unseen data. Inclusivity in model evaluation involves considering the fairness of predictions across different demographic groups and addressing potential biases that may arise in the model's outcomes.

Model optimization and validation: Based on the evaluation results, the model may need further optimization or fine-tuning. This involves adjusting hyperparameters, regularization techniques, or exploring ensemble methods to improve model performance. Once optimized, the model should be validated using an independent dataset to ensure its robustness and reliability.

Model deployment: The final step is deploying the trained model into a real-world application or system. This can involve integrating the model into an existing smart farming platform, developing application programming interfaces for easy access, or deploying the model on edge devices for real-time inference. Inclusive model deployment requires considering the accessibility and usability of the system for diverse users, including farmers with varying levels of technological infrastructure and resources.

It's important to note that the ML workflow is an iterative process, often requiring iterations and refinements at each step to improve model performance. Keeping inclusivity in mind throughout the workflow ensures that the developed models are relevant, fair, and applicable to a wide range of agricultural scenarios and stakeholders.

3.3 DATA AND PREPROCESSING

Data are the lifeblood of ML, serving as the foundation for training, validating, and deploying intelligent models. In ML, data encompass a wide array of information that feed the algorithms, enabling them to learn patterns, make predictions, and derive insights. Different types of data are encountered in ML, each carrying its own characteristics and considerations.

3.3.1 NUMERICAL DATA

Numerical data consist of continuous or discrete numerical values and is a widely used data type in smart farming. It encompasses various environmental parameters such as temperature, humidity, soil moisture, or rainfall measurements. However, inclusivity in numerical data extends beyond these parameters. It involves considering the diverse range of crops, regions, and farming practices to capture the variability within the agricultural landscape. This ensures that the ML models developed using numerical data can be applied to different agricultural contexts, considering the specific needs and characteristics of various crops and farming systems. For example, when predicting crop yield based on historical temperature and rainfall data, an inclusive approach considers the diverse range of crops grown in different regions, including both staple crops and specialty crops. It accounts for variations in crop growth requirements and environmental tolerances, ensuring that the predictive models are applicable across different crop types and geographic locations.

Data preprocessing for numerical data involves transforming and preparing the data before it can be used effectively in ML algorithms. The goal is to improve the quality and suitability of the numerical data for subsequent analysis and modeling. The following steps discuss the key concepts in data preprocessing for numerical data:

1) **Handling missing values**: Missing values can be present in numerical data due to various reasons such as sensor failures, data corruption, or incomplete data collection. Dealing with missing values is crucial to ensure accurate and reliable analysis. Common techniques for handling missing values include:
   - **Removal**: If the proportion of missing values is small, you may choose to remove the corresponding instances or features. However, this approach should be used cautiously as it can lead to information loss.

```
import pandas as pd

# Example DataFrame with null values
data'='{'A': [1, 2, None, 4],
    ' ' 'B': [5, None, 7, fl'at('nan')],
    ' ' 'C': [9, 10, 11, 12]}
```

```
df = pd.DataFrame(data)

# Remove rows with null values
cleaned _ df = df.dropna()


print(cleaned _ df)
```

- **Imputation:** Missing values can be imputed or filled in using various methods such as mean, median, mode, or regression imputation. Imputation aims to estimate reasonable values based on existing data, but it introduces uncertainty and potential bias.

```
import pandas as pd

# Example DataFrame with null values
data'='{'A': [1, 2, None, 4],
    ' ' 'B': [5, None, 7, fl'at('nan')],
    ' ' 'C': [9, 10, 11, 12]}
df = pd.DataFrame(data)

# Impute null values with the mean of each column
df.fillna(df.mean(), inplace=True)

# Impute null values with the median of each column
df.fillna(df.median(), inplace=True)

# Impute null values with the most frequent value of each column
for column in df.columns:
    most _ frequent _ value = df[column].mode().iloc[0]
    df[column].fillna(most _ frequent _ value, inplace=True)

# Impute null values using linear interpolation
df.interpolate(met'od='li'ear', inplace=True)

print(df)
```

2) **Feature scaling and normalization**: Numerical features may have different scales or units, which can affect the performance of ML algorithms. Feature scaling and normalization techniques are used to bring the features to a similar scale and facilitate fair comparisons. Common methods include:
   - **Min-max scaling:** This technique scales the features to a predefined range, typically between 0 and 1, by subtracting the minimum value and dividing by the range.

```
import pandas as pd

from sklearn.preprocessing import MinMaxScaler

# Example DataFrame with data to be normalized
```

```
data'='{'A': [1, 3, 5, 7],
    ' ' 'B': [2, 4, 6, 8]}
df = pd.DataFrame(data)

# Columns to be normalized
columns _ to _ normalize'='['''' 'B']

# Create the MinMaxScaler object
scaler = MinMaxScaler()

# Fit the scaler on the selected columns and transform them
df[columns _ to _ normalize] = scaler.fit _ transform(df[columns _ to _ normalize])

print(df)
```

- **Standardization:** Standardization transforms the features to have zero mean and unit variance by subtracting the mean and dividing by the standard deviation. This technique assumes the data follow a Gaussian distribution.

```
import pandas as pd

from sklearn.preprocessing import StandardScaler

# Example DataFrame with data to be standardized
data'='{'A': [1, 3, 5, 7],
    ' ' 'B': [2, 4, 6, 8]}
df = pd.DataFrame(data)

# Columns to be standardized
columns _ to _ standardize'='['''' 'B']

# Create the StandardScaler object
scaler = StandardScaler()

# Fit the scaler on the selected columns and transform them
df[columns _ to _ standardize] =
scaler.fit _ transform(df[columns _ to _ standardize])

print(df)
```

3) **Handling outliers:** Outliers are extreme values that deviate significantly from the normal range of the data. They can negatively impact the performance and accuracy of ML models. Dealing with outliers involves:
   - **Detection:** Outliers can be identified using statistical methods like z-score, interquartile range (IQR), or visualization techniques such as box plots or scatter plots.

```
import numpy as np

from scipy.stats import zscore
```

```
# Example data with outliers
data = np.array([2, 3, 5, 7, 8, 10, 15, 50, 100, 200])

# Z-score-based outlier detection
z _ scores = zscore(data)
outliers _ z _ score = np.abs(z _ scores) > 3

# Interquartile Range (IQR) outlier detection
Q1 = np.percentile(data, 25)
Q3 = np.percentile(data, 75)
IQR =-Q3 - Q1
lower _ bound =-Q1 - 1.5 * IQR
upper _ bound = Q3 + 1.5 * IQR
outliers _ iqr = (data < lower _ bound) | (data > upper _ bound)

pr"nt("D"ta:", data)
pr"nt("Outliers (Z-score meth"d):", data[outliers _ z _ score])
pr"nt("Outliers (IQR meth"d):", data[outliers _ iqr])
```

- **Treatment:** Outliers can be treated through methods like trimming (removing the extreme values), winsorization (replacing extreme values with the nearest non-outlier values), or transformation (applying mathematical functions to adjust the distribution).

```
import numpy as np

import scipy.stats as stats

# Example data with outliers
data = np.array([2, 3, 5, 7, 8, 10, 15, 50, 100, 200])

# Method 1: Trimming
trimmed _ data = np.clip(data, 5, 100)  # Trimming values below 5 and above
100

# Method 2: Winsorization
winsorized _ data = stats.mstats.winsorize(data,limits=[0.05, 0.05])  #
Winsorizing 5% from both tails

# Method 3: Transformation (Log Transformation)
transformed _ data = np.log1p(data)  # Adding 1 to avoid log(0) and negative
values

pr"nt("Original D"ta:", data)
pr"nt("Trimmed D"ta:", trimmed _ data)
pr"nt("Winsorized D"ta:", winsorized _ data)
pr"nt("Transformed D"ta:", transformed _ data)
```

4) **Addressing skewness:** Skewness refers to the asymmetry in the distribution of numerical data. Skewed data can impact the assumptions of ML models, especially those assuming a normal distribution. Techniques to address skewness include:

- **Logarithmic transformation:** Applying a logarithmic function to the data can reduce right-skewness and bring the data closer to a normal distribution.

```
import numpy as np

import matplotlib.pyplot as plt

# Example data with right-skewed distribution
data = np.array([1, 2, 3, 4, 5, 10, 50, 100, 500, 1000])

# Applying log transformation
data _ log _ transformed = np.log1p(data)

# Plotting the original data and the transformed data
plt.figure(figsize=(10, 5))

plt.subplot(1, 2, 1)
plt.hist(data, bins=10)
plt.ti'le('Original 'ata')
plt.xla'el('Va'ues')
plt.yla'el('Frequ'ncy')

plt.subplot(1, 2, 2)
plt.hist(data _ log _ transformed, bins=10)
plt.ti'le('Log-Transformed 'ata')
plt.xla'el('Log-Transformed Va'ues')
plt.yla'el('Frequ'ncy')

plt.tight _ layout()
plt.show()
```

- **Box-cox transformation:** This technique applies a power transformation to the data, aiming to achieve a more symmetric distribution.

```
import numpy as np

from scipy.stats import boxcox
import matplotlib.pyplot as plt

# Example data with skewness
data = np.array([1, 2, 3, 5, 10, 20, 50, 100, 200])

# Box-Cox transformation
transformed _ data, lambda _ param = boxcox(data)

pr"nt("Original D"ta:", data)
pr"nt("Transformed D"ta:", transformed _ data)
pr"nt("Lambda parame"er:", lambda _ param)
```

5) **Dimensionality reduction:** In some cases, numerical data may have a high number of features, leading to the curse of dimensionality and potential overfitting. Dimensionality reduction techniques, such as PCA or feature

selection methods, can be applied to reduce the number of features while preserving important information and minimizing redundancy.

3.3.2 CATEGORICAL DATA

Categorical data represent variables with specific categories or labels. In smart farming, categorical data can include crop types, pest or disease types, or different soil types. An inclusive approach to categorical data acknowledges the diversity of crops and pests encountered in smart farming. It considers a wide range of crop species, including both major crops and those specific to certain regions or communities. This ensures that the ML models can effectively handle the classification and prediction tasks across different crops and pests, supporting diverse farming practices and regional needs.

For instance, when classifying crop diseases based on categorical labels, an inclusive approach encompasses a comprehensive set of diseases affecting various crops, including those that predominantly impact specific crops or regions. It takes into account the varying symptoms and characteristics of diseases across different crops, ensuring that the classification models can accurately identify and distinguish between diseases in a diverse range of agricultural settings.

Data preprocessing for categorical data involves transforming and preparing the data before it can be effectively used in ML algorithms. It aims to encode categorical variables into numerical representations, handle missing values, and address class imbalance. The goal is to convert categorical data into a suitable format that can be used by ML models. In the following text, the key concepts of categorical data preprocessing are discussed:

1) **Handling missing values**: Similar to numerical data, categorical data can also contain missing values. Dealing with missing values in categorical data can be approached in various ways:
   - **Removal:** If the proportion of missing values is small, you may choose to remove the corresponding instances or features. However, caution should be exercised to ensure that important information is not lost.
   - **Imputation:** Missing values can be imputed or filled in using methods such as mode imputation, where the most frequent category is used to replace the missing values. Alternatively, advanced techniques like predictive imputation can be employed to estimate missing values based on other variables.

2) **Encoding categorical variables**
   ML algorithms typically require numerical input. Therefore, categorical variables need to be encoded into numerical representations. Common encoding techniques include:
   - **One-hot encoding:** This technique creates a binary column for each category, where a value of 1 indicates the presence of the category and 0 represents its absence. It is suitable for categorical variables without a natural ordering or hierarchy.

```
import pandas as pd

# Example DataFrame with a categorical column
data'= {'F'uit': ['A'pl'', 'Ba'an'', 'Or'ng'', 'A'pl'', 'Or'nge']}
df = pd.DataFrame(data)

# Perform One-Hot Encoding using pandas get _ dummies() function
one _ hot _ encoded _ df = pd.get _ dummies(df, colum's=['F'uit'])

pr"nt("Original DataFram":\n", df)
pr"nt("\nOne-Hot Encoded DataFram":\n", one _ hot _ encoded _ df)
```

- **Ordinal encoding:** Ordinal encoding assigns a unique numerical value to each category, preserving the ordinal relationship between categories. For example, assigning 1, 2, 3 to low, medium, high, respectively.

```
import pandas as pd

from sklearn.preprocessing import OrdinalEncoder

# Example DataFrame with a categorical column
data'= {''ize': ['S'al'', 'Me'iu'', 'L'rg'', 'L'rg'', 'S'al'', 'Me'ium']}
df = pd.DataFrame(data)

# Create the OrdinalEncoder object
ordinal _ encoder = OrdinalEncoder(categorie'=[['S'al'', 'Me'iu'',
'L'rge']])

# Fit and transform the categorical column using Ordinal Encoding
'df['Size _ Enc'ded'] = ordinal _ encoder.fit _ transform('f[['ize']])

pr"nt("Original DataFram":\n", 'f[['ize']])
pr"nt("\nOrdinal Encoded DataFram":\n", 'f[['Size _ Enc'ded']])
```

- **Binary encoding:** Binary encoding converts each category into a binary code, representing each category as a combination of 0s and 1s. This method is useful for high-cardinality categorical variables, reducing the dimensionality compared to one-hot encoding.

```
import pandas as pd

import category _ encoders as ce

# Example DataFrame with a categorical column
data'= {''ity': ['New 'or'', 'Lo'do'', 'P'ri'', 'Lo'do'', 'T'kyo']}
df = pd.DataFrame(data)

# Create the BinaryEncoder object
binary _ encoder = ce.BinaryEncoder(co's=['ity'])

# Fit and transform the categorical column using Binary Encoding
df _ encoded = binary _ encoder.fit _ transform(df)
```

```
pr"nt("Original DataFram":\n", df)
pr"nt("\nBinary Encoded DataFram":\n", df _ encoded)
```

- **Label encoding:** Label encoding assigns a numerical label to each category, ranging from 0 to the number of categories minus one. This method is suitable for categorical variables with an inherent order, but it should be used with caution as it may introduce unintended ordinality.

```
import pandas as pd

from sklearn.preprocessing import LabelEncoder

# Example DataFrame with a categorical column
data'= {''ity': ['New 'or'', 'Lo'do'', 'P'ri'', 'Lo'do'', 'T'kyo']}
df = pd.DataFrame(data)

# Create the LabelEncoder object
label _ encoder = LabelEncoder()

# Fit and transform the categorical column using Label Encoding
'df['City _ Enc'ded'] = label _ encoder.fit _ transform'df[''ity'])

pr"nt("Original DataFram":\n", 'f[[''ity']])
pr"nt("\nLabel Encoded DataFram":\n", 'f[['City _ Enc'ded']])
```

3) Handling class imbalance

In some cases, categorical data may exhibit class imbalance, where certain categories are significantly more prevalent than others. Class imbalance can negatively impact the performance of ML models, particularly in classification tasks. Techniques to handle class imbalance include:

- **Oversampling:** Oversampling increases the representation of minority categories by randomly replicating or generating synthetic samples from the minority class.

```
import pandas as pd

from collections import Counter
from imblearn.over _ sampling import RandomOverSampler

# Example DataFrame with an imbalanced class distribution
data'= {'fea'ure': [1, 2, 3, 4, 5, 6, 7, 8, 9, 10],
    '   'l'bel': [0, 0, 0, 0, 0, 0, 1, 1, 1, 1]}
df = pd.DataFrame(data)

# Count the class distribution before oversampling
pr"nt("Class distribution before oversampl"ng:", Counter'df['l'bel']))

# Create the RandomOverSampler object
oversampler = RandomOverSampler(random _ state=42)
```

```
# Perform random oversampling
X _ resampled, y _ resampled = oversampler.fit _ resample('f[['fea'ure']],
'df['l'bel'])

# Count the class distribution after oversampling
pr"nt("Class distribution after oversampl"ng:", Counter(y _ resampled))
```

- **Undersampling:** Undersampling reduces the representation of the majority class by randomly removing samples from the majority class.

```
import pandas as pd

from collections import Counter
from imblearn.under _ sampling import RandomUnderSampler

# Example DataFrame with an imbalanced class distribution
data'= {'fea'ure': [1, 2, 3, 4, 5, 6, 7, 8, 9, 10],
   '   'l'bel': [0, 0, 0, 0, 0, 0, 1, 1, 1, 1]}
df = pd.DataFrame(data)

# Count the class distribution before downsampling
pr"nt("Class distribution before downsampl"ng:", Counter'df['l'bel']))

# Create the RandomUnderSampler object
undersampler = RandomUnderSampler(random _ state=42)

# Perform random under-sampling
X _ resampled, y _ resampled = undersampler.fit _ resample('f[['fea'ure']],
'df['l'bel'])

# Count the class distribution after downsampling
pr"nt("Class distribution after downsampl"ng:", Counter(y _ resampled))
```

- **Synthetic minority over-sampling technique (SMOTE):** SMOTE generates synthetic examples for the minority class by interpolating between existing instances. This technique helps to balance the class distribution while increasing the diversity of the dataset.

```
import pandas as pd

from collections import Counter
from imblearn.over _ sampling import SMOTE

# Example DataFrame with an imbalanced class distribution
data'= {'fea'ure': [1, 2, 3, 4, 5, 6, 7, 8, 9, 10],
   '   'l'bel': [0, 0, 0, 0, 0, 0, 1, 1, 1, 1]}
df = pd.DataFrame(data)

# Count the class distribution before oversampling
pr"nt("Class distribution before oversampl"ng:", Counter'df['l'bel']))
```

```
# Create the SMOTE object
smote = SMOTE(random _ state=42)

# Perform SMOTE oversampling
X _ resampled, y _ resampled = smote.fit _ resample('f[['fea'ure']],
'df['l'bel'])

# Count the class distribution after oversampling
pr"nt("Class distribution after oversampl"ng:", Counter(y _ resampled))
```

3.3.3   TIME SERIES DATA

Time series data, consisting of observations recorded over successive time intervals, are commonly collected in smart farming applications. Inclusivity in time series data involves capturing the temporal dynamics and patterns across different crops, regions, and farming practices. It acknowledges the variations in growth patterns, phenology, and environmental responses exhibited by diverse crops. For example, when forecasting crop yield based on historical yield data, an inclusive approach accounts for variations in growth cycles, planting dates, and management practices across different crops. It considers the unique characteristics of each crop, ensuring that the time series models can effectively capture and predict yield fluctuations for a wide range of agricultural products, supporting inclusive decision-making in diverse farming systems. mage data preprocessing involves transforming and preparing the data to enhance the quality and suitability of image data for subsequent analysis and modeling.

3.3.4   IMAGE DATA

Image data are usually acquired through drones, cameras, or satellite imagery, and provides visual information in smart farming applications. Inclusivity in image data involves considering the diversity of crops, landscapes, and imaging technologies used in different agricultural contexts. It encompasses the representation of different crops, including both widely cultivated crops and those specific to certain cultural or geographical regions. It also accounts for variations in landscape characteristics, such as field topography or vegetation cover. For example, when identifying nutrient deficiencies in crops based on leaf images, an inclusive approach considers the visual characteristics of various crops, accounting for differences in leaf morphology, coloration, and growth patterns. It ensures that the image analysis models can accurately detect and classify nutrient deficiencies across a wide range of crops, supporting diverse agricultural systems and regional practices.

- **Image formatting and resizing:**
  Image data may come in various formats and sizes. To ensure consistency and compatibility, it is important to preprocess images by converting them to a standardized format, such as JPEG or PNG, and resizing them to a uniform size. This allows for easier manipulation and analysis of the image data.

- **Normalization and standardization:**

  Normalization and standardization techniques are used to transform pixel values in the image data. This ensures that the pixel values fall within a specific range, enabling algorithms to handle the data more effectively. Common techniques include:

  - **Normalization:** Normalizing the pixel values to a range between 0 and 1 by dividing each pixel value by the maximum pixel value in the image.
  - **Standardization:** Standardizing the pixel values by subtracting the mean pixel value across the entire dataset and dividing by the standard deviation. This brings the pixel values to a similar scale and facilitates fair comparisons.

```
import cv2

import numpy as np
from sklearn.preprocessing import StandardScaler
import matplotlib.pyplot as plt

# Load an example image (repl'ce 'path _ to _ i'age' with the actual path to
your image)
image = cv2.imr'ad('path _ to _ i'age')

# Convert the image to float32 for further processing
image = image.astype(np.float32)

# Image normalization (scaling pixel values to [0, 1])
normalized _ image = image / 255.0

# Image standardization (zero mean and unit variance)
standard _ scaler = StandardScaler()
reshaped _ image = image.reshape(-1, 3)   # Reshape image to a 2D array
(pixels as rows, channels as columns)
standardized _ image = standard _ scaler.fit _ transform(reshaped _ image)
standardized _ image = standardized _ image.reshape(image.shape)

# Plot the original, normalized, and standardized images
plt.figure(figsize=(10, 4))
plt.subplot(131)
plt.imshow(cv2.cvtColor(image.astype(np.uint8), cv2.COLOR _ BGR2RGB))
plt.ti'le('Original I'age')
plt.a'is('off')

plt.subplot(132)
plt.imshow(cv2.cvtColor(normalized _ image, cv2.COLOR _ BGR2RGB))
plt.ti'le('Normalized I'age')
plt.a'is('off')

plt.subplot(133)
plt.imshow(cv2.cvtColor(standardized _ image.astype(np.uint8), cv2.
COLOR _ BGR2RGB))
plt.ti'le('Standardized I'age')
plt.a'is('off')
```

```
plt.tight_layout()
plt.show()
```

- **Handling noise and artifacs:**
  Image data can contain noise, artifacts, or unwanted elements that may interfere with the analysis or modeling process. Preprocessing techniques for handling noise and artifacts include:
  - **Denoising:** Image denoising techniques are used to remove or reduce noise from images, improving their visual quality and enhancing the accuracy of subsequent analysis tasks. There are various methods for denoising images, ranging from traditional filters (e.g., Gaussian smoothing, median filtering, total variation denoising, wavelet denoising, non-local means denoising) to advanced deep learning-based approaches (see Table 3.2).

```
import cv2

import numpy as np
from scipy import ndimage
from skimage.restoration import denoise_tv_chambolle, denoise_wavelet,
denoise_nl_means
import matplotlib.pyplot as plt

# Read the image using OpenCV
image_pat' = 'path_to_your_image'jpg'
image = cv2.imread(image_path, cv2.IMREAD_GRAYSCALE)

# Add noise to the image (optional, for demonstration purposes)
noise = np.random.normal(0, 25, image.shape)
noisy_image = np.clip(image + noise, 0, 255).astype(np.uint8)

# Apply Gaussian Smoothing
gaussian_smoothed_image = cv2.GaussianBlur(noisy_image, (5, 5), 0)

# Apply Median Filtering
median_filtered_image = cv2.medianBlur(noisy_image, 5)

# Apply Total Variation Denoising
tv_denoised_image = denoise_tv_chambolle(noisy_image, weight=0.1)

# Apply Wavelet Denoising
wavelet_denoised_image = denoise_wavelet(noisy_image, wave'et='db1',
m'de=''oft', multichannel=False)

# Apply Non-local Means Denoising
nl_means_denoised_image = denoise_nl_means(noisy_image, h=10,
patch_size=7, patch_distance=13)

# Display the original and denoised images
plt.figure(figsize=(12, 8))
plt.subplot(2, 3, 1), plt.imshow(noisy_image, c'ap=''ray'),
plt.ti'le('Noisy I'age')
```

TABLE 3.2

Comparative Review of the Popular Image Denoising Techniques.

Denoising Technique	Advantages	Disadvantages	Noise Type	Complexity	Applicability	Parameter Tuning	Fine grain	Edge Preserve	Texture Preserve
Gaussian Smoothing	Simple and fast. Preserves image structure	Blurs fine details; May cause loss of image sharpness	Gaussian or random noise	Low	General	None	Moderate	Moderate	Moderate
Median Filtering	Effective for salt-and-pepper noise removal; Preserves edges and details	Smoothing effect on textures; may introduce blurring in homogeneous areas	Salt-and-pepper noise	Low	General	None	High	High	Moderate
Total Variation Denoising	Preserves edges and fine details; effective for removing Gaussian and salt-and-pepper noise; can handle complex noise patterns	May oversmooth textures; requires careful selection of regularization parameter	Gaussian or salt-and-pepper noise	Moderate	General	Moderate	High	Moderate	Moderate
Wavelet Denoising	Effective for a wide range of noise types; preserves image details; can handle both low and high noise levels	Requires tuning of thresholding parameters; may introduce artifacts in highly textured areas	Various noise types	Moderate to High	General	Moderate	High	High	High

Method	Advantages	Disadvantages	Noise Type						
Non-local Means Denoising	Preserves image details and textures; effective for removing Gaussian and salt-and-pepper noise; robust to various noise levels	Can be computationally expensive for large images; may oversmooth thin structures	Gaussian or salt-and-pepper noise	High	General	Moderate	Moderate	Moderate	High
Deep Learning-based Denoising	High denoising performance; can handle complex noise patterns; learns from large-scale datasets	Requires training on large datasets; higher computational complexity	Various noise types	High	General	High	High	High	High
BM3D (Block-Matching 3D)	Effective for removing additive white Gaussian noise; preserves image details and textures; handles various noise levels	May introduce ringing artifacts; requires careful parameter tuning	Additive white Gaussian noise	Moderate to High	Specific (AWGN)	Moderate	High	High	High
Adaptive Wiener Filtering	Adjusts filtering based on local image characteristics; preserves edges and details; reduces noise without oversmoothing	May introduce blurring in textured regions; sensitive to parameter settings	Various noise types	Moderate	Specific	High	High	High	Moderate

(Continued)

TABLE 3.2 (Continued)

Denoising Technique	Advantages	Disadvantages	Noise Type	Complexity	Applicability	Parameter Tuning	Fine grain	Edge Preserve	Texture Preserve
Non-Local Bayes Denoising	Preserves fine details and textures; effective for removing Gaussian and impulse noise; robust to noise variations	Requires careful selection of parameters; higher computational complexity	Gaussian or impulse noise	High	Specific (Gaussian, impulse)	High	High	High	High
Guided Image Filtering	Preserves image details and edges; smoothens noise without blurring textures;	Limited performance for high noise levels; sensitive to guidance image quality	Various noise types	Low to Moderate	Specific	Moderate	High	High	High

```
plt.subplot(2, 3, 2), plt.imshow(gaussian _ smoothed _ image, c'ap=''ray'),
plt.ti'le('Gaussian Smoot'ing')
plt.subplot(2, 3, 3), plt.imshow(median _ filtered _ image, c'ap=''ray'),
plt.ti'le('Median Filte'ing')
plt.subplot(2, 3, 4), plt.imshow(tv _ denoised _ image, c'ap=''ray'),
plt.ti'le('Total Variation Denoi'ing')
plt.subplot(2, 3, 5), plt.imshow(wavelet _ denoised _ image, c'ap=''ray'),
plt.ti'le('Wavelet Denoi'ing')
plt.subplot(2, 3, 6), plt.imshow(nl _ means _ denoised _ image, c'ap=''ray'),
plt.ti'le('Non-local Means Denoi'ing')
plt.show()
```

- **Artifact removal:** Removing unwanted elements or artifacts from the image, such as sensor dust, lens flares, or motion blur, using techniques like noise reduction filters, deblurring techniques, compression artifacts removal, image inpainting, ghosting and reflection removal, streak and banding artifact removal, color correction and white balance, and super-resolution (see Table 3.3).
- **Data augmentation**

Data augmentation techniques are used to artificially increase the size and diversity of the image dataset. This helps to improve the robustness and generalization of the ML models. Image data augmentation methods can be categorized into basic and advanced techniques, each offering distinct approaches to augmenting the training dataset (see Table 3.4). The basic data augmentation methods can be further divided into traditional image manipulation, image erasing–based methods, and image-mix-based methods. Traditional image manipulation techniques encompass simple and widely used transformations such as rotation, flipping, translation, scaling, shear, and zoom. These techniques alter the image's spatial properties, providing variations in orientation, position, and scale. Additionally, color and contrast manipulation, as well as noise injection, fall under this category, offering adjustments to the image's color distribution and introducing random noise to enhance the model's robustness. Image erasing–based methods involve selective removal or occlusion of regions within the image. Techniques like cutout randomly mask out rectangular regions, encouraging the model to rely on other features and contextual information. By simulating occlusions or partial object appearances, these methods promote resilience to incomplete or obstructed visual information. Image-mix-based methods combine multiple images to create new training samples. These methods include techniques like Mixup and CutMix, where images are blended or overlaid with each other, respectively. By combining samples, these methods introduce inter-class relationships and promote better generalization by forcing the model to learn from diverse image contexts. On the other hand, advanced augmentation techniques leverage more sophisticated approaches. Auto augment–based methods automate the selection and application of augmentation policies using optimization or reinforcement learning. These methods search for the most effective combinations of transformations tailored to the specific dataset and task, optimizing the model's performance.

TABLE 3.3

Comparative Review of the Popular Artifact Removal Techniques.

Technique	Advantages	Disadvantages	Suitable Artifacts	Computational Complexity	Applicability	Parameter Tuning	Preserve Details	Use Case
Noise Reduction Filters	- Simple and computationally efficient	- May blur fine details	Gaussian noise	Low	General	None	Moderate	Image preprocessing, object detection
Deblurring Techniques	- Restores sharpness and clarity to blurred images	- Requires knowledge or estimation of blur kernel	Blurred or out-of-focus images	Moderate	General	Moderate	High	Crop disease diagnosis, quality assessment
Compression Artifacts Removal	- Removes compression-related artifacts	- May result in loss of some image details	JPEG or other compressed image formats	Moderate	Specific (compression artifacts)	Moderate	High	Image storage and transmission, document analysis
Image Inpainting	- Fills in missing or corrupted image regions	- Requires estimation or prediction of missing data	Missing or damaged regions in images	Moderate	Specific (missing data)	High	High	Object recognition, image restoration
Ghosting and Reflection Removal	- Removes ghosting and reflection artifacts	- May not handle complex or overlapping artifacts	Images with ghosting or reflection artifacts	Moderate	Specific (ghosting, reflection artifacts)	Moderate	High	Precision agriculture, fruit quality inspection
Streak and Banding Artifact Removal	- Reduces streaks and banding artifacts	- May introduce slight blurring or loss of details	Images with streaks or banding artifacts	Moderate	Specific (streaks, banding artifacts)	Moderate	High	Satellite imagery analysis, plant disease detection

Technique	Description	Limitation	Applicable to		Specificity			Applications
Color Correction and White Balance	- Corrects color artifacts and white balance issues	- May alter the overall color appearance of the image	Images with color cast or incorrect white balance	Low to moderate	Specific (color artifacts, white balance)	Low to Moderate	Moderate	Plant phenotyping, crop health assessment
Super-resolution	- Enhances image resolution and level of detail	- May introduce artifacts or amplify noise	Low-resolution images or videos	High	Specific (low-resolution images)	High	High	Remote sensing, precision agriculture
JPEG Artifact Removal	- Specifically targets removal of JPEG compression artifacts	- May result in loss of fine details	JPEG-compressed images	Moderate to high	Specific (JPEG compression artifacts)	Moderate	High	Image storage and transmission, document analysis
Moiré Pattern Removal	- Eliminates moiré patterns caused by interference effects	- Requires detection and analysis of moiré patterns	Images with moiré patterns	Moderate to high	Specific (moiré patterns)	Moderate	High	Crop monitoring, pattern analysis
Chromatic Aberration Correction	- Corrects color fringing and distortion in images	- Requires estimation or modeling of chromatic aberration	Images with chromatic aberration	Moderate	Specific (chromatic aberration)	Moderate	High	Agricultural imaging, precision farming

TABLE 3.4

Comparative Review of the Popular Augmentation Techniques.

Category	Method	Popular Techniques	Advantages	Disadvantages	Complexity	Use Case in Smart Farming
Basic Data Augmentation Methods	Traditional image manipulation	Rotation, Flip, Translation, Scaling, Shear, Zoom	- Simple and computationally efficient	- Limited augmentation capabilities	Low	Image preprocessing, object detection
	Image erasing–based methods	Cutout, Occlusion	- Simulates occlusions and partial object appearances	- May introduce unrealistic patches or artifacts	Low to Moderate	Object recognition, anomaly detection
	Image mix–based methods	Mixup, CutMix	- Encourages model robustness and generalization	- May require careful balancing of mix ratios	Low to Moderate	Image classification, semantic segmentation
Advanced Methods	Auto-augment-based methods	AutoAugment, RandAugment	- Optimizes augmentation policies automatically	- Requires additional training for policy search	Moderate	Object detection, image classification
	Feature augmentation Techniques	Cutout++, Mixup++	- Enhances augmentation with additional techniques	- May increase computational complexity	Moderate	Object recognition, image restoration
	Deep Generative Models	GANs, VAEs	- Generates realistic synthetic images for augmentation	- Requires training of generative models	High	Data augmentation, model training

Feature augmentation techniques focus on augmenting the feature space rather than the image space. Methods like random erasing or style transfer modify the image's features or texture, respectively, while preserving the semantic content. This enables the model to learn more robust and discriminative features. Deep generative models, such as generative adversarial networks (GANs) and variational autoencoders (VAEs), offer a novel approach to data augmentation. These models learn to generate new synthetic images that resemble real samples, introducing novel and diverse data points to expand the training dataset.

- **Feature Extraction:**

In some cases, the raw pixel values may be too high-dimensional for modeling. In such scenarios, feature extraction techniques, such as convolutional neural networks (CNNs) or pretrained models like VGGNet or ResNet, can be used to extract meaningful features from the images. These extracted features can then be used as inputs to ML algorithms.

3.3.5 TEXTUAL DATA

Textual data, such as agricultural research papers, weather reports, or farmer notes, provide unstructured information that can be valuable in smart farming. Inclusivity in textual data involves considering the diverse sources, languages, and terminologies used in agricultural literature and documentation. It encompasses incorporating research papers, reports, and farmer knowledge from different regions and cultures, supporting a broad range of perspectives and practices.

For example, when extracting information from weather reports to inform irrigation decisions, an inclusive approach considers weather data and reports from various meteorological agencies and sources, ensuring that the models can handle diverse formats and terminologies. It also accounts for regional and local knowledge, incorporating farmer notes and experiences to enhance the accuracy and relevance of the extracted information for different farming communities.

Text preprocessing is an essential step in transforming raw text into a format that can be effectively used by ML algorithms. This typically encompasses several key steps:

- **Text cleaning:** Text cleaning involves removing any irrelevant or noisy elements from the text. This can include removing special characters, punctuation, and numerical values. Additionally, it may involve converting the text to lowercase to ensure consistency in word representations.
  - **Tokenization:** Tokenization is the process of splitting the text into individual units or tokens. These tokens can be words, sentences, or even subwords, depending on the specific task and requirements. Tokenization allows for better analysis and manipulation of the text data.

```
import nltk

nltk.downl'ad('p'nkt')   # Download the punkt tokenizer data

from nltk.tokenize import word _ tokenize
```

```
# Example text
tex" = "Natural Language Processing (NLP) is a subfield of artificial
intellige"ce."

# Tokenize the text
tokens = word _ tokenize(text)

pr"nt("Original T"xt:", text)
pr"nt("Tokenized T"xt:", tokens)
```

- **Stopword removal:** Stopwords are commonly occurring words in a language that do not carry significant meaning for analysis, such as "the," "is," or "and." Removing stopwords can help reduce the noise in the text and improve computational efficiency. However, it is important to consider the context and task at hand, as sometimes stopwords can carry important information.

```
import nltk

nltk.downl'ad('stopw'rds')  # Download the stopwords data

from nltk.corpus import stopwords
from nltk.tokenize import word _ tokenize

# Example text
tex" = "Natural Language Processing (NLP) is a subfield of artificial
intellige"ce."

# Tokenize the text
tokens = word _ tokenize(text)

# Get the list of English stopwords
stop _ words = set(stopwords.wo'ds('eng'ish'))

# Remove stopwords from the tokens
filtered _ tokens = [word for word in tokens if word.lower() not in
stop _ words]

pr"nt("Original T"xt:", text)
pr"nt("Tokenized T"xt:", tokens)
pr"nt("Filtered Text (without stopwor"s):", filtered _ tokens)
```

- **Stemming and lemmatization:** Stemming and lemmatization are techniques used to normalize words by reducing them to their base or root form. Stemming involves removing prefixes and suffixes from words, while lemmatization maps words to their dictionary or lemma form. These techniques help in reducing word variations and grouping together words with similar meanings.

```
import nltk

nltk.downl'ad('p'nkt')  # Download the punkt tokenizer data
nltk.downl'ad('wor'net')  # Download the WordNet lemmatizer data
```

```
from nltk.stem import PorterStemmer
from nltk.tokenize import word_tokenize

# Example text
tex" = "Stemming is a technique used for processing wo"ds."

# Tokenize the text
tokens = word_tokenize(text)

# Initialize the PorterStemmer
stemmer = PorterStemmer()

# Perform stemming on the tokens
stemmed_tokens = [stemmer.stem(word) for word in tokens]

pr"nt("Original T"xt:", text)
pr"nt("Tokenized T"xt:", tokens)
pr"nt("Stemmed T"xt:", stemmed_tokens)

import nltk
nltk.downl'ad('p'nkt')  # Download the punkt tokenizer data
nltk.downl'ad('wor'net')  # Download the WordNet lemmatizer data

from nltk.stem import WordNetLemmatizer
from nltk.tokenize import word_tokenize

# Example text
tex" = "Lemmatization is the process of converting words to their base
f"rm."

# Tokenize the text
tokens = word_tokenize(text)

# Initialize the WordNetLemmatizer
lemmatizer = WordNetLemmatizer()

# Perform lemmatization on the tokens
lemmatized_tokens = [lemmatizer.lemmatize(word) for word in tokens]

pr"nt("Original T"xt:", text)
pr"nt("Tokenized T"xt:", tokens)
pr"nt("Lemmatized T"xt:", lemmatized_tokens)
```

- **Normalization:** Normalization involves transforming words with similar meanings into a common representation. It can include techniques like spell correction, abbreviations expansion, or converting contractions to their full forms. Normalization ensures consistency and improves the accuracy of text analysis.
  - **Removing rare words:** In some cases, rare or infrequently occurring words may not contribute much to the overall analysis and can be removed to reduce the feature space. This can be done based on

predefined frequency thresholds or by using statistical measures like term frequency-inverse document frequency (TF-ID).

```
import nltk

from nltk.corpus import stopwords
from nltk.tokenize import word_tokenize
from collections import Counter

# Example text
tex" = "This is an example sentence. It contains some words that may be
r"re."

# Tokenize the text
tokens = word_tokenize(text)

# Remove stopwords
stop_words = set(stopwords.wo'ds('eng'ish'))
filtered_tokens = [word for word in tokens if word.lower() not in
stop_words]

# Count the frequency of each word
word_freq = Counter(filtered_tokens)

# Define the threshold frequency for rare words
threshold_freq = 1

# Filter out rare words
filtered_words = [word for word in filtered_tokens if word_freq[word] >
threshold_freq]

# Join the words back to form a cleaned sentence
cleaned_tex" " " ".join(filtered_words)

pr"nt("Original T"xt:", text)
pr"nt("Cleaned T"xt:", cleaned_text)
```

- Handling Missing Data: Textual data may contain missing values or incomplete text entries. It is important to handle missing data appropriately, either by removing the incomplete entries or by applying techniques like imputation to fill in the missing values.
  - Vectorization: To represent textual data numerically, it needs to be converted into a numerical format. This is typically done through vectorization techniques like bag-of-words (BoW), term frequency-inverse document frequency, or word embeddings such as Word2Vec or GloVe. Vectorization allows ML algorithms to process and analyze the text data effectively.

```
from sklearn.feature_extraction.text import CountVectorizer

# Example text corpus
```

```
corpus = [
"    "This is the first docum"nt.",
"    "This document is the second docum"nt.",
"    "And this is the third "ne.",
"    "Is this the first docum"nt?",
]


# Create the CountVectorizer object
vectorizer = CountVectorizer()

# Fit and transform the corpus to generate the bag-of-words representation
bow _ representation = vectorizer.fit _ transform(corpus)

# Get the feature names (words) from the vectorizer
feature _ names = vectorizer.get _ feature _ names _ out()

# Print the bag-of-words representation and feature names
pr"nt("Bag-of-Words Representatio":\n", bow _ representation.toarray())
pr"nt("\nFeature Names (Words":\n", feature _ names)

from sklearn.feature _ extraction.text import TfidfVectorizer

# Example text corpus
corpus = [
"    "This is the first docum"nt.",
"    "This document is the second docum"nt.",
"    "And this is the third "ne.",
"    "Is this the first docum"nt?",
]

# Create the TfidfVectorizer object
vectorizer = TfidfVectorizer()

# Fit and transform the corpus to generate the TF-IDF representation
tfidf _ representation = vectorizer.fit _ transform(corpus)

# Get the feature names (words) from the vectorizer
feature _ names = vectorizer.get _ feature _ names _ out()

# Print the TF-IDF representation and feature names
pr"nt("TF-IDF Representatio":\n", tfidf _ representation.toarray())
pr"nt("\nFeature Names (Words":\n", feature _ names)
```

3.5.6 SPATIAL DATA

A kind of data representing information related to geographical locations or coordinates is essential in smart farming. Inclusivity in spatial data involves considering the diverse geographic contexts, field sizes, and land tenure systems encountered in agriculture. It encompasses the representation of different regions, including smallholder farms, large-scale commercial farms, and community-managed lands, ensuring that the spatial models and analyses can cater to various agricultural settings. For example, when analyzing satellite imagery to assess crop health, an inclusive approach considers the diverse landscapes and field sizes, accounting for variations in crop layouts, intercropping systems, and field boundaries. It ensures that the spatial analysis models can accurately detect and monitor crop health across different spatial scales, supporting diverse farming practices and land management approaches.

Data preprocessing for spatial data involves preparing and transforming geographic or spatial information to make it suitable for analysis and modeling. Spatial data often include information related to locations, coordinates, geometries, and attributes associated with specific points, lines, or polygons on the earth's surface. The following are key concepts in spatial data preprocessing:

- **Data integration:** Spatial data may come from various sources and formats, such as GPS devices, satellite imagery, geographic databases, or sensor networks. Data integration involves merging and combining these diverse data sources into a unified dataset for analysis. This step ensures consistency and compatibility among the different spatial data layers.
- **Geometric validation and cleaning:** Spatial datasets can contain errors, inconsistencies, or inaccuracies in their geometries. Geometric validation and cleaning involve checking the integrity of the spatial data, removing duplicate or overlapping features, correcting geometric errors (e.g., self-intersections), and ensuring the dataset adheres to defined standards and rules.
- **Coordinate reference system (CRS) transformation:** Spatial data are typically referenced to a specific coordinate system or CRS. CRS transformation involves converting spatial data from one coordinate system to another, allowing for seamless integration and analysis with other spatial datasets that may use different reference systems.
- **Spatial interpolation:** Spatial interpolation is used when dealing with missing or incomplete spatial data. It involves estimating the values of unknown locations based on the values of neighboring known locations. Interpolation methods, such as inverse distance weighting, kriging, or splines, can be used to generate continuous and complete spatial datasets.
- **Spatial aggregation:** Spatial aggregation involves combining fine-grained spatial data into coarser spatial units or regions. Aggregation can be performed based on administrative boundaries, grid cells, or other predefined spatial units. This process reduces the complexity of the data, facilitates analysis, and helps maintain privacy when dealing with sensitive spatial information.
- **Spatial join and overlay:** Spatial join and overlay operations combine spatial datasets based on their spatial relationships. These operations allow for the integration of attributes from multiple spatial layers, enabling analysis and modeling based on combined information. Spatial joins can link data based on proximity, containment, or intersection, while overlay operations combine geometries and attributes based on spatial intersections.
- **Feature extraction:** Feature extraction involves deriving additional spatial attributes or characteristics from the raw spatial data. This can include

calculating distances, areas, centroids, or deriving new variables based on spatial relationships (e.g., nearest neighbor distances or density measures). Feature extraction enhances the richness of spatial data and provides additional information for analysis.

- **Spatial filtering:** Spatial filtering techniques are used to extract specific features or patterns from spatial data. This can involve applying filters based on attributes (e.g., selecting features based on a certain range of values) or spatial criteria (e.g., extracting features within a specific distance buffer). Filtering helps focus the analysis on specific areas of interest or specific spatial patterns.

3.5.7 GRAPH DATA

Graph data represent relationships or connections between entities in a network. In the context of smart farming, graph data can capture various agricultural relationships, such as plant-pollinator networks, co-occurrence patterns of pests and diseases, or social networks of farmers. An inclusive approach to graph data acknowledges the diversity of these relationships and networks, accounting for variations across different crops, regions, and farming systems.

For example, in analyzing plant-pollinator networks, an inclusive approach considers the diverse range of crops and pollinator species encountered in different agricultural landscapes. It takes into account variations in pollinator behavior, preferences, and abundance, ensuring that the graph-based models can capture and analyze pollination dynamics in diverse crop species and regions. In the case of co-occurrence patterns of pests and diseases, an inclusive approach encompasses a comprehensive set of pests and diseases affecting different crops, accounting for variations in geographic distribution, host range, and interactions. This allows the graph-based models to capture complex relationships among pests, diseases, and crops, enabling more accurate predictions and targeted management strategies in diverse agricultural contexts. Additionally, an inclusive approach to graph data in smart farming recognizes the social networks and collaborations among farmers. It considers the diversity of farmer communities, their interactions, and knowledge-sharing practices. By incorporating social network analysis techniques, such as community detection or influence analysis, the models can uncover patterns of information flow, identify influential farmers, and support inclusive decision-making processes in agriculture.

Data preprocessing for graph data involves preparing and transforming graph-based datasets to make them suitable for analysis and modeling. Graph data represent entities or objects as nodes and their relationships or interactions as edges or connections. The following are key concepts in graph data preprocessing:

- **Graph construction**: Graph data preprocessing starts with constructing the graph structure from the available data. This involves defining nodes and edges based on the entities and relationships of interest. Nodes represent individual entities, while edges represent the connections or interactions between them. The construction process may vary depending on the type of graph, such as directed or undirected, weighted or unweighted, and labeled or unlabeled.

- **Node and edge attribute extraction**: Graph data often include attributes associated with nodes and edges. These attributes provide additional information and context about the entities and relationships in the graph. Preprocessing involves extracting relevant attributes and assigning them to the corresponding nodes or edges. Examples of node attributes in smart farming could be crop type, soil type, or weather conditions, while edge attributes could represent measures of similarity, distance, or strength of interaction between nodes.

- **Graph cleaning**: Graph data can contain noise, inconsistencies, or incomplete information. Cleaning the graph involves identifying and handling missing or erroneous data, removing duplicate nodes or edges, and addressing any data quality issues. Cleaning ensures the graph data is reliable and accurate for subsequent analysis.

- **Graph transformation**: Graph data may need to be transformed to enhance the analysis or to meet specific requirements. Transformation techniques include graph scaling, normalization, or logarithmic transformations of node or edge attributes. These transformations can help standardize the data or adjust the scales for better analysis or model performance.

- **Feature extraction**: Graph data preprocessing may involve extracting additional features from the graph structure. These features can capture higher-level patterns or characteristics of the graph. Examples of graph feature extraction techniques include calculating node centrality measures (e.g., degree centrality, betweenness centrality) or graph motifs (recurring subgraph patterns). Extracted features provide valuable insights for subsequent analysis or modeling tasks.

- **Graph partitioning**: Graph partitioning divides the graph into smaller subgraphs or clusters based on certain criteria. Partitioning techniques like community detection or clustering algorithms group nodes with similar characteristics or connectivity patterns together. Partitioning can facilitate analysis by focusing on specific subgraphs or identifying functional units within the graph.

- **Graph embedding**: Graph embedding techniques aim to represent the graph data in a low-dimensional vector space while preserving important structural and relational information. Embedding methods, such as node2vec, GraphSAGE, or graph convolutional networks (GCNs), map nodes or subgraphs to continuous vectors. These embeddings enable the use of traditional machine learning algorithms or deep learning models for graph-based analysis.

- **Graph sampling**: Graph datasets can be large and computationally expensive to analyze. Graph sampling techniques select a subset of nodes or edges from the graph while preserving the overall structure and properties. Sampling can be random or based on specific criteria such as node degrees or attributes. Sampling reduces computational complexity and allows for faster analysis and modeling.

3.4   CLASSIFICATION OF MACHINE LEARNING

ML algorithms may be trained in a variety of methods, each with advantages and dis-advantages. ML is widely classified into four groups based on these methodologies and modes of learning: supervised learning, unsupervised learning, semi-supervised learn-ing, and reinforcement learning (Greener et al., 2021; Goyal, 2023; Dayal et al., 2023).

3.4.1   SUPERVISED LEARNING

Supervised ML models are trained using labeled datasets, allowing the models to learn and improve over time. For example, an algorithm may be taught using images of dogs and other objects that have all been identified by humans, and the machine could then learn how to recognize images of dogs on its own. Today, the most popu-lar kind is supervised ML. In particular, supervised ML is differentiated by the way it uses labeled datasets to train devices to appropriately identify data or anticipate out-comes. As input data are fed into the model, the weights are modified until the model is adequately fitted, which occurs as part of the cross-validation process. Supervised ML helps us uncover a variety of answers to real-world problems, such as categoriz-ing spam in a separate folder from your email.

For instance, consider the following input dataset: parrot and crow photos. Ini-tially, the system is trained to recognize the images, which include the color, eyes, form, and size of the parrot and crow. Following training, an image of a parrot is presented as input, and the machine is supposed to identify the item and forecast the result. To create a final prediction, the trained computer examines the input image for numerous aspects of the item, such as color, eyes, form, and so on. In supervised ML, this is the process of identifying objects. The supervised learning technique's primary goal is to translate the input variable into the output variable. There are two major categories of supervised ML. Next, they will be discussed.

3.4.1.1   Classification

Classification is described as the act of recognizing, comprehending, and classifying things and thoughts into predefined categories, that is, "sub-populations." With the use of these pre-categorized training datasets, classification in ML systems employs a wide range of methods to classify future datasets into corresponding and relevant categories. In particular, ML classification algorithms employ input training data to estimate the likelihood or probability that the data that follows will fall into one of the specified categories. One of the most prominent uses of classification is to categorize emails as "spam" or "non-spam," as employed by today's leading email service providers. In summary, categorization is a sort of "pattern recognition." In this case, classification algorithms used to the training data discover the same pattern (similar numerical sequences, words or attitudes, and so on) in subsequent datasets. We will investigate classification algorithms in depth.

The classification algorithm is a supervised learning approach that uses training data to categorize fresh observations. In classification, the software learns how to cat-egorize new observations into distinct classes or groupings by using the dataset or observations supplied. For example, 0 or 1, red or blue, yes or no, spam or not spam,

TABLE 3.5

The Categories of Classification Algorithms.

Category	Sub-category Algorithms
Linear classifiers	Logistic Regression
	Naive Bayes Classifier
	Fisher's Linear Discriminant
Support vector machines	Least Squares Support Vector Machines
Quadratic classifiers	-
Kernel estimation	K-Nearest Neighbor
Decision trees	Random Forest
Neural networks	-
Learning vector quantization	-

and so forth. Classes can be described using targets, labels, or categories. Because it is a supervised learning approach using input and output data, the classification algorithm employs labeled input data. In the classification process, a discrete output function (y) is assigned to an input variable (x). To sum up, classification is a kind of pattern recognition in which classification algorithms are applied to training data to detect the same pattern in other datasets. Classification algorithms can be roughly grouped into the categories depicted in Table 3.5. Next, several algorithm examples will be discussed.

Logistic regression is a statistical approach for developing ML models using dichotomous dependent variables, that is, binary. Logistic regression is a statistical technique used to describe data and the connection between one dependent variable and one or more independent variables. Independent variables may be nominal, ordinal, or interval in nature. The term "logistic regression" is derived from the logistic function that it employs. The sigmoid function is another name for the logistic function. This logistic function has a value between zero and one. In particular, logistic regression is a classification algorithm rather than a regression algorithm. Based on a collection of independent variables, it estimates discrete values (binary values such as 0/1, yes/no, true/false). Simply described, it forecasts the likelihood of an event occurring by fitting data to a logit function. As a result, it's also known as logit regression. Because it forecasts the probability, the values obtained will always be between 0 and 1. For instance, assume you have a sum on your calculus test. There can only be two outcomes, right? Either you solve it or you don't (and don't presume method points here). Consider being given a variety of amounts in an attempt to determine which chapters you have a good understanding of. The study's findings would be as follows: if you are given a trigonometry-based issue, you are 70% likely to solve it. On the other hand, if it's a calculus issue, your chances of receiving a solution are only 30%. This is what logistic regression offers. The assumptions of the logistic regression algorithm can be listed as follows:

- The dependent variable in a binary logistic regression must be binary.
- The intended outcome should be represented by the factor level one of the dependent variables in a binary regression.

TABLE 3.6

Differences between Logistic and Linear Regressions.

Logistic Regression	Linear Regression
Classification problems are solved using this method.	Regression problems are solved using this method.
The response variable is categorical.	The response variables are of a continuous type.
It aids in calculating the likelihood of a specific occurrence happening.	As the independent variable changes, it aids in estimating the dependent variable.
It is a Sigmoid curve.	It is a straight line.

- Only relevant variables should be included.
- The independent variables should be unrelated to one another. This suggests that there should be minimal or no multicollinearity in the model.
- The log odds are linearly connected to the independent variables.
- Logistic regression necessitates large sample sizes.

As observed, the logistic regression is completely different from linear regression. Table 3.6 shows the main difference between them.

A random forest algorithm is a supervised ML method that is widely used for classification and regression issues. We know that a forest is made up of many trees, and the more trees there are, the more vigorous the forest is. Similarly, the more trees in a random forest algorithm, the greater its accuracy and problem-solving capability. Random forest is a classifier that uses the average of many decision trees on different subsets of a given dataset to increase its predicting accuracy. It is built on the idea of ensemble learning, which is the act of integrating numerous classifiers to solve a complicated issue and enhance the model's performance.

Naive Bayes classifier is a classification strategy based on the premise of predictor independence, often known as Bayes' theorem. A Naive Bayes classifier, in basic words, posits that the existence of one feature in a class is independent of the presence of any other feature. For example, if a fruit is red, spherical, and roughly 3 inches in diameter, it is classified as an apple. Even if these traits are reliant on each other or on the existence of the other features, a Naive Bayes classifier would consider all of these attributes to contribute independently to the likelihood that this fruit is an apple. Building a Bayesian model is straightforward and especially useful when dealing with large datasets. In addition to its simplicity, Naive Bayes is known to outperform complicated classification systems.

K-nearest neighbor is a classification and prediction technique that uses distance between data points to partition data into groups. The K-nearest neighbor algorithm posits that data points that are adjacent to one another must be similar, and hence the data point to be classed is grouped with the closest cluster.

In support vector machine, each data item is plotted as a point in n-dimensional space (where n is the number of features you have), with the value of each feature being the value of a certain coordinate. For example, if we just possessed two attributes of a person, such as height and hair length, we would first plot these two variables in two-dimensional space, with each point having two coordinates (these coordinates are known as support vectors). Now we'll look for a line that divides the data into two differently classed sets of data. This will be the line along which the distances from the nearest location in each of the two groups are the greatest. Finally, based on where the testing data falls on either side of the line, we may classify the new data.

3.4.1.2 Types of Learners in Classification Problems

In ML classification problems, there are two categories of learners: lazy learners and eager learners. Eager learners are ML algorithms that construct a model from the training dataset before making predictions on subsequent datasets. They spend more time during the training phase because they want to improve their generalization from learning the weights, but they need less time to produce predictions. The following are some instances of eager learners in ML algorithms:

- Logistic regression
- Support vector machine
- Decision trees
- Artificial neural networks

On the other hand, lazy learners do not generate any model instantly from the training data, which is where the lazy element comes from. They just memorize the training data, and if a prediction is required, they seek the nearest neighbor from the whole training data, making them highly sluggish during prediction. Examples of this kind include:

- K-nearest neighbor
- Case-based reasoning

Note: Certain techniques such as BallTrees and KDTrees can be utilized to reduce prediction latency.

3.4.1.3 Types of Classification Tasks

There are four types of classification tasks in ML: binary, multi-class, multi-label, and imbalanced. We will discuss each task in detail in the following text.

Binary classification difficulties sometimes necessitate creation of two classes, one reflecting the normal condition and the other the aberrant state. For example, the normal state is "not spam," but the abnormal state is "spam." Another example is when a medical test task has a normal condition of "cancer not found" and an adverse condition of "cancer discovered." Class label 0 is assigned to the class in its normal state, whereas class label 1 is assigned to the class in its abnormal state. A binary classification problem is usually represented by a model that anticipates a Bernoulli probability distribution for each occurrence. The Bernoulli distribution is a discrete probability distribution that deals with events that have binary outcomes of 0 or 1.

In terms of categorization, this means that the model predicts that an example will fall into class 1, or the abnormal condition. The following binary classification methods are the most popular ones:

- Logistic regression
- Support vector machines
- Decision trees

Certain algorithms, such as support vector machines and logistic regression, were designed specifically for binary classification and do not accept more than two classes by default.

In contrast to binary classification, *multi-class classification* does not contain the concept of normal and abnormal results. Instances are instead classified into one of many well-known classes. In some circumstances, the number of class labels may be rather large. For example, in a facial recognition system, a model may predict that a photograph belongs to one of thousands or tens of thousands of faces. Text translation models and other word prediction issues might be classified as a subset of multi-class classification. Each word in the sequence of words to be predicted requires a multi-class classification, with the number of potential classes determined by the vocabulary size, which can range from tens of thousands to hundreds of thousands of words. A model that anticipates a Multinoulli probability distribution for each case is commonly used to represent multiclass classification jobs. Several binary classification approaches may be used for multi-class classification. An approach known as "one-vs-rest" or "one model for each pair of classes" is used to do this, which involves fitting multiple binary classification models with each class versus all other classes (called one-vs-one). These multi-class classification approaches can be used by the following binary classification algorithms:

- Support vector machine
- Logistic regression

Note: "One-vs-one" means fitting a single binary classification model to each pair of classes. Whereas "one-vs-rest" means fitting a single binary classification model versus all other classes for each class.

Multi-label classification tasks include two or more class labels and enable one or more class labels to be predicted for each case. Consider the photo categorization example. In this case, a model can predict the presence of numerous known items in a photograph, such as "person," "apple," and "bicycle". A photograph may contain many things in the scene. This is in stark contrast to multi-class and binary classification, which assume a single-class label for each occurrence. A model that anticipates numerous outcomes is widely used to represent multi-label classification problems, with each result anticipated as a Bernoulli probability distribution. This method, in essence, predicts many binary classifications for each case. Multi-label classification algorithms used for multi-class or binary classification cannot be directly used. The algorithms with multiple labels, which are specialized variants of typical classification algorithms, include:

- Multi-label gradient boosting
- Multi-label random forests
- Multi-label decision trees

The phrase "*imbalanced classification*" refers to classification tasks in which the distribution of instances within each class is not uniform. A majority of the examples in the training dataset belong to the normal class, while a minority belong to the abnormal class, resulting in binary classification problems in general. Specialized techniques can be used to change the sample composition in the training dataset by oversampling the minority class or under-sampling the dominant class. Specialized modeling approaches, such as cost-sensitive ML algorithms, can be used to give the minority class additional attention while fitting the model to the following training datasets:

- Cost-sensitive support vector machines
- Cost-sensitive decision trees
- Cost-sensitive logistic regression

3.4.1.4 Regression

Regression is a technique for determining the connection between independent variables or characteristics and a dependent variable or result. After the link between the independent and dependent variables has been estimated, outcomes may be predicted. Regression is a statistical branch of study that is essential in machine learning forecast models. It's used in predictive modeling to anticipate continuous outcomes; therefore, it's useful for forecasting and predicting data outputs. In general, ML regression entails sketching a line of greatest fit through the data points. To create the best-fit line, the distance between each point and the line is minimized. Together with classification, regression is a major application of supervised ML. Classification is the classification of things based on learned characteristics, whereas regression is the prediction of continuous outcomes. Both involve predictive modeling issues. Because classification and regression models rely on labeled input and output training data, supervised ML is essential in both circumstances. The training data's characteristics and output must be labeled so that the model can grasp the link. Regression analysis is used to investigate the connection between a set of independent factors and a single dependent variable or result. Regression techniques will be used to train models that anticipate or predict trends and outcomes. With labeled training data, these models will learn the link between input and output data. It may then estimate future trends or predict outcomes based on previously unknown input data, or it can be used to fill gaps in historical data. Special care should be taken, as with any supervised ML, to ensure that the labeled training data is representative of the general population. If the training data are unrepresentative, the prediction model will overfit to input that does not reflect new or previously unknown data. After the model is applied, this will result in erroneous forecasts. Since regression analysis covers the connections between characteristics and outcomes, care must be given to incorporate the appropriate features.

In predictive analytics, ML regression models are primarily used to anticipate trends and predict outcomes. To understand the link between different independent variables and a result, regression models will be trained. As a result, the model can comprehend the several aspects that may result in the desired conclusion. The produced models can be utilized in a number of ways and circumstances. Results may be forecasted using new and previously unknown data, market swings can be predicted and compensated for, and campaigns can be tested by adjusting several independent factors. In practice, a model will be trained using labeled data to learn about the link between data characteristics and the dependent variable. The model can forecast the result of fresh and unknown data by estimating this connection. This might be used to anticipate missing historical data as well as forecast future results. In a sales setting, a company may utilize regression ML to forecast next month's revenue based on a variety of parameters. In a medical setting, an organization might anticipate long-term health patterns in the broader population. Generally, supervised ML models are employed for classification or regression issues. Classification is the process of training a model to categorize an item based on its attributes. This might involve face recognition software or detecting spam emails behind a firewall. To identify the exact characteristics that categorize a tagged item, a model will be trained using labeled input and output data. A regression problem, on the other hand, occurs when a model is employed to predict continuous outcomes or values. This may be a model that predicts income increases, home values, or retail sales. To identify the strength of correlations between data attributes and output, the model is trained using labeled input and output data. Regression is used to find patterns and correlations in a dataset that can subsequently be applied to fresh and previously unexplored data. As a result, regression is an important component of machine learning in finance, and it is frequently used to estimate portfolio performance or stock costs and trends. Models may be taught to grasp the link between a wide range of characteristics and a desired outcome. In most circumstances, ML regression gives businesses insight into certain outcomes. Yet, because this technique has the potential to affect an organization's decision-making process, the explainability of ML is critical. Table 3.7 shows the main differences between regression and classification algorithms.

To do regression, ML employs a variety of techniques. To perform ML regression, many prominent methods are utilized. The various strategies may use a varied number of independent variables or analyze various types of data. ML regression models of various sorts may potentially assume a distinct connection between the independent and dependent variables. Linear regression approaches, for example, presume that the connection is linear and would be ineffective with nonlinear datasets. Some of the most prevalent regression approaches in ML may be classified as follows:

- Simple linear regression
- Multiple linear regression
- Logistic regression

TABLE 3.7

Differences between Regression and Classification Algorithms.

Regression Algorithms	Classification Algorithms
The output variable must be of either continuous or real value.	The output variable must be discrete in nature.
The regression method aims to transfer an input value (x) to a continuous output variable (y).	The classification algorithm's job is to transfer the input variable x to the discrete output variable y.
They work with continuous data.	They are employed when dealing with discrete data.
It attempts to identify the best-fit line, which more precisely forecasts the output.	Classification seeks to identify the decision boundary that separates the dataset into distinct classes.
Regression algorithms are used to tackle regression issues such as home price forecasting and weather forecasting.	Classification algorithms are used to tackle issues such as recognizing spam e-mails, detecting cancer cells, and voice recognition.
Regression techniques are further subdivided into linear and non-linear regression.	Classification algorithms are further subdivided into binary classifiers and multi-class classifiers.

Simple linear regression is an approach that draws a straight line among data points to minimize the error between the line and the data points. It is one of the most fundamental and straightforward forms of ML regression. In this scenario, the connection between the independent and dependent variables is considered to be linear. This method is straightforward since it is used to investigate the connection between the dependent variable and one independent variable. Because of the straight line of best fit, outliers may be prevalent in basic linear regression.

Multiple linear regression is a technique that is utilized when more than one independent variable is involved. Polynomial regression is an example of a multivariate linear regression approach. It is a sort of multiple linear regression that is used when there is more than one independent variable. When numerous independent variables are present, it achieves a better fit than basic linear regression. When displayed in two dimensions, the outcome is a curved line fitted to the data points.

When the dependent variable can take one of two values, such as true or false, or success or failure, *logistic regression* is utilized. Logistic regression models may be used to forecast the likelihood of a dependent variable happening. In general, the output values must be binary. A sigmoid curve can be used to depict the connection between the dependent and independent variables.

3.4.2 UNSUPERVISED LEARNING

Unsupervised and supervised ML are typically addressed in tandem. Unsupervised learning, as opposed to supervised learning, makes use of unlabeled data. It identifies patterns in the data that aid in the resolution of clustering or association difficulties. When subject matter experts are unclear of common qualities within a dataset, this is very valuable. Semi-supervised learning happens when just a portion of the incoming data is labeled. Unsupervised and semi-supervised learning may be more tempting options since relying on domain expertise to categorize data accurately for supervised learning may be time consuming and costly. In particular, unsupervised learning, also known as unsupervised ML, analyzes and clusters unlabeled information using ML techniques. Without the need for human interaction, these algorithms uncover hidden patterns or data groupings. Because of its capacity to detect similarities and contrasts in data, it is a perfect option for exploratory data analysis, cross-selling techniques, consumer segmentation, and picture identification. Hierarchical, K-means, and Gaussian mixture models are common clustering techniques. Clustering, association, and dimensionality reduction are the three major tasks performed by unsupervised learning models. Each learning technique will be defined subsequently, along with typical algorithms and ways for carrying them out efficiently.

3.4.2.1   Clustering

Clustering is a data mining technique that organizes unlabeled data into groups based on similarities and differences. Clustering techniques are used to arrange raw, unclassified data items into groups represented by information structures or patterns. Clustering methods are classified into four types: exclusive, overlapping, hierarchical, and probabilistic.

Exclusive clustering is a type of grouping in which a data point can only reside in one cluster. This is sometimes referred to as "hard" clustering. Exclusive clustering is demonstrated via the K-means clustering technique. K-means clustering is a popular example of an exclusive clustering approach in which data points are assigned to one of K groups depending on their distance from the centroid of each group. The data points closest to a specific centroid will be grouped together. A higher K number indicates smaller groups with more granularity, whereas a lower K value indicates bigger groupings with less granularity. Market segmentation, document clustering, picture segmentation, and image compression all employ K-means clustering.

> **Note:** Overlapping clusters differ from exclusive clustering in that data points can belong to many clusters with different degrees of membership. Overlapping clustering is illustrated by "soft" or fuzzy K-means clustering.

Hierarchical clustering, also known as hierarchical cluster analysis (HCA), is an unsupervised clustering technique that may be divided into two types: agglomerative clustering and divisive clustering. Agglomerative clustering is a "bottoms-up" method. Its data points are initially segregated as individual groups and then blended together repeatedly based on similarity until one cluster is produced. To quantify similarity, four alternative approaches are typically used:

1. **Ward's linkage:** According to this technique, the distance between two clusters is measured by the increase in the sum of squares after the clusters have been merged.
2. **The average relationship:** The mean distance between two sites in each cluster is used to define this approach.

3. **Full (or maximum) linkage:** The greatest distance between two locations in each cluster defines this approach.
4. **A single (or minimal) link:** The minimal distance between two locations in each cluster defines this approach.

The most frequent metric used to determine these distances is Euclidean distance; however, other metrics, such as Manhattan distance, are often mentioned in clustering literature. Divisive clustering is the inverse of agglomerative clustering; instead, it employs a "top-down" strategy. A single data cluster is separated in this example depending on the discrepancies between data points. Although divisive clustering is not often utilized, it is worth mentioning in the context of hierarchical clustering. A dendrogram, a tree-like figure that depicts the merging or splitting of data points at each iteration, is commonly used to display these clustering processes.

Probabilistic clustering is an unsupervised strategy that aids in the resolution of density estimation or "soft" clustering issues. Data points are grouped in probabilistic clustering based on their likelihood of belonging to a specific distribution. One of the most often used probabilistic clustering algorithms is the Gaussian mixture model (GMM). GMMs are mixture models, which implies they are composed of an unknown number of probability distribution functions. They are generally used to identify whether a particular data point conforms to a Gaussian or normal probability distribution. If we know the mean or variance, we may tell which distribution a particular data point belongs to. Nevertheless, because these factors are unknown in GMMs, we must assume the existence of a latent, or hidden, variable to cluster data points properly. While the expectation-maximization (EM) technique is not needed, it is typically used to estimate the assignment probability for a given data point to a certain data cluster.

3.4.2.2 Association Rules

A rule-based approach for determining associations between variables in a given dataset is known as an association rule. These techniques are commonly employed in market basket analysis, helping businesses to better understand the linkages between various items. Knowing client consumption habits allows organizations to create stronger cross-selling tactics and recommendation engines. Amazon's "Customers Who Bought This Item Also Purchased" and Spotify's "Discover Weekly" playlists are also examples of this. While other methods, including Apriori, Eclat, and FP-Growth, are used to build association rules, the Apriori technique is the most extensively utilized.

Apriori algorithms are used in transactional datasets to find frequent item sets, or groupings of items, to predict the likelihood of consuming one product based on the consumption of another. For example, if I start playing Black Sabbath's radio on Spotify with "Orchid," one of the other songs on this channel will very certainly be a Led Zeppelin song, such as "Over the Hills and Far Away." This is based on my previous listening habits as well as the listening patterns of others. Apriori methods count item sets using a hash tree, traversing the dataset breadth-first.

3.4.2.3 Dimensionality Reduction

While more data typically give more accurate findings, it can also influence the performance of ML algorithms (e.g., overfitting) and make dataset visualization challenging. When the number of characteristics, or dimensions, in a given data-set is too large, dimensionality reduction is performed. It minimizes the amount of data inputs to a reasonable quantity while keeping the dataset's integrity as much as feasible. It is often employed at the preprocessing data stage, and there are several dimensionality reduction methods available, including:

Principal component analysis (PCA) is a dimensionality reduction approach that uses feature extraction to eliminate redundancies and compress datasets. A linear transformation is used in this approach to generate a new data representation, gener-ating a set of "principal components." The first principal component is the direction that maximizes the dataset's variance. While the second main component finds the most variation in the data, it is fully uncorrelated to the first, producing a direc-tion that is perpendicular, or orthogonal, to the first. This process is repeated for each dimension, with the next main component being the direction orthogonal to the preceding components with the largest variation.

Singular value decomposition (SVD) is another dimensionality reduction method that divides a matrix, A, into three low-rank matrices. The formula for SVD is A = USVT, where U and V are orthogonal matrices. S is a diagonal matrix, and S values are regarded as singular values of matrix A. It, like PCA, is often used to decrease noise and compress Data, such as picture files.

t-distributed stochastic neighbor embedding (t-SNE) is a nonlinear dimensionality reduction technique primarily used for visualization. It aims to map high-dimensional data onto a low-dimensional space, typically two or three dimensions, while preserv-ing local relationships between data points. t-SNE constructs a probability distribu-tion over pairs of high-dimensional data points and a similar probability distribution over the corresponding low-dimensional points. It minimizes the divergence between these two distributions using gradient descent, effectively creating a mapping that reveals the underlying structure and clusters in the data.

Autoencoders use neural networks to compress data before recreating a new rep-resentation of the original data. The following graphic shows how the hidden layer functions as a bottleneck to compress the input layer before rebuilding inside the output layer. Encoding refers to the stage from the input layer to the hidden layer, while decoding refers to the stage from the hidden layer to the output layer.

3.4.3 REINFORCEMENT LEARNING

One significant disadvantage of ML is the massive quantity of data required to train models. The more complicated a model, the more data it may necessitate. Never-theless, we may not have access to this information. It might not exist, or we might not have access to it. Also, the data gathered may be untrustworthy. It may contain incorrect or missing values, or it may be out of date. Therefore, learning from a tiny fraction of activities will not assist in broadening the huge range of possible solutions to a specific problem. This will slow the rate of technological advancement. Robots must learn to do things on their own, rather than only from humans. Reinforcement learning solves all of these issues.

Reinforcement learning is a process that is dependent on feedback. Here, the AI component uses the hit-and-trial approach to autonomously assess its surroundings, take action, learn from experiences, and improve performance. The component is awarded for each correct action and punished for each incorrect motion. As a result, the reinforcement learning component seeks to maximize rewards by completing positive activities. Unlike supervised learning, reinforcement learning does not use labeled data, and agents learn only via their experiences. Take, for example, video games. The game describes the environment in this case, and each move of the reinforcement agent determines its state. The agent is entitled to input in the form of punishment and rewards, which affects the total game score. The agent's ultimate objective is to get a high score.

In the reinforcement learning problem, an agent explores an unfamiliar environment to attain a goal. The premise that all objectives may be characterized by the maximizing of predicted cumulative reward underpins reinforcement learning. To maximize reward, the agent must learn to perceive and disturb the state of the environment through its activities. The formal foundation for reinforcement learning is inspired by the optimum control of Markov decision processes (MDP). The value function, which correctly reflects the "goodness" of a state, is a helpful abstraction of the reward signal. Whereas the reward signal indicates the immediate advantage of being in a certain state, the value function records the cumulative reward that is projected to be gathered from that state onward. A reinforcement learning algorithm's goal is to find the action strategy that maximizes the average value extracted from every state of the system. There are two types of reinforcement learning algorithms: model-free and model-based.

3.4.3.1   Model-Free Algorithms

Model-free algorithms do not construct an explicit model of the environment, or, to be more precise, the MDP. They are more similar to trial-and-error algorithms, which execute tests with the environment using actions and directly derive the best policy from it. Value-based or policy-based algorithms are the two types of model-free algorithms. Value-based algorithms believe optimum policy to be the direct outcome of precisely calculating the value function of each state. The agent interacts with the environment to sample state and reward trajectories using a recursive connection given by the Bellman equation. The value function of the MDP may be calculated given enough trajectories. Once the value function is known, determining the optimal policy is as simple as behaving greedily with regard to the value function at each stage of the process. State-action-reward-state-action (SARSA) and Q-learning are two popular value-based algorithms. In contrast, policy-based algorithms directly estimate the best policy without modeling the value function. They convert the learning problem into an explicit optimization problem by explicitly parametrizing the policy with learnable weights. The agent, like value-based algorithms, samples state and reward trajectories; however, this information is utilized to actively enhance the policy by maximizing the average value function over all states. Monte Carlo policy gradient (REINFORCE) and deterministic policy gradient are two popular policy-based reinforcement learning methods. Policy-based techniques have a significant degree of variation, which emerges as instabilities during the training process. Value-based techniques, while more stable, are insufficient for modeling continuous action spaces. The actor-critic algorithm, one of the most powerful reinforcement learning algorithms, is created by integrating value-based and policy-based techniques. Both the policy (actor) and the value function (critic) in this approach are parametrized to allow for effective use of training data while maintaining steady convergence.

3.4.3.2 Model-Based Algorithms

By sampling states, executing actions, and monitoring the rewards, reinforcement learning algorithms construct a model of the world. The model forecasts the expected reward and the predicted future state for each state and feasible action. The first is a regression problem, whereas the second is a density estimation problem. The reinforcement Learning agent may plan its activities without directly interacting with the environment if it is given a model of the environment. This is similar to a thought experiment that a human could perform while attempting to solve an issue. When the planning process is intertwined with the policy estimation process, the Reinforcement Learning agent's capacity to learn improves.

3.5   FROM NEURAL NETWORKS TO DEEP LEARNING

Artificial neural networks (ANNs) form the foundation of modern deep learning algorithms. They are inspired by the structure and functionality of biological neural networks in the human brain. ANNs consist of interconnected nodes called artificial neurons or perceptron, organized in layers. The basic components of an ANN include input layer, hidden layers, and output layer.

> **Input layer**: The input layer is the starting point of the neural network. It receives the input data and passes it forward to the next layer. Each neuron in the input layer represents a feature or attribute of the input data. For example, in image classification tasks, each neuron in the input layer could represent a pixel value of the image.
> **Hidden layers**: Hidden layers are the intermediate layers between the input and output layers. They play a crucial role in extracting and learning complex representations and patterns from the input data. A neural network can have one or more hidden layers, and each layer consists of multiple neurons. The number of hidden layers and the number of neurons in each layer can vary based on the complexity of the problem and the network architecture.
> **Output layer**: The output layer is the final layer of the neural network. It provides the predictions or outputs based on the learned representations from the input data. The number of neurons in the output layer depends on the type of task. For example, in a binary classification problem, the output layer may have a single neuron representing the probability of belonging to one class. In a multi-class classification problem, the output layer may have multiple neurons, with each neuron representing the probability of belonging to a specific class.

Each neuron in the neural network is associated with weights and biases. During the training process, these weights and biases are adjusted iteratively to minimize the difference between the predicted outputs and the actual outputs. This adjustment is achieved through a process called backpropagation, where the error is propagated backward from the output layer to the hidden layers, updating the weights and biases along the way. The strength and effectiveness of neural networks lie in their ability to learn complex patterns and relationships in data. Through training on large labeled datasets, neural networks can adapt their internal representations and optimize their parameters to make accurate predictions. This capability has revolutionized various fields, including image and speech recognition, natural language processing, and smart farming applications such as crop yield prediction, disease detection, and agricultural decision-making.

Activation functions introduce nonlinearity to ANNs, enabling them to model complex relationships between inputs and outputs. They are applied to the outputs of individual neurons within the network. Here are some commonly used activation functions:

Sigmoid function: The sigmoid function, also known as the logistic function, is a popular activation function. It maps the input value to a range between 0 and 1, which can be interpreted as a probability. The formula for the sigmoid function is as follows:

$$f(x) = \frac{1}{(1 + \exp(-x))} \, f(x) = \frac{1}{(1 + \exp(-x))} \tag{1}$$

The sigmoid function is useful in binary classification tasks, where the output represents the probability of belonging to a particular class. However, it can suffer from the "vanishing gradient" problem, which can impede the training of deep neural networks.

Rectified linear nit (ReLU): The ReLU activation function is widely used in deep learning models. It is defined as:

$$f(x) = \max(0, x) \tag{2}$$

ReLU is computationally efficient and addresses the vanishing gradient problem. It introduces nonlinearity and helps the neural network learn complex representations. However, ReLU can suffer from the "dying ReLU" problem, where some neurons get stuck at zero and cease to learn.

Hyperbolic tangent (Tanh): The Tanh function is similar to the sigmoid function but maps the input to a range between −1 and 1. It is defined as follows:

$$f(x) = \frac{(\exp(x) - \exp(-x))}{(\exp(x) + \exp(-x))}$$

Tanh is useful when the output range needs to be symmetric around zero. It can be used in both classification and regression tasks.

SoftMax: The SoftMax function is commonly used in multi-class classification problems. It takes a vector of real numbers as input and normalizes them into a probability distribution over multiple class. The SoftMax function is defined as follows:

$$f(x_i) = \frac{\exp(x_i)}{\text{sum}(\exp(x_j))}, \text{ for all } i \qquad (3)$$

The output of the SoftMax function represents the probabilities of the input belonging to each class, ensuring that the sum of the probabilities adds up to 1.

Loss functions quantify the difference between the predicted outputs of the neural network and the actual target values during the training process. They provide a measure of how well the network is performing. The choice of loss function depends on the type of task and the desired behavior of the neural network. Here are two commonly used loss functions:

Mean squared error (MSE): The MSE is commonly used in regression tasks. It calculates the average squared difference between the predicted values and the actual values. The formula for MSE is as follows:

$$\text{MSE} = (1/n) * \text{sum}\left(\left(y_{pred} - y_{actual}\right)^2\right) \qquad (4)$$

Minimizing the MSE encourages the network to produce predictions that are close to the actual values, penalizing larger deviations more heavily.

Cross-entropy loss: Cross-entropy loss is typically used in classification tasks, particularly when dealing with multi-class classification problems. It measures the dissimilarity between the predicted probability distribution and the true distribution of the target labels. The formula for cross-entropy loss is:

$$\text{Cross} - \text{Entropy} = -\sum y_{actual} * log\left(y_{pred}\right) \qquad (5)$$

where y_{actual} represents the true label and y_{pred} represents the predicted probability distribution over classes. Minimizing cross-entropy loss encourages the network to assign higher probabilities to the correct class labels.

The backpropagation algorithm is a key component of training ANNs by iteratively updating the network weights to minimize the difference between predicted outputs and actual outputs. Here's a step-by-step explanation of the backpropagation algorithm:

Step 1, forward pass: In the forward pass, the input data is propagated through the network, layer by layer, to generate predicted outputs. Each neuron computes a weighted sum of its inputs, applies an activation function, and passes the result to the next layer.

Step 2, compute loss: After the forward pass, the network's predicted outputs are compared with the actual target outputs. A loss function, such as MSE or cross-entropy loss, is used to quantify the difference between the predicted and actual outputs.

Step 3, backward pass: The backward pass is the core of the backpropagation algorithm. It involves calculating the gradients of the loss function with respect to the weights of the network. The gradients indicate the direction and magnitude of weight adjustments required to minimize the loss.

Step 4, gradient calculation: Starting from the output layer, the gradients of the loss function with respect to the weights are calculated using the chain rule of calculus. The gradient of the loss function with respect to the output layer's activations is computed first. Then, this gradient is backpropagated to the previous layers, and the gradients are successively computed for each layer.

Step 5, weight update: With the gradients calculated, the weights of the network are updated using an optimization algorithm, typically gradient descent or one of its variants. The weights are adjusted in the direction that minimizes the loss, based on the calculated gradients and a learning rate hyperparameter.

Step 6, iteration: Steps 1–5 are repeated for multiple iterations or epochs, allowing the network to gradually converge toward better weight configurations and reduced loss. The training process continues until a stopping criterion, such as reaching a maximum number of iterations or achieving satisfactory performance, is met. The backpropagation algorithm leverages the chain rule of calculus to efficiently compute the gradients of the loss function with respect to the network weights. By propagating the error backward through the network, the algorithm adjusts the weights in a way that improves the network's ability to make accurate predictions. It's important to note that there are variations and enhancements to the basic backpropagation algorithm, such as mini-batch updates, regularization techniques, and momentum-based optimization, which can improve the training process and the generalization ability of the neural network.

Deep learning has emerged as a revolutionary field within the broader domain of ANNs, enabling the development of highly sophisticated models capable of learning and making accurate predictions. The evolution of deep learning can be understood by tracing its progression from traditional neural networks to the advanced architectures that form the foundation of deep learning today. The journey begins with the advent of basic artificial neural networks, which were inspired by the structure and functioning of biological neural networks. These early networks consisted of interconnected nodes or neurons, organized into layers. Each neuron performed a weighted sum of its inputs and applied an activation function to produce an output. This simple yet powerful concept paved the way for subsequent advancements. Over time, researchers discovered that deeper neural networks, comprising multiple hidden layers, could learn more complex representations and capture intricate patterns in the data. This realization led to the development of deep neural networks, marking a significant milestone in the evolution of deep learning. Deep neural networks demonstrated enhanced capabilities in areas such as image and speech recognition, natural language processing, and recommendation systems. One of the critical factors behind the success of deep neural networks was the introduction of more sophisticated activation functions. Traditional activation functions, like the sigmoid function, suffered from limitations such as the vanishing gradient problem. In response, researchers explored novel activation functions, including ReLU. ReLU addressed the vanishing gradient problem and significantly improved the training and performance of deep neural networks.

Moreover, advancements in computational power and the availability of large-scale datasets acted as catalysts in the evolution of deep learning. Deep neural networks require substantial computational resources and extensive labeled datasets to train effectively. The availability of powerful GPUs and parallel computing techniques enabled researchers to train deeper networks efficiently. Additionally, the growth of the Internet and digital technologies resulted in vast amounts of labeled data, which proved instrumental in training deep learning models. The breakthrough moment in deep learning came with the introduction of CNNs and recurrent neural networks (RNNs). CNNs, with their specialized convolutional layers, exhibited exceptional performance in image and video analysis tasks. RNNs, on the other hand, demonstrated remarkable abilities in sequential data processing, making them suitable for tasks such as speech recognition and natural language processing. The continued exploration of deep learning architectures led to the development of more advanced techniques, such as deep reinforcement learning, GANs, and transformers. Deep reinforcement learning combines deep neural networks with reinforcement learning algorithms, enabling the training of agents capable of learning optimal decision-making policies in complex environments. GANs revolutionized the field of generative modeling, allowing the generation of realistic and high-quality synthetic data. Transformers, with their attention mechanism, brought significant advancements in natural language processing and achieved state-of-the-art results in machine translation and language understanding tasks.

Today, deep learning has established itself as a powerful paradigm within machine learning and artificial intelligence. Its applications span various domains, including healthcare, finance, robotics, and, notably, smart farming. Deep learning models have shown immense potential in crop yield prediction, disease detection, precision agriculture, and optimization of farming practices. As deep learning continues to evolve, researchers and practitioners are exploring advanced architectures, optimization algorithms, and techniques to further enhance the capabilities and interpretability of deep learning models. The field holds tremendous promise for tackling increasingly complex problems and pushing the boundaries of AI.

3.6 THE ROLE OF MACHINE LEARNING IN SMART AGRICULTURE

Agriculture has faced several challenges, including temperature changes, a lack of suitable irrigation systems, food scarcity, groundwater density, significant waste, and so on. Smart farming facilitated by ML also helps farmers deal with genuine challenges that arise as a result of autonomous solutions and decision-making. In farming, ML has a wide range of applications (Alanazi and Alrashdi, 2023; Batool and Khan, 2022). As a result, the apps must be dependable and strong. Changes in external situations can be handled by very efficient ML techniques. It also assists them in making real-time decisions and assuring an adequate platform or framework for contextual data collecting. ML and other cognitive solutions have the potential to transform the fate of farming. Nonetheless, there is still much to be done in agricultural research and development on a broad scale, but there are several applications and advanced technology tools on the market that may improve the whole system. Next, we will propose some examples of the advantages of ML-based solutions.

3.6.1 AUTOMATIC IDENTIFICATION OF RIPENED CROPS AND DROUGHT PATTERNS

Precision agriculture is being revolutionized by AI and ML, which are converting farms into smart farmlands. Individuals may automatically identify drought trends and trace crop ripening patterns thanks to a unique mix of technologies such as big data, AI, IoT, ML, and cloud and their applications. Furthermore, the introduction of smart tractors makes it easier for them to filter out unhealthy and infected plants. The technology is widely utilized in agriculture for safety, research analysis, terrain scanning, monitoring soil moisture, geographical analysis, and identifying yield difficulties (Alfred et al., 2021). Smart drones with ML and AI capabilities detect unhealthy plants and aid in the accurate spraying of pesticides on farmlands.

They also aid in the addition of macro- and micronutrients as well as the examination of physical qualities such as chemical properties, moisture, pH balance of soil, and others. The combination of precision agriculture and AI-powered applications enables humans to detect the match case and discover the illness that has halted plant development, matching it with the diseases mentioned in the imaging database.

Farmers may create remedial measures at an early stage after learning about the disease in real time, potentially eliminating the possibility of loss. Precision agriculture has limitless potential with data analytics, AI, and ML. The data is then gathered, measured, and evaluated before being distributed to the farmers.

3.6.2 REAL-TIME CHATBOT-BASED ANSWERS TO AGRICULTURAL CHALLENGES

Chatbots are AI-powered advanced technologies that perform automatic interactions with people. They are built utilizing ML techniques, which allow users to comprehend the language of the users and generate individualized interactions with them. The chatbots are primarily designed for use in media, agriculture, retail, and travel (Rezk et al., 2021). The service not only supports farmers, but it also allows them to obtain real-time replies and solutions to their questions.

Now, we are moving toward AI-enabled smart farming, in which technology handles farming procedures. Farmers have long struggled with many internal and external concerns such as insect infestations, unpredictable weather, water scarcity, and so on. By utilizing big data and AI analytics, the tendency may now be reversed. It aids in the optimization of the entire farmland while ensuring that each piece is used efficiently. The sophisticated technology also scans each plant to track its development and health. Any pest problems are recognized at an early stage and individuals are alerted. That was not practicable with traditional farming practices.

3.6.3   OPTIMIZATION OF THE FARMING PROCESS BY ML-POWERED SOLUTIONS

In smart greenhouses, fish farming, and animal monitoring, the integration of big data analytics, AI and ML, and smart edge devices such as drones, GPS, and sensors is frequently employed (Ip et al., 2018). The deployment of advanced blockchain technology accelerates the transformation of agriculture. It promotes openness, speedy processing, and greater accountability. Furthermore, the improvement helps to optimize the supply chain while adding value to the agricultural process.

3.6.4   CROP YIELD OPTIMIZATION

Seed quality and diversity of choices are critical for optimal plant performance. The ML-enabled technologies aid in the rapid and healthy growth of crops. Also, the quantity of output is affected by hybrid seed selection. Farmers' needs should be met by the seed. Farmers may use AI and ML to learn how different varieties of seedlings behave in different weather circumstances and soil types. This information enables farmers to make the best decision at the correct moment to eliminate crop loss caused by diseases or other factors (Rakhra et al., 2022). Farmers may also use technology to adapt to shifting market trends, customer wants, and annual results. It assists farmers in increasing the value of their produce. As a result, farmers may boost their productivity by 6–7 times per acre and make better use of their acreage.

3.6.5   MORE ADVANCEMENT

AI technology has improved to the point that tractor machinery is now capable of picking away rotten or sick plants. Moreover, satellite photography depicts various drought patterns. There are also AI- and ML-powered applications that farmers may utilize as diagnostic tools. These apps are designed to offer farmers with detailed information about plants (Jagtap et al., 2022). It also aids in the discovery of remedial actions to tackle the problem. But, agriculture specialists, technology businesses, and thought leaders must continue to create, exploit, and increase the potential of new technologies. Furthermore, it is the responsibility of governments to extend the role and value of precision agriculture. Farmers should be motivated and trained to use emerging technologies such as ML and AI, which have the potential to significantly boost agricultural produce and productivity.

REFERENCES

Alanazi, B., & Alrashdi, I. (2023). Anomaly detection in smart agriculture systems on network edge using deep learning technique. *Sustainable Machine Intelligence Journal, 3,* 1–31. https://doi.org/10.61185/SMIJ.2023.33104.

Alfred, R., Obit, J. H., Chin, C. P. Y., Haviluddin, H., & Lim, Y. (2021). Towards paddy rice smart farming: A review on big data, machine learning, and rice production tasks. *IEEE Access, 9,* 50358–50380. https://doi.org/10.1109/ACCESS.2021.3069449

Batool, I., & Khan, T. A. (2022). Software fault prediction using data mining, machine learning and deep learning techniques: A systematic literature review. *Computers and Electrical Engineering, 100,* 107886. https://doi.org/10.1016/J.COMPELECENG.2022.107886

Boehmke, B., & Greenwell, B. (2019). *Hands-on machine learning with R.* https://doi.org/10.1201/9780367816377

Dayal, M., Gupta, M., Gupta, M., Bara, A. R., & Chaubey, C. (2023). *Introduction to machine learning methods with application in agriculture* (pp. 184–203). https://services.igi-global.com/resolvedoi/resolve.aspx?doi=10.4018/978-1-6684-6413-7.ch012. https://doi.org/10.4018/978-1-6684-6413-7.CH012

Dong, J., Valzania, L., Maillard, A., Pham, T., Gigan, S., & Unser, M. (2023). Phase retrieval: From computational imaging to machine learning: A tutorial. *IEEE Signal Proces sing Magazine*, *40*(1), 45–57. https://doi.org/10.1109/MSP.2022.3219240

Goyal, S. (2023). Software measurements from machine learning to deep learning. In *Computational intelligence applications for software engineering problems* (pp. 119–134). https://doi.org/10.1201/9781003283195-6

Greener, J. G., Kandathil, S. M., Moffat, L., & Jones, D. T. (2021). A guide to machine learning for biologists. *Nature Reviews Molecular Cell Biology*, *23*(1), 40–55. https://doi.org/10.1038/s41580-021-00407-0

Hatzilygeroudis, I., Tsihrintzis, G. A., & Jain, L. C. (2023). *Introduction to fusion of machine learning paradigms* (pp. 1–4). https://doi.org/10.1007/978-3-031-22371-6_1

Ip, R. H. L., Ang, L. M., Seng, K. P., Broster, J. C., & Pratley, J. E. (2018). Big data and machine learning for crop protection. *Computers and Electronics in Agriculture*, *151*, 376–383. https://doi.org/10.1016/J.COMPAG.2018.06.008

Jagtap, S. T., Phasinam, K., Kassanuk, T., Jha, S. S., Ghosh, T., & Thakar, C. M. (2022). Towards application of various machine learning techniques in agriculture. *Materials Toda y: Proceedings*, *51*, 793–797. https://doi.org/10.1016/J.MATPR.2021.06.236

Rakhra, M., Sanober, S., Quadri, N. N., Verma, N., Ray, S., & Asenso, E. (2022). Implementing machine learning for smart farming to forecast farmers' interest in hiring equipment. *Journal of Food Quality*, *2022*. https://doi.org/10.1155/2022/4721547

Rezk, N. G., Hemdan, E. E. D., Attia, A. F., El-Sayed, A., & El-Rashidy, M. A. (2021). An efficient IoT based smart farming system using machine learning algorithms. *Multimedia Tools and Applications*, *80*(1), 773–797. https://doi.org/10.1007/S11042-020-09740-6/TABLES/14

4 From Field to Database

*Sensors, Data Collection,
and Efficient Management
in Smart Farming*

4.1 INTRODUCTION TO SENSOR TECHNOLOGY IN SMART FARMING

In recent years, the agricultural industry has witnessed a remarkable transformation with the integration of advanced sensor technologies in smart farming practices. Sensors, which are at the heart of precision agriculture, have revolutionized the way farmers monitor, measure, and manage various aspects of crop production. These sensors, ranging from soil moisture sensors to weather sensors and plant health sensors, provide real-time data on critical parameters that directly influence agricultural outcomes. By capturing precise and continuous information from the field, sensor technology empowers farmers with valuable insights and enables data-driven decision-making (Musat et al., 2018).

The significance of sensor technology in agriculture cannot be overstated. One of the primary advantages lies in its ability to offer a granular understanding of crop and environmental conditions, enabling farmers to optimize resource allocation and enhance overall productivity. For instance, soil moisture sensors help monitor soil moisture levels, allowing farmers to apply irrigation water precisely when and where needed, reducing water waste and preventing over- or under-irrigation. Similarly, weather sensors provide accurate data on temperature, humidity, wind speed, and precipitation, facilitating informed decisions about planting, pest control, and disease management. Moreover, sensor technology plays a crucial role in early detection and prevention of crop diseases and pests. Plant health sensors can detect subtle changes in leaf reflectance and chlorophyll content, signaling the presence of diseases or nutrient deficiencies before they become visually apparent. This early warning system enables farmers to take timely action, implementing targeted interventions and minimizing crop losses. By continuously monitoring crop health and growth parameters, sensors enable farmers to optimize the use of fertilizers, pesticides, and other inputs, resulting in improved yield quality and reduced environmental impact (Almalki et al., 2021).

The advent of Internet of Things (IoT) technology has ushered in a new era of sensing and data collection in smart farming, revolutionizing the way agricultural processes are monitored and managed. IoT devices, equipped with sensors and connected through robust networks, have enabled farmers to gather real-time, granular data from every corner of their fields. This vast network of interconnected devices has

DOI: 10.1201/9781003400103-4

transformed traditional farms into smart, data-driven ecosystems, offering unprecedented visibility into crop health, soil conditions, weather patterns, and equipment performance. With IoT technology, farmers can make informed decisions based on accurate and timely information, unlocking the full potential of precision agriculture.

One of the key strengths of IoT technology in smart farming lies in its ability to create a seamless web of data connectivity across the farm. Soil moisture sensors, temperature and humidity sensors, and other environmental sensors collect data continuously, transmitting it wirelessly to centralized platforms or cloud-based systems. This data is then processed, analyzed, and presented to farmers in an easily accessible format, empowering them with real-time insights. IoT-enabled data collection has eliminated the need for manual data recording and reduced human errors, saving time and resources while improving data accuracy. Moreover, IoT technology has enabled a higher degree of automation in smart farming practices. From automated irrigation systems that respond to soil moisture readings to autonomous drones equipped with imaging sensors for crop health assessment, IoT devices have streamlined labor-intensive tasks and optimized resource utilization. This level of automation ensures that crops receive the right amount of water, nutrients, and protection at precisely the right time, leading to increased yields and resource efficiency. Additionally, IoT-driven data analytics and machine learning algorithms enable predictive and prescriptive capabilities, forecasting potential issues and suggesting optimal solutions for improved crop management (Saiz-Rubio and Rovira-Más, 2020).

4.2   TAXONOMY OF AGRICULTURAL SENSORS

In this section, we present a comprehensive taxonomy of sensors used in smart farming, categorizing them based on their role and specific use cases. By understanding the different types of sensors available, farmers can effectively harness their capabilities to monitor and manage various aspects of crop production. Environmental sensors form a crucial category of sensors in smart farming. Soil moisture sensors enable farmers to measure the water content in the soil, providing valuable insights for optimizing irrigation practices. Temperature and humidity sensors monitor ambient conditions, aiding in assessing crop health and preventing disease outbreaks. Weather sensors capture data on temperature, humidity, wind speed, rainfall, and solar radiation, enabling accurate weather forecasting and facilitating informed crop management decisions (Mohamed, 2023).

Plant health sensors play a vital role in assessing and monitoring the well-being of crops. Chlorophyll sensors measure the chlorophyll content in plants, helping identify nutrient deficiencies and stress levels. Leaf area index sensors estimate vegetation density and health, facilitating crop growth analysis and biomass estimation. Canopy sensors assess overall plant health, vigor, and biomass by measuring light reflectance and transmittance. These plant health sensors provide valuable data for optimizing nutrient application, detecting plant stress, and improving overall crop management practices.

The presented taxonomy also includes sensors for monitoring nutrient levels, crop yield, pest and disease detection, animal monitoring, water quality, imaging, and equipment monitoring. Each category encompasses specific sensors tailored to address the unique challenges and requirements of smart farming. By leveraging these sensor technologies, farmers can gain real-time insights into their crops, make data-driven decisions, and optimize their agricultural practices for improved productivity, sustainability, and profitability.

4.2.1 ENVIRONMENTAL SENSORS

Environmental sensors play a crucial role in smart farming by providing real-time data on various environmental factors that directly impact crop health and productivity. These sensors are designed to monitor and measure parameters such as soil moisture, temperature, humidity, weather conditions, light intensity, and gas concentrations. By collecting accurate and timely information about the farming environment, farmers can make informed decisions regarding irrigation scheduling, nutrient management, pest control, and overall crop management practices. Environmental sensors enable precision agriculture, helping farmers optimize resource utilization, minimize environmental impact, and improve crop yield and quality. Through the integration of advanced sensor technologies, smart farming systems can create a dynamic and responsive environment where farmers can monitor and manage the agricultural ecosystem with greater precision and efficiency.

Environmental sensors in smart farming encompass a wide range of sensors that help monitor and analyze various aspects of the farming environment. Let's delve into some additional sensors and their subcategories within this category

4.2.1.1 Soil Moisture Sensors

Soil moisture sensors are valuable devices used in agriculture and smart farming to measure the water content in the soil. These sensors play a critical role in optimizing irrigation practices and ensuring the efficient use of water resources. By providing real-time data on soil moisture levels, farmers can make informed decisions about when and how much to irrigate, leading to better crop yield and resource conservation. These sensors are often integrated into IoT systems, enabling remote monitoring and data analysis, which further enhances the overall efficiency and productivity of agricultural practices (Madushanki et al., 2019).

Tensiometers: Tensiometers, also known as soil moisture tension sensors or soil water potential sensors, are essential instruments used in smart farming to measure the soil's moisture content and tension. These sensors play a crucial role in optimizing irrigation practices, enabling farmers to make informed decisions about when and how much to irrigate, leading to more efficient water usage and improved crop yield. The working principle of a tensiometer is based on the measurement of the soil water potential or tension. Soil water potential is a measure of the energy required by plants to extract water from the soil. It represents the force that water molecules adhere to soil particles, and it influences the plant's ability to absorb water from the soil. When soil water potential is low (negative tension), it indicates that the soil is moist, and plants can easily extract water. Conversely, when soil water potential is high (positive tension), the soil is dry, and plants face difficulty in obtaining water from the soil. Tensiometers typically consist of a porous ceramic cup or tube attached to a pressure transducer or a water-filled tube connected to a vacuum gauge. The ceramic cup is buried in the soil at a specific depth, and as the soil moisture level changes, water moves in or out of the ceramic cup, causing changes in pressure or water level within the tube. These changes are then translated into readings that indicate the soil water potential or tension. In smart farming, tensiometers are integrated into the IoT and data collection systems, providing real-time soil moisture information. This data is then transmitted to cloud-based platforms or farm management software, where it can be analyzed and visualized. Farmers can access this data remotely, either through web or mobile applications, and receive alerts when the soil moisture reaches critical levels (Triantafyllou et al., 2019).

Capacitance sensors: A capacitive soil moisture sensor is a type of sensor used in agriculture and smart farming to measure the moisture content in the soil. It operates on the principle of changes in the dielectric constant of the soil with varying moisture levels. The sensor consists of two or more electrodes, typically made of metal or conductive material that are inserted into the soil. The soil acts as a dielectric material between these electrodes. When the soil is dry, it has a lower dielectric constant, which results in less electrical capacitance between the electrodes. As the soil moisture increases, the dielectric constant also increases, leading to higher electrical capacitance.

Time-domain reflectometry (TDR) sensors: The TDR sensor is a sophisticated and widely used type of soil moisture sensor in agriculture and environmental monitoring. TDR sensors operate on the principle of measuring the travel time of an electromagnetic pulse along a probe inserted into the soil. This technology provides accurate and reliable measurements of soil moisture content. The working principle of a TDR sensor involves sending a short electromagnetic pulse down a transmission line or waveguide inserted into the soil. The pulse travels along the waveguide at the speed of light until it encounters a change in the dielectric constant, which occurs at the soil–water interface. The amount of time taken for the pulse to reflect back to the sensor is directly proportional to the soil's dielectric constant, which, in turn, is related to its moisture content. The dielectric constant is a measure of how well a material can store electrical energy, and it varies with soil moisture levels. Dry soil has a lower dielectric constant, whereas wet soil has a higher dielectric constant due to the presence of water (Lytos et al., 2020).

4.2.1.2 Temperature and Humidity Sensors

Ambient temperature sensors: These are devices used to measure and monitor the surrounding air temperature in the agricultural environment. These sensors play a crucial role in smart farming by providing real-time data on temperature variations, which directly impact crop growth, livestock health, and overall farm management. By monitoring ambient temperature, farmers can optimize planting schedules, adjust irrigation and ventilation systems, and implement protective measures during extreme weather conditions. These sensors are often integrated into smart farming systems, enabling remote monitoring and data transmission through web or mobile applications. With accurate and timely temperature data, farmers can make informed decisions, improve resource management, and enhance the efficiency and productivity of their farming operations (Biradar and Shabadi, 2017).

Leaf temperature sensors: These are specialized devices used to measure the temperature of plant leaves. These sensors are essential in smart farming as they provide valuable insights into the health and stress levels of crops. Leaf temperature is closely related to plant transpiration and water stress, making it a crucial parameter for irrigation management and crop health monitoring. By monitoring leaf temperature, farmers can detect early signs of water deficiency, nutrient imbalances, or disease, allowing for targeted interventions and optimized irrigation strategies. Leaf temperature sensors are often deployed in conjunction with other environmental sensors to provide a comprehensive understanding of crop conditions and optimize crop management practices for increased yields and resource efficiency.

Wet-bulb and dry-bulb hygrometers: These are instruments used to measure the humidity level in the air. These sensors play a significant role in smart farming by providing critical data on the moisture content in the environment, which influences plant growth, disease prevalence, and livestock comfort. Wet bulb hygrometers measure the temperature of a wet surface exposed to the air, while dry bulb hygrometers measure the ambient air temperature. By comparing the two readings, the relative humidity can be determined. Monitoring humidity levels helps farmers optimize irrigation schedules, prevent fungal diseases, and improve animal husbandry conditions. Integrating wet and dry bulb hygrometers into smart farming systems allows for real-time monitoring and remote data access, enabling farmers to make data-driven decisions and enhance the overall efficiency and sustainability of their farming practices.

4.2.1.3   Weather Sensors

Anemometers: These are sensors used to measure and monitor wind speed and direction in the agricultural environment. In smart farming, anemometers play a crucial role in providing real-time data on wind conditions, which have significant implications for various farming activities. Wind speed data is essential for assessing the potential risk of wind damage to crops and structures, optimizing pesticide and herbicide application to minimize drift, and evaluating microclimates within the farm. Additionally, knowing wind direction helps farmers plan for proper crop orientation, optimize ventilation in greenhouses, and enhance weather forecasting for more informed decision-making. By integrating anemometers into smart farming systems, farmers can remotely access wind data through web or mobile applications, enabling proactive measures to mitigate potential wind-related challenges and enhance farm safety and productivity.

Rain gauges: These are sensors designed to measure and record the amount of rainfall in a given area. In smart farming, rain gauges are essential for accurate and timely precipitation data, enabling farmers to monitor water availability, manage irrigation schedules, and assess potential flood risks. By knowing precise rainfall amounts, farmers can optimize water usage, prevent overwatering or under-watering of crops, and implement conservation practices during periods of excess rainfall. Rain gauges also aid in assessing soil moisture levels, which are critical for effective crop management and water resource planning. Integrating rain gauges into smart farming systems allows farmers to remotely access rainfall data, enabling data-driven decisions for improved water management and sustainable agricultural practices.

Pyranometers: These are sensors used to measure the total solar irradiance received on a horizontal surface. In smart farming, pyranometers provide crucial data on solar radiation levels, which directly influence crop growth and photosynthesis rates. Monitoring solar irradiance helps farmers optimize planting schedules, assess crop health and vigor, and plan for potential solar energy generation. By understanding solar radiation patterns, farmers can implement shade management strategies, protect sensitive crops from excessive sunlight, and optimize the positioning of solar panels for maximum energy production. Integrating pyranometers into smart farming systems allows for real-time solar radiation data collection and remote access, enabling farmers to make informed decisions and enhance resource utilization for sustainable and efficient farming practices.

Barometers: These are sensors used to measure atmospheric pressure in the agricultural environment. In smart farming, barometers play a critical role in providing data on changes in atmospheric pressure, which can have implications for weather forecasting and crop health. Atmospheric pressure fluctuations are associated with weather patterns, and sudden changes in pressure often indicate the approach of weather systems, such as storms or fronts. Monitoring barometric pressure allows farmers to anticipate weather conditions, make timely decisions regarding planting, harvesting, or protection of crops, and take measures to protect farm structures and livestock from extreme weather events. Integrating barometers into smart farming systems enables remote data access and weather monitoring, empowering farmers to respond proactively to changing weather conditions and optimize farming practices for increased resilience and productivity.

4.2.1.4   Light Sensors

Quantum sensors: Quantum sensors, also known as photosynthetically active radiation (PAR) sensors, are devices used to measure the quantity of photosynthetically active radiation that plants receive. In smart farming, quantum sensors play a critical role in providing data on the amount of light available for photosynthesis, which directly impacts crop growth and productivity. Monitoring PAR levels helps farmers optimize crop planting densities, assess light availability in greenhouses, and implement precise light management strategies to enhance crop yield and quality. Quantum sensors are particularly important for indoor or greenhouse farming, where natural light availability may be limited, and artificial lighting is used to supplement plant growth. Integrating quantum sensors into smart farming systems allows for real-time monitoring of light levels and remote data access, enabling farmers to make data-driven decisions for efficient and sustainable crop cultivation.

Lux meters: These are sensors used to measure illuminance, which represents the amount of visible light falling on a surface. In smart farming, lux meters are essential for assessing the intensity of natural or artificial light in the agricultural environment. Monitoring illuminance levels helps farmers optimize the placement and intensity of artificial lighting in indoor or greenhouse settings, ensuring optimal growth conditions for crops. Lux meters are particularly useful for evaluating the effectiveness of grow lights, determining light distribution in different areas of the farm, and assessing shading effects on plant growth.

4.2.1.5 Gas Sensors

Carbon dioxide (CO_2) sensors: Carbon dioxide (CO_2) sensors are devices used to measure and monitor the concentration of CO_2 in the agricultural environment. In smart farming, CO_2 sensors play a critical role in providing data on the level of carbon dioxide present, which directly affects plant growth and photosynthesis rates. Monitoring CO_2 levels helps farmers optimize greenhouse ventilation and assess crop health. In closed environments like greenhouses, excessive CO_2 levels can lead to reduced plant growth and productivity, while inadequate levels can limit photosynthesis.

Ozone sensors: These are devices used to measure and monitor ozone gas concentrations in the agricultural environment. In smart farming, ozone sensors play a crucial role in providing data on the levels of ozone, which can have both positive and negative effects on plants and crops. Ozone is a reactive gas that can be beneficial in the upper atmosphere, protecting plants from harmful ultraviolet radiation. However, at ground level, elevated ozone levels can be harmful to plants, leading to reduced growth, yield losses, and increased susceptibility to diseases and pests.

4.2.2 Plant Health Sensors

Plant health sensors are instrumental in smart farming as they provide invaluable insights into the well-being and vitality of crops. These sensors employ various techniques to assess the health status of plants, including measuring chlorophyll content, estimating leaf area index, and analyzing canopy characteristics. By monitoring these plant health indicators, farmers can detect nutrient deficiencies, identify signs of stress, and optimize fertilization and irrigation practices accordingly. Plant health sensors enable early detection of diseases, pests, and other abnormalities, allowing for timely intervention and targeted treatments. By leveraging plant health sensors, farmers can proactively manage crop health, maximize yield potential, and minimize the use of chemicals, leading to more sustainable and environmentally friendly farming practices (Bandara et al., 2020).

Plant health sensors encompass a diverse array of technologies that aid in assessing the well-being and condition of plants. Here are some additional sensors and their subcategories within the plant health sensor category.

4.2.2.1   Chlorophyll Fluorescence Sensors

Active fluorescence sensors: These are specialized devices used to measure the fluorescence emitted by plants when they are excited by a light source. In smart farming, active fluorescence sensors play a critical role in providing valuable data on the photosynthetic efficiency and stress levels of crops. When plants absorb light during photosynthesis, some of the absorbed energy is re-emitted as fluorescence. The intensity and characteristics of this fluorescence can indicate the health and physiological state of the plants. Active fluorescence sensors can detect changes in fluorescence patterns caused by factors such as water stress, nutrient deficiencies, and disease infections. By monitoring fluorescence, farmers can assess crop stress and health, optimize irrigation and nutrient management practices, and implement timely interventions to prevent yield losses. Integrating active fluorescence sensors into smart farming systems allows for real-time monitoring and remote data access, enabling farmers to make data-driven decisions and enhance crop productivity and resource efficiency.

Passive fluorescence sensors: These are devices that measure the natural fluorescence emitted by plants without applying any external light source. In smart farming, passive fluorescence sensors provide valuable data on plant health and photosynthetic activity. Chlorophyll in plants naturally emits fluorescence when exposed to sunlight. The intensity and spectral characteristics of this fluorescence can indicate the efficiency of photosynthesis and overall plant health. These sensors can detect changes in fluorescence patterns caused by environmental stressors such as water availability, nutrient imbalances, and pathogen infections. With the monitoring of passive fluorescence, farmers can gain insights into plant stress levels, assess the impact of environmental conditions on crop health, and implement targeted management strategies. Integrating passive fluorescence sensors into smart farming systems enables continuous monitoring and remote data access, empowering farmers to make informed decisions for sustainable and efficient crop cultivation (Codeluppi et al., 2020).

4.2.2.2   Leaf Area Index Sensors

Optical leaf area index (LAI) sensors: Use optical measurements to estimate the leaf area index, providing insights into vegetation density and growth patterns.

Hemispherical photography: Capture images of plant canopies to calculate the leaf area index and assess light interception.

4.2.2.3 Canopy Sensors

Multispectral sensors: Optical LAI sensors are specialized devices used to measure and estimate the leaf area index of crops in the agricultural environment. LAI is a crucial parameter in smart farming as it represents the amount of leaf surface area relative to the ground area and is directly related to photosynthetic potential and biomass production. Optical LAI sensors use various optical techniques, such as light transmission or reflection, to quantify the density and distribution of leaves in the canopy.

Hyperspectral sensors: Hemispherical photography is a technique used to capture images of the sky and canopy from below the plant canopy. In smart farming, hemispherical photography plays a vital role in providing valuable information on light availability and interception in the agricultural environment. By analyzing hemispherical images, farmers can quantify metrics such as canopy openness, canopy cover, and light transmission through the canopy. This data is crucial for understanding light distribution within the crop canopy, which directly influences plant growth and photosynthesis. Farmers can use hemispherical photography to optimize crop planting densities, adjust canopy management strategies, and implement precise light management practices in controlled environments such as greenhouses. Integrating hemispherical photography into smart farming systems allows farmers to capture and analyze canopy images remotely, enabling data-driven decisions for enhanced light utilization, improved crop health, and increased productivity.

4.2.2.4 Disease and Pest Detection Sensors

Spectral imaging sensors: Spectral imaging sensors are advanced devices used to capture and analyze detailed spectral information from objects in the agricultural environment. In smart farming, these sensors play a crucial role in providing data-rich images that contain spectral signatures of different materials and crops. Spectral imaging sensors can capture data across numerous narrow and contiguous bands within the electromagnetic spectrum, beyond the capabilities of conventional RGB cameras. By analyzing the spectral data, farmers can gain valuable insights into crop health, disease detection, nutrient status, and stress levels. Spectral imaging enables the identification of specific plant characteristics, such as chlorophyll content and water stress, allowing for precise and targeted management strategies (Mohamed et al., 2021).

Electro-antennogram (EAG) sensors: EAG sensors are specialized devices used to detect and measure the electrical responses of insect antennae to specific chemical stimuli, known as semiochemicals. In smart farming, EAG sensors play a crucial role in pest management and insect monitoring. When insects detect certain chemicals released by plants or other insects, their antennae respond with electrical signals. EAG sensors capture and measure these electrical signals, providing insights into the sensory responses of insects to different compounds. By using EAG sensors, farmers can identify specific chemical cues that attract or repel pests, enabling the development of more targeted and effective pest control strategies. Additionally, EAG sensors aid in early detection of insect infestations, allowing farmers to implement timely and precise measures for pest control, reducing the need for broad-spectrum pesticides and minimizing potential environmental impacts. Integrating EAG sensors into smart farming systems facilitates real-time insect monitoring and remote data access, empowering farmers to make data-driven decisions for integrated pest management and sustainable agriculture practices.

4.2.3 NUTRIENT SENSORS

Nutrient sensors play a vital role in smart farming by enabling accurate and real-time monitoring of nutrient levels in soil, plants, or irrigation systems. These sensors provide valuable insights into the availability and distribution of essential nutrients such as nitrogen, phosphorus, potassium, and micronutrients. By measuring nutrient concentrations, farmers can optimize fertilizer application, prevent nutrient imbalances, and ensure that plants receive the necessary elements for healthy growth and development. Nutrient sensors can be deployed in various forms, including soil probes, sap flow sensors, or plant tissue analyzers, allowing farmers to assess nutrient status at different stages of plant growth. With the help of nutrient sensors, farmers can implement precision nutrient management strategies, reduce fertilizer waste, and enhance crop productivity while minimizing environmental impact.

Nutrient sensors encompass a range of technologies that enable precise monitoring and management of nutrient levels in smart farming. Here are some additional sensors and their subcategories within the nutrient sensor category.

4.2.3.1   Soil Nutrient Sensors

Electrical conductivity (EC) sensors: EC sensors are devices used to measure the ability of a soil solution to conduct an electric current. In smart farming, EC sensors play a critical role in providing valuable data on soil salinity levels and nutrient content. Soil salinity affects the availability of water and nutrients to plants, and excessive salinity can lead to reduced crop growth and productivity. By measuring EC, farmers can assess soil quality, identify areas with high salinity levels, and implement appropriate soil management practices, such as leaching or soil amendments, to improve soil conditions and crop health. Additionally, EC sensors can be used to estimate soil moisture levels, allowing for efficient irrigation scheduling and water management. Integrating EC sensors into smart farming systems enables continuous monitoring of soil salinity and moisture levels, empowering farmers to make data-driven decisions for sustainable irrigation and nutrient management, leading to enhanced crop productivity and water-use efficiency (Iaksch et al., 2021).

Ion-specific electrodes: Ion-specific electrodes are specialized sensors used to measure the concentration of specific ions in soil solutions. In smart farming, ion-specific electrodes are valuable tools for assessing soil nutrient levels and ion imbalances. These sensors are capable of detecting and measuring specific ions such as potassium (K+), nitrate (NO3–), ammonium (NH4+), calcium (Ca2+), and others. By monitoring ion concentrations, farmers can optimize fertilization practices, ensure balanced nutrient availability to plants, and prevent nutrient deficiencies or toxicities. Ion-specific electrodes are particularly useful for precision agriculture, where site-specific nutrient management is essential to maximize crop yield and minimize environmental impact. Integrating ion-specific electrodes into smart farming systems allows for real-time monitoring of soil nutrient levels and remote data access, empowering farmers to implement precise and efficient nutrient management strategies for sustainable and productive crop cultivation.

Soil moisture and nutrient tension sensors: Soil moisture and nutrient tension sensors are specialized devices used to measure the water availability and nutrient tension in the soil. In smart farming, these sensors play a crucial role in providing real-time data on soil moisture content and nutrient availability, which are essential factors for optimizing irrigation and nutrient management practices. Soil moisture sensors measure the volumetric water content in the soil, helping farmers determine the optimal timing and amount of irrigation required to maintain adequate soil moisture levels for plant growth. Nutrient tension sensors, on the other hand, measure the availability of nutrients to plants in the soil, providing valuable information for precision nutrient application and avoiding nutrient leaching. By monitoring soil moisture and nutrient tension, farmers can efficiently allocate water and nutrients to crops, minimize water and nutrient wastage, and enhance overall resource use efficiency. Integrating soil moisture and nutrient tension sensors into smart farming systems allows for continuous monitoring and remote data access, enabling data-driven decisions for optimal irrigation and nutrient management, leading to improved crop health, productivity, and sustainable agricultural practices.

4.2.3.2 Plant Sap Analysis Sensors

Plant sap pH Sensors: These sensors are specialized devices used to measure the pH level of the sap extracted from plants. In smart farming, plant sap pH sensors play a critical role in providing valuable data on the acid-alkaline balance within the plant tissues. pH is a measure of the hydrogen ion concentration in a solution and is essential for determining the physiological status and nutrient availability in plants. The pH level of plant sap can provide insights into nutrient uptake and assimilation, as well as the presence of any nutrient imbalances or deficiencies. Plant sap pH sensors aid in precision agriculture by enabling site-specific nutrient management and early detection of nutrient-related issues, leading to enhanced crop growth, quality, and overall farm productivity. Integrating plant sap pH sensors into smart farming systems allows for real-time monitoring and remote data access, empowering farmers to make data-driven decisions and implement precise and efficient nutrient management practices for sustainable and high-yield crop production (Schönfeld et al., 2018).

Electrical conductivity (EC) sensors: EC sensors are recognized as essential instruments that play a crucial part in enhancing agricultural methodologies. The purpose of these sensors is to assess the electrical conductivity of a solution, which is strongly correlated with the concentration of dissolved ions in the soil. The increasing significance of precision agriculture is accompanied by the crucial role of EC sensors in delivering instantaneous information on soil salinity and nutrient concentrations. These sensors let farmers to remotely oversee and regulate soil conditions, hence facilitating decision-making based on data. The methodical use of EC sensors provides farmers with a comprehensive comprehension of the electrical conductivity of their fields. This knowledge enables them to customize their irrigation and fertilization approaches in order to optimize crop output and resource utilization. The strategic implementation of EC sensors in the context of smart farming extends beyond the sole purpose of data collection. Instead, it serves as a crucial component within an intricate network of interconnected improvements. By incorporating EC sensors with other devices like weather stations, drones, and automated irrigation systems, a holistic and up-to-date understanding of the agricultural environment is obtained. The utilization of data synergy enables the implementation of real-time modifications to irrigation programs, taking into account the prevailing soil conditions, hence mitigating the risks of excessive watering or inadequate nutrient supply. In addition, EC sensors play a significant role in facilitating predictive analytics, allowing farmers to proactively anticipate and address potential issues such as soil deterioration or nutrient deficits. The adoption of this integrated strategy not only improves the effectiveness of agricultural operations but also fosters the implementation of sustainable practices by reducing the unnecessary utilization of resources. Within the dynamic realm of smart agriculture, the incorporation of EC sensors serves as a testament to the dedication towards precision, sustainability, and the astute administration of agricultural resources.

4.2.3.3 Leaf Nutrient Sensors

Leaf nitrogen sensors: These are specialized devices used to measure the nitrogen content in plant leaves. In smart farming, leaf nitrogen sensors play a crucial role in providing valuable data on the nutritional status and health of plants. Nitrogen is an essential element for plant growth and is a key component of chlorophyll, which is responsible for photosynthesis. Monitoring leaf nitrogen levels helps farmers assess the nitrogen status of crops, optimize fertilization practices, and identify potential nutrient deficiencies or excesses.

Chlorophyll meters: These are specialized devices used to measure the chlorophyll content in plant leaves. In smart farming, chlorophyll meters play a crucial role in providing valuable data on the photosynthetic health and vigor of plants. Chlorophyll is the green pigment found in plant leaves that is responsible for capturing light energy during photosynthesis. By measuring chlorophyll content, farmers can assess the photosynthetic capacity of crops, monitor plant health, and identify any stress factors affecting photosynthesis. Chlorophyll meters are particularly useful for diagnosing nutrient deficiencies, water stress, and pest or disease infestations, as these factors can impact chlorophyll levels and, therefore, the plant's ability to produce energy through photosynthesis.

4.2.3.4 Hydroponic Nutrient Sensors

Dissolved oxygen (DO) sensors: DO sensors are specialized devices used to measure the amount of oxygen dissolved in water. In the context of smart farming, these sensors play a critical role in monitoring water quality in various agricultural applications. Oxygen is essential for the health and survival of aquatic organisms, including fish and other aquatic life present in irrigation ponds, aquaculture systems, and hydroponic setups. Monitoring DO levels is crucial in these systems to ensure that the water maintains sufficient oxygen content to support life and prevent detrimental effects of low oxygen, such as fish kills and poor plant growth. DO sensors are also used in monitoring water bodies like rivers, streams, and lakes within agricultural landscapes, as low DO levels can indicate pollution or excessive nutrient runoff, affecting the overall ecosystem health (Andrianto and Faizal, 2022).

pH and conductivity sensors: These are essential tools used in smart farming to measure the pH level and electrical conductivity of various solutions, particularly soil and water. pH sensors measure the acidity or alkalinity of a solution, such as soil or water. In agriculture, the pH level of soil significantly influences nutrient availability to plants. Different crops have specific pH preferences, and by monitoring pH, farmers can adjust soil pH through appropriate soil amendments to create optimal growing conditions for crops. Maintaining the correct pH level ensures that essential nutrients are available to plants, promoting healthy growth and maximizing yield potential. Conductivity sensors, on the other hand, measure the electrical conductivity of a solution, typically water or nutrient solutions. Electrical conductivity is directly related to the concentration of dissolved ions, including nutrients, in the solution. In hydroponic systems or irrigation water, conductivity sensors are invaluable for optimizing nutrient management. By monitoring conductivity, farmers can adjust nutrient solution strength and composition, ensuring that plants receive the right balance of essential nutrients for optimal growth and productivity (Lee et al., 2019).

4.2.3.5 Nutrient Monitoring Systems

IoT nutrient monitoring system: This refers to advanced and interconnected platforms that leverage sensor technology and data analytics to monitor and manage nutrient levels in agricultural environments. These systems play a vital role in precision agriculture, enabling farmers to optimize nutrient management practices, enhance crop productivity, and promote sustainable farming practices.

4.2.4 Crop Yield Sensors

Crop yield sensors play a crucial role in smart farming by accurately measuring and assessing crop production and yield. These sensors are designed to capture data related to crop biomass, fruit size, grain weight, or overall yield throughout the growth cycle. By providing real-time and precise information on crop yield, farmers can make data-driven decisions to optimize harvesting schedules, estimate crop profitability, and evaluate the effectiveness of various agronomic practices. Crop yield sensors utilize technologies such as optical sensors, weight-based sensors, or image analysis to capture data at the individual plant or field level. By integrating crop yield sensors into smart farming systems, farmers can enhance productivity, improve resource allocation, and make informed decisions to maximize crop yield and profitability. Crop yield sensors encompass a variety of technologies that enable accurate and efficient measurement of crop yield in smart farming. Here are some additional sensors and their subcategories within the crop yield sensor category.

4.2.4.1 Optical Sensors

Near-infrared (NIR) sensors: NIR sensors are specialized devices used to measure and analyze the near-infrared region of the electromagnetic spectrum. In agriculture and smart farming applications, NIR sensors play a crucial role in providing valuable information about the chemical composition and quality of various materials, including crops, soil, and agricultural products.

Hyperspectral sensors: Hyperspectral sensors are advanced imaging devices used in various fields, including agriculture and smart farming, to capture detailed and high-resolution spectral data across a wide range of wavelengths. Unlike traditional RGB cameras that capture three primary color bands (red, green, and blue), hyperspectral sensors can capture hundreds of narrow and contiguous bands within the electromagnetic spectrum (Raja and Vyas, 2019).

4.2.4.2 Weight-Based Sensors

Load cells: Load cells are specialized sensors used to measure force or weight in various applications, including smart farming and agricultural machinery. These sensors are essential for precise weight measurements, ensuring accurate data for various agricultural processes and systems.

Grain flow sensors: Grain flow sensors are specialized devices used to measure and monitor the flow rate of grains and other bulk materials during transportation and handling processes. In agriculture and smart farming applications, grain flow sensors play a critical role in ensuring efficient and accurate grain handling, storage, and logistics.

4.2.4.3 Image Analysis Sensors

Drones: Drones, also known as unmanned aerial vehicles (UAVs), are unmanned aircraft that are remotely piloted or operated autonomously. In agriculture and smart farming, drones have become invaluable tools for various applications, revolutionizing the way farmers manage their crops and land. Equipped with cameras and image analysis software, drones can capture high-resolution images of crops, enabling yield estimation through advanced image processing techniques.

Ground-based cameras: Placed strategically in fields, these cameras can capture images of crops from different angles to assess crop density and yield potential.

4.2.4.4 Crop Canopy Sensors

LiDAR (Light Detection and Ranging) sensors: LiDAR sensors are remote sensing devices that use laser pulses to measure distances and create detailed three-dimensional (3D) maps of the surrounding environment. In agriculture and smart farming, LiDAR sensors have emerged as powerful tools for comprehensive landscape analysis. Mounted on drones, tractors, or ground-based platforms, LiDAR sensors can capture precise elevation data, vegetation height, and canopy structures. This information enables farmers to accurately assess topography, soil erosion, and drainage patterns, aiding in land management and irrigation planning. Additionally, LiDAR data can be used to optimize planting density, assess tree health in orchards, and even estimate crop biomass, facilitating better crop management and resource allocation. The rapid advancements in LiDAR technology have made it an indispensable component of precision agriculture, revolutionizing the way farmers analyze their fields and make data-driven decisions for increased productivity and sustainable farming practices (Farooq et al., 2019).

Ultrasonic sensors: These are devices that use ultrasonic waves, or sound waves with frequencies beyond the range of human hearing (typically above 20 kHz), to measure distances and detect objects. In agriculture and smart farming, ultrasonic sensors are employed in various applications due to their ability to provide accurate and reliable distance measurements.

4.2.4.5 Wireless Sensor Networks

Distributed sensor networks: Comprise a network of sensors strategically placed in fields to collect data on crop growth and yield, providing spatially distributed yield information.

4.2.4.6 Yield Monitoring Systems

Combine yield monitors: Installed on combine harvesters, these systems measure yield during harvesting and create yield maps for different parts of the field.

Yield mapping software: Analyzes data from yield monitors and sensors to create detailed yield maps, enabling precision agriculture practices.

4.2.5 ANIMAL MONITORING SENSORS

Animal monitoring sensors play a vital role in smart farming by providing real-time data and insights into the health, behavior, and well-being of livestock. These sensors, equipped with advanced technologies such as GPS tracking, health monitoring, and activity sensors, enable farmers to remotely monitor animal location, track grazing behavior, detect health issues, and ensure optimal conditions for their livestock. By collecting and analyzing data on parameters like body temperature, heart rate, activity levels, and milk production, animal monitoring sensors empower farmers to make informed decisions regarding animal care, disease prevention, and overall herd management. With the help of these sensors, farmers can improve animal welfare, increase productivity, and optimize resource utilization, contributing to sustainable and efficient livestock farming practices. Animal monitoring sensors encompass various technologies that enable the tracking, health monitoring, and behavior analysis of livestock in smart farming (Dahane et al., 2020).

4.2.5.1 GPS Trackers

Collar-mounted GPS trackers: Attachable to collars or ear tags, these trackers use GPS technology to monitor animal location and movement patterns, enabling farmers to track grazing behavior, monitor herd movement, and prevent livestock theft.

Leg-mounted GPS trackers: Designed specifically for larger animals such as cattle, these trackers are attached to the animal's leg or ear and provide accurate real-time location data for monitoring and management purposes.

4.2.5.2 Health Monitoring Sensor

Body temperature sensors: Measure the body temperature of animals to monitor health conditions, detect fever or illnesses, and identify potential signs of disease.

Heart rate monitors: Track the heart rate and heart rate variability of animals to assess stress levels, monitor overall health, and detect abnormalities.

4.2.5.3 Activity and Behavior Sensors

Accelerometers: Measure animal movement, activity levels, and behavior patterns, providing insights into grazing behavior, rest patterns, and overall animal well-being.

Proximity sensors: Utilize radio-frequency identification (RFID) or near field communication technology to track animal presence, detect grouping or separation behavior, and monitor social interactions within the herd.

4.2.5.4 Rumination Monitors

Bolus rumination sensors: Implanted in an animal's rumen, these sensors measure rumination time, cud-chewing patterns, and rumen pH levels to assess digestive health and nutritional well-being.

4.2.5.5 Milk Production Sensors

Milk yield sensors: Installed in milking parlors or milking robots, these sensors monitor milk yield, flow rate, and milk composition, providing insights into the productivity and health of dairy cows (Colezea et al., 2018).

4.2.5.6   Environmental Sensors

Temperature and humidity sensors: Monitor ambient temperature and humidity levels in livestock housing or barns, ensuring optimal environmental conditions for animal comfort and welfare.

Air quality Sensors: Measure parameters such as ammonia levels, carbon dioxide, or methane concentrations to assess air quality and detect potential health hazards for animals.

4.2.6   Water Quality Sensors

Water quality sensors are essential tools in smart farming that enable accurate and continuous monitoring of the quality and condition of water sources used in agricultural operations. These sensors are designed to measure various parameters such as pH levels, dissolved oxygen, conductivity, turbidity, and nutrient concentrations in water bodies such as rivers, lakes, ponds, or irrigation systems. By collecting real-time data on water quality, farmers can assess the suitability of water for irrigation, detect potential contaminants or pollutants, and take proactive measures to ensure the health of plants, animals, and the environment. Water quality sensors empower farmers to make informed decisions about water usage, implement precise irrigation strategies, and prevent the negative impacts of poor water quality on crop health and overall agricultural sustainability. By utilizing these sensors, farmers can promote efficient water management, conserve resources, and safeguard the long-term viability of their farming operations. Water quality sensors encompass various technologies and subcategories that enable comprehensive monitoring and assessment of water quality in smart farming (Muangprathub et al., 2019).

4.2.6.1   pH Sensors

Glass electrode pH sensors: Utilize a glass electrode to measure the hydrogen ion concentration in water, providing information on water acidity or alkalinity.

Solid-state pH Sensors: Employ solid-state materials to measure pH levels, offering durable and reliable pH monitoring in various water environments.

4.2.6.2   Dissolved Oxygen Sensors

Optical dissolved oxygen Sensors: Measure oxygen concentration based on the luminescence quenching principle, providing noninvasive and accurate dissolved oxygen readings.

Electrochemical dissolved oxygen sensors: Utilize an electrochemical cell to measure the partial pressure of oxygen, offering continuous and real-time dissolved oxygen monitoring.

4.2.6.3   Conductivity Sensors

Electrode conductivity sensors: Measure the electrical conductivity of water, which correlates with the concentration of dissolved ions and salinity levels.

Inductive conductivity sensors: Use electromagnetic induction to measure water conductivity, offering accurate readings in challenging water conditions.

4.2.6.4 Turbidity Sensors

Nephelometric turbidity sensors: Measure water turbidity by assessing the amount of scattered light caused by suspended particles in the water.

Absorption turbidity sensors: Analyze the absorption of light by suspended particles to determine water turbidity levels.

4.2.6.5 Metal Ion Sensors

Ion-selective electrode sensors: Measure specific metal ion concentrations, such as calcium, magnesium, or heavy metals, providing information on water contamination levels.

Voltammetric sensors: Employ electrochemical techniques to measure metal ion concentrations, offering sensitive detection and analysis of trace metal pollutants (Ragazou et al., 2022).

4.2.7 Imaging Sensors

Imaging sensors have revolutionized smart farming by providing powerful tools for non-invasive, high-resolution imaging and analysis of crops, fields, and livestock. These sensors encompass various technologies such as visible light cameras, infrared cameras, hyperspectral imaging systems, and thermal imaging devices. By capturing images across different spectra, imaging sensors enable farmers to monitor crop health, detect diseases or nutrient deficiencies, assess plant vigor, and identify areas of stress or pest infestation. Additionally, imaging sensors can be used for precision mapping of fields, assessing soil conditions, and monitoring livestock behavior and well-being. The detailed and real-time visual information obtained from imaging sensors helps farmers make data-driven decisions, optimize resource allocation, and implement targeted interventions, ultimately leading to increased yields, improved efficiency, and sustainable agricultural practices.

4.2.7.1 Multispectral Sensors

Multispectral cameras: These are imaging devices used in smart farming to capture light across multiple specific and predefined spectral bands. Unlike traditional RGB cameras that capture only three bands (red, green, and blue), multispectral cameras can capture data in several discrete bands within the visible and/or non-visible parts of the electromagnetic spectrum. Each band corresponds to a specific wavelength range, providing unique spectral information about the objects and materials being imaged.

Multispectral drones: Mounted with multispectral cameras, these drones provide aerial imaging capabilities for large-scale crop monitoring and analysis.

4.2.7.2 Hyperspectral Sensors

Hyperspectral cameras: These are advanced imaging devices used in smart farming to capture data across a wide range of wavelengths, going beyond the human visible spectrum. These cameras enable farmers to obtain detailed spectral information about crops and vegetation, allowing for precise analysis and monitoring of agricultural conditions and health. Unlike conventional cameras that capture red, green, and blue (RGB) bands, hyperspectral cameras can capture hundreds or even thousands of narrow and contiguous bands across the electromagnetic spectrum. Each band corresponds to a specific wavelength, providing a unique spectral signature for different materials and objects (Fote et al., 2020).

Imaging spectrometers: Imaging spectrometers in smart farming are advanced sensors that combine the capabilities of a camera with the spectral resolution of a spectrometer. These sensors can capture images across multiple narrow and contiguous spectral bands, providing detailed spectral information about the objects and materials in the scene. Imaging spectrometers play a crucial role in modern agriculture by enabling farmers to perform precise and data-rich analyses of crops, soil, and vegetation. The operation of imaging spectrometers is based on the principle of spectroscopy, which involves measuring the intensity of light at different wavelengths. Each pixel in the image corresponds to a spectrum of reflectance values across multiple wavelengths, creating a hyperspectral image. These images contain rich data on the unique spectral signatures of different materials, allowing for detailed analysis and identification of specific elements or compounds.

4.2.7.3 Thermal Sensors

Thermal cameras: These are advanced devices used in smart farming to capture and record infrared radiation emitted by objects and living organisms based on their temperature. These cameras play a crucial role in modern agriculture by providing valuable thermal imagery and temperature data, enabling farmers to monitor and manage various aspects of their farm operations more effectively. Thermal cameras operate on the principle of thermography, which involves detecting and visualizing the heat signatures of objects and surfaces. Unlike traditional cameras that capture visible light, thermal cameras focus on the infrared spectrum, which is not visible to the human eye. Each object emits different levels of infrared radiation based on its temperature, and thermal cameras convert these temperature differences into visual representations, creating thermal images.

Infrared (IR) sensors: These are devices that detect and measure infrared radiation emitted by objects and living organisms based on their temperature. These sensors play a crucial role in modern agriculture by providing valuable data on temperature variations, enabling farmers to monitor and manage various aspects of their farm operations more effectively. IR sensors operate on the principle that all objects emit infrared radiation as a function of their temperature. The higher the temperature, the more intense the infrared radiation emitted. IR sensors are designed to detect this radiation and convert it into electrical signals, which can then be processed and used for various applications.

4.2.7.4 LiDAR Sensors

Terrestrial LiDAR: In smart farming, terrestrial LiDAR is used on the ground to capture highly accurate and detailed 3D point cloud data of the agricultural landscape. LiDAR is an advanced remote sensing technology that uses laser pulses to measure distances and create detailed digital representations of the environment. In smart farming applications, terrestrial LiDAR provides valuable data for precision agriculture, land management, and crop monitoring. The process of terrestrial LiDAR involves a laser scanner mounted on a tripod or vehicle, which emits laser pulses toward the surrounding landscape. The emitted laser beams bounce off objects such as plants, trees, terrain, and structures, and the reflected signals are captured by the LiDAR sensor.

Airborne LiDAR: It refers to the use of LiDAR technology mounted on aerial platforms, such as airplanes or drones, to capture detailed and high-resolution 3D point cloud data of the agricultural landscape from above. Airborne LiDAR is an advanced remote sensing technique that offers extensive coverage and rapid data acquisition, making it well-suited for large-scale agricultural applications. In airborne LiDAR, the LiDAR sensor mounted on the aerial platform emits laser pulses toward the ground. The emitted laser beams bounce off objects such as crops, vegetation, buildings, and terrain, and the reflected signals are captured by the LiDAR sensor. By measuring the time, it takes for the laser pulses to return, the system calculates the distance to each point on the ground, creating a dense and accurate 3D representation of the surveyed area (Yoon et al., 2018).

4.2.8 EQUIPMENT MONITORING SENSORS

Equipment monitoring sensors play a crucial role in smart farming by providing real-time data and insights into the condition, performance, and utilization of agricultural machinery and equipment. These sensors are designed to monitor various parameters such as engine temperature, fuel levels, hydraulic pressure, vibration, and usage metrics. By collecting and analyzing data from equipment monitoring sensors, farmers can ensure timely maintenance, detect potential issues or malfunctions, optimize equipment utilization, and minimize downtime. With the help of these sensors, farmers can enhance operational efficiency, reduce costs, and improve overall productivity. Equipment monitoring sensors contribute to the effective management of farm machinery, enabling farmers to make data-driven decisions and implement preventive measures, ultimately leading to more sustainable and successful farming practices. Equipment monitoring sensors in smart farming encompass various technologies and subcategories that enable comprehensive monitoring and management of agricultural machinery and equipment (Navarro et al., 2020).

4.2.8.1 Engine Health Sensors

Engine temperature sensors: Engine temperature sensors are devices used in smart farming to measure and monitor the temperature of the engine in agricultural machinery and equipment. These sensors play a vital role in modern agriculture by providing real-time data on engine temperature, helping farmers ensure optimal engine performance, prevent overheating, and avoid potential engine damage. Engine temperature sensors are typically integrated into the engine cooling system of vehicles and machinery, such as tractors, harvesters, and other agricultural equipment. They use various technologies, such as thermistors or temperature-sensitive resistors, to measure the engine's temperature. The data collected by these sensors is then transmitted to central databases or cloud-based platforms as part of smart farming systems, allowing farmers to remotely monitor and analyze engine temperature.

Oil pressure sensors: In smart farming, oil pressure sensors are devices used to measure and monitor the oil pressure in agricultural machinery and equipment. These sensors play a critical role in modern agriculture by providing real-time data on oil pressure, helping farmers ensure proper lubrication and prevent engine damage. Oil pressure sensors are typically integrated into the engine or lubrication system of vehicles and machinery, such as tractors, harvesters, and other agricultural equipment. They use various technologies, such as pressure transducers or piezoelectric sensors, to measure the pressure of the engine oil. The data collected by these sensors is then transmitted to central databases or cloud-based platforms as part of smart farming systems, allowing farmers to remotely monitor and analyze oil pressure levels.

Coolant level sensors: Coolant level sensors are devices used in smart farming to measure and monitor the amount of coolant or antifreeze present in agricultural machinery and equipment. These sensors play a critical role in modern agriculture by providing real-time data on coolant levels, helping farmers ensure proper cooling and prevent engine overheating. Coolant level sensors are typically integrated into the coolant reservoir or cooling system of vehicles and machinery, such as tractors, harvesters, and other agricultural equipment. They use various technologies, such as float sensors or capacitive sensors, to detect the level of coolant in the reservoir. The data collected by these sensors is then transmitted to central databases or cloud-based platforms as part of smart farming systems, allowing farmers to remotely monitor and analyze coolant levels.

4.2.8.2 Fuel Monitoring Sensors

Fuel level sensors: Fuel level sensors in smart farming are devices used to measure and monitor the quantity of fuel present in agricultural machinery and equipment. These sensors play a crucial role in modern agriculture by providing real-time data on fuel levels, enabling farmers to manage fuel usage, plan refueling, and optimize operational efficiency. Fuel level sensors are typically integrated into fuel tanks or reservoirs of vehicles and machinery, such as tractors, harvesters, and irrigation pumps. They use various technologies, such as ultrasonic or capacitive sensors, to determine the fuel level within the tank. The data collected by these sensors is then transmitted to central databases or cloud-based platforms as part of smart farming systems, allowing farmers to remotely monitor and analyze fuel levels.

Fuel consumption Sensors: Fuel consumption sensors are devices used in smart farming to measure and monitor the amount of fuel consumed by agricultural machinery and equipment. These sensors play a significant role in modern agriculture by providing valuable data on fuel usage, enabling farmers to optimize fuel efficiency, reduce operational costs, and implement sustainable farming practices. Fuel consumption sensors are typically integrated into vehicles and machinery such as tractors, harvesters, and irrigation pumps. They use various technologies, such as flow meters or fuel level sensors, to measure the amount of fuel consumed during operation. The data collected by these sensors is then transmitted to central databases or cloud-based platforms as part of smart farming systems, allowing farmers to remotely monitor and analyze fuel usage (Ünal, 2020).

4.2.8.3   Vibration Sensors

Vibration sensors are advanced devices used in smart farming to detect and measure vibrations and mechanical movements within agricultural equipment and machinery. These sensors play a crucial role in modern agriculture by monitoring the performance and health of machinery such as tractors, harvesters, and irrigation systems. Vibration sensors are typically integrated into smart farming systems, enabling farmers to remotely monitor and analyze the condition of their machinery. This proactive approach to equipment maintenance ensures timely repairs and prolongs the lifespan of agricultural assets, contributing to increased productivity and reduced costs on the farm.

Accelerometers: Accelerometers are sensors used in smart farming to measure acceleration, vibration, and changes in motion within agricultural equipment and machinery. These sensors play a critical role in modern agriculture by providing valuable data on the performance and condition of various agricultural assets, including tractors, harvesters, irrigation systems, and vehicles. By detecting changes in acceleration and vibration, farmers can monitor machinery health, identify potential issues, and implement timely maintenance, thereby enhancing operational efficiency and reducing downtime. Accelerometers typically consist of microelectro-mechanical systems (MEMS) that sense acceleration and motion changes. When subjected to acceleration or movement, the MEMS elements generate electrical signals proportional to the applied force. These signals are then converted into useful data that can be analyzed and interpreted. In smart farming applications, accelerometers are often integrated into IoT platforms, enabling real-time data transmission and remote monitoring.

Farmers can access this data through web or mobile applications, facilitating proactive decision-making and preventive maintenance.

Vibration monitors: Vibration monitors are specialized devices used in smart farming to continuously measure and analyze vibrations and mechanical movements within agricultural equipment and machinery. These monitors are an essential component of modern agriculture, providing real-time data on the condition and performance of various agricultural assets, including tractors, harvesters, irrigation systems, and vehicles. Vibration monitors typically consist of advanced sensors, such as accelerometers or piezoelectric sensors, capable of detecting minute vibrations and translating them into electrical signals. These signals are then processed and analyzed by the monitor's onboard electronics to provide actionable insights and alerts. In smart farming applications, vibration monitors are often integrated into IoT platforms, enabling remote monitoring and data transmission. Farmers can access real-time vibration data through web or mobile applications, facilitating proactive decision-making and defensive maintenance.

4.2.8.4 Usage Monitoring Sensors

Hour meters: Hour meters are utilized as precision instruments for the purpose of measuring and documenting the total duration, in hours, during which a specific agricultural apparatus or machinery has been actively engaged in operation. These meters are essential tools for tracking usage and monitoring maintenance intervals, allowing farmers to optimize equipment performance and extend its lifespan. In smart farming applications, hour meters are integrated into IoT systems, enabling remote monitoring and data collection for improved farm management. Hour meters typically consist of electronic counters or timers that record the cumulative running time of equipment. They are commonly installed on tractors, harvesters, irrigation pumps, and other machinery that undergo regular usage on the farm. The hour meter starts recording when the equipment is turned on and stops when it is turned off, providing an accurate measure of the operational hours.

Load sensors: Smart farming relies on load sensors, which are used to track and record the amount of force exerted on various pieces of farm machinery and storage facilities. The information these sensors provide on the weight of harvested crops, the burden on machines, and the amount of stored produce is invaluable to modern farmers. With these sensors, farmers can optimize equipment usage, ensure proper handling of agricultural products, and implement efficient logistics and storage practices. Load sensors can be integrated into various components of smart farming systems, such as conveyor belts, grain bins, storage silos, harvesters, and other equipment. They typically consist of strain gauges, load cells, or other transducers that convert the applied force or weight into electrical signals. These signals are then processed and analyzed to provide real-time load data.

4.2.8.5   GPS Tracking Sensors

Global positioning system (GPS) trackers: GPS trackers in smart farming are devices equipped with GPS technology that allow farmers to track and monitor the location of vehicles, equipment, and assets on their farm. These trackers play a vital role in modern agriculture by providing real-time location data, enabling farmers to optimize fleet management, improve operational efficiency, enhance security, and make informed decisions. GPS trackers typically consist of a GPS receiver, a communication module (such as GSM, GPRS, or LoRa), and a power source (e.g., battery or solar panel). The GPS receiver determines the device's precise location by receiving signals from multiple satellites, while the communication module transmits this location data to a central server or cloud-based platform. Farmers can access this data through the web or mobile applications, allowing them to monitor their assets remotely.

4.2.8.6   Condition Monitoring Sensors

Temperature sensors: Temperature sensors in smart farming are devices used to measure and monitor the ambient temperature in the agricultural environment. These sensors play a crucial role in modern farming practices by providing real-time temperature data, enabling farmers and agricultural stakeholders to make informed decisions and optimize various aspects of agricultural operations. Temperature sensors are an integral part of the IoT and smart farming systems, contributing to increased efficiency, sustainability, and crop yield.

Pressure sensors: Pressure sensors in smart farming are devices used to measure and monitor various pressures within the agricultural environment. These sensors play a crucial role in modern farming practices by providing valuable data related to water pressure, gas pressure, air pressure, and more. By collecting real-time pressure information, farmers and agricultural stakeholders can optimize irrigation systems, manage water resources efficiently, and ensure the proper functioning of equipment and facilities. There are different types of pressure sensors used in smart farming, each with specific applications, such as water pressure sensors, gas pressure sensors, and air pressure sensors.

Fluid level sensors: Fluid level sensors in smart farming are devices used to measure and monitor the levels of liquids, such as water or fertilizers, in various agricultural applications. These sensors play a critical role in optimizing water management, controlling irrigation systems, and ensuring the efficient distribution of liquids in agricultural processes. By providing real-time data on fluid levels, farmers can make informed decisions, prevent wastage, and improve overall farm productivity.

4.3   DATA COLLECTION METHODS IN SMART FARMING

In this section, we explore various techniques and approaches used to collect data in the context of smart farming. Effective data collection is vital for generating meaningful insights and driving informed decision-making in agriculture. Smart farming leverages advanced technologies to gather diverse data types from multiple sources, enabling farmers to monitor and manage their operations with greater precision and efficiency (Schönfeld et al., 2018; Andrianto and Faizal, 2022; Lee et al., 2019; Raja and Vyas, 2019).

4.3.1 ON-FIELD DATA COLLECTION

On-field data collection in the context of smart farming refers to the process of gathering real-time information and measurements directly from agricultural fields. It involves the deployment of various sensors and instruments to monitor key parameters such as weather conditions, soil characteristics, and plant health. On-field data collection provides farmers with valuable insights into the immediate conditions of their fields, enabling them to make informed decisions regarding irrigation, fertilization, pest control, and overall crop management. By collecting and analyzing on-field data, farmers can implement precision agriculture practices, optimize resource allocation, and enhance the productivity and sustainability of their farming operations.

In this context, on-field data collection plays a crucial role in gathering real-time information about the environmental conditions and soil characteristics within agricultural fields. This data is essential for making informed decisions related to irrigation, fertilization, pest control, and overall crop management. On-field data collection involves the deployment of various sensors and instruments that measure and monitor key parameters.

One important aspect of on-field data collection is the use of weather stations, which consist of sensors that capture weather-related variables such as temperature, humidity, wind speed, and rainfall. These stations are typically installed in strategic locations across the field to provide localized and accurate weather information. This data is valuable for understanding the microclimatic conditions within the field and helps farmers make precise decisions regarding irrigation scheduling, disease management, and harvesting operations. Another critical component of on-field data collection is soil moisture sensing. Soil moisture sensors are placed at different depths in the soil profile to measure the water content. These sensors provide insights into soil moisture distribution, helping farmers optimize irrigation practices and prevent under- or over-watering. Soil moisture data, combined with weather data, enables farmers to implement precise irrigation scheduling based on the specific needs of the crops and the prevailing environmental conditions. In addition to weather and soil moisture sensors, on-field data collection may also involve the use of sensors to measure other parameters such as soil temperature, pH levels, nutrient concentrations, and light intensity. Soil temperature sensors provide information about the thermal conditions of the soil, which is crucial for seed germination and root development. pH sensors help assess soil acidity or alkalinity, allowing farmers to adjust soil pH levels for optimal crop growth. Nutrient sensors provide insights into the nutrient content of the soil, enabling farmers to apply fertilizers more precisely and avoid nutrient imbalances. Light intensity sensors help monitor the availability of sunlight in different parts of the field, aiding in crop growth analysis and shade management. The on-field data collection process typically involves the installation and calibration of sensors, regular monitoring and data recording, and the use of data loggers or wireless networks to transmit the collected data to a central database or farm management system. This data can be analyzed and visualized, providing farmers with valuable insights into the dynamics of their fields and supporting informed decision-making. On-field data collection enables farmers to implement precision agriculture practices, optimize resource allocation, and achieve more efficient and sustainable farming operations (Codeluppi et al., 2020; Mohamed et al., 2021; Iaksch et al., 2021; Schönfeld et al., 2018).

4.3.2 REMOTE SENSING–BASED DATA COLLECTION

Remote sensing–based data collection in the context of smart farming refers to the utilization of aerial or satellite platforms to capture data from a distance. This approach involves the use of specialized sensors and imaging technologies to gather information about crop health, vegetation indices, water stress, and other relevant parameters. Remote sensing allows for the monitoring of large agricultural areas and provides valuable insights into the spatial variability of field conditions. By analyzing remote sensing data, farmers can identify patterns, anomalies, and trends that impact crop productivity. This information enables them to make data-driven decisions regarding crop management, resource allocation, and targeted interventions. Remote sensing–based data collection plays a crucial role in enabling farmers to assess field conditions over larger areas, detect potential issues, and implement precision farming techniques for optimal agricultural outcomes (Biradar and Shabadi, 2017; Bandara et al., 2020).

Remote sensing–based data collection is a powerful tool in smart farming that allows for the collection of valuable information about agricultural fields from a distance. This approach involves the use of remote sensing platforms such as satellites, drones, or aircraft equipped with specialized sensors and imaging technologies. These sensors capture data in the form of images or spectral measurements, which can be further processed and analyzed to gain insights into various aspects of crop health, vegetation dynamics, and environmental conditions.

One key advantage of remote sensing–based data collection is its ability to provide a comprehensive view of agricultural landscapes. Satellites equipped with high-resolution sensors orbiting the earth capture images at regular intervals, covering large areas and enabling the monitoring of crop conditions on a regional or even global scale. This allows farmers to assess the spatial variability of their fields, identify trends, and detect potential issues that may impact crop productivity.

Remote sensing data can be processed and analyzed to derive various vegetation indices, such as the normalized difference vegetation index or the enhanced vegetation index. These indices provide quantitative measures of vegetation vigor and health, indicating areas of high or low biomass and helping farmers identify regions that require specific attention or interventions. Another important application of remote sensing–based data collection is the assessment of water stress in crops. By analyzing thermal infrared imagery, which captures the temperature variations of vegetation, farmers can detect areas experiencing water scarcity and prioritize irrigation efforts accordingly (Lytos et al., 2020). This enables them to optimize water usage, prevent water stress-induced crop losses, and promote sustainable water management practices.

Remote sensing also allows for the monitoring of crop growth stages and the detection of anomalies or diseases. By analyzing multispectral or hyperspectral imagery, farmers can identify areas of crop stress, nutrient deficiencies, or pest infestations. This information helps them take timely corrective measures, such as targeted fertilization or pest control, to mitigate potential losses and ensure crop health and productivity.

4.3.3 SENSOR INTEGRATION IN FARM MACHINERY FOR DATA

The integration of sensors with farm machinery and equipment has revolutionized the way data is collected in real time in smart farming. By incorporating sensors into various agricultural machinery and equipment, farmers can gather valuable data directly from the field during farming operations. This real-time data collection enables farmers to make informed decisions and implement precision agriculture practices (Codeluppi et al., 2020).

One key area where sensor integration has had a significant impact is in the domain of precision agriculture. Tractors, combines, and other farm machinery can be equipped with sensors to capture data such as soil moisture, temperature, and nutrient levels as they move across the field. This data is then transmitted wirelessly or stored locally for later analysis. By integrating sensors with farm machinery, farmers can collect a wealth of information about the field's conditions in real time, allowing for immediate adjustments and optimizations in the farming processes.

Another area where sensor integration has been instrumental is in livestock management. Sensors can be integrated into livestock monitoring systems to collect data on animal health, behavior, and productivity. For example, wearable sensors can track the activity levels and rumination patterns of cattle, providing insights into their overall health and well-being. Real-time data collection through sensor integration enables farmers to closely monitor livestock conditions, detect early signs of disease or distress, and take prompt action to ensure the welfare of the animals (Iaksch et al., 2021).

Additionally, sensor integration with farm machinery and equipment has extended to crop protection and pesticide application. Sprayers and drones equipped with sensors can detect crop pests, diseases, or weeds in real-time, allowing for targeted and precise application of pesticides or herbicides. This not only minimizes the use of chemicals but also reduces the environmental impact and increases the efficiency of crop protection practices.

The integration of sensors with farm machinery and equipment also facilitates data connectivity and interoperability. Sensors can be connected to centralized farm management systems, allowing for seamless data transmission, storage, and analysis. This integration enables farmers to access real-time data from multiple sources, make data-driven decisions, and automate various farming processes.

4.4 DATA MANAGEMENT INFRASTRUCTURE

4.4.1 DESIGNING A DATA MANAGEMENT SYSTEM FOR SMART FARMING

Designing an effective data management system is crucial for smart farming, as it involves handling and processing large volumes of sensor data. A well-designed data management system should address aspects such as data collection, storage, retrieval, and analysis. It should consider the specific requirements of smart farming applications and the integration of data from various sources, including sensors, IoT devices, and farm machinery. The system should also ensure data quality, data integrity, and data interoperability to enable seamless integration and analysis of the collected data. Additionally, considerations such as scalability, real-time processing, and integration with other farm management systems should be taken into account during the design process. The ultimate goal is to create a robust and efficient data management system that empowers farmers with actionable insights for improved decision-making and optimized farming practices.

4.4.2 Database Architectures for Storing and Organizing Sensor Data

In smart farming, the storage and organization of sensor data are critical for efficient data management and analysis. Various database architectures can be employed to handle the specific characteristics and requirements of sensor data. One common approach is the use of relational databases, which offer a structured and organized way to store data using tables, columns, and rows. Relational databases provide the ability to define relationships between different data entities, facilitating complex querying and analysis. Another approach is the utilization of NoSQL databases, which are well-suited for handling large volumes of unstructured or semi-structured sensor data. NoSQL databases provide scalability, flexibility, and faster data retrieval, making them suitable for real-time and big data applications in smart farming. Additionally, other database technologies such as time-series databases or spatial databases may be employed to handle specific types of sensor data. The choice of the appropriate database architecture depends on factors such as data volume, data complexity, scalability requirements, and the specific needs of the smart farming application.

4.4.3 Securing Data in Smart Farming

As smart farming relies heavily on data collection and analysis, ensuring data security, privacy, and responsible data sharing is of utmost importance. Data security measures should be implemented to protect the confidentiality, integrity, and availability of sensor data. This includes implementing encryption techniques, access controls, and secure communication protocols to prevent unauthorized access or data breaches. Data privacy considerations involve anonymizing or de-identifying personal or sensitive information, adhering to privacy regulations, and obtaining appropriate consent for data collection and usage. Furthermore, data sharing in smart farming can bring numerous benefits, such as collaborative research, knowledge exchange, and decision support. However, it should be done in a controlled and responsible manner. Data sharing agreements, data usage policies, and data governance frameworks should be established to define the rights, responsibilities, and restrictions associated with data sharing. Additionally, farmers should have the ability to retain ownership and control over their data, and mechanisms for secure and selective data sharing should be in place to protect the interests of all stakeholders involved in the smart farming ecosystem.

4.5 DATA QUALITY AND PREPROCESSING

4.5.1 Ensuring Data Accuracy and Reliability in Smart Farming

In smart farming, ensuring the accuracy and reliability of sensor data is crucial for making informed decisions and optimizing farming practices. Several factors can affect data accuracy, including sensor calibration, environmental conditions, and sensor placement. It is essential to calibrate sensors regularly to maintain their accuracy and account for any drift or deviation over time. Proper sensor installation and placement in the field, considering factors such as height, orientation, and distance from the target, can also enhance data accuracy. Additionally, environmental factors like temperature, humidity, and lighting conditions should be monitored and accounted for to minimize their impact on sensor measurements. Quality control measures, such as data validation and verification, can be implemented to identify and rectify any inaccuracies or anomalies in the collected data. Moreover, cross-validation techniques, where data from multiple sensors or sources are compared and analyzed, can provide insights into data consistency and reliability. By ensuring data accuracy and reliability, farmers can have confidence in the data-driven decisions they make and optimize their farming operations accordingly (Saiz-Rubio and Rovira-Más, 2020; Mohamed, 2023; Madushanki et al., 2019; Triantafyllou et al., 2019; Lytos et al., 2020).

4.5.2 Data Preprocessing for Cleaning and Filtering Sensor Data

Data preprocessing is an essential step in smart farming to clean and filter sensor data before analysis. Sensor data can be susceptible to noise, outliers, and missing values, which can adversely affect the quality and reliability of the data analysis. Data cleaning techniques involve identifying and removing or correcting inconsistencies, errors, and noise in the data. This can be achieved through various methods such as filtering, smoothing, and interpolation. Filtering techniques, such as moving average or median filters, can help remove high-frequency noise from the data. Smoothing techniques, such as low-pass filters, can reduce the impact of random fluctuations and improve the signal-to-noise ratio. Interpolation methods, such as linear or spline interpolation, can be used to estimate missing data points based on the available data. Additionally, outlier detection algorithms can be applied to identify and handle outliers, which are data points significantly deviating from the expected range or distribution. By applying appropriate data preprocessing techniques, farmers can obtain cleaner and more reliable sensor data for subsequent analysis and decision-making.

4.5.3 Dealing with Missing Data and Outliers in Sensor Measurements

Sensor measurements in smart farming applications may sometimes contain missing data or outliers due to various reasons such as sensor malfunction, communication issues, or environmental factors. Handling missing data is crucial to avoid biases and ensure the completeness of the data analysis. Several techniques can be employed, including imputation methods such as mean imputation, regression imputation, or multiple imputation, which estimate the missing values based on the available data.

Another approach is to discard the incomplete records; however, this may lead to a reduction in the dataset size and potential loss of valuable information. Outliers, on the other hand, are data points that significantly deviate from the expected patterns or range (Muangprathub et al., 2019; Ragazou et al., 2022; Fote et al., 2020; Yoon et al., 2018). They can be detected using statistical methods such as Z-score, modified Z-score, or box plots. Outliers can be treated by either removing them if they are due to data entry errors or by applying robust statistical techniques that are less sensitive to extreme values. Proper handling of missing data and outliers in sensor measurements ensures that the subsequent data analysis and decision-making processes are based on accurate and reliable information, leading to improved farming practices in smart farming.

4.6   REAL-TIME DATA PROCESSING AND ANALYSIS

4.6.1   Techniques for Real-Time Data Processing in Smart Farming

Real-time data processing plays a vital role in smart farming, enabling timely decision-making and proactive management of agricultural operations. Various techniques are employed to process sensor data in real time. One common approach is stream processing, where data is processed as it arrives, allowing for immediate analysis and response. Stream processing frameworks, such as Apache Kafka and Apache Flink, provide the infrastructure for handling high-volume, high-velocity data streams and performing real-time computations. These frameworks enable real-time data aggregation, filtering, and transformation, allowing farmers to extract valuable insights from sensor data as it is generated. Other techniques include complex event processing, where patterns and rules are defined to identify meaningful events or anomalies in the data stream. ML algorithms can also be integrated into the real-time processing pipeline, enabling predictive analytics and anomaly detection. By employing these techniques, smart farming systems can process sensor data in real time, facilitating proactive decision-making and optimization of farming practices (Farooq et al., 2019; Dahane et al., 2020; Colezea et al., 2018).

4.6.2   Implementing Edge Computing for On-Site Data Analysis

Edge computing has emerged as a powerful paradigm in smart farming, enabling on-site data analysis and reducing reliance on cloud infrastructure. With edge computing, sensor data is processed and analyzed at the edge of the network, closer to the data source. This approach offers several advantages, including reduced latency, enhanced data privacy, and improved reliability in areas with limited or intermittent connectivity. On-site data analysis using edge computing allows for real-time decision-making without the need to transmit data to a centralized server. Edge devices, such as gateways or edge servers, are equipped with computing capabilities and machine learning algorithms, enabling them to perform advanced analytics directly on the sensor data. This facilitates immediate response and enables autonomous actions in smart farming applications. Moreover, edge computing enables the integration of contextual information, such as local weather conditions or historical data, into the analysis, resulting in more accurate and context-aware decision-making. By implementing edge computing for on-site data analysis, smart farming systems can leverage the benefits of real-time analytics while ensuring data privacy, reducing network latency, and enhancing overall system reliability (Biradar and Shabadi, 2017).

4.6.3 Real-Time Analytics for Decision-Making in Precision Agriculture

Real-time analytics has transformative applications in precision agriculture, enabling data-driven decision-making and optimization of farming operations. By processing sensor data in real time and applying advanced analytics techniques, farmers can gain valuable insights into various aspects of their agricultural practices. For instance, real-time analytics can be used for crop monitoring, allowing farmers to assess plant health, detect diseases or pests, and optimize irrigation and fertilization schedules. It can also facilitate yield prediction, helping farmers estimate crop production and plan harvest activities. Real-time analytics can aid in predicting weather patterns and micro-climate changes, enabling farmers to take proactive measures to protect crops from adverse conditions. Additionally, it can support livestock management by monitoring animal behavior, health, and well-being in real time. Real-time analytics in precision agriculture also paves the way for autonomous systems, such as automated irrigation or robotic harvesting, which can respond dynamically to changing conditions based on real-time data analysis (Mohamed, 2023; Madushanki et al., 2019; Triantafyllou et al., 2019).

4.7 DATA INTEGRATION AND FUSION

4.7.1 Integrating Data from Multiple Sensors and Sources

In smart farming, a wide range of sensors are deployed to monitor various aspects of agricultural operations, such as environmental conditions, soil moisture, crop health, and animal behavior. Integrating data from multiple sensors and other sources is essential for obtaining a holistic view of the farming system and making informed decisions. Data integration involves collecting data from different sensors and sources, aligning them in a unified format, and merging them into a single cohesive dataset. This integration enables correlation and analysis across different dimensions, providing a comprehensive understanding of the farming environment. Integration can be achieved through standardized protocols and data formats, ensuring compatibility and interoperability among different sensors and systems. By integrating data from multiple sensors and sources, farmers can gain deeper insights into the complex interactions within the farming ecosystem, enabling them to optimize resource allocation, detect anomalies, and improve overall efficiency.

4.7.2 Sensor Data Fusion Techniques for Combining Heterogeneous Data Streams

Sensor data fusion is a process of combining data from multiple sensors to generate a more accurate and comprehensive representation of the monitored phenomena.

In smart farming, where diverse sensors with different modalities and measurement capabilities are employed, sensor data fusion becomes crucial for extracting meaningful information and reducing uncertainties. Various techniques are used for sensor data fusion, including statistical methods, ML algorithms, and expert systems. Statistical methods, such as weighted averaging or Bayesian estimation, are commonly used to combine sensor measurements and estimate the true state of the environment. ML techniques, such as ensemble methods or deep learning architectures, can learn the relationships and dependencies between different sensor data streams and produce fused outputs. Expert systems leverage domain knowledge and rules to make decisions based on inputs from multiple sensors. These fusion techniques aim to exploit the complementary information provided by different sensors and improve the accuracy, reliability, and robustness of the derived insights (Saiz-Rubio and Rovira-Más, 2020; Mohamed, 2023; Madushanki et al., 2019; Triantafyllou et al., 2019).

4.7.3   Benefits of Data Fusion for Smart Farming Systems

Data fusion in smart farming offers several benefits that contribute to improved accuracy and efficiency of agricultural systems. Firstly, by combining data from multiple sensors, farmers can obtain a more complete and accurate understanding of the farming environment. This enables precise decision-making and targeted interventions, leading to optimized resource utilization, reduced costs, and enhanced crop yields. Secondly, data fusion helps mitigate the limitations and uncertainties associated with individual sensors. By integrating data from multiple sources, errors or biases in individual measurements can be minimized, and outliers can be identified and filtered out. This leads to increased reliability and robustness in the derived information. Thirdly, data fusion enables the detection of complex relationships and patterns that may not be evident in isolated sensor data streams. By combining different modalities and measurements, hidden correlations can be revealed, leading to insights that can drive proactive management strategies. Moreover, data fusion facilitates real-time monitoring and decision-making, allowing farmers to respond promptly to changing conditions and optimize their operations (Bandara et al., 2020; Codeluppi et al., 2020; Mohamed et al., 2021; Iaksch et al., 2021).

4.8   DATA VISUALIZATION AND DECISION SUPPORT

4.8.1   Visualizing Sensor Data for Intuitive Understanding and Insights

Visualizing sensor data plays a crucial role in smart farming by providing intuitive understanding and valuable insights to farmers and agronomists. By representing sensor data in visual formats such as line charts, bar charts, scatter plots, and heatmaps, complex data patterns and trends can be easily identified. For example, visualizing temperature and humidity data over time can reveal daily and seasonal variations, helping farmers optimize irrigation schedules and manage crop growth accordingly. Additionally, spatial visualizations on maps can highlight variations in soil moisture levels or nutrient distribution across the field, enabling targeted interventions for improved crop health and yield. Furthermore, visualizing sensor data in real time can provide immediate feedback on environmental conditions, allowing farmers to respond promptly to changing conditions. Interactive visualizations and dashboards empower stakeholders to explore the data, zoom in on specific time periods or regions of interest, and gain deeper insights into the performance and behavior of crops, livestock, or environmental conditions. By effectively visualizing sensor data, farmers can make informed decisions, optimize resource allocation, and enhance overall farm management practices.

4.8.2 Developing Decision Support Systems Based on Sensor Data Analysis

Decision support systems (DSS) leverage advanced sensor data analysis techniques to provide farmers with actionable recommendations and insights. By applying ML algorithms and statistical models to sensor data, DSS can predict crop yields, detect disease outbreaks, optimize irrigation and fertilization strategies, and facilitate pest management. For example, using historical sensor data and weather information, ML models can forecast crop yields for different scenarios, allowing farmers to make informed decisions about harvesting, storage, and market planning. DSS can also integrate data from multiple sensors and sources, such as weather stations, soil moisture sensors, and satellite imagery, to provide comprehensive and holistic insights into farm operations. These systems can generate real-time alerts and notifications to farmers, enabling them to take timely actions and mitigate risks. Additionally, DSS can incorporate optimization algorithms to determine optimal planting densities, crop rotations, and resource allocation strategies, maximizing productivity and profitability. By harnessing the power of sensor data analysis and ML, decision support systems empower farmers to make data-driven decisions, improve resource efficiency, and achieve sustainable agricultural practices (Lee et al., 2019; Raja and Vyas, 2019; Farooq et al., 2019; Dahane et al., 2020).

4.8.3 Data Visualization and Decision-Making Tools in Smart Farming

A variety of tools and techniques are available to support data visualization and decision-making in smart farming. Data visualization tools, such as Tableau, Power BI, and Python libraries like Matplotlib, Seaborn, and Plotly, offer a wide range of options for creating visually appealing representations of sensor data. These tools allow farmers to customize and create interactive dashboards, charts, and maps to suit their specific needs. Geographic Information Systems (GIS) software, such as ArcGIS and QGIS, enable spatial analysis and mapping of sensor data, facilitating site-specific decision-making and precision agriculture practices. DSS can be developed using programming languages like Python or R, leveraging machine learning libraries such as scikit-learn, TensorFlow, or PyTorch for data analysis and model development. Cloud-based platforms and frameworks, such as Microsoft Azure, Google Cloud Platform, or Amazon Web Services, provide a scalable and efficient infrastructure for storing, processing, and analyzing large volumes of sensor data. Furthermore, emerging technologies like augmented reality and virtual reality offer new possibilities for immersive data visualization and decision-making experiences in smart farming. These technologies enable farmers to visualize sensor data in 3D space, simulate scenarios, and interact with virtual farm environments, enhancing their understanding and decision-making capabilities. By utilizing these tools and techniques, farmers and agricultural professionals can unlock the full potential of sensor data, gain deeper insights, and optimize their farming practices for improved productivity, sustainability, and profitability (Biradar and Shabadi, 2017; Bandara et al., 2020; Codeluppi et al., 2020; Mohamed et al., 2021; Iaksch et al., 2021; Schönfeld et al., 2018; Andrianto and Faizal, 2022).

4.9 SCALABILITY AND CONNECTIVITY

4.9.1 Scaling Up Sensor Networks for Large-Scale Farming Operations

As smart farming practices continue to expand, the scalability of sensor networks becomes paramount for large-scale farming operations. Scaling up sensor networks involves deploying a higher number of sensors across vast agricultural landscapes to capture comprehensive data. This requires careful consideration of sensor placement, coverage, and density to ensure adequate data collection without compromising cost-effectiveness. Additionally, managing the power supply and connectivity of a large number of sensors becomes crucial. Implementing wireless sensor networks (WSNs) with long-range connectivity options, such as LoRaWAN or NB-IoT, can facilitate the seamless integration and communication of sensors across the farm. Furthermore, the use of mesh network topologies and gateway devices can extend the network coverage and overcome connectivity challenges in remote areas. By scaling up sensor networks, farmers can gather extensive data from various points in their operations, enabling a more accurate and holistic understanding of their farms' conditions and performance (Codeluppi et al., 2020; Mohamed et al., 2021; Iaksch et al., 2021).

4.9.2 Ensuring Connectivity and Network Infrastructure

To enable seamless data collection from sensors in smart farming, ensuring robust connectivity and network infrastructure is essential. Reliable connectivity ensures that data can be transmitted in real time from the sensors to the data collection system. This requires establishing a stable and secure network infrastructure that can handle the volume and frequency of data generated by the sensors. Depending on the farm's size and geographical layout, farmers may need to consider the installation of wireless access points or repeaters to ensure connectivity across the entire farm. Additionally, utilizing cellular networks or satellite communications can provide connectivity options in areas with limited network coverage. Furthermore, integrating edge computing capabilities within the network infrastructure can facilitate localized data processing and reduce latency, enabling near real-time data collection and analysis. By ensuring connectivity and a robust network infrastructure, farmers can overcome data collection challenges, optimize sensor data transmission, and make informed decisions based on up-to-date information (Lee et al., 2019).

4.9.3 Challenges and Solutions for Managing Big Farming Data

The proliferation of sensors in smart farming generates a massive volume of data, leading to the challenge of managing and processing big data effectively. Handling large datasets requires scalable storage solutions and efficient data management techniques. Cloud-based platforms and distributed file systems, such as Hadoop and Apache Spark, offer scalable storage and processing capabilities for big data in smart farming. These technologies allow farmers to store and analyze data from multiple sensors, perform complex computations, and extract valuable insights. Data compression and aggregation techniques can also be employed to reduce storage requirements and enhance processing efficiency. Furthermore, implementing data preprocessing pipelines, which include data cleaning, filtering, and transformation steps, helps to improve data quality and remove noise or outliers before analysis. Moreover, advanced analytics techniques, such as machine learning and data mining algorithms, can be applied to extract patterns, detect anomalies, and predict future trends from the big sensor data. By effectively managing and processing big data, farmers can harness the full potential of sensor-generated information, enabling data-driven decision-making, optimization of farm operations, and the discovery of new opportunities for improving productivity and sustainability in smart farming.

4.10 IMPLICATION ON EGYPTIAN AGRICULTURE

The implications of farming sensors, IoT, data collection, and management technologies in Egyptian agriculture are profound, holding immense promise for the sector's sustainable development. As Egypt faces the challenges of ensuring food security, optimizing resource utilization, and mitigating environmental impact, the integration of these advanced technologies offers transformative opportunities. By harnessing the power of sensor data, connectivity, and data-driven decision-making, Egyptian farmers can revolutionize their agricultural practices. This chapter explores the implications of farming sensors, IoT, data collection, and management technologies on Egyptian agriculture, delving into their role in enhancing productivity, resource efficiency, and sustainable agricultural practices. Furthermore, we discuss the integration of these technologies, highlighting the synergies and collective benefits that can be derived when they work together harmoniously. Through this comprehensive exploration, we aim to shed light on the immense potential these technologies hold for shaping the future of Egyptian agriculture and driving sustainable development in the sector (Raja and Vyas, 2019).

Farming sensors have profound implications for sustainable development in Egyptian agriculture. For instance, soil moisture sensors play a crucial role in optimizing irrigation practices by providing accurate measurements of soil moisture content. This enables farmers to apply precise amounts of water, avoiding over-irrigation and water wastage. By implementing precision irrigation techniques, such as drip irrigation or variable rate irrigation, farmers can conserve water resources and ensure efficient water usage, particularly in water-scarce regions of Egypt. This not only supports sustainable water management but also enhances crop productivity and reduces energy consumption associated with pumping water. Plant health sensors offer another significant implication for sustainable agriculture. These sensors monitor various indicators of crop health, such as leaf temperature, chlorophyll levels, and disease symptoms. By detecting early signs of plant stress or disease, farmers can take proactive measures to address the issues promptly. This allows for targeted interventions, such as applying appropriate treatments or adjusting nutrient levels, reducing the need for excessive use of pesticides and fertilizers. By minimizing the use of agrochemicals, farmers can mitigate environmental pollution, protect beneficial insects, and safeguard ecosystem health. Environmental sensors, including weather stations and climate sensors, contribute to climate-smart farming practices in Egypt. By collecting data on temperature, humidity, solar radiation, and wind speed, these sensors provide valuable insights into local weather conditions and climate patterns. Farmers can leverage this information to optimize their planting schedules, manage pest outbreaks, and mitigate the impact of extreme weather events. For example, they can adjust irrigation schedules based on weather forecasts, preventing waterlogging or drought stress. This level of precision and adaptability helps farmers optimize resource usage, minimize crop losses, and adapt to climate change, enhancing the resilience of Egyptian agriculture.

The IoT revolutionizes sustainable development in Egyptian agriculture by enabling real-time data collection, analysis, and decision-making. IoT devices, such as wireless sensor networks, drones, and satellite imagery, provide a wealth of data on various aspects of farming, including crop conditions, soil moisture, pest infestations, and equipment performance. This data-driven approach empowers farmers to make informed decisions based on accurate and up-to-date information, leading to optimized resource usage and improved agricultural practices. An example of IoT's implication in sustainable agriculture is the integration of IoT devices with precision agriculture techniques. By combining GPS technology, sensors, and actuators, farmers can implement site-specific management strategies tailored to the specific needs of different areas within their fields. This allows for targeted application of fertilizers and pesticides, minimizing input usage and reducing environmental impact. Furthermore, IoT enables remote monitoring and control of irrigation systems, facilitating efficient water management and conservation. IoT also contributes to sustainable livestock management. Animal monitoring sensors, such as wearable devices or RFID tags, collect data on animal health, behavior, and location. This information helps farmers identify and address potential health issues, optimize feeding regimes, and ensure animal welfare.

Effective data collection and management technologies have profound implications for sustainable development in Egyptian agriculture. The ability to gather, store, and analyze vast amounts of data from multiple sources empowers farmers and stakeholders to make informed decisions and implement sustainable farming practices. Data analytics techniques applied to agricultural data offer valuable insights for optimizing resource allocation, improving crop management, and reducing waste. For instance, by analyzing historical weather data, crop yields, and soil conditions, predictive models can be developed to forecast crop performance and optimize planting schedules. This helps farmers maximize productivity while minimizing resource consumption, leading to more sustainable agricultural practices. The integration of data collection and management technologies also facilitates traceability and quality control in the agricultural supply chain. Through the use of blockchain technology, for example, farmers can securely record and verify every stage of production, from seed to harvest to distribution. This level of transparency and traceability enhances consumer confidence, ensures food safety, and promotes sustainable and ethical farming practices. Moreover, data-driven decision support systems enable precision agriculture practices, such as variable rate application of inputs. Based on the analysis of spatial and temporal variations in soil fertility, crop health, and weather conditions, farmers can tailor their interventions, such as fertilizer application or pesticide spraying, to specific areas within their fields. This targeted approach minimizes input waste, reduces environmental contamination, and improves overall farm efficiency (Navarro et al., 2020; Ünal, 2020).

The integration of farming sensors, IoT, data collection, and management technologies forms a holistic approach to sustainable development in Egyptian agriculture. By combining real-time data from various sensors and IoT devices, farmers can gain comprehensive insights into their farming operations, optimize resource usage, and minimize environmental impact. For example, by integrating soil moisture sensors with IoT networks, farmers can receive real-time data on soil moisture levels across their fields. This information can be analyzed alongside weather data and crop water requirements to develop efficient irrigation schedules and prevent water wastage. Similarly, the integration of environmental sensors, such as weather stations, with IoT platforms enables farmers to access weather forecasts, pest alerts, and disease outbreak predictions. This empowers them to take proactive measures to protect crops, minimize chemical inputs, and optimize production. The seamless integration of data collection and management technologies enables the aggregation and analysis of large-scale datasets. This allows for the development of advanced analytics models and decision support systems that assist farmers in making sustainable and data-driven decisions. For instance, by integrating satellite imagery, weather data, and crop health sensors, farmers can create precise prescription maps for variable rate application of inputs. This targeted approach optimizes resource allocation, reduces waste, and enhances overall farm sustainability (Saiz-Rubio and Rovira-Más, 2020; Mohamed, 2023).

REFERENCES

Almalki, F. A., Soufiene, B. O., Alsamhi, S. H., & Sakli, H. (2021). A low-cost platform for environmental smart farming monitoring system based on IoT and UAVs. *Sustainability, 13*(11), 5908.

Andrianto, H., & Faizal, A. (2022, November). Future research on smart farming platforms. In *2022 International Conference on Information Technology Systems and Innovation (ICITSI)* (pp. 358–362). IEEE.

Bandara, T. M., Mudiyanselage, W., & Raza, M. (2020, November). Smart farm and monitoring system for measuring the environmental condition using wireless sensor network-IOT technology in farming. In *2020 5th International Conference on Innovative Technologies in Intelligent Systems and Industrial Applications (CITISIA)* (pp. 1–7). IEEE.

Biradar, H. B., & Shabadi, L. (2017, May). Review on IOT based multidisciplinary models for smart farming. In *2017 2nd IEEE International Conference on Recent Trends in Electronics, Information & Communication Technology (RTEICT)* (pp. 1923–1926). IEEE.

Codeluppi, G., Cilfone, A., Davoli, L., & Ferrari, G. (2020). LoRaFarM: A LoRaWAN-based smart farming modular IoT architecture. *Sensors*, *20*(7), 2028.

Colezea, M., Musat, G., Pop, F., Negru, C., Dumitrascu, A., & Mocanu, M. (2018). CLUeFARM: Integrated web-service platform for smart farms. *Computers and Electronics in Agriculture*, *154*, 134–154.

Dahane, A., Benameur, R., Kechar, B., & Benyamina, A. (2020, October). An IoT based smart farming system using machine learning. In *2020 International Symposium on Networks, Computers and Communications (ISNCC)* (pp. 1–6). IEEE.

Farooq, M. S., Riaz, S., Abid, A., Abid, K., & Naeem, M. A. (2019). A survey on the role of IoT in agriculture for the implementation of smart farming. *IEEE Access*, *7*, 156237–156271.

Fote, F. N., Mahmoudi, S., Roukh, A., & Mahmoudi, S. A. (2020, November). Big data storage and analysis for smart farming. In *2020 5th International Conference on Cloud Computing and Artificial Intelligence: Technologies and Applications (CloudTech)* (pp. 1–8). IEEE.

Iaksch, J., Fernandes, E., & Borsato, M. (2021). Digitalization and big data in smart farming–a review. *Journal of Management Analytics*, *8*(2), 333–349.

Lee, M., Kim, H., & Yoe, H. (2019). ICBM-based smart farm environment management system. In: Lee, R. (eds) *Software Engineering, Artificial Intelligence, Networking and Parallel/Distributed Computing SNPD 2018. Studies in Computational Intelligence*, vol 790 (pp. 42–56). Springer. https://doi.org/10.1007/978-3-319-98367-7_4

Lytos, A., Lagkas, T., Sarigiannidis, P., Zervakis, M., & Livanos, G. (2020). Towards smart farming: Systems, frameworks and exploitation of multiple sources. *Computer Networks*, *172*, 107147.

Madushanki, A. R., Halgamuge, M. N., Wirasagoda, W. S., & Syed, A. (2019). Adoption of the Internet of Things (IoT) in agriculture and smart farming towards urban greening: A review. *International Journal of Advanced Computer Science and Applications*, *10*(4), 11–28.

Mohamed, E. S., Belal, A. A., Abd-Elmabod, S. K., El-Shirbeny, M. A., Gad, A., & Zahran, M. B. (2021). Smart farming for improving agricultural management. *The Egyptian Journal of Remote Sensing and Space Science*, *24*(3), 971–981.

Mohamed, M. (2023). Agricultural sustainability in the age of deep learning: Current trends, challenges, and future trajectories. *Sustainable Machine Intelligence Journal*, *4*(4), 1–20. https://doi.org/10.61185/SMIJ.2023.44102

Muangprathub, J., Boonnam, N., Kajornkasirat, S., Lekbangpong, N., Wanichsombat, A., & Nillaor, P. (2019). IoT and agriculture data analysis for smart farm. *Computers and Electronics in Agriculture*, *156*, 467–474.

Musat, G. A., Colezea, M., Pop, F., Negru, C., Mocanu, M., Esposito, C., & Castiglione, A. (2018). Advanced services for efficient management of smart farms. *Journal of Parallel and Distributed Computing*, *116*, 3–17.

Navarro, E., Costa, N., & Pereira, A. (2020). A systematic review of IoT solutions for smart farming. *Sensors*, *20*(15), 4231.

Ragazou, K., Garefalakis, A., Zafeiriou, E., & Passas, I. (2022). Agriculture 5.0: A new strategic management mode for a cut cost and an energy efficient agriculture sector. *Energies*, *15*(9), 3113.

Raja, L., & Vyas, S. (2019). The study of technological development in the field of smart farming. In *Smart Farming Technologies for Sustainable Agricultural Development* (pp. 1–24). IGI Global.

Saiz-Rubio, V., & Rovira-Más, F. (2020). From smart farming towards agriculture 5.0: A review on crop data management. *Agronomy*, *10*(2), 207.

Schönfeld, M. V., Heil, R., & Bittner, L. (2018). Big data on a farm—smart farming. *Big Data in Context*, 109–120.

Triantafyllou, A., Tsouros, D. C., Sarigiannidis, P., & Bibi, S. (2019, May). An architecture model for smart farming. In *2019 15th International Conference on Distributed Computing in Sensor Systems (DCOSS)* (pp. 385–392). IEEE.

Ünal, Z. (2020). Smart farming becomes even smarter with deep learning—a bibliographical analysis. *IEEE Access, 8,* 105587–105609.

Yoon, C., Huh, M., Kang, S. G., Park, J., & Lee, C. (2018, February). Implement smart farm with IoT technology. In *2018 20th International Conference on Advanced Communication Technology (ICACT)* (pp. 749–752). IEEE.

5 Maximizing Yield, Minimizing Water

Machine Intelligence for Precision Irrigation and Water Management

5.1 INTRODUCTION

Managing water for agricultural purposes is a time-consuming and important part of maintaining hydrological, climatological, and agronomic equilibrium. In this chapter, we'll look at four analyses created primarily to calculate evapotranspiration on a daily, weekly, or monthly basis. For efficient utilization of resources in agricultural production and for the planning and operation management of irrigation systems, a precise prediction of evapotranspiration is a complicated task. The chapter also explores ML solutions' potential in different water management tasks, such as covering water demand forecasting, leakage and contamination detection, sewer defect assessment, wastewater system state prediction, asset monitoring, and urban flooding (Chaudhry and Garg, 2019).

Farmers are continually at the mercy of nature's whims: winds, frosts, and heat—environmental effects constitute a huge risk. A harvest loss is a huge economic danger, especially for small-scale farmers. Farmers have typically relied on intuition, experience, and obsolete historical data to adjust for losses and improve harvests. For instance, several sectors of Japan (agriculture, forestry, fisheries, and the food sector) rely largely on highly trained people. Yet, the average age of Japanese farmers is increasing, while young persons' interest in farming is diminishing. At the same time, cropland is in short supply, and food self-sufficiency has reached a new low in recent years. Environmental concerns are becoming a major threat. As a countermeasure, even the most conventional industries, such as agriculture, are increasingly employing IoT, big data, and AI. These technologies are projected to alleviate the effects of rising food demand and climate change. Using current technology as part of larger digital transformation projects has become an important prerequisite for decreasing labor and ensuring manpower. The overarching goal of smart agriculture operations is to attain greater self-sufficiency and higher profits by reducing crop failure risks and improving overall output quality (Obaideen et al., 2022).

Water is necessary for life. Over thousands of years, human habitation and development have been influenced by a consistent supply of clean, safe water. People thrived, migrated, or died in the face of a volatile supply chain. While the necessity

 DOI: 10.1201/9781003400103-5

to manage water properly and efficiently has not changed over time, the management technologies available on the market have. Water utilities now have access to data-driven technologies that allow them to extract previously unachievable information on water supply and demand, allowing water managers to plan for a dependable clean water future.

AI in agriculture is quickly becoming the foundation of automation. It aids with the automation of routine and boring operations such as collecting field data, labeling and analyzing data, creating reports, and sending notifications. The influence of these simple adjustments on agricultural practices may be evident quickly. Smart irrigation reduces water usage, reduces human labor, provides a unified picture of soil features, and improves long-term landscape health while saving money. To accomplish these benefits, several types of water irrigation systems now widely integrate IoT sensors and AI technologies. The types of water irrigation systems can be listed as follows:

- **Sprinkler irrigation:** To schedule the next watering, an AI-based irrigation system receives data from thermal and auditory rain sensors that assess the intensity of rainfall. Following data analysis and computation, the system delivers automatic messages to sprinklers to prevent overwatering or excessive water usage.
- **Center pivot irrigation:** In-field sensors supply data insights to the AI-based system which manages circle irrigation sprinklers and regulates the stream or angle of water flow. Rather than overwatering nearby plants, this allows water to reach plants farther away from the source.
- **Drip and micro irrigation:** Water is supplied directly to the plant's roots, ensuring equal distribution, reducing evaporation and runoff, and improving irrigation efficiency. AI algorithms may be used to precisely regulate the quantity of water applied to a given crop.

5.2 EVAPOTRANSPIRATION MODELING

Evapotranspiration (ET) is a fundamental hydrological process that describes the combined loss of water vapor from the soil surface through evaporation and from plant surfaces through transpiration. It plays a critical role in the movement of water in the earth's atmosphere and is a key component of the water cycle. Evaporation refers to the process by which water is converted from a liquid state to a vapor state and released into the atmosphere. It occurs from exposed water bodies, such as lakes, rivers, and reservoirs, as well as from the moist soil surface in agricultural fields and natural landscapes. Transpiration, on the other hand, is the process by which water is taken up by plant roots and released into the atmosphere through tiny pores called stomata in the leaves. It is an essential mechanism for plants to cool themselves, transport nutrients, and maintain their structural integrity. ET is a vital component in the water balance of ecosystems, watersheds, and agricultural fields. It influences the availability of water resources, soil moisture levels, and groundwater recharge. Understanding ET is crucial for water resources management, as it helps estimate the amount of water loss from different landscapes, guiding decisions on water allocation and irrigation practices (Rohith et al., 2021; Saraf and Gawali, 2017).

In agricultural water management, accurate knowledge of evapotranspiration is critical for optimizing irrigation scheduling and ensuring that crops receive the appropriate amount of water for healthy growth. Over-irrigation can lead to wastage of valuable water resources, while under-irrigation can adversely affect crop yields and agricultural productivity. Furthermore, evapotranspiration is a key component in environmental studies and ecological research. It influences climate patterns, energy balance, and local microclimates. It affects the functioning of ecosystems, including forest health, wetland habitats, and wildlife survival. In areas with limited water resources, understanding ET is essential for assessing the ecological impacts and potential stress on ecosystems (Dahane et al., 2022).

ET is a complex process involving three main components: soil evaporation, plant transpiration, and interception loss. Soil evaporation occurs when water from the moist soil surface transitions into vapor due to energy received from the surrounding environment. Plant transpiration, on the other hand, is the release of water vapor into the atmosphere through small pores in plant leaves known as stomata. This mechanism facilitates the upward movement of water and nutrients from the roots to the leaves, vital for the cooling and nutrition of plants. Additionally, interception loss takes place when precipitation, such as rain or dew, is intercepted by the canopy of vegetation before reaching the ground. Some of this intercepted water evaporates directly from the leaf surfaces, contributing to the overall ET. Understanding these components is crucial as they collectively govern the overall water vapor loss from different parts of the landscape, playing a critical role in the water cycle (Goap et al., 2018).

The rates of ET are influenced by various factors, making it a dynamic process. Weather conditions, including temperature, humidity, wind speed, and solar radiation, significantly impact ET rates. Higher temperatures and lower humidity promote faster evaporation and transpiration, while windy conditions enhance the transport of water vapor away from the surfaces, increasing ET rates. Additionally, vegetation type plays a crucial role, as different plant species exhibit varying transpiration rates due to their unique morphological and physiological characteristics. For instance, plants with broad leaves generally have higher transpiration rates than those with narrow leaves. The leaf area index (LAI), which represents the total leaf area per unit ground area, is directly related to transpiration rates. A higher LAI indicates more foliage for water vapor release, leading to increased transpiration. Soil properties, such as soil type, texture, and moisture content, also influence soil evaporation rates. Sandy soils with low water-holding capacity tend to promote faster evaporation, while clayey soils with higher water retention capacity result in slower evaporation rates. Furthermore, the availability of water in the soil plays a critical role in determining both soil evaporation and plant transpiration rates. When soil water is limited, both processes are reduced, affecting overall ET rates (Vij et al., 2020).

The estimation of evapotranspiration is essential for various applications in water management, agriculture, and environmental studies. In water balance studies, accurate knowledge of ET aids in assessing the availability and movement of water resources within a region. For agricultural water management, understanding ET is crucial for optimizing irrigation scheduling and ensuring crops receive the appropriate amount of water for healthy growth. Over-irrigation can lead to wastage of valuable water resources, while under-irrigation can adversely affect crop yields and agricultural productivity. Additionally, evapotranspiration is a key component in environmental studies and ecological research. It influences climate patterns, energy balance, and local microclimates, which, in turn, affects the functioning of ecosystems, including forest health, wetland habitats, and wildlife survival. In areas with limited water resources, understanding ET is essential for assessing the ecological impacts and potential stress on ecosystems. Therefore, accurate estimation and monitoring of evapotranspiration provide valuable insights into water balance, agricultural productivity, and ecological health, contributing to informed decision-making and sustainable management of our precious water resources (Akhund et al., 2022).

Different methods are employed to measure ET, each catering to specific scales and settings, and offering unique advantages and limitations. One commonly used method is the lysimeter, which directly measures water loss from a representative soil column or planted area. Lysimeters are divided into two types: weighing and non-weighing lysimeters. Weighing lysimeters involves the continuous weighing of the entire soil-plant system, providing accurate and direct measurements of ET. However, their installation and maintenance can be labor-intensive and expensive. Non-weighing lysimeters, on the other hand, estimate ET based on soil water content changes within the lysimeter. While non-weighing lysimeters are easier to install and maintain, they may lack the precision of weighing lysimeters. Lysimeters are well-suited for research purposes and small-scale studies, offering detailed information on ET dynamics under controlled conditions. Another popular method is the eddy covariance technique, which measures the vertical flux of water vapor between the land surface and the atmosphere. This method utilizes fast-response gas analyzers and sonic anemometers to capture fluctuations in wind velocity and water vapor concentration. Eddy covariance provides continuous, high-frequency measurements of ET over large areas, making it suitable for monitoring ecosystem-scale water fluxes. It is particularly effective in natural ecosystems, such as forests and grasslands, where the exchange of water vapor is significant. However, the eddy covariance method requires advanced instrumentation and data processing, making it more challenging to implement than other techniques (Raghuvanshi et al., 2022).

The Bowen ratio method is based on the measurement of sensible and latent heat fluxes, allowing for the calculation of ET. It involves sensors that measure air temperature and humidity gradients and requires a Bowen ratio constant specific to the surface being studied. The Bowen ratio method is relatively simple and cost-effective, making it suitable for continuous ET measurements over agricultural fields and managed landscapes. However, it relies on several assumptions, such as steady-state conditions, which may limit its accuracy under certain circumstances. Microlysimeters are small devices buried in the soil to measure soil water evaporation directly. They consist of a container with a known amount of water, and as the water evaporates from the container, the weight change is used to calculate soil evaporation. Microlysimeters are relatively inexpensive and easy to deploy, making them suitable for field-scale measurements. However, they may underestimate total ET, as they only account for soil evaporation and not transpiration from vegetation (Abioye et al., 2022).

The choice of method depends on the scale of the study, available resources, and the specific research objectives. Lysimeters and microlysimeters are better suited for small-scale investigations and controlled experiments, offering detailed and precise measurements. On the other hand, eddy covariance and Bowen ratio methods are more appropriate for large-scale and continuous monitoring of ET in natural ecosystems and agricultural landscapes. Integrating multiple measurement methods can provide a comprehensive understanding of ET dynamics across various scales and settings, enabling more informed water management decisions and sustainable land use practices.

Estimating crop-specific evapotranspiration (ETc), also known as crop water requirements, is essential for efficient and sustainable water management in agriculture. Different methods have been developed to estimate ETc, considering factors such as climate, crop type, and growth stages. Three widely used methods are the FAO-56 dual crop coefficient approach, the Blaney-Criddle method, and crop-specific adjustment factors. The FAO-56 dual crop coefficient approach is a widely adopted method for estimating ETc. It involves calculating two coefficients: the basal crop coefficient (Kcb) and the actual crop coefficient (Kc). The basal crop coefficient represents the ratio of reference evapotranspiration (ET0) to potential evapotranspiration (ETp) under specific climatic conditions. The actual crop coefficient (Kc) is then determined by adjusting the basal crop coefficient based on the crop's development stages and growth patterns. This approach accounts for the water needs of the crop at different growth stages, considering factors such as root development, canopy coverage, and crop senescence. By incorporating crop-specific parameters, the FAO-56 method allows for more accurate ETc estimation and enables optimized irrigation scheduling throughout the crop's lifecycle.

The Blaney-Criddle method is a simplified approach for estimating ETc based on temperature data. It calculates ETc using average monthly temperature values and crop-specific coefficients. While the Blaney-Criddle method is easy to apply, it may not account for variations in climatic conditions and crop characteristics accurately. Therefore, it is more suitable for quick estimations and rough approximations of ETc in areas with limited data availability. Crop-specific adjustment factors are another approach to estimating ETc, taking into account the specific water needs of different crop types. These factors are derived from field observations and experiments and are applied to the reference evapotranspiration (ET0) to obtain ETc values. This method is beneficial when detailed crop coefficients are not available, and it allows for a tailored approach to water management for different crops. However, the accuracy of the crop-specific adjustment factors relies on the availability of reliable field data, which may not always be readily accessible (Touil et al., 2022).

The accurate estimation of crop-specific evapotranspiration is crucial for optimizing irrigation practices and ensuring efficient water use in agriculture. Different crops have varying water requirements at different growth stages, considering crop characteristics is vital for precise ETc estimation. A crop's root depth, canopy coverage, leaf area index, and physiological response to environmental factors all play significant roles in determining its water needs. By accounting for these crop-specific parameters, irrigation can be timed and managed more effectively, leading to improved crop yields and water use efficiency. Furthermore, the accurate estimation of ETc is crucial in regions facing water scarcity or limited water resources. Over-irrigation can lead to wastage of valuable water, while under-irrigation can result in reduced crop productivity. By adopting appropriate methods for estimating ETc and considering crop characteristics and growth stages, farmers and water managers can make informed decisions and implement sustainable irrigation practices, contributing to both agricultural productivity and water resource conservation.

Remote sensing technologies, particularly satellite-based thermal and optical sensors, have revolutionized the monitoring and mapping of ET over large areas. These advanced sensors provide valuable data on land surface temperature, vegetation indices, and water vapor content, enabling researchers and water managers to estimate ET at regional and global scales. Satellite-based remote sensing offers a comprehensive and cost-effective approach to assessing water usage and vegetation health, making it an indispensable tool in various water management applications. One of the primary applications of remote sensing in water management is the estimation of actual evapotranspiration (ETa) and crop water requirements. By integrating satellite-derived data, such as land surface temperature and vegetation indices, with meteorological data, researchers can estimate ETa over vast agricultural areas. This information is invaluable for optimizing irrigation scheduling, as it allows farmers to precisely apply water resources to meet crop demands. Additionally, the data can be used to assess crop water stress and identify areas where irrigation needs may be higher due to adverse weather conditions or soil moisture deficiencies (Viani, 2016).

Drought monitoring is another critical application of remote sensing in water management. Satellite-based ET mapping provides real-time information on vegetation health and water usage, enabling the timely detection of drought-prone regions. By continuously monitoring ET rates over large areas, authorities can identify drought-affected areas and implement appropriate water conservation measures, such as water use restrictions and drought contingency plans. This proactive approach helps mitigate the impacts of drought on agriculture, ecosystems, and water resources. Furthermore, remote sensing data is crucial in supporting irrigation planning and water allocation decisions. By mapping ET and monitoring water consumption over time, water managers can assess the efficiency of irrigation systems and identify areas with excessive water usage. This information enables the implementation of targeted water-saving strategies and the allocation of water resources based on crop water requirements and environmental considerations. Satellite-based ET data also facilitates the assessment of water availability and the identification of potential water sources for irrigation in areas with limited water resources.

5.3   SMART WATER MANAGEMENT

The efficient use of water through irrigation has always been intricately related to agricultural progress and successful farming. Yet, managing natural water resources effectively while also doing a conventional cost-benefit analysis for technology and infrastructure overheads is a tricky balancing act. Reduced water usage is critical, especially given that agriculture is expected to account for more than 70% of worldwide water use. With food consumption only increasing, water use is predicted to rise by 15% to satisfy this need.

Smart water management is the enhancement of water management through the use of intelligent systems that include a variety of hardware and software, meters, sensors, and data storage, processing, and visualization tools to monitor, control, and regulate water quality, water flow, and system-related equipment. Modern water technology is a collection of IoT devices and software based on cutting-edge technology that links farmers to their crops. These systems are intelligent because they can link devices and have extensive data processing capabilities, allowing them to develop systems that interact directly with the management. Based on real-world data, this system is capable of identifying, measuring, and perceiving issues, as well as correcting them and providing new solutions. This sophisticated technology also automates and reduces human mistakes. Next, two examples of AI-based water management applications will be discussed.

5.3.1 Optimizing Irrigation Scheduling and Distribution

It is critical to identify locations that are being overwatered or underwatered. A daily duty that can be difficult to analyze for any farmer or agronomist is determining the appropriate amount of water to get the best production and quality. Overwatering can potentially be dangerous depending on the type of plant. Over-irrigated cotton crops, for example, will result in the growth of more leaves rather than the cotton blooms that hold the crop's worth. Farmers strive to develop an appropriate watering plan for their crops that maximizes output and quality while minimizing expenditures.

ET has been a critical measure in developing a plant-specific irrigation system. It is the product of evaporation from the ground surface and transpiration from plants. Current satellite imaging and weather forecasts assist farmers in better estimating evapotranspiration. Nevertheless, advances in IoT sensor technology enable far more precise irrigation decisions by detecting plant behavior instead of (or in addition to) soil and meteorological conditions.

Data inputs from satellite, aircraft, or drone photography may be processed and analyzed by powerful AI engines. Deep learning algorithms, for example, can assist us in interpreting data from photos and identifying patterns that highlight irrigation difficulties (as well as other issues such as pests). When photography is paired with soil- and plant-based sensors, data can provide an extraordinarily precise read of irrigation demands in real time while also alerting us to possible problems.

5.3.2 Detecting Irrigation Problems or Leaks

Water waste, particularly in locations where water is scarce, is a major concern (and expense) for farmers and food growers worldwide. While there are methods such as drip irrigation and complex controlled environments such as soilless greenhouses at one end of the spectrum, they include technology and systems that are pricey and hence unsuitable for broad agriculture (or lower-value crops). The detection of faults, such as leaks in irrigation systems, is one area that may be greatly improved.

It used to take a personal check to spot a damaged piece of equipment or detect a leak. IoT devices imply that software can notify when anything is incorrect or suspicious—and this is only possible when devices are linked together. An irrigation sensor may identify an irregularity and relate it to the underlying issue or variable in this manner, especially if it is linked to other data points such as weather data, which allows it to rule out other probable causes.

Suppose that a grower oversees 2,630 hectares of farmland in east central Idaho, where temperatures can vary by up to 25°C in two days. His most difficult problem is controlling irrigation. With 80 irrigation pivots to switch on when it gets hot, any problem may rapidly become a major one as the ground dries up. They may obtain aerial pictures and other data on the field, including thermal imaging of each plant, by using AI-based products like Valley Insights©. The collected footage and AI field analysis may deliver precise alerts that pinpoint the specific problem areas, including irrigation difficulties that require prompt action. This means they can deal with problems like pivot-related leaks, which are difficult to spot with the human eye. The power of AI extends beyond highlighting a problem. It describes how to correct an irrigation inconsistency.

5.3.3   Data-Driven Water Management Decisions Using AI Analytics

Crop quality is determined by the optimum quantity of watering since both overwatering and underwatering can harm or hamper crop development. Also, the soil must be wet, and the necessary humidity must be maintained. Farmers, however, continue to struggle with determining the optimal amount of water to achieve the desired production and quality. Furthermore, it is a time-consuming, labor-intensive, and complicated procedure that necessitates high-quality, localized data inputs.

AI's capabilities extend well beyond increasing agricultural productivity and lowering production costs. AI-based agriculture systems that utilize a variety of datasets such as satellite images, temperature, humidity, climate, and weather predictions can aid in the development of a new irrigation automation control. This will help farmers make better water management decisions, wasting less water and preserving energy.

Evapotranspiration, a water cycle that includes both evaporation and transpiration, has long been considered an important factor in designing a crop-specific irrigation system. Modern satellite images, weather forecasting, and remote sensing assist farmers in estimating and improving their assessments of daily rainfall and potential evapotranspiration without the requirement for site-specific calibration. Weather sensors mixed with data from a GIS-based system can also aid in the generation of more accurate water projections.

5.4   PRECISION IRRIGATION SYSTEMS

As mentioned before, the primary objective of smart farming is to increase food self-sufficiency and profitability by mitigating environmental hazards associated with crop failures and improving overall yield quality. Classic irrigation has long been ripe for reform in our planet. Watering crops and gardens by hand is just a waste of time, and irrigation based on timers cannot account for changes in weather or soil moisture levels. We now rely on smart irrigation technologies to overcome this and take irrigation to the next level. A smart irrigation system is one that defines its watering procedures based on the weather or soil conditions. This implies that irrigation is tailored for the specific region that is being watered, saving water and optimizing crop or plant development (see Figure 5.1).

FIGURE 5.1   Example of Smart Irrigation.

5.4.1   Smart Irrigation's Main Characteristics

The existence of a smart irrigation controller is the easiest way to characterize smart irrigation. These devices assess either local weather temperatures or soil moisture and alter their watering schedules accordingly, as well as other user-inputted demands. As a result, the most distinguishing aspect of these systems is their changeable watering or sprinkling schedules. Smart irrigation is a system that enables precise control of a big farm's water demands, saving both money and water in the long term. Even more crucially, because of the system's enhanced precision, you can ensure that your plants are constantly at the proper moisture level, resulting in a better growth cycle.

Furthermore, like with most, if not all, smart systems on the market today, you can connect your smart irrigation system to your smartphone or tablet for further control. This enables you to alter the settings on the fly using a simple app, as well as get notifications and regularly updated information about your lawn or garden directly to your preferred device. This level of control enables you to regulate the exact watering patterns and demands of various sections within a single garden, giving smart irrigation systems a level of control that is game-changing in the field of irrigation.

5.4.2 WORKING OF A PRECISION IRRIGATION SYSTEM

As previously stated, the smart irrigation controller is a critical component of these systems. These controllers are sophisticated sensors that determine the needed intensity of watering for the system depending on either temperature or soil moisture levels and are therefore the heart of the entire irrigation system. Because of the way they function, weather-based controllers are also known as evapotranspiration controllers. These controllers gather meteorological information to determine how frequently they should water the garden or lawn, taking into account the projected evaporation and transpiration in a system. Weather controllers are grouped into three kinds based on the manner they employ to acquire information:

- **Signal-based controllers** acquire their data from a public source, which wirelessly transmits it to the controller.
- **Historic controllers** consider historical water consumption in a specific region and act on these averages.
- **On-site controllers** use their own sensors to determine temperature and react to the exact temperature in the region.

Instead, soil moisture sensors are used by soil-based controls. A sensor is put at the root level of the garden to continually determine the volumetric water content. That is, how much water is now present in the soil. Based on this information, the owner and system may determine an acceptable water threshold. When the volumetric water level falls below this level, the system recognizes that it has to start watering again.

5.4.3 COMPONENTS OF A PRECISION IRRIGATION SYSTEM

While the controller is the most important component of a smart irrigation system, it is far from the only one, and the total system's quality is dependent on every component. The initial components are, of course, the controller and its associated sensors, but they are also accompanied by the device that will be used to control the system itself. There are dedicated control pads, however depending on the model, the control method might simply be your smartphone. Following that, the components of a smart irrigation system are generally the same as those of any automated sprinkling system:

- A water supply for the system, which is often a link to a valve.
- Agriculture pipes are used to connect running water to each sprinkler.
- Water is distributed using rotors or sprinklers.
- Drip tubing is used in systems that rely on it rather than overhead sprinkling.

Smart irrigation is now conserving water in agricultural irrigation. Most farmers are interested in the precise water savings. Smart irrigation has a place in agriculture. When utilized for farming, sophisticated weather systems provide highly precise readings, allowing up to 13% of the total water normally necessary for sprinkling to be saved. This not only saves water but also makes crops healthier in the long term.

5.5 DECISION SUPPORT SYSTEMS

The development of decision support systems (DSS) for precision irrigation management represents a significant advancement in modern agricultural practices. Precision irrigation aims to optimize water usage by providing the right amount of water, at the right time, and in the right place, tailored to the specific needs of individual crops. DSS for precision irrigation integrates data from various sources, including weather forecasts, soil moisture sensors, satellite imagery, and crop growth models. These systems leverage advanced algorithms and machine learning techniques to process and analyze the data, allowing farmers to make informed decisions about irrigation strategies. By providing real-time insights and recommendations, DSS for precision irrigation empowers farmers to enhance water efficiency, reduce water waste, and improve crop yields, while simultaneously minimizing environmental impact (Sleem, 2022).

The development of DSS for precision irrigation management has become increasingly inclusive, catering to farmers of all scales and technological backgrounds. With the advent of user-friendly interfaces and mobile applications, DSS adoption is not limited to large commercial farms but extends to smallholders and subsistence farmers. Moreover, these systems consider diverse agricultural practices, crop types, and geographical regions, making them adaptable to various farming scenarios. Additionally, the inclusive nature of DSS development involves engaging stakeholders from different sectors, including farmers, researchers, agricultural experts, and policymakers. By incorporating local knowledge and feedback, DSS designers ensure that these systems align with the specific needs and challenges faced by farmers in different regions. The result is a more accessible, context-specific, and scalable solution that empowers farmers worldwide to embrace precision irrigation as a sustainable water management strategy.

The development of DSS for precision irrigation management is part of a broader shift toward sustainable and climate-smart agricultural practices. As water resources become scarcer and climatic conditions become more unpredictable, precision irrigation becomes crucial for ensuring food security and reducing the impact of agriculture on water ecosystems. By integrating climate data and weather predictions, DSS for precision irrigation can anticipate droughts, heatwaves, or heavy rainfall events, enabling farmers to adjust irrigation schedules accordingly. Furthermore, these systems promote the use of sensor-based technologies and IoT devices, fostering the adoption of smart farming practices. The inclusive development of DSS encourages collaboration between technology providers, agronomists, and water management experts, facilitating knowledge exchange and innovation in the agriculture sector (Singh et al., 2022; Dos Santos et al., 2023).

The integration of machine intelligence with crop models and simulation tools represents a powerful synergy that revolutionizes agricultural decision-making and crop management practices. Crop models and simulation tools have long been essential in predicting crop growth, yield, and response to various environmental conditions.

However, these models often rely on simplified assumptions and require manual parameterization, which may limit their accuracy and adaptability. By incorporating machine intelligence, such as AI and ML, into crop models and simulation tools, we can enhance their capabilities significantly. ML algorithms can process vast amounts of data from diverse sources, including weather data, soil properties, crop characteristics, and historical yield records. With this wealth of information, the models can be trained to learn complex relationships and patterns, leading to more precise and data-driven predictions of crop behavior (Dos Santos et al., 2023; Zhang et al., 2021).

The integration of machine intelligence enables dynamic and adaptive crop management. These enhanced crop models can continuously learn from real-time data, adjusting their predictions and recommendations as environmental conditions change. For example, they can automatically optimize irrigation schedules based on soil moisture levels and weather forecasts or suggest the most suitable crop varieties based on climate and soil conditions. Moreover, machine intelligence can facilitate model parameterization and calibration. Traditionally, parameterizing crop models involved laborious manual tuning. With ML techniques, the models can learn from observed data and automatically optimize their parameters, streamlining the model setup process and improving accuracy. The integration of machine intelligence also allows for improved DSS in agriculture. Farmers can leverage these advanced tools to receive personalized and actionable insights, enabling them to make informed choices about crop planning, resource allocation, and risk management. The combination of crop models, simulation tools, and machine intelligence fosters a more precise, efficient, and sustainable approach to agricultural practices, leading to increased crop productivity, resource conservation, and better resilience to climate variability. As technology continues to advance and more data becomes available, the integration of machine intelligence with crop models and simulation tools will play a pivotal role in shaping the future of precision agriculture and sustainable food production (Abioye et al., 2022; Touil et al., 2022; Viani, 2016; Singh et al., 2022; Dos Santos et al., 2023).

Visualization and user-friendly interfaces are pivotal components in facilitating informed decision-making in precision irrigation and water management. These elements play a crucial role in transforming complex data and insights into easily understandable and actionable information for farmers, agronomists, and water resource managers. By leveraging data visualization techniques, such as interactive charts, graphs, and maps, precision irrigation systems can present real-time information on soil moisture levels, weather forecasts, crop health, and water usage in a visually engaging manner. These visualizations allow users to quickly grasp the current state of their fields, identify patterns, and detect anomalies that may require immediate attention. For example, color-coded maps can indicate areas with excessive moisture levels or drought stress, guiding farmers to apply irrigation resources more effectively and efficiently.

User-friendly interfaces are designed to accommodate users with varying levels of technical expertise, making precision irrigation accessible to a broader range of stakeholders. Intuitive interfaces enable farmers to interact with the system effortlessly, customize irrigation schedules, and set specific water management goals. The interfaces may also include options to view historical data, track trends, and compare different management strategies, empowering users to make data-driven decisions that align with their unique farming practices. Moreover, visualization and user-friendly interfaces foster data-driven precision agriculture. By integrating data from sensors, drones, and satellite imagery, these systems can generate predictive models that anticipate crop water requirements and optimize irrigation practices accordingly. Farmers can receive timely alerts and recommendations, enabling them to respond proactively to changing conditions and mitigate potential risks.

Beyond the farm level, these interfaces facilitate data sharing and collaboration among multiple stakeholders involved in water management, including water authorities, policymakers, and environmental agencies. Access to shared visualizations and insights enhances communication and coordination, promoting collective efforts in sustainable water resource management. The combination of visualization and user-friendly interfaces enhances transparency and trust in precision irrigation and water management practices. By providing users with a clear understanding of water usage, efficiency, and environmental impact, these systems encourage responsible water stewardship and promote conservation efforts (Zhang et al., 2021).

5.6 CASE STUDY

The availability of safe drinking water is of utmost importance for maintaining good health and is considered a fundamental human right. It is an integral part of effective health protection policies at the national, regional, and local levels. Moreover, investing in water supply and sanitation can lead to significant economic benefits, as the reduction in adverse health effects and healthcare costs outweighs the expenses of implementing such interventions.

In our case study, we have analyzed water quality data from 3,276 different water bodies, each containing various variables representing different water quality metrics. These metrics are essential in evaluating the overall quality of water and its suitability for human consumption.

pH Value: The pH value indicates the acid-base balance of water and its acidic or alkaline condition. The World Health Organization (WHO) recommends a maximum permissible pH range of 6.5–8.5 for drinking water. In our investigation, the pH values ranged from 6.52 to 6.83, falling within the WHO standards.

Hardness: Water hardness is primarily caused by calcium and magnesium salts dissolved from geological deposits. The length of time water stays in contact with hardness-producing materials affects the hardness level. Hardness was originally defined as the capacity of water to precipitate soap due to the presence of calcium and magnesium.

Solids (total dissolved solids, TDS): TDS refer to the inorganic and some organic minerals or salts present in water, such as potassium, calcium, sodium, bicarbonates, chlorides, magnesium, and sulfates. High TDS values indicate highly mineralized water. The desirable limit for TDS in drinking water is 500 mg/l, with a maximum limit of 1000 mg/l.

Chloramines: Chlorine and chloramine are commonly used disinfectants in public water systems. Chloramines are formed when ammonia is added to chlorine for water treatment. Chlorine levels up to 4 milligrams per liter (mg/L) or 4 parts per million (ppm) are considered safe in drinking water.

Sulfate: Sulfates occur naturally in minerals, soil, rocks, ambient air, groundwater, plants, and food. They are also used in the chemical industry. Sulfate concentrations in freshwater typically range from 3 to 30 mg/L, but certain locations may have higher concentrations (up to 1000 mg/L).

Conductivity: Conductivity measures the ability of water to conduct electric current, which is influenced by the concentration of ions present in water. WHO standards dictate that the electrical conductivity (EC) value should not exceed 400 µS/cm.

Organic Carbon: Total organic carbon (TOC) in water originates from decaying natural organic matter and synthetic sources. There are specific guidelines for TOC levels in treated and source water set by the US EPA.

Trihalomethanes: THMs are chemicals that may be present in water treated with chlorine. The concentration of THMs depends on the level of organic material, chlorine dosage, and water temperature. THM levels up to 80 ppm are considered safe for drinking water.

Turbidity: Turbidity is a measure of the quantity of solid matter suspended in water. It affects the light-emitting properties of water and indicates the quality of waste discharge with respect to colloidal matter. The WHO recommends a turbidity value of 5.00 NTU or lower.

Potability: it indicates whether the water is harmless for human consumption, with a value of 1 indicating potable water and 0 indicating non-potable water.

To model water quality and assess its potability using exploratory data analysis (EDA) and ML techniques, we will first conduct a comprehensive EDA of the water_potability dataset. This involves visualizing and understanding the distribution, relationships, and patterns among the water quality metrics. EDA will help identify outliers, missing values, and potential data preprocessing requirements. Subsequently, we will employ various ML algorithms such as decision trees, random forests, support vector machines, or gradient boosting to build predictive models. The ML models will be trained on a subset of the data with labeled potability values and evaluated using appropriate metrics to measure their accuracy and performance. Feature importance analysis derived from the ML models will help us discern the most influential water quality metrics affecting potability. The EDA and ML approach will enable us to gain valuable insights into the complex relationships between water quality parameters and potability, aiding in better water management decisions for smart farming practices and ensuring safe access to drinking water.

In the first step of our implementation, we need to perform the necessary imports of libraries and modules that will be used throughout the data analysis and ML process. Below are the essential Python libraries we want to import:

```
# Basic Libraries
import numpy as np
```

```python
import pandas as pd
from warnings import filterwarnings
from collections import Counter

# Visualizations Libraries
import matplotlib.pyplot as plt
import seaborn as sns
import plotly
import plotly.offline as pyo
import plotly.express as px
import plotly.graph_objs as go
pyo.init_notebook_mode()
import plotly.figure_factory as ff
import missingno as msno

# Data Pre-processing Libraries
from sklearn.preprocessing import StandardScaler,MinMaxScaler
from sklearn.model_selection import train_test_split

# Import Machine Learning Algorithms
from sklearn.linear_model import LogisticRegression
from sklearn.linear_model import RidgeClassifier
from sklearn.linear_model import SGDClassifier
from sklearn.linear_model import PassiveAggressiveClassifier
from sklearn.linear_model import Perceptron

from sklearn.naive_bayes import BernoulliNB
from sklearn.naive_bayes import GaussianNB

from sklearn.svm import SVC
from sklearn.svm import LinearSVC
from sklearn.svm import NuSVC

from sklearn.neighbors import KNeighborsClassifier
from sklearn.neighbors import NearestCentroid
from sklearn.neighbors import RadiusNeighborsClassifier

from sklearn.tree import DecisionTreeClassifier
from sklearn.tree import ExtraTreeClassifier

from sklearn.ensemble import RandomForestClassifier
from sklearn.ensemble import AdaBoostClassifier
from sklearn.ensemble import GradientBoostingClassifier
from sklearn.ensemble import IsolationForest
from sklearn.ensemble import ExtraTreesClassifier
from sklearn.ensemble import StackingClassifier
from sklearn.ensemble import VotingClassifier
from sklearn.ensemble import HistGradientBoostingClassifier

# Evaluation & CV Libraries
from sklearn.metrics import precision_score,accuracy_score
from sklearn.model_selection import RandomizedSearchCV
from sklearn.model_selection import GridSearchCV
from sklearn.model_selection import RepeatedStratifiedKFold
```

Q. What is the proportion of potable water samples in the dataset?

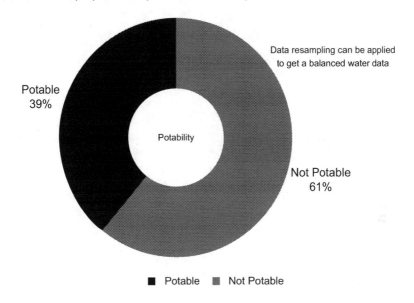

FIGURE 5.2   Visualization of Potability Distribution.

To gain a clear understanding of the proportion of potable and non-potable water samples in our dataset, we employed data visualization techniques, such as a pie chart. The pie chart effectively illustrated the distribution of potability labels, representing the relative sizes of the two categories (see Figure 5.2). This visualization enabled us to visually grasp the balance between potable and non-potable water samples in our dataset. Such a visualization is essential as it provides an initial glimpse into the class distribution, which can influence the choice of appropriate evaluation metrics and guide us in addressing potential class imbalance issues during the modeling process. Below is the essential Python function to do this visualization:

```
def plot _ pie _ chart(df, column _ name):
    """
    Generate a pie chart for the given column in the DataFrame.

    Parameters:
        df (pd.DataFrame): The input DataFrame.
        column _ name (str): The column that contains the potability values.
    """
    d = pd.DataFrame(df[column _ name].value _ counts())

    fig = px.pie(d,
                values=column _ name,
                names=['Not Potable','Potable'],
                hole=0.4,template='presentation',
                color _ discrete _ sequence=[colors _ green[1],
colors _ blue[1]],
```

```
                          labels={'label': column _ name, column _ name: 'No. Of
Samples'})

    fig.add _ annotation(text='Data resampling can be applied <br> to get a
balanced water data',
                          x=1.3, y=0.9, showarrow=False, font _ size=15,
font _ family='sans-serif')

    fig.add _ annotation(text=column _ name,
                          x=0.5, y=0.5, showarrow=False, font _ size=14,
font _ family='sans-serif')

    fig.update _ layout(
        font _ family='sans-serif',
        title=dict(text=f'Q. What is the proportion of potable water
samples in the dataset?',
                          x=0.47, y=0.98, font=dict(color=colors _ dark[2],
size=20)),
        legend=dict(x=0.37, y=-0.05, orientation='h',
traceorder='reversed'),
        hoverlabel=dict(bgcolor='white'))

    fig.update _ traces(textposition='outside', textinfo='percent+label')

    fig.show()
# Given DataFrame df and the column name 'Potability'
plot _ pie _ chart(df, 'Potability')
```

In order to understand the distribution of the "hardness" variable, a critical water quality metric, we utilized data visualization techniques to create a histogram (see Figure 5.3). This visualization allowed us to observe the spread and concentration of hardness values across the dataset. By examining the hardness distribution, we could identify any potential outliers or skewness in the data. Additionally, understanding the hardness distribution is crucial as it helps us comprehend the variability of this parameter in the water bodies under consideration. This knowledge will be valuable in later stages of the analysis when selecting appropriate data preprocessing techniques or when interpreting the results of the ML models based on the hardness variable.

```
import pandas as pd
import plotly.express as px

def plot _ distribution _ of _ hardeness(df, column _ name):
    """
    Generate a histogram with vertical lines and annotations for
the given column in the DataFrame.

    Parameters:
        df (pd.DataFrame): The input DataFrame.
        column _ name (str): The name of the column for which to
generate the histogram.
    """
```

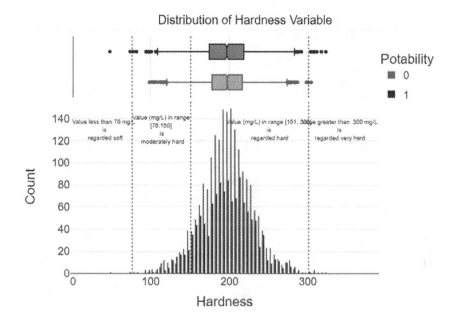

FIGURE 5.3   Visualization of Distribution of Hardness Variable in Our Case Study.

```
fig = px.histogram(df,
                    x=column _ name,
                    y=Counter(df[column _ name]),
                    color='Potability',
                    template='presentation',
                    marginal='box',
                    nbins=100,
                    color _ discrete _ sequence=[colors _ green[3],
colors _ blue[3]],
                    barmode='group',
                    histfunc='count')

    fig.add _ vline(x=151, line _ width=1, line _ color=colors _ dark[1],
line _ dash='dot')
    fig.add _ vline(x=301, line _ width=1, line _ color=colors _ dark[1],
line _ dash='dot')
    fig.add _ vline(x=76, line _ width=1, line _ color=colors _ dark[1],
line _ dash='dot')

    fig.add _ annotation(text='Value less than 76 mg/L <br>is<br> regarded
soft', x=40, y=130, showarrow=False, font _ size=10)
    fig.add _ annotation(text='Value (mg/L) in range <br>[76,150] <br> is
<br> moderately hard', x=114, y=130, showarrow=False, font _ size=10)
    fig.add _ annotation(text='Value (mg/L) in range [151, 300]<br> is <br>
regarded hard', x=250, y=130, showarrow=False, font _ size=10)
    fig.add _ annotation(text='Value greater than  300 mg/L<br> is <br>
regarded very hard', x=340, y=130, showarrow=False, font _ size=10)

    fig.update _ layout(
        font _ family='sans-serif',
```

```
                title=dict(text=f'Distribution of {column _ name} Variable', x=0.53,
        y=0.95, font=dict(color=colors _ dark[2], size=20)),
                xaxis _ title _ text=column _ name,
                yaxis _ title _ text='Count',
                legend=dict(x=1, y=0.96, bordercolor=colors _ dark[3],
        borderwidth=0, tracegroupgap=5),
                bargap=0.4,
            )
        fig.show()
        # Assuming you have your DataFrame df and the column name 'Hardness'
        plot _ distribution _ of _ hardeness(df, 'Hardness')
```

To gain insights into the distribution of the "pH level" variable, a fundamental water quality parameter, we leveraged data visualization techniques
to create a histogram (see Figure 5.4), which enable grasping the frequency
and spread of pH values across the dataset. Understanding the pH level distribution is crucial as it provides essential information about the acidity or alkalinity of the water bodies in question. This knowledge will be instrumental
in subsequent stages of the analysis, aiding in data preprocessing decisions
and contributing to the interpretability of ML model results based on the pH
level variable.

```
def plot _ distribution _ pHlevel(df, column _ name):
        """
        Generate a histogram with vertical lines and annotations for the
        given column in the DataFrame.
```

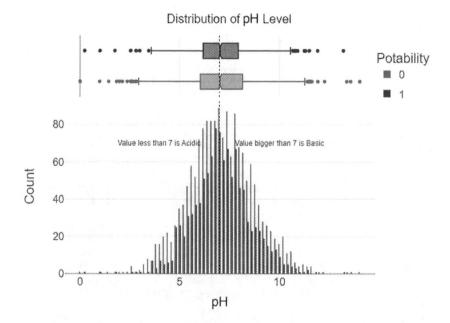

FIGURE 5.4   Visualization of Distribution of pH-Level Variable in Our Case Study.

```
    Parameters:
        df (pd.DataFrame): The input DataFrame.
        column _ name (str): The name of the column for which to generate
the histogram.
    """


    fig = px.histogram(df, x=column _ name,
y=Counter(df[column _ name]),color='Potability',
                        template='presentation',marginal='box',nbins=100,
color _ discrete _ sequence=[colors _ green[3], colors _ blue[3]],
                        barmode='group', histfunc='count')

    fig.add _ vline(x=7, line _ width=1, line _ color=colors _ dark[1],
line _ dash='dot')

    fig.add _ annotation(text='Value less than 7 is Acidic', x=4, y=70,
showarrow=False, font _ size=12)
    fig.add _ annotation(text='Value bigger than 7 is Basic', x=10, y=70,
showarrow=False, font _ size=12)


    fig.update _ layout(
        font _ family='sans-serif',
        title=dict(text=f'Distribution of {column _ name} Level', x=0.5,
y=0.95, font=dict(color=colors _ dark[2], size=20)),
        xaxis _ title _ text=column _ name,
        yaxis _ title _ text='Count',
        legend=dict(x=1, y=0.96, bordercolor=colors _ dark[4],
borderwidth=0, tracegroupgap=5),
        bargap=0.4,
    )
    fig.show()


# Assuming you have your DataFrame df and the column name 'ph'
plot _ distribution _ pHlevel(df, 'ph')
```

To explore the distribution of the "TDS" variable, a significant indicator of water mineralization, we utilized data visualization techniques to create a histogram (see Figure 5.5). This visualization allowed us to observe the frequency and spread of TDS values across the dataset. With the analysis of TDS distribution, we could identify potential trends, outliers, or concentration patterns in the data. Understanding the distribution of TDS is vital, as it provides valuable insights into the mineral content of the water bodies under consideration. This plays a pivotal role in subsequent stages of our analysis, guiding us in making informed decisions during data preprocessing and influencing the interpretation of machine learning model outcomes, particularly in relation to water quality and its potential impact on potability.

```
def plot _ distribution _ of _ TDS(df, column _ name):
    """
    Generate a histogram for TDS column in the water data.

    Parameters:
        df (pd.DataFrame): The input DataFrame.
```

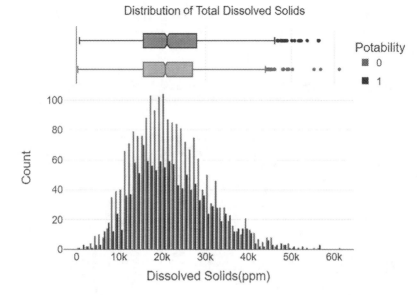

FIGURE 5.5   Visualization of Distribution of the TDS Variable in Our Case Study.

```
        column _ name (str): The name of the column containing TDS
values.
    """
    fig = px.histogram(df,
                       x=column _ name,y=Counter(df[column _ name]),
                       color='Potability',
                       template='presentation',
                       marginal='box',
                       nbins=100,
                       color _ discrete _ sequence=[colors _ green[3],
colors _ blue[3]],
                       barmode='group',
                       histfunc='count')

    fig.update _ layout(
        font _ family='sans-serif',
        title=dict(text=f'Distribution Of Total Dissolved {column _ name} ',
x=0.5, y=0.95, font=dict(color=colors _ dark[2], size=20)),
        xaxis _ title _ text='Dissolved '+column _ name+'(ppm)',
        yaxis _ title _ text='Count',
        legend=dict(x=1, y=0.96, bordercolor=colors _ dark[4],
borderwidth=0, tracegroupgap=5),
        bargap=0.3,
    )
    fig.show()

plot _ distribution _ of _ TDS(df, 'Solids')
```

To explore the distribution of the "chloramines" variable, a key aspect of water disinfection, we employed a histogram (see Figure 5.6). This

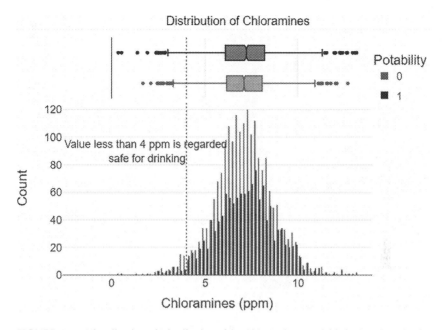

FIGURE 5.6   Visualization of Distribution of the Chloramines Variable in Our Case Study.

visualization allowed us to examine the frequency and variability of chloramines values within the dataset. Analysis of the distribution of chloramines is crucial, as it provides important information about the level of disinfectants used in treating the water. This information is significant in subsequent stages of the analysis, as it aids in data preprocessing decisions and helps us interpret the results of ML models, particularly in assessing the relationship between chloramines and water potability in the context of smart farming water management.

```
import pandas as pd
import plotly.express as px

def plot _ distribution _ of _ chloramines(df, column _ name):
    """
    Generate a histogram for the chloramines variable in water data.

    Parameters:
        df (pd.DataFrame): The input DataFrame.
        column _ name (str): The name of the column containing chloramines
values.
    """

    fig = px.histogram(df,
                       x=column _ name,
                       y=Counter(df[column _ name]),
                       color='Potability',
                       template='presentation',
```

```
                              marginal='box',
                              nbins=100,
                              color _ discrete _ sequence=[colors _ green[3],
colors _ blue[3]],

                              barmode='group',
                              histfunc='count')

    fig.add _ vline(x=4, line _ width=1, line _ color=colors _ dark[1],
line _ dash='dot')

    fig.add _ annotation(text='Value less than 4 ppm is regarded<br> safe
for drinking', x=1.8, y=90, showarrow=False)

    fig.update _ layout(
        font _ family='sans-serif',
        title=dict(text=f'Distribution of {column _ name}', x=0.53, y=0.95,
font=dict(color=colors _ dark[2], size=20)),
        xaxis _ title _ text=f'{column _ name} (ppm)',
        yaxis _ title _ text='Count',
        legend=dict(x=1, y=0.96, bordercolor=colors _ dark[4],
borderwidth=0, tracegroupgap=5),
        bargap=0.4,
    )
    fig.show()


    # Assuming you have your DataFrame df and the column name
'Chloramines'
plot _ distribution _ of _ chloramines(df, 'Chloramines')
```

To examine the distribution of the "sulfate" variable, an important water quality parameter, we utilized data visualization techniques like histograms (see Figure 5.7). This visualization allowed us to gain insights into the frequency and spread of sulfate values across the dataset. By analyzing the sulfate distribution, we could identify any potential patterns, anomalies, or concentrations in the data. This knowledge is essential in subsequent stages of our analysis, as it guides us in data preprocessing decisions and helps in interpreting the results of ML models, especially in assessing the impact of sulfate levels on water potability in the context of smart farming water management.

```
import pandas as pd
import plotly.express as px

def plot _ distribution _ of _ sulfate(df, column _ name):
    """
    Generate a histogram with a vertical line and annotation for the
given column in the DataFrame.

    Parameters:
        df (pd.DataFrame): The input DataFrame.
        column _ name (str): The name of the column for which to generate
the histogram.
    """
```

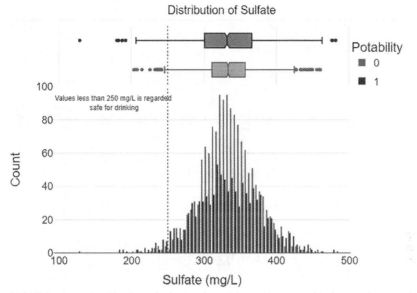

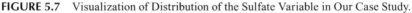

FIGURE 5.7   Visualization of Distribution of the Sulfate Variable in Our Case Study.

```
fig = px.histogram(df,
                   x=column _ name,
                   y=Counter(df[column _ name]),
                   color='Potability',
                   template='presentation',
                   marginal='box',
                   nbins=100,
                   color _ discrete _ sequence=[colors _ green[3],
colors _ blue[3]],
                   barmode='group',
                   histfunc='count')

    fig.add _ vline(x=250, line _ width=1, line _ color=colors _ dark[1],
line _ dash='dot')

    fig.add _ annotation(text='Values less than 250 mg/L is regarded<br>
safe for drinking', x=175, y=90, showarrow=False,font _ size=12)

    fig.update _ layout(
        font _ family='sans-serif',
        title=dict(text=f'Distribution of {column _ name}', x=0.53, y=0.95,
font=dict(color=colors _ dark[2], size=20)),
        xaxis _ title _ text=column _ name + ' (mg/L)',
        yaxis _ title _ text='Count',
        legend=dict(x=1, y=0.96, bordercolor=colors _ dark[4],
borderwidth=0, tracegroupgap=5),
        bargap=0.3,
    )
    fig.show()
# Assuming you have your DataFrame df and the column name 'Sulfate'
plot _ distribution _ of _ sulfate(df, 'Sulfate')
```

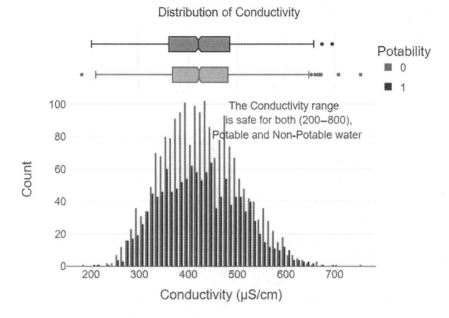

FIGURE 5.8   Visualization of Distribution of the Conductivity Variable in Our Case Study.

In order to investigate the distribution of the "conductivity" variable, a critical indicator of water's electrical properties, we employed histograms plot (see Figure 5.8). This visualization enabled us to examine the frequency and dispersion of conductivity values across the dataset. By analyzing the conductivity distribution, we gained insights into potential trends, outliers, or variations in the data. Understanding the distribution of conductivity is vital, as it provides essential information about the ion concentration and the ability of water to transmit electric current. This knowledge plays a pivotal role in subsequent stages of our analysis, guiding us in data preprocessing decisions and influencing the interpretation of ML model outcomes, particularly in relation to water quality assessment and its relevance to potability in the context of smart farming water management.

```
import pandas as pd
import plotly.express as px

def plot_distribution_of_conductivity(df, column_name):
    """
    Generate a histogram with an annotation for the given column in the
DataFrame.

    Parameters:
        df (pd.DataFrame): The input DataFrame.
        column_name (str): The name of the column for which to
generate the histogram.
    """
```

```
fig = px.histogram(df,
                    x=column_name,
                    y=Counter(df[column_name]),
                    color='Potability',
                    template='presentation',
                    marginal='box',
                    nbins=100,
                    color_discrete_sequence=[colors_green[3],
colors_blue[3]],
                    barmode='group',
                    histfunc='count')

    fig.add_annotation(text='The Conductivity range <br> is safe for both
(200-800),<br> Potable and Non-Potable water',
                    x=600, y=90, showarrow=False)


    fig.update_layout(
        font_family='sans-serif',
        title=dict(text=f'Distribution of {column_name} ', x=0.5, y=0.95,
font=dict(color=colors_dark[2], size=20)),
        xaxis_title_text=f'{column_name} (μS/cm)',
        yaxis_title_text='Count',
        legend=dict(x=1, y=0.96, bordercolor=colors_dark[4],
borderwidth=0, tracegroupgap=5),
        bargap=0.3,
    )
    fig.show()
# Assuming you have your DataFrame df and the column name 'Conductivity'
plot_distribution_of_conductivity(df, 'Conductivity')
```

To explore the distribution of the "OrganicCarbon" variable, a significant measure of organic compounds in water, a histograms plot is displayed in Figure 5.9. This visualization allowed us to examine the frequency and variability of OrganicCarbon values within the dataset. By studying the OrganicCarbon distribution, we gained insights into potential patterns, outliers, or concentrations in the data. Understanding the distribution of OrganicCarbon is crucial, as it provides valuable information about the amount of natural and synthetic organic matter present in water sources. This knowledge is significant in subsequent stages of our analysis, as it guides us in data preprocessing decisions and helps interpret the results of ML models, particularly in assessing the relationship between OrganicCarbon levels and water potability in the context of smart farming water management.

```
import pandas as pd
import plotly.express as px

def plot_distribution_of_OrganicCarbon(df, column_name):
    """
    Generate a histogram with a vertical line and annotation for the
given column in the DataFrame.

    Parameters:
        df (pd.DataFrame): The input DataFrame.
```

```
          column _ name (str): The name of the column for which to generate
the histogram.
      """
      fig = px.histogram(df,
                        x=column _ name,
                        y=Counter(df[column _ name]),
                        color='Potability',
                        template='presentation',
                        marginal='box',
                        nbins=100,
                        color _ discrete _ sequence=[colors _ green[3],
colors _ blue[3]],
                        barmode='group',
                        histfunc='count')

      fig.add _ vline(x=10, line _ width=1, line _ color=colors _ dark[1],
line _ dash='dot')

      fig.add _ annotation(text='Standard level of Organic Carbon<br> is
upto 10 ppm', x=5.3, y=110, showarrow=False, font _ size=12)

      fig.update _ layout(
          font _ family='sans-serif',
          title=dict(text=f'Distribution of {column _ name}', x=0.5, y=0.95,
font=dict(color=colors _ dark[2], size=20)),
          xaxis _ title _ text=f'{column _ name} (ppm)',
          yaxis _ title _ text='Count',
          legend=dict(x=1, y=0.96, bordercolor=colors _ dark[4],
borderwidth=0, tracegroupgap=5),
```

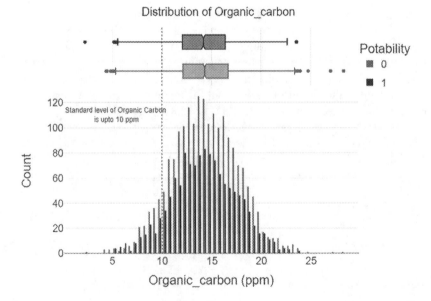

FIGURE 5.9 Visualization of Distribution of the OrganicCarbon Variable in Our
Case Study.

```
        bargap=0.4,
    )
    fig.show()
# Assuming you have your DataFrame df and the column name 'Organic_
carbon'
plot_distribution_of_OrganicCarbon(df, 'Organic_carbon')
```

In order to investigate the distribution of the "trihalomethanes" variable, a crucial parameter associated with water disinfection using chlorine, we employed data visualization techniques namely histograms (see Figure 5.10). This visualization allowed us to examine the frequency and dispersion of trihalomethanes values across the dataset. By analyzing the trihalomethanes distribution, we gained insights into potential trends, outliers, or concentrations in the data. Understanding the distribution of trihalomethanes is essential as it provides vital information about the level of disinfectants used in water treatment.

```
import pandas as pd
import plotly.express as px

def plot_distribution_of_trihalomethanes(df, column_name):
    """
    Generate a histogram for Trihalomethanes in the water data.

    Parameters:
        df (pd.DataFrame): The input DataFrame.
```

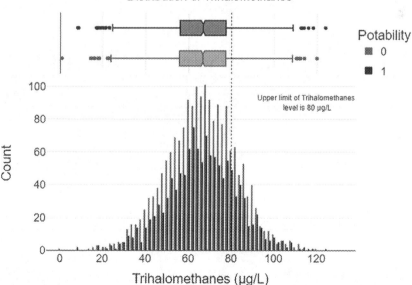

FIGURE 5.10 Visualization of Distribution of Trihalomethanes Variable in Our Case Study.

```
          column _ name (str): The name of the column containing
Trihalomethanes values.
     """

    fig = px.histogram(df,
                          x=column _ name,
                          y=Counter(df[column _ name]),
                          color='Potability',
                          template='presentation',
                          marginal='box',
                          nbins=100,
                          color _ discrete _ sequence=[colors _ green[3],
colors _ blue[3]],
                          barmode='group',
                          histfunc='count')

    fig.add _ vline(x=80, line _ width=1, line _ color=colors _ dark[1],
line _ dash='dot')

    fig.add _ annotation(text='Upper limit of Trihalomethanes<br> level is
80 µg/L', x=115, y=90, showarrow=False, font _ size=12)

    fig.update _ layout(
        font _ family='sans-serif',
        title=dict(text=f'Distribution of {column _ name}', x=0.5, y=0.95,
font=dict(color=colors _ dark[2], size=20)),
        xaxis _ title _ text=f'{column _ name} (µg/L)',
        yaxis _ title _ text='Count',
        legend=dict(x=1, y=0.96, bordercolor=colors _ dark[4],
borderwidth=0, tracegroupgap=5),
        bargap=0.3,
    )
    fig.show()
plot _ distribution _ of _ trihalomethanes(df, 'Trihalomethanes')
```

To examine the distribution of the "turbidity" variable, an important parameter representing the quantity of solid matter in water, we visualize this variable using histograms shown in Figure 5.11. This visualization allowed us to explore the frequency and spread of turbidity values across the dataset. By studying the turbidity distribution, we gained insights into potential patterns, outliers, or variations in the data. Understanding the distribution of turbidity is crucial as it provides valuable information about the quality of water and the presence of suspended particles.

```
import pandas as pd
import plotly.express as px

def plot _ distribution _ of _ turbidity(df, column _ name):
     """
    Generate a histogram with a vertical line and annotation for the
given column in the DataFrame.

    Parameters:
        df (pd.DataFrame): The input DataFrame.
```

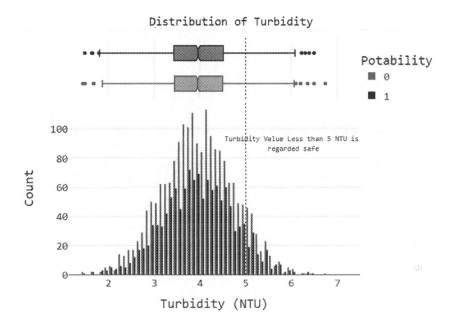

FIGURE 5.11   Visualization of Distribution of the Turbidity Variable in Our Case Study.

```
        column _ name (str): The name of the column for which to
generate the histogram.
    """

    fig = px.histogram(df,
                        x=column _ name,
                        y=column _ name,
                        color='Potability',
                        template='presentation',
                        marginal='box',
                        nbins=100,
                        color _ discrete _ sequence=[colors _ green[3],
colors _ blue[3]],
                        barmode='group',
                        histfunc='count')

    fig.add _ vline(x=5, line _ width=1, line _ color=colors _ dark[1],
line _ dash='dot')

    fig.add _ annotation(text='Turbidity Value Less than 5 NTU is<br>
regarded safe', x=6, y=90,font _ size=12, showarrow=False)

    fig.update _ layout(
        font _ family='monospace',
        title=dict(text=f'Distribution of {column _ name}', x=0.5, y=0.95,
font=dict(color=colors _ dark[2], size=20)),
        xaxis _ title _ text=f'{column _ name} (NTU)',
        yaxis _ title _ text='Count',
```

```
          legend=dict(x=1, y=0.96, bordercolor=colors _ dark[4],
borderwidth=0, tracegroupgap=5),
          bargap=0.3,
   )
   fig.show()
plot _ distribution _ of _ turbidity(df, 'Turbidity')
```

To gain a comprehensive understanding of the relationships and interactions between different water quality variables in our dataset, we employed a pairplot for visualization (see Figure 5.12). A pairplot is a powerful data visualization tool that allows us to create scatterplots between all pairs of variables, while also displaying histograms of each individual variable's distribution along the diagonal. By generating the pairplot, we can visually identify any correlations, patterns, or potential outliers in the data. This visualization aids us in exploring how different water quality metrics are interrelated, providing valuable insights into the overall structure of the dataset. Understanding these relationships is crucial in selecting appropriate features for our ML models

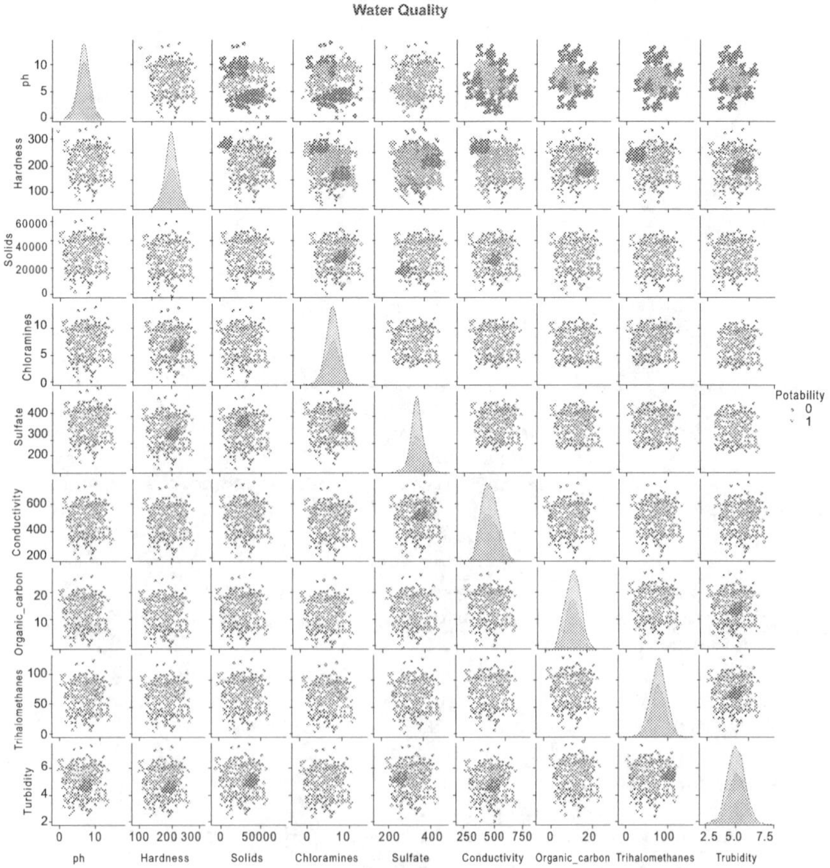

FIGURE 5.12 Visualization of Pairplots for Different Pairs of Variables in Our Case Study.

and can contribute to improved model performance by capturing meaningful interactions between variables.

```
import seaborn as sns

# Create the pairplot
ax = sns.pairplot(df, hue="Potability", diag_kind="kde", kind="scatter",
palette="hls")

# Set the size of the plot
ax.fig.set_size_inches(15, 15)

# Set the title of the plot
ax.fig.suptitle('Water Quality', y=1.08, size=26, color=colors_blue[1],
weight='bold')
```

To further investigate the relationships between water quality variables and assess their linear associations, we displayed a Pearson correlation map for our dataset. The Pearson correlation map is a heatmap that visually represents the correlation coefficients between pairs of variables (see Figure 5.13). It provides a quick and intuitive way to identify both positive and negative correlations between different metrics. By examining the correlation map, we can pinpoint strong correlations (either positive or negative) between specific variables, which can help us uncover potential dependencies and redundancies among the features. This knowledge is valuable in feature selection for our ML models, as it allows us to choose the most relevant and uncorrelated variables, leading to

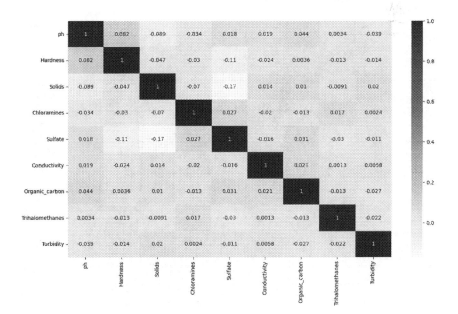

FIGURE 5.13 Visualization of Pearson Correlation Map in Our Case Study.

improved model generalization and interpretability. Additionally, understanding the correlations between water quality metrics helps us gain deeper insights into the underlying dynamics of the dataset and aids in making informed decisions during the model building process, contributing to the effectiveness of water quality modeling and potability prediction in the context of smart farming water management.

```
cor=df.drop('Potability',axis=1).corr(method='pearson')
plt.figure(figsize=(14,8))
sns.heatmap(cor, annot=True, cmap='Blues')
```

In addition to the Pearson correlation map, we also utilized the Kendall correlation map to explore the relationships between water quality variables in our dataset. The Kendall correlation is a nonparametric measure of correlation that assesses the strength and direction of monotonic relationships between variables (see Figure 5.14). By displaying the Kendall correlation map, we can uncover potential nonlinear associations and dependencies among the water quality metrics. This visualization complements the Pearson correlation map, offering a more robust analysis that is less sensitive to outliers and can capture relationships that may not be linear. Understanding the Kendall correlations helps us identify important connections between variables that might be overlooked by a purely linear correlation analysis. By considering both Pearson and Kendall correlation maps, we gain a comprehensive view of the interrelationships among water quality metrics, enhancing our ability to select relevant features for our ML models and improving the accuracy and interpretability

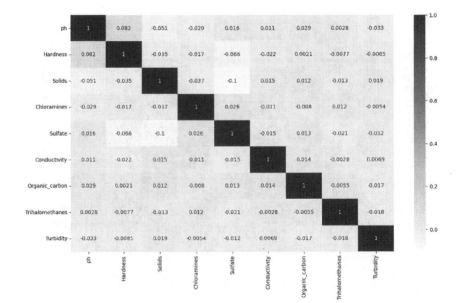

FIGURE 5.14 Visualization of the Kendall Correlation Map in Our Case Study.

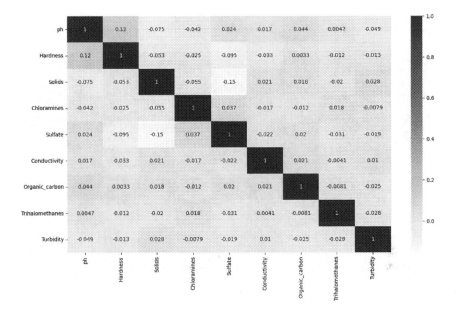

FIGURE 5.15   Visualization of the Spearman Correlation Map in Our Case Study.

of our water quality modeling for potability prediction in the context of smart farming water management.

```
cor=df.drop('Potability',axis=1).corr(method='kendall')
plt.figure(figsize=(14,8))
sns.heatmap(cor, annot=True, cmap='Blues')
```

In addition to the Pearson and Kendall correlation maps, we also employed the Spearman correlation map to further investigate the relationships between water quality variables in our dataset. The Spearman correlation is a nonparametric measure that assesses the monotonic relationships between variables, similar to the Kendall correlation. By displaying the Spearman correlation map, we can gain additional insights into potential non-linear associations and dependencies among the water quality metrics (see Figure 5.15). This visualization complements the previous correlation analyses, providing a robust assessment of the relationships that are not affected by outliers and can capture complex connections between variables. Understanding the Spearman correlations enhances our understanding of the underlying patterns in the data, assisting in feature selection for our ML models.

```
cor=df.drop('Potability',axis=1).corr(method='spearman')
plt.figure(figsize=(14,8))
sns.heatmap(cor, annot=True, cmap='Blues')
```

To address missing data and assess its impact on our analysis, we displayed a missing number map for our dataset. This visualization provides valuable

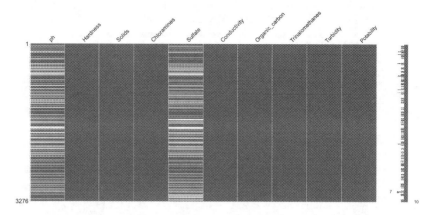

FIGURE 5.16   Visualization of the Missing Values Map in Our Case Study.

insights into the extent and distribution of missing values across different water quality variables (see Figure 5.16). By examining the missing number map, we can identify the variables with significant missing data, helping us prioritize our data imputation strategies or decide whether to exclude certain features from our analysis.

Understanding the extent of missing data is crucial for ensuring the integrity and reliability of our water quality modeling and potability prediction. It allows us to implement appropriate data imputation techniques or consider alternative modeling approaches to mitigate the potential biases introduced by missing values. By displaying the missing number map, we can take necessary steps to handle missing data effectively and ensure the robustness of our smart farming water management analysis.

```
fig = msno.matrix(df,color=(0,0.5,0.5))
```

To gain a comprehensive understanding of the water quality metrics in both potable and non-potable data subsets, we tabulated descriptive statistics for each group. These statistics provide valuable summary measures, such as mean, standard deviation, minimum, maximum, and quartiles, for each water quality variable. By comparing the descriptive statistics between the potable and non-potable data, we can identify potential differences in the distribution and variability of the metrics, which may offer valuable insights into the factors influencing water potability. This analysis helps us understand the characteristics of water bodies deemed potable and non-potable, guiding us in identifying key features that play a significant role in determining water quality. Moreover, the tabulated descriptive statistics serve as a basis for further exploratory analysis and model building, contributing to more informed decision-making in smart farming water management and water quality modeling for potability prediction.

```
df[df['Potability']==0].describe()
```

TABLE 5.1

Summary of Descriptive Statistics for Non-potable Samples in Our Case Study.

	count	mean	std	min	25%	50%	75%	max
pH	1684.00	7.09	1.68	0.00	6.04	7.04	8.16	14.00
Hardness	1998.00	196.73	31.06	98.45	177.82	197.12	216.12	304.24
Solids	1998.00	21777.49	8543.07	320.94	15663.06	20809.62	27006.25	61227.20
Chloramines	1998.00	7.09	1.50	1.68	6.16	7.09	8.07	12.65
Sulfate	1510.00	334.56	36.75	203.44	311.26	333.39	356.85	460.11
Conductivity	1998.00	426.73	80.05	181.48	368.50	422.23	480.68	753.34
Organic_Carbon	1998.00	14.36	3.33	4.37	12.10	14.29	16.65	28.30
Trihalomethanes	1891.00	66.30	16.08	0.74	55.71	66.54	77.28	120.03
Turbidity	1998.00	3.97	0.78	1.45	3.44	3.95	4.50	6.74
Potability	1998.00	0.00	0.00	0.00	0.00	0.00	0.00	0.00

```
df[df['Potability']==1].describe()
```

TABLE 5.2

Summary of Descriptive Statistics for Potable Samples in Our Case Study.

	count	mean	std	min	25%	50%	75%	max
pH	1101.00	7.07	1.45	0.23	6.18	7.04	7.93	13.18
Hardness	1278.00	195.80	35.55	47.43	174.33	196.63	218.00	323.12
Solids	1278.00	22383.99	9101.01	728.75	15668.99	21199.39	27973.24	56488.67
Chloramines	1278.00	7.17	1.70	0.35	6.09	7.22	8.20	13.13
Sulfate	985.00	332.57	47.69	129.00	300.76	331.84	365.94	481.03
Conductivity	1278.00	425.38	82.05	201.62	360.94	420.71	484.16	695.37
Organic_Carbon	1278.00	14.16	3.26	2.20	12.03	14.16	16.36	23.60
Trihalomethanes	1223.00	66.54	16.33	8.18	56.01	66.68	77.38	124.00
Turbidity	1278.00	3.97	0.78	1.49	3.43	3.96	4.51	6.49
Potability	1278.00	1.00	0.00	1.00	1.00	1.00	1.00	1.00

In order to address missing data in our dataset, we employed a simple imputation technique by filling null values with the average of each respective water quality metric. By inputting missing values with the average, we aim to maintain the overall central tendency of the data and reduce potential bias introduced by missing data points. This imputation method ensures that the general distribution and variability of the water quality metrics remain relatively unchanged, allowing us to retain valuable information for analysis and modeling.

```
df['ph'].fillna(value=df['ph'].mean(),inplace=True)
df['Sulfate'].fillna(value=df['Sulfate'].mean(),inplace=True)
df['Trihalomethanes'].fillna(value=df['Trihalomethanes'].
mean(),inplace=True)
```

To prepare our data for machine learning, we performed a train-test split with a test size of 30%, using the appropriate Python library. This split allows us to divide the dataset into two subsets: the training set, which we will use to build and train our machine learning model, and the test set, which we will use to evaluate the model's performance on unseen data. By setting the test size to 30%, we allocated 70% of the data to the training set and 30% to the test set. This ensures that we have a sufficiently large training set to build a robust model while also having enough test data to assess its generalization to new, unseen samples. The train-test split is a fundamental step in the machine learning workflow, as it enables us to measure the model's accuracy and performance before deploying it in real-world scenarios.

```
X = df.drop('Potability',axis=1).values
y = df['Potability'].values
X_train, X_test, y_train, y_test = train_test_split(X, y,
test_size=0.3, random_state=101)
```

After performing the train-test split, we further preprocessed the training data by normalizing it. Normalization is a crucial step in preparing the data for ML, especially when working with features that have different scales or units. It involves transforming the data so that each feature has a mean of 0 and a standard deviation of 1. This process ensures that all features contribute equally to the model training, preventing any single feature from dominating the learning process due to its larger magnitude.

```
scaler = StandardScaler()
scaler.fit(X_train)
X_train = scaler.transform(X_train)
X_test = scaler.transform(X_test)
```

After preprocessing the data, including the train-test split and normalization, we proceeded to train multiple machine learning classifiers on the training data. We experimented with various algorithms, such as decision trees, random forests, SVM, and gradient boosting, among others, to explore their effectiveness in predicting water potability in smart farming. Each classifier was trained using the training data and its corresponding potability labels.

Next, we evaluated the performance of each classifier using the test data, which the models had not seen during training. We calculated various performance metrics, such as accuracy, precision, recall, and F1-score, to assess the models' ability to correctly predict potable and non-potable water samples. The accuracy metric gives us an overall measure of how many predictions were correct out of all predictions made. Precision measures the proportion of true potable samples among all samples predicted as potable, while recall (also known as sensitivity or true positive rate) measures the proportion of true potable samples that were correctly predicted. The F1-score provides a balance between precision and recall.

```
# Ignore warnings
warnings.filterwarnings('ignore')
```

```
models = [
    ("LR", LogisticRegression(max_iter=1000)),
    ("SVC", SVC()),
    ('KNN', KNeighborsClassifier(n_neighbors=10)),
    ("DTC", DecisionTreeClassifier()),
    ("GNB", GaussianNB()),
    ("SGDC", SGDClassifier()),
    ("Perc", Perceptron()),
    ("NC", NearestCentroid()),
    ("Ridge", RidgeClassifier()),
    ("NuSVC", NuSVC()),
    ("BNB", BernoulliNB()),
    ('RF', RandomForestClassifier()),
    ('ADA', AdaBoostClassifier()),
    ('XGB', GradientBoostingClassifier()),
    ('PAC', PassiveAggressiveClassifier())
]

results = []
finalResults = []
confusion_matrices = {}

for name, model in models:
    model.fit(X_train, y_train)
    model_results = model.predict(X_test)

    precision = precision_score(y_test, model_results, average='macro')
    recall = recall_score(y_test, model_results, average='macro')
    accuracy = accuracy_score(y_test, model_results)
    f1 = f1_score(y_test, model_results, average='macro')
    roc_auc = roc_auc_score(y_test, model_results)
    cappa = cohen_kappa_score(y_test, model_results)
    confusion = confusion_matrix(y_test, model_results)

    results.append((precision, recall, accuracy, f1, roc_auc, cappa))
    finalResults.append((name, precision, recall, accuracy, f1, roc_auc,
cappa))
    confusion_matrices[name] = confusion

finalResults.sort(key=lambda k: k[1], reverse=True)

# Convert finalResults to a DataFrame
df_final_results = pd.DataFrame(finalResults, columns=['Model',
'Precision', 'Recall', 'Accuracy', 'F1-Score', 'ROC-AUC', 'Cappa'])

# Display the finalResults in a table
df_final_results
```

After training and evaluating each machine learning classifier, we displayed the confusion matrix for each algorithm. The confusion matrix is a vital tool in assessing the performance of a classification model and understanding its predictive capabilities. It provides a tabular representation of the true positive (TP), true negative (TN), false positive (FP), and false negative (FN) predictions made by the model. For each ML algorithm, the

TABLE 5.3

Quantitative Results of ML Algorithms on the Test Set of Our Case Study.

Model	Precision	Recall	Accuracy	F1-Score	ROC-AUC	Cappa
SVC	0.6926	0.6015	0.6765	0.5863	0.6015	0.2294
RF	0.6767	0.6157	0.6796	0.6105	0.6157	0.2551
NuSVC	0.6452	0.6281	0.6673	0.6306	0.6281	0.2676
XGB	0.6420	0.5795	0.6531	0.5622	0.5795	0.1786
KNN	0.6149	0.5650	0.6389	0.5452	0.5650	0.1458
GNB	0.6114	0.5624	0.6368	0.5416	0.5624	0.1401
DTC	0.5689	0.5706	0.5860	0.5692	0.5706	0.1391
ETC	0.5670	0.5681	0.5860	0.5673	0.5681	0.1350
ADA	0.5600	0.5388	0.6073	0.5212	0.5388	0.0857
PAC	0.5192	0.5178	0.5565	0.5164	0.5178	0.0367
Perc	0.5175	0.5184	0.5178	0.5113	0.5184	0.0349
NC	0.5028	0.5029	0.5137	0.5007	0.5029	0.0057
SGDC	0.4955	0.4959	0.5392	0.4925	0.4959	-0.0085
LR	0.3067	0.5000	0.6134	0.3802	0.5000	0.0000
Ridge	0.3067	0.5000	0.6134	0.3802	0.5000	0.0000
BNB	0.3067	0.5000	0.6134	0.3802	0.5000	0.0000
LSVC	0.3067	0.5000	0.6134	0.3802	0.5000	0.0000
RKNN	0.3067	0.5000	0.6134	0.3802	0.5000	0.0000
IF	0.1272	0.3035	0.3520	0.1792	0.4901	-0.0073

confusion matrix allows us to determine how well the model correctly classified potable and non-potable water samples (see Figure 5.17). From the confusion matrix, we can calculate additional performance metrics such as precision, recall, and F1-score, providing a comprehensive assessment of the classifier's abilities.

```
# Display the confusion matrix for each model
for name, confusion _ matrix in confusion _ matrices.items():
    plt.figure(figsize=(5, 4))
    plt.imshow(confusion _ matrix, interpolation='nearest',
cmap=plt.cm.Blues)
    plt.title(f'Confusion Matrix for {name}')
    plt.colorbar()
    classes = np.unique(y _ test)
    tick _ marks = np.arange(len(classes))
    plt.xticks(tick _ marks, classes)
    plt.yticks(tick _ marks, classes)

    thresh = confusion _ matrix.max() / 2.0
    for i, j in itertools.product(range(confusion _ matrix.shape[0]),
range(confusion _ matrix.shape[1])):
        plt.text(j, i, format(confusion _ matrix[i, j], 'd'),
                horizontalalignment="center",
```

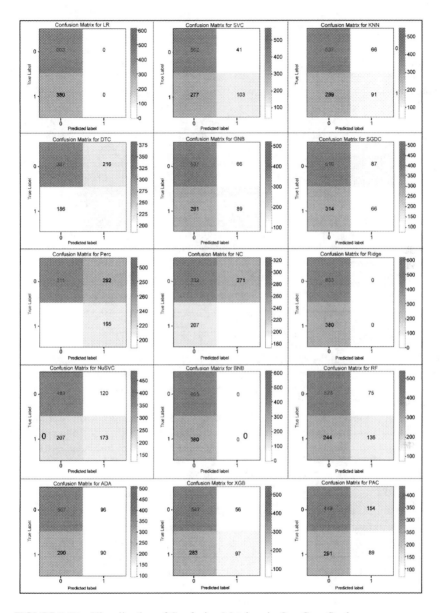

FIGURE 5.17 Visualization of Confusion Matrices in Our Case Study.

```
                    color="white" if confusion _ matrix[i, j] > thresh else
"black")

    plt.ylabel('True label')
    plt.xlabel('Predicted label')
    plt.tight _ layout()
    plt.show()
```

REFERENCES

Abioye, E. A., Hensel, O., Esau, T. J., Elijah, O., Abidin, M. S. Z., Ayobami, A. S., . . . Nasirahmadi, A. (2022). Precision irrigation management using machine learning and digital farming solutions. *AgriEngineering, 4*(1), 70–103.

Akhund, T. M. N. U., Newaz, N. T., Zaman, Z., Sultana, A., Barros, A., & Whaiduzzaman, M. (2022). IoT-based low-cost automated irrigation system for smart farming. *Lecture Notes in Networks and Systems, 333*, 83–91. https://doi.org/10.1007/978-981-16-6309-3_9/FIGURES/5

Chaudhry, S., & Garg, S. (2019). *Smart irrigation techniques for water resource management* (pp. 196–219). https://Services.Igi-Global.Com/Resolvedoi/Resolve.Aspx?Doi=10.4018/978-1-5225-5909-2.Ch009; https://doi.org/10.4018/978-1-5225-5909-2.CH009

Dahane, A., Benameur, R., & Kechar, B. (2022). An IoT low-cost smart farming for enhancing irrigation efficiency of smallholders farmers. *Wireless Personal Communications, 127*(4), 3173–3210. https://doi.org/10.1007/S11277-022-09915-4/METRICS

Dos Santos, R. P., Beko, M., & Leithardt, V. R. (2023, March). Package proposal for data preprocessing for machine learning applied to precision irrigation. In *2023 6th Conference on Cloud and Internet of Things (CIoT)* (pp. 141–148). IEEE.

Goap, A., Sharma, D., Shukla, A. K., & Rama Krishna, C. (2018). An IoT based smart irrigation management system using machine learning and open source technologies. *Computers and Electronics in Agriculture, 155*, 41–49. https://doi.org/10.1016/J.COMPAG.2018.09.040

Obaideen, K., Yousef, B. A. A., AlMallahi, M. N., Tan, Y. C., Mahmoud, M., Jaber, H., & Ramadan, M. (2022). An overview of smart irrigation systems using IoT. *Energy Nexus, 7*, 100124. https://doi.org/10.1016/J.NEXUS.2022.100124

Raghuvanshi, A., Singh, U. K., Sajja, G. S., Pallathadka, H., Asenso, E., Kamal, M., Singh, A., & Phasinam, K. (2022). Intrusion detection using machine learning for risk mitigation in IoT-enabled smart irrigation in smart farming. *Journal of Food Quality, 2022*. https://doi.org/10.1155/2022/3955514

Rohith, M., Sainivedhana, R., & Sabiyath Fatima, N. (2021). IoT enabled smart farming and irrigation system. In *Proceedings—5th International Conference on Intelligent Computing and Control Systems, (ICICCS 2021)*, (pp. 434–439). https://doi.org/10.1109/ICICCS51141.2021.9432085

Saraf, S. B., & Gawali, D. H. (2017). IoT based smart irrigation monitoring and controlling system. In *RTEICT 2017–2nd IEEE International Conference on Recent Trends in Electronics, Information and Communication Technology, Proceedings, 2018-January*, (pp. 815–819). https://doi.org/10.1109/RTEICT.2017.8256711

Singh, D. K., Sobti, R., Kumar Malik, P., Shrestha, S., Singh, P. K., & Ghafoor, K. Z. (2022). IoT-driven model for weather and soil conditions based on precision irrigation using machine learning. *Security and Communication Networks, 2022*.

Sleem, A. (2022). Empowering smart farming with machine intelligence: An approach for plant leaf disease recognition. *Sustainable Machine Intelligence Journal, 1*(1), 1–11. https://doi.org/10.61185/SMIJ.2022.1013

Touil, S., Richa, A., Fizir, M., Argente García, J. E., & Skarmeta Gómez, A. F. (2022). A review on smart irrigation management strategies and their effect on water savings and crop yield. *Irrigation and Drainage, 71*(5), 1396–1416. https://doi.org/10.1002/IRD.2735

Viani, F. (2016). Experimental validation of a wireless system for the irrigation management in smart farming applications. *Microwave and Optical Technology Letters, 58*(9), 2186–2189. https://doi.org/10.1002/MOP.30000

Vij, A., Vijendra, S., Jain, A., Bajaj, S., Bassi, A., & Sharma, A. (2020). IoT and machine learning approaches for automation of farm irrigation system. *Procedia Computer Science, 167*, 1250–1257. https://doi.org/10.1016/J.PROCS.2020.03.440

Zhang, J., Guan, K., Peng, B., Jiang, C., Zhou, W., Yang, Y., . . . Cai, Y. (2021). Challenges and opportunities in precision irrigation decision-support systems for center pivots. *Environmental Research Letters, 16*(5), 053003.

6 Innovations in Livestock Monitoring
A Machine Learning Journey

6.1 INTRODUCTION

This chapter discusses animal welfare and livestock production as two subcategories under livestock management. Monitoring animal behavior for illness identification and prevention at an early stage is the primary application of machine learning (ML) in the field of animal welfare, which is concerned with the health and well-being of animals. On the other hand, livestock production is concerned with problems in the production system, and the primary objective of ML applications in this sector is the precise estimation of economic balances for producers based on the monitoring of production lines. The advancements in agricultural and animal production during the past century have been astounding. Complete automation of crop harvest or environmental monitoring would have seemed unattainable a few decades ago, but it is now the norm (Iwasaki et al., 2019). We have discovered ways to enhance output in various industries using technology and modern machinery, not just for profit but also to meet the requirements of the world's rising population. There are, however, two sides to every coin. The cost of advancement was high. Certain circumstances have deteriorated as a result of the expansion of large-scale farming. As the demand for animal products has increased, farming facilities have grown in size while decreasing space consumption to maintain cost-effectiveness. Increasing demand also causes quality assurance problems. It is far more difficult to make the industrial agricultural environment completely safe under the constraints dictated by mass production. Another issue to address is the industry's environmental effect. Pollution, soil depletion, and, most crucially, its carbon footprint have all become worse in recent decades, despite increasingly stringent laws (Singh et al., 2022).

Ultimately, AI enables us to address these difficulties without jeopardizing production. In fact, when utilized wisely, AI promotes it while also promoting sustainability and enhancing animal care. With customers increasingly concerned about the ethical elements of agricultural processes, AI can assist farmers in meeting their changing expectations. The digital age is here, and with it a new era of smart farming. ML and AI are being utilized to transform cattle management and monitoring. AI-based solutions boost livestock productivity and management in anything from poultry to dairy cows. ML algorithms are an essential component of precision livestock production. Farmers use it to automate the monitoring of animal behavior and well-being, anticipate disease outbreaks, and improve feeding schedules (Wagner et al., 2020).

In other words, ML technology gives livestock producers the capacity to greatly increase the well-being of their animals. It is critical not just for the quality of their products, but also from an ethical and regulatory standpoint. Smart equipment and innovative software make it simpler than ever to monitor the living circumstances of animals and discover any irregularities that might harm them. Simultaneously, the system records animal behavioral patterns and associates them with certain factors and their combinations. This enables farmers to continually adjust their conditions to encourage output while maintaining the greatest quality (Wagner et al., 2020).

Utilizing AI technologies, livestock farmers may reduce their environmental effects while also eliminating problematic methods that are both ethically questionable and unsustainable. Particularly when it comes to lowering the carbon footprint, AI provides unrivaled assistance, allowing farmers to reduce resource usage while improving the sustainability of their feeding practices and overall farm output. Next, the meaning of livestock management and several examples of AI applications will be discussed.

6.2 DATA COLLECTION AND SENSORS IN LIVESTOCK MONITORING

Livestock monitoring relies on the collection of comprehensive and accurate data to gain valuable insights into animal behavior, health, and productivity. In modern livestock farming, a wide array of sensors and data collection methods are employed to monitor various aspects of animal life. These include global positioning system (GPS) tracking for animal location and movement analysis, radio-frequency identification (RFID) tags for individual identification, temperature sensors to monitor environmental conditions, and activity monitors to assess animal behavioral patterns. Collecting diverse data streams enables a more holistic understanding of livestock dynamics, thereby facilitating evidence-based decision-making for optimal management practices (Fuentes et al., 2020).

While data collection technologies offer invaluable benefits, they also present certain challenges that demand attention in livestock monitoring. One significant hurdle is the integration of data from different sources and sensors, which often follow diverse formats and protocols. Ensuring seamless data integration is crucial to avoid discrepancies and maintain the integrity of the collected information. Moreover, data quality assurance is of utmost importance as inaccuracies or inconsistencies can lead to faulty analyses and decisions. Farmers must be vigilant in regularly calibrating and maintaining sensors, as well as implementing rigorous data validation procedures to enhance the reliability and accuracy of the collected data.

The vast amounts of data collected through various sensors hold great potential for generating actionable insights into livestock management. Leveraging ML algorithms, researchers and farmers can analyze these datasets to gain real-time insights into livestock health, behavior, and productivity. For instance, health monitoring systems can use temperature and activity data to detect early signs of illness, alerting farmers to intervene promptly. Additionally, behavioral analysis can reveal patterns related to feeding habits and social interactions, enabling farmers to tailor management strategies for improved animal welfare and productivity. These data-driven insights empower farmers with evidence-based decision-making capabilities, ultimately leading to enhanced agricultural practices (Akhigbe et al., 2021).

The field of data collection in livestock monitoring continues to advance rapidly, promising even greater capabilities for precision farming. Emerging technologies, such as wearable sensors and Internet of Things (IoT) devices, offer more sophisticated data collection approaches. Wearable devices can provide continuous and noninvasive monitoring of vital signs, while IoT integration allows seamless communication between various sensors and data hubs. These developments pave the way for more comprehensive and interconnected livestock management systems. As data collection technologies mature and become more accessible, it is crucial for researchers and stakeholders to collaborate and standardize data formats, enabling seamless data sharing and promoting advancements in the field (Farooq et al., 2022).

6.3 MACHINE LEARNING FOR LIVESTOCK HEALTH MONITORING

ML has emerged as a powerful tool for enhancing livestock health monitoring and disease detection. By harnessing the capabilities of ML algorithms, researchers and farmers can analyze large volumes of sensor data collected from individual animals and herds. Supervised learning methods, such as support vector machines (SVM) and random forests, can be trained on labeled datasets, enabling the classification of health states and identification of potential diseases. Additionally, unsupervised learning techniques like clustering can help in identifying subtle patterns and anomalies within the data that may indicate early stages of illnesses or stress. The ability of ML to process complex data and recognize intricate patterns offers a promising avenue for early disease diagnosis and timely intervention. One of the key advantages of employing ML in livestock health monitoring is the potential for early disease detection. By continuously monitoring physiological data, such as body temperature, heart rate, and activity levels, ML models can establish baseline health profiles for individual animals. Deviations from these baselines can serve as warning signs for potential health issues. To effectively leverage ML for livestock health monitoring, seamless integration into existing livestock management systems is vital. This requires the development of user-friendly interfaces that enable farmers and animal health professionals to interact with ML algorithms and interpret the generated insights (See Figure 6.1). Visualizations

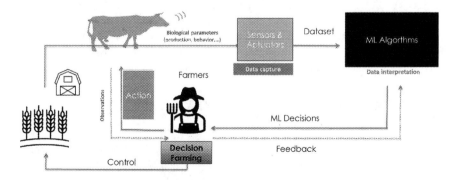

FIGURE 6.1   Visualization of General Workflow of ML for Decision-Making in Livestock.

and interpretable models can help bridge the gap between complex algorithms and practical decision-making, empowering end-users to make informed choices for their livestock's well-being. Moreover, continuous model retraining with new data ensures that the ML models remain up-to-date and adaptive to changing livestock health patterns. Successful integration of ML into livestock health management holds the potential to revolutionize disease prevention and overall animal welfare practices (Fuentes et al., 2022).

6.4 PREDICTIVE ANALYTICS FOR LIVESTOCK PRODUCTIVITY

Predictive analytics in livestock management involves the application of advanced statistical and ML techniques to forecast future productivity metrics of individual animals or entire herds. By utilizing historical data on various factors such as growth rates, milk production, and egg-laying rates, predictive models can be developed to estimate future performance. Supervised learning algorithms, such as regression and time-series analysis, are commonly employed to create predictive models based on past data patterns. These models provide valuable insights to farmers, allowing them to anticipate and plan for future productivity, thus optimizing resource allocation and breeding strategies (Neethirajan and Kemp, 2021).

Predictive analytics plays a pivotal role in enhancing livestock breeding programs and reproductive management. Through the integration of genomic and phenotypic data, ML models can predict the genetic potential of individual animals for desired traits like milk yield, meat quality, or disease resistance. This information empowers farmers to make informed decisions when selecting breeding pairs, leading to improved offspring with desired characteristics. Additionally, predictive models can forecast the optimal timing for artificial insemination and calving, minimizing the gestation period and ensuring reproductive efficiency. By implementing data-driven breeding strategies, farmers can consistently improve the overall genetic quality and productivity of their livestock populations. In addition to breeding improvements, predictive analytics aids in optimizing resource allocation and improving feed efficiency on livestock farms. By analyzing historical data on feed consumption and weight gain, ML models can estimate the optimal feed rations for different growth stages and environmental conditions. Farmers can adjust feeding regimens, accordingly, reducing feed waste and associated costs while maximizing growth rates. Moreover, predictive analytics helps identify periods of low feed efficiency or abnormal weight gain, which may signal health or management issues. By promptly addressing these concerns, farmers can mitigate potential economic losses and ensure the overall well-being of their livestock (Sultan et al., 2023).

6.5 ENVIRONMENTAL MONITORING AND RESOURCE OPTIMIZATION

AI-driven livestock management or precision livestock farming (PLF) is a collection of instruments that allow farmers to regulate and enhance their animals' health and well-being, living circumstances, and reproduction. AI is increasingly being used in these operations because it helps farmers to draw better inferences from their data and integrate all of the pieces (cameras, microphones, scanners, sensors) into a cohesive system that supports decision-making, accurate forecasts, and anomaly detection.

Although PLF relates to tools, smart farming describes how information is processed. Its goal is to leverage existing data to enhance farming procedures across the board. It's worth mentioning that the smart approach does not always include the use of modern gear and full automation. The key here is data: clever farmers aim to acquire as much relevant information as possible and make sense of it. To make this feasible, they integrate AI-powered software into their operations, which are frequently connected with IoT sensors that gather data on the state of farming facilities, product quality, and so on. Smart farming and precision livestock farming practices complement each other, assisting livestock producers in improving animal health and outcomes. AI can help to simplify cattle husbandry in a variety of ways. Several of them rely on computer vision and sophisticated predictive analytics. Let's look at some of the most prevalent use cases to get a sense of the range of AI's possibilities in this industry (Sultan et al., 2023).

6.5.1 IDENTIFICATION OF ANIMALS

Identification of livestock is needed by regulatory bodies, but it also ensures safety and helps farmers enhance the quality of their products and the care of their animals. Farmers used to know their animals' health history, age, reproduction, growth, birth date, dietary habits, and so on. With the rise of agriculture, we can keep this excellent practice going with a little aid from technology. From the day of birth, each animal's route is registered and monitored in many livestock agricultural facilities. This necessitates the development of an identification system that will keep track of many factors, therefore growing the knowledge base on each unique animal. AI aids in the analysis of this data and the extraction of insights from it. Farmers may completely automate animal identification by using computer vision. To get all the important information about a certain animal's status and history, simply scan the identification number of the code. Even smaller animals, such as chickens, may be detected individually rather than in groups using AI. This reduces the epidemiological risk and makes it easier to improve well-being in these very difficult settings.

ML techniques have revolutionized the field of animal identification, offering efficient and accurate solutions for distinguishing individual animals within a population. Traditionally, animal identification relied on physical methods such as ear tags, branding, or tattoos, which were time-consuming and prone to errors. With the advent of ML, noninvasive and automated identification methods have emerged, utilizing various data sources like images, biometric features, or vocalizations. Supervised learning algorithms, including deep neural networks and SVM, are commonly employed to classify and identify animals based on their unique characteristics. This shift toward data-driven and technology-based identification methods has significantly enhanced the speed and accuracy of animal identification processes (Akbar et al., 2020).

Image-based identification is one of the prominent applications of ML in animal identification. By utilizing photographs or video footage of animals, deep learning models like convolutional neural networks (CNNs) can be trained to recognize distinctive patterns, markings, and coloration unique to each animal. These models excel at feature extraction and can identify animals even in challenging conditions, such as varying lighting and poses. The use of image-based identification is particularly valuable in wildlife conservation, where remote cameras capture images of endangered species for monitoring and research. Through ML, researchers can efficiently analyze vast image datasets, identifying individual animals and tracking their movements and behavior for population studies and habitat conservation efforts.

Beyond image-based identification, ML is also applied to biometric and vocal recognition techniques. Biometric features like fingerprints, nose prints, or iris patterns can serve as unique identifiers for animals, similar to human biometric authentication. ML models can be trained on biometric data to accurately distinguish between individual animals, enabling noninvasive and reliable identification methods. Additionally, vocal recognition involves analyzing and classifying animal vocalizations, which can be species-specific and contain individual variations. ML algorithms, such as hidden Markov models and Gaussian mixture models, can process audio data to identify individual animals by their unique vocal signatures. These advanced identification approaches offer exciting possibilities for wildlife monitoring, livestock management, and research applications (Akbar et al., 2020).

6.5.2 WEIGHING AUTOMATION SYSTEMS

Weighing is essential for quality control. Individual animals or groups of animals can be weighed (that, again, refers more to poultry and other small animals). What's more, weighing is frequently a source of worry for the animals who try to avoid the scale. This has an impact on both their well-being and the process's efficacy. That is why it is critical to make the entire procedure as simple and quick as feasible. Automation can assist with this. Sensitive sensors can precisely identify weight in a fraction of a second and instantly register the findings in the database, eliminating the need to manually scan them. Furthermore, an improper weight might suggest a health problem or poor nutrition habits. An AI system can evaluate this data and extract insights from it, allowing farming conditions to be improved. The algorithm can uncover links between an animal's weight and its history by recognizing it. This simplifies quality assurance procedures (Fote et al., 2020).

6.6 LIVESTOCK BEHAVIOR ANALYSIS AND WELFARE

While being subject to strict quality control standards, large-scale industrial farming generates favorable conditions for epidemic threats to emerge. As a result, rigorous monitoring is critical and required. AI has the potential to greatly increase animal welfare while also lowering epidemiological hazards. Here's a full explanation of how it's feasible.

6.6.1 OBSERVING DRINKING AND FEEDING HABITS

IoT devices driven by computer vision can detect trends in animal drinking and feeding behaviors, giving farmers useful data. The sensors aid in this process by recording the amount and rate of ingestion throughout the day and night to monitor animal behavior and discover irregularities. Farmers may discover animals with atypical dietary patterns using data processed by the AI system, which might be a symptom of health or behavioral concerns. Simultaneously, they may utilize the collected data to discover correlations between the specific diet and the health and weight of the cattle. As a result, it becomes a vital tool for quality control. ML techniques have revolutionized the monitoring of drinking and feeding habits in animals, providing automated and nonintrusive solutions for collecting valuable behavioral data. Traditional methods of observation often involved manual recording, which could be labor-intensive, time-consuming, and prone to human errors. ML algorithms, particularly those based on computer vision, enable automatic recognition and tracking of animal behaviors in real time. By analyzing video footage or sensor data from feeding and watering stations, these models can identify instances of drinking and feeding, quantify consumption rates, and detect changes in behavior patterns. The application of ML in this context not only provides precise data but also reduces the need for constant human supervision, allowing researchers and farmers to gain comprehensive insights into animal habits efficiently (Akbar et al., 2020; Fote et al., 2020; Warner et al., 2020).

The adoption of ML for observing drinking and feeding habits carries significant implications for both livestock management and wildlife studies. In livestock farming, these automated monitoring systems enable continuous assessment of animal nutrition and hydration, ensuring the well-being and productivity of the herd. By accurately tracking feeding and drinking patterns, farmers can identify potential health issues or irregularities in consumption, allowing for timely intervention and improved resource allocation. Moreover, ML-based observations can optimize feed distribution, minimizing waste and operational costs. In the context of wildlife studies, the application of ML facilitates noninvasive behavioral research. Researchers can deploy cameras and sensors in the natural habitats of wild animals, gathering data on their drinking and feeding behaviors without disturbing their natural routines. This approach offers crucial insights into the ecological dynamics and conservation needs of various species, aiding in the development of targeted conservation strategies and wildlife management initiatives (Neethirajan and Kemp, 2021; Sultan et al., 2023).

6.6.2 STUDY OF ACTIVITY PATTERNS, MOVEMENT, AND POSTURE

The same methods mentioned above may be used to investigate additional patterns that are important for good quality control. Variables such as activity during the day and night, mobility, and posture can all be useful indications of an animal's health. ML algorithms combined with computer vision may recognize, categorize, and relate them to the symptoms of a certain condition, generating an alarm automatically.

6.6.3 IDENTIFICATION OF FECES

Feces can provide valuable information about animal well-being. Farmers can use computer vision to automate their inspection rather than performing it manually to find irregularities. If the animal is contaminated with germs, the feces will contain it as well. Based on the examined sample, the AI system may instantly identify the possible hazard of contamination and give insights to the farmer. ML techniques have revolutionized the process of fecal identification in ecological and wildlife studies. Traditional methods for feces identification require manual examination by experts, which could be time-consuming and subjective. With the advancement of ML, automated fecal identification systems have emerged, enabling efficient and accurate analysis of fecal samples. Computer vision algorithms, particularly those based on deep learning models like CNNs, can be trained on large datasets of fecal images from different species. These models can then recognize distinctive visual patterns and characteristics specific to each species, allowing for rapid and precise identification.

The adoption of ML-based fecal identification offers numerous advantages and finds applications across various fields. In wildlife ecology, the rapid identification of feces aids in studying animal behavior, habitat use, and species interactions. By understanding the diet and distribution of different species, researchers can assess ecological dynamics and implement targeted conservation strategies. Moreover, the application of ML in fecal identification extends to noninvasive monitoring of endangered species, helping in population estimation and tracking changes in animal numbers over time. In agricultural settings, ML-based fecal identification is essential for livestock management. By automating the identification of animal feces, farmers can monitor herd health, identify nutritional deficiencies, and assess the impact of feed supplements on livestock digestion. The efficiency and accuracy provided by ML enhance animal welfare and optimize agricultural practices (Neethirajan and Kemp, 2021).

6.6.4 TEMPERATURE ANALYSIS FOR HEAT STRESS MONITORING

Monitoring heat stress is another method artificial intelligence may improve animal well-being. Because of the large concentration of livestock in a relatively small space, farm animals can be subjected to high temperatures, which can have a catastrophic effect on both their physical and mental health—especially in the long run. Sensors coupled with the AI-based system may gather temperature data, extracting insights about its increases and falls, and tying it to certain events or actions. The ML algorithm detects trends that increase the danger of heat stress and delivers a real-time notice when the temperature hits the risky threshold. ML has proven to be a valuable tool for automating temperature analysis in heat stress monitoring for livestock and animals. Heat stress can have severe implications on animal health, productivity, and welfare, making it essential to accurately monitor and mitigate its effects. Traditional methods of temperature monitoring involved manual measurements at various intervals, which could be labor-intensive and prone to human errors. ML algorithms, particularly those based on time-series analysis, can analyze continuous temperature data from sensors installed in barns, shelters, or pastures. These models can identify temperature patterns and trends associated with heat stress, triggering early warning systems when certain thresholds are exceeded. The application of ML in temperature analysis not only enables real-time monitoring but also facilitates proactive interventions to ensure the well-being of animals and optimize livestock management practices (Akhigbe et al., 2021).

The adoption of ML-based temperature analysis offers significant advantages and finds broad applications in heat stress monitoring for various animal populations.

In livestock farming, heat stress can lead to reduced feed intake, lower milk production, and compromised reproductive performance. With deployment of ML-based temperature monitoring systems, farmers can identify heat stress episodes promptly, allowing for the implementation of cooling measures and shade provision to alleviate its impact on animals. Moreover, ML models can consider additional factors, such as humidity and air movement, to generate more accurate heat stress predictions tailored to specific environments and animal species. Beyond livestock, ML is also applied in wildlife conservation to monitor heat stress in endangered species, especially during extreme weather events. By understanding how climate change affects different ecosystems and animal habitats, conservationists can devise strategies to protect vulnerable populations and preserve biodiversity.

6.6.5 KEEPING AN EYE ON LIVESTOCK VOCALIZATIONS

ML has become a powerful tool for automated analysis of livestock vocalizations, offering significant advantages in monitoring animal behavior, health, and well-being. Livestock, such as cattle, sheep, and pigs, use vocalizations as a means of communication, expressing various emotions, social interactions, and stress levels. Traditional methods of vocalization analysis relied on manual observation and interpretation by experts, limiting the scale and accuracy of data collection. ML algorithms, particularly those based on pattern recognition and natural language processing, can process large datasets of audio recordings to identify and classify different vocalizations. These models can distinguish between various vocalization types, such as distress calls, mating calls, and mother–offspring communications. By automating vocalization analysis, researchers and farmers can gain valuable insights into livestock behavior and well-being, facilitating timely interventions for improved animal care and management.

The adoption of ML-based vocalization analysis holds numerous applications and benefits for livestock management and research. In animal welfare studies, automated vocalization analysis allows for continuous monitoring of livestock well-being, enabling early detection of signs of stress, discomfort, or illness. Identifying distress calls or abnormal vocalizations promptly can lead to timely interventions, reducing potential negative impacts on animal health and productivity. Additionally, ML-based vocalization analysis finds application in reproductive management. By recognizing specific mating calls or vocal cues during estrus, farmers can optimize breeding programs and enhance reproductive efficiency. Furthermore, automated vocalization analysis facilitates precision livestock farming by enabling real-time monitoring of animal behavior in large-scale livestock operations. The insights gained from ML models assist in optimizing feeding regimens, identifying environmental stressors, and enhancing overall animal welfare and productivity.

6.7 MONITORING AND MODIFYING SHED AND AQUACULTURE CONDITIONS

ML has emerged as a valuable technology for real-time monitoring of shed and aquaculture conditions, providing farmers and aquaculturists with precise and up-to-date insights into their operations. In intensive livestock and aquaculture systems, maintaining optimal environmental conditions is crucial for animal health, growth, and overall productivity. Traditional methods of monitoring involved manual data collection and observation, which could be time consuming and limited in scope. ML algorithms, particularly those based on sensor data analysis, can process information from various environmental sensors such as temperature, humidity, water quality, and air quality. These models can recognize patterns and anomalies in the data, alerting farmers to deviations from ideal conditions (Neethirajan and Kemp, 2021; Sultan et al., 2023).

One of the significant advantages of ML in shed and aquaculture conditions is its potential for adaptive control and precision management. As ML algorithms continually analyze and learn from environmental data, they can develop predictive models that anticipate future trends and requirements. These insights allow for proactive adjustments to shed climate, ventilation, feeding systems, or water quality parameters to prevent adverse conditions and enhance efficiency. In aquaculture, ML can optimize feeding schedules, considering factors like water temperature, fish behavior, and growth rates, leading to reduced feed waste and improved fish health. Moreover, the integration of ML with automated control systems enables real-time adjustments based on accurate predictive models. This adaptive control approach ensures that shed and aquaculture conditions are consistently optimized, minimizing resource usage, and reducing environmental impacts, while maximizing productivity and profitability (Fote et al., 2020).

6.8   EVALUATING PASTURE

ML has proven to be a valuable tool for automating the evaluation of pasture conditions, offering significant advantages in assessing forage quality and vegetation dynamics. Traditionally, pasture evaluation required manual sampling and laborious data collection, which could be time consuming and challenging to execute on large or remote grazing lands. ML algorithms, particularly those based on remote sensing and image analysis, can process data from satellite imagery, aerial surveys, or drone footage to assess vegetation cover, biomass, and species distribution across pastures. These models can classify different vegetation types, identify areas of high forage density, and detect indicators of pasture degradation or overgrazing (Sultan et al., 2023).

The adoption of ML-based pasture evaluation has broad applications and offers numerous benefits for sustainable grazing management and environmental conservation. In livestock farming, precise assessments of pasture conditions lead to improved livestock performance, as animals graze on nutrient-rich forage and avoid areas of poor quality. ML models can support decisions on pasture rotation and rest periods, promoting sustainable land use and preventing overgrazing, which can lead to soil erosion and reduced biodiversity. Moreover, in conservation efforts, ML-based pasture evaluation aids in habitat monitoring and wildlife management. By tracking changes in vegetation cover and species distribution, researchers can assess the impacts of grazing practices on ecosystems and design conservation plans to preserve biodiversity and restore degraded areas. Overall, the integration of ML in pasture evaluation contributes to more informed land management decisions, sustainable grazing practices, and the enhancement of both livestock productivity and ecosystem health (Akbar et al., 2020).

6.9 ENHANCING HATCHERIES

Hatcheries allow farmers to provide ideal circumstances for the development of embryos in eggs. It is not possible to accomplish it in the typical fashion that employs animals in industrial manufacturing. As a result, producers are faced with the difficulty of replicating the environmental factors that the eggs acquire during natural hatching. It necessitates accuracy and continual monitoring, as changes in temperature and humidity can disrupt the incubation process. The AI system, which is linked to sensors and incubators, can extract and assess important data to notice any situation changes that might disrupt embryo development. Based on these observations, they can make changes to sustain the incubation process. Simultaneously, it analyzes the impact of certain situations on fertility, learning from this and continually improving its suggestions.

In addition, early detection of non-hatchable and sterile eggs saves farmers money by optimizing hatchery area utilization and increasing overall yield. They can accomplish this by combining near-infrared hyperspectral imaging methods with ML. ML systems trained on datasets comprising photos of viable and infertile eggs categorize them so that farmers may remove the latter as soon as feasible from the hatchery.

6.10 MONITORING THE DEVELOPMENT OF EMBRYOS

ML has emerged as a powerful tool for automating the monitoring of embryo development in various fields, such as assisted reproduction, fertility research, and animal breeding programs. Traditionally, embryo development monitoring involved manual observation and assessment by embryologists, which could be subjective and labor-intensive. ML algorithms, particularly those based on image analysis and pattern recognition, can process time-lapse imaging data of developing embryos. These models can analyze morphological changes, cell division patterns, and embryo quality indicators, accurately tracking the progression of embryo development. By harnessing the power of ML, embryologists can receive real-time insights into embryo health and viability, allowing for precise embryo selection and timely interventions to improve the success rates of fertility treatments and breeding programs.

The adoption of ML-based embryo development monitoring holds numerous applications and advantages in reproductive medicine and livestock breeding. In human fertility treatments, such as in vitro fertilization (IVF), ML models enable embryologists to select the most viable embryos for transfer, enhancing the chances of successful pregnancy and reducing the risk of multiple births. Additionally, ML can assist in pre-implantation genetic testing, identifying genetic abnormalities in embryos, and supporting the selection of healthy embryos for transfer. In animal breeding programs, ML-based embryo monitoring optimizes genetic selection, accelerating genetic progress and improving livestock productivity and performance. Moreover, ML provides researchers with valuable insights into embryo development dynamics, shedding light on the molecular and cellular processes that influence embryonic growth and differentiation.

REFERENCES

Akbar, M. O., Shahbaz Khan, M. S., Ali, M. J., Hussain, A., Qaiser, G., Pasha, M., Pasha, U., Missen, M. S., & Akhtar, N. (2020). IoT for development of smart dairy farming. *Journal of Food Quality*, *2020*. https://doi.org/10.1155/2020/4242805

Akhigbe, I., Munir, K., Akinade, O., Akanbi, L., & Oyedele, L. O. (2021). IoT technologies for livestock management: A review of present status, opportunities, and future trends. *Big Data and Cognitive Computing*, *5*(1), 10. https://doi.org/10.3390/BDCC5010010

Farooq, M. S., Sohail, O. O., Abid, A., & Rasheed, S. (2022). A survey on the role of IoT in agriculture for the implementation of smart livestock environment. *IEEE Access*, *10*, 9483–9505. https://doi.org/10.1109/ACCESS.2022.3142848

Fote, F. N., Roukh, A., Mahmoudi, S., Mahmoudi, S. A., & Debauche, O. (2020). Toward a big data knowledge-base management system for precision livestock farming. *Procedia Computer Science*, *177*, 136–142. https://doi.org/10.1016/J.PROCS.2020.10.021

Fuentes, S., Gonzalez Viejo, C., Tongson, E., & Dunshea, F. R. (2022). The livestock farming digital transformation: Implementation of new and emerging technologies using artificial intelligence. *Animal Health Research Reviews*, *23*(1), 59–71. https://doi.org/10.1017/S1466252321000177

Fuentes, S., Viejo, C. G., Cullen, B., Tongson, E., Chauhan, S. S., & Dunshea, F. R. (2020). Artificial intelligence applied to a robotic dairy farm to model milk productivity and quality based on cow data and daily environmental parameters. *Sensors*, *20*(10), 2975. https://doi.org/10.3390/S20102975

Iwasaki, W., Morita, N., & Nagata, M. P. B. (2019). IoT sensors for smart livestock management. *Chemical, Gas, and Biosensors for Internet of Things and Related Applications*, 207–221. https://doi.org/10.1016/B978-0-12-815409-0.00015-2

Neethirajan, S., & Kemp, B. (2021). Digital twins in livestock farming. *Animals*, *11*(4), 1008. https://doi.org/10.3390/ANI11041008

Singh, A., Jadoun, Y. S., Singh Brar, P., Kour, G., Singh, A., Brar, P. S., & Kour, G. (2022). Smart technologies in livestock farming. *Smart and Sustainable Food Technologies*, 25–57. https://doi.org/10.1007/978-981-19-1746-2_2

Sultan, M., Zhou, Y., Shamshiri, R. R., Imran, M., & Neethirajan, S. (2023). The significance and ethics of digital livestock farming. *AgriEngineering*, *5*(1), 488–505. https://doi.org/10.3390/AGRIENGINEERING5010032

Wagner, N., Antoine, V., Mialon, M. M., Lardy, R., Silberberg, M., Koko, J., & Veissier, I. (2020). Machine learning to detect behavioural anomalies in dairy cows under subacute ruminal acidosis. *Computers and Electronics in Agriculture*, *170*, 105233. https://doi.org/10.1016/J.COMPAG.2020.105233

Warner, D., Vasseur, E., Lefebvre, D. M., & Lacroix, R. (2020). A machine learning based decision aid for lameness in dairy herds using farm-based records. *Computers and Electronics in Agriculture*, *169*, 105193. https://doi.org/10.1016/J.COMPAG.2019.105193

7 Enhancing Crop Health with Machine Learning

Disease and Weed Identification Strategies

7.1 INTRODUCTION

This chapter explores and investigates the potential of ML solutions in improving the productivity of smart farming systems through different crop management tasks, namely yield prediction, weed detection, disease detection, and crop quality estimation. The process of yield prediction, which is one of the most important aspects of precision agriculture, is of utmost significance for yield mapping, yield estimation, the synchronization of crop production and demand, and crop management to achieve higher profitability levels. Disease detection and yield prediction are the subcategories that contain the most articles that are included in this chapter. Controlling pests and diseases in open-air and greenhouse environments is one of the most pressing issues facing the agricultural industry today. Moreover, identifying and controlling weeds is another significant challenge in the agricultural industry. Weeds are seen by many farmers and other crop producers as the most significant obstacle to crop production. Because it is difficult to distinguish weeds from crops, accurate weed detection is of utmost importance to the practice of sustainable agriculture. Weeds cannot be easily distinguished from crops. Further, studies that have been developed to identify characteristics connected with the quality of the crop make up the penultimate subcategory for the crop category. The precise identification and classification of the quality characteristics of crops can lead to increased product prices while simultaneously reducing waste.

Agriculture and farming are among the world's oldest and most significant vocations. It is very significant in the economic sector. In other words, agriculture is a five trillion-dollar business worldwide. The global population is predicted to exceed nine billion by 2050, necessitating a 70% increase in agricultural production to meet demand. As the world's population grows, land, water, and resources become insufficient to sustain the demand-supply cycle. As a result, we must adopt a more strategic approach to farming to maximize productivity. In particular, the agricultural process can be divided into several stages:

- *Soil preparation:* This is the first stage of farming in which farmers prepare the soil for seeding. This procedure entails breaking up huge clumps of dirt and removing waste such as sticks, pebbles, and roots. In addition,

DOI: 10.1201/9781003400103-7

depending on the type of crop, add fertilizers and organic matter to produce an optimum environment for crops.

- *Sowing seeds:* At this point, you must consider the space between two seeds as well as the depth at which you will sow the seeds. Climate factors like as temperature, humidity, and rainfall are critical during this stage.
- *Applying fertilizers:* Maintaining soil fertility is critical so that farmers may continue to cultivate nutritious and healthy crops. Fertilizers are used by farmers because they contain plant nutrients such as nitrogen, phosphorus, and potassium. Fertilizers are simply planted nutrients that are given to agricultural areas to complement the components that are already present in the soil. This stage also influences the crop's quality.
- *Irrigation:* This step helps to keep the soil wet and humidity levels high. Crop development can be hampered by underwatering or overwatering, and if not done appropriately, it can result in crop damage.
- *Weed control:* Weeds are undesirable plants that grow near crops or at farm boundaries. Weed control is critical because weeds reduce yields, raise production costs, interfere with harvest, and reduce crop quality.
- *Harvesting:* It is the process of collecting mature crops from fields. This activity is labor intensive since it requires a large number of laborers. Postharvest handling, such as cleaning, sorting, packaging, and refrigeration, is also included in this step.
- *Storage:* The phase of the postharvest system in which products are held in such a way that food security is ensured other than during agricultural seasons. It also covers crop packaging and transportation.

There are several challenges that can be obstacles to the process of farming. For instance, climate conditions such as rainfall, temperature, and humidity all have a part in the agriculture lifecycle. Climate change is being caused by increased deforestation and pollution, making it difficult for farmers to make judgments on how to prepare the soil, sow seeds, and harvest. Also, every crop requires a different type of nourishment in the soil. Soil requires three major nutrients: nitrogen (N), phosphorus (P), and potassium (K). Nutrient deficit can result in poor crop quality. Moreover, weed control is critical in agriculture, as seen by the agricultural life cycle. If not regulated, it can raise production costs and take minerals from the soil, causing a nutritional deficit in the soil. All of these challenges cause the need for smart crop management.

7.2   LITERATURE REVIEW

AI technologies are being used by the agricultural industry to help yield better crops, manage pests, monitor soil and growing conditions, organize data for farmers, assist with workload, and improve a wide range of agriculture-related duties along the food supply chain. Several contributions have been offered to enhance the overall process of agriculture and crop management (Ennouri et al., 2021; Vitali et al., 2021; Dharani et al., 2021; Khan et al., 2022; Gautron et al., 2022).

For example, Rahman et al. (2019) created a model that can anticipate soil series based on land type and then recommend suitable crops based on the prediction. Soil categorization employs a variety of ML methods, including weighted K-nearest neighbor (k-NN), bagged trees, and SVM. The study used soil records from six Upazillas in the Khulna district of Bangladesh. The experimental findings reveal that the suggested SVM-based strategy outperforms numerous other methods.

Partel et al. (2019) created and tested a smart sprayer prototype based on AI. The sprayer included the you only look once (YOLO) object identification system machine vision software. It detects particular target weeds using convolutional neural networks and deep learning, and it sprays using a piece of hardware with 12 unique quick-reaction nozzles. Utilizing the GTX 1070 Ti GPU, the missed targets (portulaca weed) were decreased by 81% (from 43% to 8%), the detection system's precision and recall were raised by 20% and 77%, respectively, and the total spraying system's precision and recall were enhanced by 10% and 59%, respectively (comparing with the TX2 GPU).

Ai et al. (2020) used a CNN to detect crop diseases automatically from dataset sourced from the AI Challenger Competition with 27 illness photos from ten crops. The Inception-ResNet-v2 model was utilized for training and the evaluations demonstrated that the model can successfully identify the dataset, with an overall identification accuracy of up to 86.1%. The results validated that this hybrid network model has a greater recognition accuracy than the classic model and may be used to successfully identify and detect plant diseases and insect pests.

Mazzia et al. (2020) created and tested a real-time apple-detecting algorithm on numerous edge AI devices. The dataset for training was produced using photographs collected during a field study of an apple orchard in northern Italy, and the images used for testing were taken from a widely used Google data collection by filtering out images including apples in various situations to confirm the algorithm's resilience. The suggested study uses YOLOv3-tiny architecture to identify small objects.

Shankar et al. (2020) highlighted Xarvio's digital agricultural solutions and how they contribute to the achievement of the United Nations Sustainable Development Goals. Farmers may apply for crop protection more efficiently through targeted application by using recent advances in AI. Spray Timer, Zone Spray, Buffer Zones, and Product Recommendation are the modules given in this article that guarantee crop protection products are administered at the appropriate time and just where they are needed, while also assuring the proper product at the ideal rate. This not only decreased the environmental effect but also boosted the farmer's production and profitability. Real-world case studies in two major food-producing regions, Europe and Brazil, demonstrated the impact of our digital solutions. In Europe, the combination of AI-driven spray scheduling, variable rate application maps, and product recommendations has resulted in a 30% drop in fungicide consumption on field trial cereal crops and a 72% decrease in tank residues, decreasing environmental contamination. In Brazil, the Zone Spray weed mapping solution developed utilizing computer vision techniques resulted in an average savings of 61%, reducing herbicide and water use by nearly two-thirds. As a consequence, the ideas described in this article are in line with the United

Nations Sustainable Development Goals of achieving zero hunger and responsible consumption and production.

The user interface of expert systems should widen thinking patterns, selecting new sustainable agricultural viewpoints. Schoning and Richter (2021) introduced the technological architecture of such an expert system, as well as the user-in-the-loop idea. The AI-based expert system should handle multidimensional optimization tasks such as increasing crop diversity while taking into account local soil, climate, livestock demands, and any accessible technology. In addition to the choice of job, the expert system had to defend its decision-making foundation, because the aim is to achieve the most sustainable farming with the highest crop production, not the highest yield.

Navinkumar et al. (2021) chose the Thottiyam region for research, and irrigation management was implemented for the growth of the Navarai type of paddy grown in the region. The meteorological information in the region was obtained from the TNAU Agritech webpage. With the use of AI approaches, the goal water level necessary for each growth period has been determined, and the amount of water level to be given by irrigation has been projected. The obtained data was initially sent into a fuzzy logic controller. Based on the rules provided, this controller anticipated the values for the supplied input. These rules were developed using the information gathered. The identical inputs were fed into an artificial neural network (ANN) trained with the backpropagation technique. The network was trained several times, and the output was determined to be less error-prone than the fuzzy logic approach. The projected values were discovered to be almost correct. As a result, ANN prediction outperforms fuzzy logic output. Yet, when the amount of data to be sent to the network is large, the complexity grows.

Adami et al. (2021) focused on a smart crop management application that used computer vision and ultrasonic emission to create virtual fences that protect crops from ungulate assaults and thereby considerably minimize output losses. Beginning with an advanced device that can emit ultrasound to drive away ungulates and thus protect crops from their threat, this work provides a detailed description of the design, development, and evaluation of an intelligent animal repulsion system that can detect and recognize ungulates as well as generate ultrasonic signals tailored to each species of ungulate. Taking into consideration the limits imposed by the rural environment in terms of energy supply and network connection, the suggested system is built on IoT platforms that provide a good balance of performance, cost, and energy usage. In this paper, the authors implemented and evaluated various edge computing devices (Raspberry Pi, with or without a neural compute stick, and NVIDIA Jetson Nano) running real-time object detectors (YOLO and Tiny-YOLO) with custom-trained models to determine the most effective animal recognition HW/SW platform to be integrated with the ultrasound generator.

Huang et al. (2022) offered a smart agricultural growth monitoring system with an adaptive cryptography engine to maintain sensor data security and an edge AI-based estimator to identify pest and disease severity (PDS) of target crops. The crop growth monitoring system may execute the relevant steps to interact with the physical environment to guarantee the healthy development of crops based on the PDS and crop water needs. When a request for sensor data from a sensor platform is received by the crop growth monitoring system, it negotiates with the sensor platform to utilize the same cryptographic function. Based on the smart crop management process, cryptographic functions may be tailored to changing and real-time needs, while actuators can be programmed to interact with the physical environment to maintain crop health.

Using photos captured by UAVs, the convolutional neural network was utilized to detect weeds in a commercial crop of Chinese cabbage (Ong et al., 2023). Using the Simple Linear Iterative Clustering Superpixel technique, the obtained pictures were preprocessed and then categorized into crop, soil, and weed classes. After that, the segmented pictures were utilized to build the CNN-based classifier. The random forest (RF) method was used to compare the performance of CNN. The findings indicated that CNN obtained a greater overall accuracy of 92.41% than RF (86.18%).

7.3 CROP DISEASE MANAGEMENT

Technological advancements in agriculture monitoring systems have made it even easier for farmers to acquire precise data to improve crop management choices. Reliable environmental and soil conditions data influence crop positioning, watering, and crop protection decisions (Kaur and Gupta, 2022). Smart crop management enables organizations to increase overall efficiency, production, and sustainability while preserving critical resources (Vakula et al., 2022). This is preserved by efficient management of different farming processes that were previously discussed. Next, several examples of smart crop management tasks will be discussed.

7.3.1 WEED AND DISEASE DETECTION

We can now identify plant illnesses and pests using deep learning picture recognition technologies. And if you want to know not only if your crops have pests, but also how many there are, computer vision systems for insect identification may help with that as well. Drones fitted with computer vision AI allow for the consistent spraying of pesticides or fertilizers throughout a field. Unmanned aerial vehicle (UAV) sprayers can work with excellent precision in terms of area and amount sprayed thanks to real-time detection of target spraying regions. This minimizes the danger of polluting crops, humans, animals, and water supplies dramatically. While there is immense promise here, there are also some problems. Spraying a big field, for example, is considerably more efficient with many UAVs, but assigning precise job sequences and flight paths for individual aircraft might be challenging. Yet it doesn't imply intelligent spraying is out of the question. Virginia Tech researchers developed a smart spray system based on servo motor-operated sprayers that detect weeds using computer vision. A camera installed on the sprayer collects weed geolocation and evaluates the size, shape, and color of each troublesome plant to apply exact doses of herbicide with pinpoint accuracy. In other words, it acts as a weed killer. In other words, the computer vision system's accuracy allows it to spray with such precision that it avoids collateral harm to crops or the environment (Sleem, 2022).

Some computer vision robots are taking a more direct approach to removing undesirable plants. Currently, detecting weeds in the same manner that computer vision detects insects or unusually behaved chickens does not save the farmer any time. To be of even more assistance, the AI must locate and eliminate the weed. Physically removing weeds not only saves the farmer time but also decreases the need for chemicals, making the entire agricultural process far more ecologically friendly and sustainable. Fortunately, object detection can effectively recognize weeds and separate them from crops. The true power, however, comes when computer vision techniques are paired with machine learning to create robots capable of autonomous weeding.

7.3.2 Yield and Crop Quality Estimation

Micro and macronutrients in the soil are important variables in crop health and yield quantity and quality. Then, after crops are planted, it is critical to monitor their growth stages to maximize production efficiency. Understanding the relationships between crop development and the environment is critical for making crop health modifications. Formerly, human observation and judgment were used to evaluate soil quality and crop health. This strategy, however, is neither accurate nor timely. Instead, we can now employ drones to collect aerial picture data and train computer vision models to use them for intelligent crop and soil monitoring. This data may be analyzed and interpreted by visual sensing AI to:

- Monitor crop health
- Make precise yield projections
- Detect crop starvation considerably faster than people

AI models can alert farmers to specific problem regions, allowing them to take rapid action (Chergui and Kechadi, 2022). For example, manually observing wheat head growth phases is exactly the type of labor-intensive operation that AI may assist within precision agriculture. Researchers did this by collecting photos of wheat at different "heading" stages spanning three years and in varied lightings, which enabled them to construct a "two-step coarse-to-fine wheat ear recognition method." This computer vision model then outperformed human observation in properly recognizing wheat development phases, removing the need for farmers to make daily trips into the fields to inspect their harvest.

Returning to the significance of soil, another study sought to determine how effectively computer vision can identify soil organic carbon content (SOC). Soil evaluation normally entails farmers digging up samples and transporting them to a lab for time- and energy-intensive examination. Instead, the researchers decided to test if picture data from a low-cost portable microscope could be used to train an algorithm to perform the same thing. Moreover, the computer vision model was able to predict sand content and SOC with precision similar to expensive lab processing. Consequently, not only can computer vision reduce most of the onerous, manual work needed in crop and soil monitoring, but it can also do it more effectively than people in many circumstances.

7.4 CASE STUDY

In this chapter, we present a comprehensive case study focusing on the detection of coffee leaf disease using vision transformers (ViT) and explore the pivotal role of ML in crop disease management. Coffee is one of the world's most widely consumed beverages, and its production is crucial for the livelihood of millions of farmers worldwide. However, coffee leaf disease, caused by the fungus *Hemileia vastatrix*, poses a significant threat to coffee plantations, leading to substantial economic losses and threatening global coffee production. Traditional disease detection methods often rely on manual inspection, which can be time consuming and may not be sensitive enough to detect early-stage infections. Thus, the integration of ML and computer vision techniques offers promising solutions to revolutionize crop disease management and safeguard agricultural productivity.

In this case study, we demonstrate the potential of ViT in coffee leaf disease detection, showcasing the power of ML algorithms in identifying infected coffee leaves accurately and efficiently. ViT have emerged as a groundbreaking deep learning architecture that has demonstrated exceptional performance in various computer vision tasks, including image classification. By fine-tuning the pre-trained ViT model on a dataset of coffee leaf images, we showcase its ability to differentiate between healthy and infected coffee leaves with impressive accuracy. The successful application of ML in detecting coffee leaf disease not only expedites the identification process but also enables early intervention, preventing the spread of the disease and minimizing crop losses. This study highlights the immense promise of ML-based approaches in crop disease management and sets a precedent for the adoption of advanced technologies to ensure food security and sustainable agriculture in the face of emerging challenges. The following is an overview of the implementation of our case study on coffee leaf disease detection using ViT:

The code starts by importing the necessary libraries and modules, including TensorFlow, Keras, and the ViT model.

```
# Importing the necessary libraries

import numpy as np                    # NumPy: Library for numerical
computations in Python
import tensorflow as tf               # TensorFlow: Deep learning library
developed by Google Brain
from tensorflow import keras          # Keras: High-level API for building
and training deep learning models
from tensorflow.keras import layers   # TensorFlow's Keras layers for
building neural networks

import matplotlib.pyplot as plt        # Matplotlib: Library for data
visualization in Python

from tensorflow.keras.preprocessing.image import ImageDataGenerator  #
Data augmentation for images
from PIL import Image                 # Python Imaging Library for image
processing
```

```
import pandas as pd                    # Pandas: Library for data
manipulation and analysis
import seaborn as sb                    # Seaborn: Data visualization
library based on Matplotlib
import os                               # Operating System library for
interacting with the file system
import warnings                         # Library to manage warnings in
Python


# Ignore warnings
warnings.filterwarnings('ignore')


import glob as gb                       # Library for working with file
paths
import cv2                              # OpenCV: Computer vision library
for image and video processing
import keras                            # Keras: High-level neural networks
API


from keras import backend as K         # Keras backend for managing low-
level operations
from keras.models import Sequential, Model, load_model  # Keras classes
for creating models
from keras.callbacks import EarlyStopping, ModelCheckpoint  # Keras
callbacks for model training
from keras.layers import Dropout, Input, Add, Dense, Activation,
ZeroPadding2D, BatchNormalization, Flatten, Conv2D, AveragePooling2D,
MaxPooling2D, GlobalMaxPooling2D, MaxPool2D  # Keras layers for building
neural networks
from keras.preprocessing import image  # Image preprocessing utilities in
Keras
from keras.initializers import glorot_uniform  # Keras initializer for
Glorot uniform initializer


from sklearn.metrics import accuracy_score, precision_score, recall_score,
f1_score, roc_auc_score, classification_report  # Metrics for model
evaluation


from sklearn.preprocessing import LabelBinarizer  # LabelBinarizer: Helper
class for one-hot encoding labels
from sklearn.metrics import roc_curve, auc, roc_auc_score  # Receiver
Operating Characteristic (ROC) metrics
from itertools import cycle            # Iterator tools for creating cycles


# Setting the plot style using Seaborn
sns.set_style('whitegrid')


# More plot settings for Seaborn
import matplotlib.pyplot as plt
plt.style.library['seaborn-whitegrid']


# Importing modules for model visualization
from sklearn.metrics import confusion_matrix
from sklearn.metrics import ConfusionMatrixDisplay
```

We load the dataset containing labeled images of coffee leaves, where each image is classified into five classes.

```
# Data Augmentation Configuration
# --------------------------------
```

```
# Create a data generator for training data with the following
configurations:
# - rescale: Rescale pixel values to a range of [0, 1] by dividing by
255.0
traingen =
tf.keras.preprocessing.image.ImageDataGenerator(rescale=1.0/255.0)


# Create a data generator for test data with the same rescaling
configuration
testgen =
tf.keras.preprocessing.image.ImageDataGenerator(rescale=1.0/255.0)


# Create a data generator for validation data with the same rescaling
configuration
validgen =
tf.keras.preprocessing.image.ImageDataGenerator(rescale=1.0/255.0)


# Data Loading and Preprocessing
# -------------------------------
# Load training data from the 'train_path' directory with the following
configurations:
# - batch_size: Number of samples per batch during training (128 samples
per batch)
# - directory: Path to the directory containing the training data
# - shuffle: Whether to shuffle the data after each epoch during training
(True for shuffling)
# - target_size: Size to which all images will be resized (128x128 pixels
in this case)
# - class_mode: Type of label encoding, 'categorical' for one-hot encoded
labels
train_ds = traingen.flow_from_directory(batch_size=128,
directory=train_path, shuffle=True,
                                        target_size=(128, 128),
class_mode='categorical')


# Load test data from the 'test_path' directory with the same
configurations as the training data
test_ds = traingen.flow_from_directory(batch_size=128,
directory=test_path, shuffle=False,
                                       target_size=(128, 128),
class_mode='categorical')


# Load validation data from the 'val_path' directory with the same
configurations as the training data
val_ds = traingen.flow_from_directory(batch_size=128, directory=val_path,
shuffle=True,
                                      target_size=(128, 128),
class_mode='categorical')

# Image Processing Configuration
# -------------------------------
image_size = 128  # Size to which input images will be resized
patch_size = 12  # Size of the patches to be extracted from the input
images
num_patches = (image_size // patch_size) ** 2  # Calculate the total
number of patches in the image


# Transformer Configuration
# -------------------------
projection_dim = 64  # Dimensionality of the projected embeddings in the
transformer
num_heads = 4  # Number of attention heads in the multi-head self-attention
mechanism
```

```
transformer _ units = [
    projection _ dim * 2,   # Size of the first transformer layer
    projection _ dim,       # Size of the second transformer layer

]   # List containing the size of each transformer layer

transformer _ layers = 8  # Number of transformer layers in the model

# Multi-Layer Perceptron (MLP) Head Configuration
# -------------------------------
mlp _ head _ units = [2048, 1024]  # List containing the number of units in
each layer of the MLP head

# Number of Classes in the Classification Task
# -------------------------------
num _ classes = 5  # Number of output classes in the classification task

# Input Shape for the Model
# -------------------------------
input _ shape = (128, 128, 3)  # Shape of the input images (128x128 pixels
with 3 color channels)

class MLPLayer(tf.keras.layers.Layer):
    def _ _ init _ _ (self, hidden _ units, dropout _ rate):
        """
        Constructor for the MLP layer.

        Parameters:
            hidden _ units (int): Number of units in the hidden layer.
            dropout _ rate (float): The dropout rate used between the Dense
layers.
        """
        super(MLPLayer, self). _ _ init _ _ ()

        self.hidden _ units = hidden _ units
        self.dropout _ rate = dropout _ rate

        # Define the first Dense layer with GELU activation
        self.dense1 = layers.Dense(hidden _ units, activation=tf.nn.gelu)

        # Define the dropout layer
        self.dropout = layers.Dropout(dropout _ rate)

    def call(self, inputs, training=None):
        """
        Method to perform the forward pass through the MLP layer.

        Parameters:
            inputs (tf.Tensor): The input tensor to the MLP layer.
            training (bool): Whether the model is in training mode or not.

        Returns:
            tf.Tensor: The output tensor after passing through the MLP
layer.
        """
        x = self.dense1(inputs)
        x = self.dropout(x, training=training)
        return x
```

```python
class Patches(layers.Layer):
    def __init__(self, patch_size):
        """
        Constructor for the Patches layer.

        Parameters:
            patch_size (int): Size of the square patches to be extracted
from the images.
        """
        super(Patches, self).__init__()
        self.patch_size = patch_size

    def call(self, images):
        """
        Method to extract patches from input images.

        Parameters:
            images (tf.Tensor): The input tensor containing the images.

        Returns:
            tf.Tensor: A tensor containing patches extracted from the
input images.
        """
        # Get the batch size from the input tensor
        batch_size = tf.shape(images)[0]

        # Extract patches from the images using the specified patch size
        patches = tf.image.extract_patches(
            images=images,
            sizes=[1, self.patch_size, self.patch_size, 1],
            strides=[1, self.patch_size, self.patch_size, 1],
            rates=[1, 1, 1, 1],
            padding="VALID",
        )

        # Determine the dimensions of the extracted patches
        patch_dims = patches.shape[-1]

        # Reshape the extracted patches to have the appropriate dimensions
        patches = tf.reshape(patches, [batch_size, -1, patch_dims])

        return patches

import tensorflow as tf
from tensorflow.keras import layers

class PatchEncoder(layers.Layer):
    def __init__(self, num_patches, projection_dim):
        """
        Constructor for the PatchEncoder layer.

        Parameters:
            num_patches (int): Number of patches extracted from the
images.
            projection_dim (int): Dimensionality of the projected
embeddings for each patch.
        """
        super(PatchEncoder, self).__init__()
        self.num_patches = num_patches
```

```
            # Create a Dense layer for patch projection
            self.projection = layers.Dense(units=projection_dim)

            # Create an Embedding layer for positional embeddings
            self.position_embedding = layers.Embedding(
                input_dim=num_patches, output_dim=projection_dim
            )

    def call(self, patch):
        """
        Method to encode the input patches.

        Parameters:
            patch (tf.Tensor): A tensor containing the patches to be
encoded.

        Returns:
            tf.Tensor: A tensor containing the encoded patches.
        """
        # Create a tensor containing the positions of each patch
        positions = tf.range(start=0, limit=self.num_patches, delta=1)

        # Project the input patch using the Dense layer
        projected_patch = self.projection(patch)

        # Get the positional embeddings corresponding to each patch
position
        position_embeddings = self.position_embedding(positions)

        # Combine the projected patch with the positional embeddings
        encoded_patch = projected_patch + position_embeddings

        return encoded_patch

def Build_Coffee_ViT():
    inputs = layers.Input(shape=input_shape)
    # Augment data.
    # Create patches.
    patches = Patches(patch_size)(inputs)
    # Encode patches.
    encoded_patches = PatchEncoder(num_patches, projection_dim)(patches)

    # Create multiple layers of the Transformer block.
    for _ in range(transformer_layers):
        # Layer normalization 1.
        x1 = layers.LayerNormalization(epsilon=1e-6)(encoded_patches)
        # Create a multi-head attention layer.
        attention_output = layers.MultiHeadAttention(
            num_heads=num_heads, key_dim=projection_dim, dropout=0.1
        ) (x1, x1)
        # Skip connection 1.
        x2 = layers.Add()([attention_output, encoded_patches])
        # Layer normalization 2.
        x3 = layers.LayerNormalization(epsilon=1e-6)(x2)
        # MLP.
        x3 = MLPLayer (x3, hidden_units=transformer_units,
dropout_rate=0.1)
```

```
        # Skip connection 2.
        encoded_patches = layers.Add()([x3, x2])


    # Create a [batch_size, projection_dim] tensor.
    representation = layers.LayerNormalization(epsilon=1e-
6)(encoded_patches)
    representation = layers.Flatten()(representation)
    representation = layers.Dropout(0.5)(representation)
    # Add MLP.
    features = MLPLayer(representation, hidden_units=mlp_head_units,
dropout_rate=0.5)
    # Classify outputs.
    logits = layers.Dense(num_classes)(features)
    # Create the Keras model.
    model = keras.Model(inputs=inputs, outputs=logits)
    return model


# Create the Coffee ViT model using the Build_Coffee_ViT() function
model = Build_Coffee_ViT()


# Create an EarlyStopping callback to monitor validation loss and stop
training if it doesn't improve for 10 epochs
callback = tf.keras.callbacks.EarlyStopping(monitor='val_loss',
patience=10)


# Compile the model with the specified loss, optimizer, and metrics
model.compile(
    loss=keras.losses.CategoricalCrossentropy(from_logits=True),  #
Categorical cross-entropy loss for multi-class classification
    optimizer='adam',  # Adam optimizer with default learning rate
    metrics=[keras.metrics.CategoricalAccuracy(name="accuracy")],  # Track
categorical accuracy during training
)


# Train the model using the training data generator 'my_gen' and validate
it using the validation data 'val_ds'
# The fit() function will train the model for 5 epochs
history = model.fit(
    gen(train_ds),  # Training data generator that yields batches of data
    steps_per_epoch=len(train_ds),  # Number of steps (batches) per epoch
for training data
    validation_data=val_ds,  # Validation data
    validation_steps=len(val_ds),  # Number of steps (batches) per epoch
for validation data
    epochs=5,  # Number of epochs to train the model
    callbacks=[callback],  # List of callbacks to be applied during
training (EarlyStopping in this case)
    verbose=1,  # Set to 1 to see the progress during training
)
```

To demonstrate the model's predictions, we visualize some sample images along with the model's classification results. This allows us to gain a better understanding of the model's strengths and weaknesses and identify any misclassifications that might occur (see Figure 7.1).

In our case study on coffee leaf disease detection using ViT, we go beyond just achieving high accuracy and delve into the interpretability and visualization

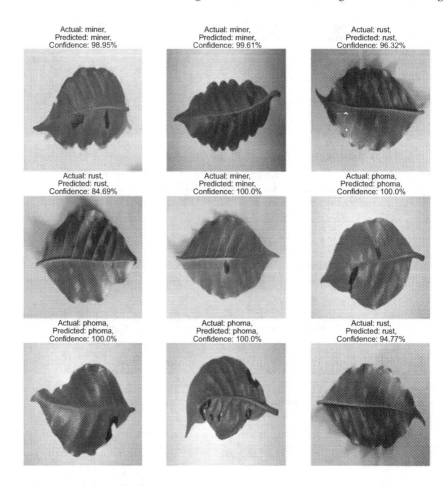

FIGURE 7.1   Visualization of Model Predictions.

of the model's performance. Visualization plays a crucial role in understanding how the ML model is making decisions and provides valuable insights into its behavior.

The receiver operating characteristic (ROC) curve and its corresponding area under the curve (AUC) provide a comprehensive evaluation of the model's performance across different classification thresholds. The AUC value summarizes the ROC curve's performance in a single metric, where higher values (closer to 1) indicate better model performance. In our case study, the ROC-AUC curve allows us to quantify the model's ability to distinguish between healthy and infected coffee leaves and helps in determining the optimal classification threshold for real-world deployment (see Figure 7.2).

The confusion matrix is a powerful visualization tool that provides a detailed breakdown of the model's predictions. It tabulates the true positive (TP), true negative (TN), false positive (FP), and false negative (FN) classifications. By

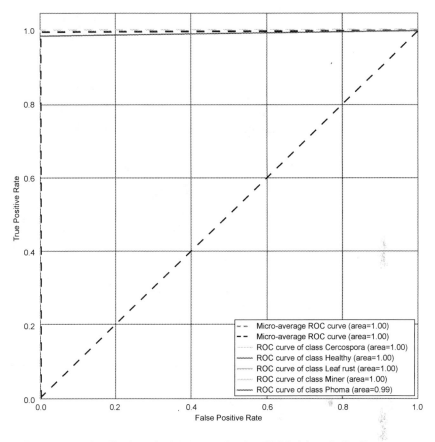

FIGURE 7.2   Visualization of ROC Curves for the ViT Model on Coffee Data.

visually representing these values in a matrix, we gain insights into how well the model is correctly identifying true positives and negatives and where it might be misclassifying instances. The confusion matrix (Figure 7.3) aids in understanding the strengths and weaknesses of ViT, allowing us to identify specific classes that may require further attention or data imbalance issues that need to be addressed.

T-SNE is a dimensionality reduction technique that allows us to visualize high-dimensional data in a lower-dimensional space. In our case, we can use T-SNE to visualize the representations learned by the ViT model in a 2D or 3D space. By projecting the features extracted from the coffee leaf images onto a lower-dimensional plane, we can observe if the model is able to effectively separate healthy and infected leaves or if there is any clustering pattern that might reveal valuable information about the data distribution. T-SNE enables us to validate if the ViT model has learned meaningful representations and if it can discern between different classes with distinct patterns (see Figure 7.4).

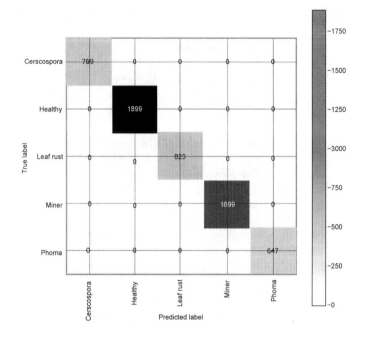

FIGURE 7.3   Visualization of Confusion Matrix for the ViT Model on Coffee Data.

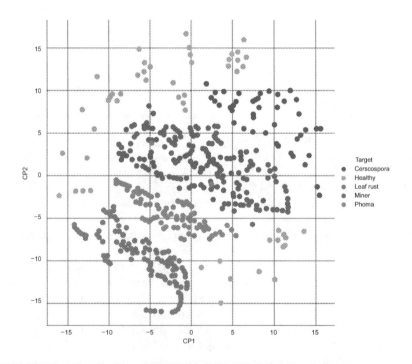

FIGURE 7.4   Visualization of T-SNE plot for the ViT Model on Coffee Data.

REFERENCES

Adami, D., Ojo, M. O., & Giordano, S. (2021). Design, development and evaluation of an intelligent animal repelling system for crop protection based on embedded edge-AI. *IEEE Access, 9*, 132125–132139. https://doi.org/10.1109/ACCESS.2021.3114503

Ai, Y., Sun, C., Tie, J., & Cai, X. (2020). Research on recognition model of crop diseases and insect pests based on deep learning in harsh environments. *IEEE Access, 8*, 171686–171693. https://doi.org/10.1109/ACCESS.2020.3025325

Chergui, N., & Kechadi, M. T. (2022). Data analytics for crop management: A big data view. *Journal of Big Data, 9*(1), 1–37. https://doi.org/10.1186/S40537-022-00668-2

Dharani, M. K., Thamilselvan, R., Natesan, P., Kalaivaani, P. C. D., & Santhoshkumar, S. (2021). Review on crop prediction using deep learning techniques. *Journal of Physics: Conference Series, 1767*(1), 012026. https://doi.org/10.1088/1742-6596/1767/1/012026

Ennouri, K., Smaoui, S., Gharbi, Y., Cheffi, M., Ben Braiek, O., Ennouri, M., & Triki, M. A. (2021). Usage of artificial intelligence and remote sensing as efficient devices to increase agricultural system yields. *Journal of Food Quality, 2021*. https://doi.org/10.1155/2021/6242288

Gautron, R., Maillard, O. A., Preux, P., Corbeels, M., & Sabbadin, R. (2022). Reinforcement learning for crop management support: Review, prospects and challenges. *Computers and Electronics in Agriculture, 200*, 107182. https://doi.org/10.1016/J.COMPAG.2022.107182

Huang, C. H., Chen, B. W., Lin, Y. J., & Zheng, J. X. (2022). Smart crop growth monitoring based on system adaptivity and edge AI. *IEEE Access, 10*, 64114–64125. https://doi.org/10.1109/ACCESS.2022.3183277

Kaur, N., & Gupta, V. (2022). Climate dependent crop management through data modeling. *Lecture Notes on Data Engineering and Communications Technologies, 91*, 739–767. https://doi.org/10.1007/978-981-16-6285-0_59/FIGURES/5

Khan, M. H. U., Wang, S., Wang, J., Ahmar, S., Saeed, S., Khan, S. U., Xu, X., Chen, H., Bhat, J. A., & Feng, X. (2022). Applications of artificial intelligence in climate-resilient smart-crop breeding. *International Journal of Molecular Sciences, 23*(19), 11156. https://doi.org/10.3390/IJMS231911156

Mazzia, V., Khaliq, A., Salvetti, F., & Chiaberge, M. (2020). Real-time apple detection system using embedded systems with hardware accelerators: An edge AI application. *IEEE Access, 8*, 9102–9114. https://doi.org/10.1109/ACCESS.2020.2964608

Navinkumar, T. M., Kumar, R. R., & Gokila, P. V. (2021). Application of artificial intelligence techniques in irrigation and crop health management for crop yield enhancement. *Materials Today: Proceedings, 45*, 2248–2253. https://doi.org/10.1016/J.MATPR.2020.10.227

Ong, P., Teo, K. S., & Sia, C. K. (2023). UAV-based weed detection in Chinese cabbage using deep learning. *Smart Agricultural Technology, 4*, 100181. https://doi.org/10.1016/J.ATECH.2023.100181

Partel, V., Charan Kakarla, S., & Ampatzidis, Y. (2019). Development and evaluation of a low-cost and smart technology for precision weed management utilizing artificial intelligence. *Computers and Electronics in Agriculture, 157*, 339–350. https://doi.org/10.1016/J.COMPAG.2018.12.048

Rahman, S. A. Z., Mitra, K. C., & Islam, S. M. M. (2019). Soil classification using machine learning methods and crop suggestion based on soil series. In *2018 21st International Conference of Computer and Information Technology, ICCIT 2018*. https://doi.org/10.1109/ICCITECHN.2018.8631943

Schoning, J., & Richter, M. L. (2021). AI-based crop rotation for sustainable agriculture worldwide. In *2021 11th IEEE Global Humanitarian Technology Conference, GHTC 2021* (pp. 142–146). https://doi.org/10.1109/GHTC53159.2021.9612460

Shankar, P., Werner, N., Selinger, S., & Janssen, O. (2020). Artificial intelligence driven crop protection optimization for sustainable agriculture. In *2020 IEEE/ITU International*

Conference on Artificial Intelligence for Good, AI4G 2020 (pp. 1–6). https://doi. org/10.1109/AI4G50087.2020.9311082

Sleem, A. (2022). Empowering smart farming with machine intelligence: An approach for plant leaf disease recognition. *Sustainable Machine Intelligence Journal, 1*(1), 1–11. https://doi.org/10.61185/SMIJ.2022.1013

Vakula Rani, J., Aishwarya, J., & Hamsini, K. (2022). *Crop Management Using Machine Learning* (pp. 575–584). https://doi.org/10.1007/978-981-16-2543-5_49

Vitali, G., Francia, M., Golfarelli, M., & Canavari, M. (2021). Crop management with the IoT: An interdisciplinary survey. *Agronomy, 11*(1), 181. https://doi.org/10.3390/ AGRONOMY11010181

8 Automated Harvesting and Robotics in Agriculture

8.1 INTRODUCTION

Automated harvesting represents a paradigm shift in the agriculture industry, wherein traditional manual harvesting methods are replaced or complemented by advanced technologies and robotics. It involves the integration of cutting-edge automation, machine learning (ML) algorithms, and robotics systems into the harvesting process, aiming to improve efficiency, precision, and sustainability. The significance of automated harvesting lies in its potential to address critical challenges faced by modern agriculture, such as labor shortages, rising production demands, and environmental concerns. By optimizing the harvesting process, farmers can reduce reliance on human labor, increase crop yields, minimize wastage, and promote resource-efficient practices. Moreover, automated harvesting plays a vital role in the broader concept of smart farming, wherein data-driven decision-making and precision agriculture techniques converge to create a more productive and environmentally conscious agricultural ecosystem (Thangavel and Murthi, 2017).

The roots of automated harvesting can be traced back to the early developments in agricultural machinery during the Industrial Revolution. Mechanical reapers and threshers were some of the first innovations that aimed to streamline labor-intensive harvesting tasks. Over the years, advancements in electronics, sensors, and computing have propelled the evolution of agricultural automation. In recent decades, the emergence of sophisticated robotics, GPS technology, and artificial intelligence (AI) has accelerated the adoption of automated harvesting systems. Today, modern farms deploy an array of automated machinery, such as robotic pickers, autonomous tractors, and drones, to revolutionize traditional farming practices. This progression from basic mechanization to autonomous systems has not only transformed the efficiency of harvest but has also opened up new possibilities for sustainable and environmentally friendly agriculture.

Despite the numerous advantages, the implementation of automated harvesting in agriculture is not without challenges. High initial costs, especially for small-scale farmers, pose a barrier to entry for adopting these technologies. Integration with existing farming practices and infrastructure can also be complex, requiring specialized training and technical expertise. Additionally, ensuring robust and reliable performance under diverse environmental conditions remains a concern. However, the motivation to overcome these challenges is strong, driven by the pressing need to increase food production to meet the demands of a growing global population. Moreover, the environmental benefits of precision agriculture and reduced chemical usage are compelling incentives to explore and invest in automated harvesting. As agricultural automation continues to evolve, it is imperative to strike a balance between technological advancements and inclusive adoption, ensuring that all farmers can harness the potential of these innovations to build a sustainable and resilient agricultural future (Horng et al., 2020).

Climate change is linked to agriculture in two ways: it is caused by agricultural emissions and, of course, it impacts farming. Consumerism, population expansion, and increased purchasing power of some segments of the global population are threatening the food production of many nations at an alarming rate. We have seen the catastrophic devastation that climate change has brought to agriculture in recent years; the impact on farms has been so severe that worldwide prices for many products have skyrocketed, pushing them out of reach for many. A transition from the traditional, processed food system to sustainable farming can be quite promising, especially in the long run, for a planet bedeviled by uncertainties such as droughts, floods, and erratic weather conditions—thanks to ever-rising temperatures—and facing challenges when it comes to energy demand. We can no longer deny the truth that industrial agriculture has dramatically increased groundwater depletion and soil health deterioration.

According to the Intergovernmental Panel on Climate Change (IPCC), the world's leading climate change assessment organization, agricultural activities account for around one-fifth of greenhouse gas (GHG) emissions caused by human activity. The quantity of CO_2 in the earth's atmosphere is now over 412 parts per million (ppm), and it is steadily increasing. This is a 47% increase since the beginning of the industrial period, when concentrations were about 280 ppm, and an 11% increase since 2000, when they were 370 ppm. Agricultural operations such as rice growing, cattle raising, and biomass burning are responsible for 22–46% of global methane emissions. Paddy fields are the major contributors to methane emissions, responsible for 15–20% of total world emissions caused by human activity. These figures highlight the critical importance of creating climate-conscious alternatives and substitutes for current farming practices that contribute to GHG emissions, to ensure that economic activity does not occur at the cost of the environment and eventually account for mankind's demise. This ensures that a Climate-Smart Sustainable Agriculture program is implemented, which seeks to safeguard farmers from altered precipitation events by distributing a relevant package of practices focusing on reduced water use (more crop per drop), yield improvement, and climate-resilient varieties, as well as the adoption of appropriate mechanization.

The agricultural business has gone a long way in the previous several decades, from traditional farming practices to contemporary agriculture technologies. The issues of rural agriculture have finally been overcome by technology, which is continually looking for new methods to improve productivity. The purpose of smart farming technology is to help farmers cultivate high-yield crops to feed the world's rising population. AI, robots, and IoT have resulted in the creation of several extraordinary gadgets that have been shown to be enormously beneficial for farmers in addressing some fundamental challenges in the agricultural process. For example, the introduction of robots in harvesting tools has made agricultural harvesting considerably easier and more time-efficient for farmers. The agricultural business has seen various advances, including the introduction of extremely advanced smart harvesting tools on the market. Let us first examine how smart harvesting works (Astanakulov et al., 2021).

8.2   AUTOMATED HARVESTING

Harvesting robots and autonomous harvesters are used in smart harvesting. Sensors and imaging systems used by smart harvesting robots and autonomous harvesters include single-shot multibox detectors, ultrasonic sensors, compass sensors, 3D sensors, global navigation satellite systems (GNSS), radio-frequency identification (RFID), depth camera, and red, green, blue (RGB) camera. Moreover, smart harvesters employ a number of on-premises and cloud-based apps. All of these components help farmers manage and enhance their fieldwork (Horng et al., 2020; Astanakulov et al., 2021). A smart harvesting system also allows for the collection of real-time data from any location. Real-time data is useful for keeping track of all in-field machinery's operating hours and reducing mechanical damage during shaking activities. Smart harvesting equipment also helps with day-to-day monitoring and racking, from sweeping to shaking and plucking. The smart harvest industry is predicted to increase rapidly due to several benefits. According to a BIS Research analysis, the worldwide smart harvest market was valued at $8.38 billion in 2021, with a CAGR of 12.50% estimated to reach $16.85 billion by 2027 (Muthusinghe et al., 2019).

Crop harvesting is a physically taxing, repetitive, and time-consuming job. It needs a certain level of knowledge as well as a delicate touch. Agricultural autonomous robots gather crops with a range of robotic elements that allow them to operate in harsh temperatures and adverse situations. Using advanced computer vision and ML algorithms, these robots tackle the sensitive nature of crops while rejecting underripe or unhealthy products. A fruit harvesting robot, for example, can detect when some fruit is ripe, allowing it to choose each fruit and vegetable without hurting or discarding any. Many startups, as well as major agricultural organizations, are investing in fruit harvesting robots.

Beyond automated harvesting robots, technological behemoths like Microsoft are building a comprehensive set of digital tools based on AI, ML, and cloud computing. Microsoft Research is open sourcing its agricultural data and connectivity technologies to enhance farmers' yields while cutting costs and aiding the agriculture industry in taking full responsibility for its role in climate change.

The Project FarmVibes is an innovative endeavor within the field of precision agriculture, which places a strong emphasis on the open sharing of agricultural data and the utilization of networking technology. The objective of this initiative is multifarious, encompassing the improvement of farmers' crop yields, the reduction of operational expenses, and the promotion of proactive steps within the agriculture industry to mitigate its impact on climate change. The primary approach entails using cutting-edge technologies and knowledge acquired from diverse sources to establish a comprehensive and user-friendly platform with the aim of supporting farmers.

The central focus of Project FarmVibes revolves around FarmVibes.AI, an advanced technological platform that aims to leverage artificial intelligence and data analytics in order to facilitate sustainable and accurate agricultural methods. The platform effectively incorporates the latest advancements in precision agriculture by integrating data from various sources and establishing collaborations. Microsoft, a prominent participant in this endeavor, provides its specialized knowledge in data collection and synchronization, engaging in close collaboration with significant agricultural entities such as Land O'Lakes and Bayer.

FarmVibes.AI is made up of two major components. The first consists of data intake and post routines that aid in collecting data for data fusion models designed specifically for agriculture. It also provides examples of model training notebooks that make it straightforward to change existing models and set up data preprocessing. The second component is a computational engine that permits data intake as well as altering existing workflows and generating new ones using the updated model. With this project, the company hopes to enable researchers, practitioners, and data scientists to develop low-cost digital tools to assist farmers in estimating emissions from their operations, preparing for climate change by forecasting weather variations, and selecting the best management strategies for increasing soil health (Wang et al., 2022).

8.3   MACHINE LEARNING-BASED AUTOMATED HARVESTING

ML algorithms have emerged as a transformative force in the realm of automated harvesting, revolutionizing traditional agricultural practices and paving the way for more efficient and sustainable crop production. At its core, ML involves the development of computer algorithms that can learn from data and make informed decisions without explicit programming. In the context of automated harvesting, ML techniques are harnessed to imbue agricultural robots and machinery with the ability to perceive, analyze, and adapt to the dynamic conditions of the farm. By leveraging vast amounts of data collected from sensors, drones, and other IoT devices, ML algorithms can accurately identify crops, assess their maturity, predict optimal harvest timing, and make real-time decisions for precise and gentle harvesting. This data-driven approach not only enhances the speed and accuracy of the harvesting process but also optimizes resource allocation, minimizes wastage, and improves overall farm productivity. As ML continues to advance, its integration with automated harvesting systems holds the promise of addressing critical challenges in modern agriculture and contributing to sustainable and resilient food production systems (Xiong et al., 2020).

Application of ML algorithms in automated harvesting tasks is multifaceted, encompassing various aspects of agricultural automation. One key area where ML shines is crop detection and recognition. Through computer vision techniques and deep learning models like convolutional neural networks (CNNs), agricultural robots can discern different crops amidst diverse backgrounds, enabling precise and selective harvesting. ML-based crop recognition also facilitates the monitoring of crop health, allowing for targeted interventions such as disease detection and early pest management. Furthermore, ML plays a vital role in harvest timing and yield prediction. By analyzing historical data on crop development and combining it with real-time environmental variables like weather patterns and soil conditions, ML models can forecast the optimal moment for harvesting, maximizing crop yield and quality.

The integration of ML with robotic path planning and navigation further empowers agricultural robots to maneuver autonomously, avoiding obstacles and minimizing crop damage. Through reinforcement learning algorithms, robots can learn from their experiences to optimize harvesting trajectories and reduce energy consumption. Additionally, ML algorithms contribute to postharvest activities, such as sorting and quality control. By classifying harvested produce based on various attributes like size, color, and ripeness, ML-driven systems ensure that only the highest-quality crops reach the market, reducing food waste and enhancing economic viability. As ML technologies evolve and become more accessible, their potential in automated harvesting tasks continues to expand, promising a future where intelligent agricultural robots work hand-in-hand with farmers to create sustainable and resilient food production systems (Bac et al., 2014).

8.3.1 Machine Learning-Based Crop Recognition

The implementation of ML in automated harvesting tasks begins with leveraging computer vision techniques to identify and recognize crops in the field. Computer vision algorithms are designed to process visual data from images or videos and extract meaningful information. In the context of automated harvesting, these algorithms play a crucial role in enabling agricultural robots to perceive and understand their surroundings. By analyzing images captured by cameras mounted on robots or drones, ML-powered systems can distinguish between different types of crops, even in complex and cluttered environments. This capability is essential for precise and selective harvesting, as it allows the robotic systems to identify the target crops and leave the rest undisturbed. As computer vision technology advances, ML models have become increasingly adept at handling varying lighting conditions, occlusions, and changes in vegetation, making them highly reliable tools for crop detection and recognition (Kurita et al., 2017).

In the domain of automated harvesting, image processing and feature extraction are fundamental steps in the crop detection process. Once images are captured by sensors or cameras, they undergo preprocessing to enhance their quality and remove noise. Image processing techniques, such as filtering, thresholding, and morphological operations, are applied to clean the images and ensure that only relevant features are retained for analysis. Following preprocessing, features specific to crops are extracted from the images. These features may include color, shape, texture, and spatial information, which provide distinctive characteristics for different crop types. By extracting relevant features from the images, ML algorithms can build effective models that can accurately distinguish between various crops, enabling precise identification and subsequent decision-making during harvesting operations.

Two powerful classes of ML models that have shown exceptional performance in crop recognition are convolutional neural networks (CNNs) and Vision Transformers (ViTs). CNNs are deep learning models specifically designed to process visual data, making them particularly suitable for image-based tasks such as crop recognition. By using multiple layers of convolution and pooling, CNNs can automatically learn hierarchical features from images, effectively capturing complex patterns and structures that aid in accurate crop classification. On the other hand, ViTs, a relatively newer architecture, have demonstrated remarkable success in various computer vision tasks. ViTs process images by dividing them into patches and treating the task as a sequence-to-sequence problem, allowing for efficient and scalable image recognition. Both CNNs and ViTs have shown exceptional performance in large-scale crop recognition applications, showcasing the potential of ML in advancing automated harvesting practices and contributing to more sustainable and efficient agriculture. As research and development in ML continue to progress, these models are expected to become even more effective in crop detection, ultimately leading to smarter and more proficient harvesting systems (Kang et al., 2020).

8.3.2 HARVEST TIMING AND YIELD PREDICTION

ML models have proven to be invaluable tools for predicting the optimal harvest timing based on crop maturity. The prediction of the ideal harvesting window is critical for ensuring maximum crop yield and quality. ML algorithms can leverage a wide range of data inputs, including historical climate data, soil conditions, crop development stages, and phenotypic characteristics. By analyzing these variables, ML models can identify patterns and correlations that are beyond human perception. For instance, ML algorithms can learn to detect subtle indicators of crop maturity that might not be apparent to the naked eye. These models can be trained on large datasets, encompassing various crops and geographical regions, to improve their accuracy and generalization. As a result, farmers can make informed decisions about the optimal timing for harvesting, ensuring that crops are collected at their peak condition and minimizing potential yield losses due to overripening or premature harvesting.

To estimate crop yield accurately, ML-based systems rely on both historical data and real-time monitoring. Historical data, such as past yield records, weather patterns, and agronomic practices, provide valuable insights into yield trends and variations over time. This data can be used to train ML models, enabling them to learn from past patterns and make informed predictions about future yields. Real-time monitoring, on the other hand, involves the use of remote sensing technologies, IoT devices, and drones to continuously collect data during the growing season. These real-time data streams allow ML models to adapt dynamically to changing environmental conditions, crop health, and resource availability. By integrating historical data and real-time monitoring, ML-driven yield estimation systems become more robust and accurate, as they can account for unforeseen events and seasonal variations that may impact the final crop yield.

While ML-based yield prediction holds great promise for enhancing agricultural productivity, several factors influence the accuracy of these predictions. One crucial factor is the availability and quality of data. ML models heavily rely on data, and inaccurate or incomplete data can lead to biased or unreliable predictions. Hence, efforts must be made to ensure that data collection methods are rigorous and standardized. Additionally, the choice of features and variables used as input to the ML models is essential. Identifying the most relevant and informative features that correlate with crop yield is critical for accurate predictions. Moreover, external factors like extreme weather events, diseases, and pest infestations can significantly affect yield outcomes and may not be entirely predictable by historical or real-time data. Therefore, while ML models can account for many factors, there may always be some degree of uncertainty in yield predictions. Continuous improvement and fine-tuning of ML models through iterative learning and adaptation are crucial to overcoming these challenges and achieving higher accuracy in yield estimation, ultimately enabling farmers to optimize their harvesting practices and ensure food security (Mohamed , 2023).

8.3.3 MACHINE LEARNING IN HARVEST POSTPROCESSING AND QUALITY CONTROL

ML has revolutionized postharvest processes in agriculture, particularly in sorting, grading, and quality control of harvested produce. Traditionally, these tasks were labor-intensive and subjective, leading to inconsistencies in quality and potential market waste. ML algorithms have brought automation and objectivity to these processes, ensuring uniformity and precision. By analyzing various attributes of the harvested crops, such as size, color, shape, and defects, ML models can accurately sort and grade the produce based on predefined quality criteria. Advanced computer vision techniques, including deep learning models like CNNs, allow for the rapid and reliable assessment of large quantities of produce. This level of automation and efficiency not only reduces labor costs but also minimizes human errors and ensures that only high-quality crops reach the market, thus enhancing consumer satisfaction and brand reputation.

ML-driven quality assessment has proven to be a game-changer in determining the overall quality of harvested produce. ML models can be trained on vast datasets containing images and sensor data from different batches of produce, along with corresponding quality ratings provided by human experts. By learning from this labeled data, ML algorithms can generalize the patterns and characteristics associated with good and poor-quality produce. As a result, these models can assess the quality of new batches of produce accurately and efficiently, even without the need for human intervention. By combining data from various sources, such as visual data, spectroscopy, and other sensor readings, ML models can detect subtle defects, measure ripeness, and assess internal quality factors that may not be evident through visual inspection alone. This comprehensive quality assessment allows farmers and agribusinesses to optimize the allocation of produce to different markets or processing channels, thus maximizing revenue and minimizing waste.

One of the most significant advantages of ML-driven quality control in postharvest processes is its role in reducing food waste. By accurately assessing the quality of harvested crops, ML models can identify produce that falls below market standards or is at risk of spoilage. Such crops can be diverted to alternative uses, such as processing into value-added products or livestock feed, preventing them from going to waste. Additionally, ML algorithms can aid in predicting the shelf life of perishable produce based on its quality characteristics, allowing for better inventory management and reducing the risk of spoilage during storage and transportation. By efficiently managing the supply chain and ensuring that only high-quality produce reaches consumers, ML-driven quality control can enhance market value for farmers and agribusinesses. This, in turn, incentivizes sustainable agricultural practices, encourages better crop management, and fosters a more resilient and environmentally friendly food system. As ML technology continues to advance, the potential for further optimization of postharvest processes and quality control becomes increasingly promising, contributing to a more efficient and sustainable food supply chain (Astanakulov et al., 2021).

8.4   ROBOTICS IN AGRICULTURE

Robotic technologies have ushered in a new era of automation and efficiency in agriculture, transforming the way farming operations are carried out. In the modern agricultural landscape, a diverse array of robotics technologies is deployed, ranging from ground-based autonomous vehicles to aerial drones and underwater robots. Ground-based robots, equipped with advanced sensors and navigation systems, perform a myriad of tasks, including automated plowing, planting, weeding, and harvesting. These robots can operate in various terrains and adverse weather conditions, enabling farmers to optimize resource utilization and reduce labor-intensive efforts. Aerial drones have emerged as indispensable tools for precision agriculture, conducting aerial surveys, crop monitoring, and spraying operations. By capturing high-resolution imagery and multispectral data, drones provide valuable insights into crop health, nutrient deficiencies, and pest infestations, facilitating data-driven decision-making for farmers. Furthermore, underwater robots are employed in aquaculture to monitor water quality, inspect underwater structures, and assist in fish farming practices. As the capabilities of robotics continue to evolve, these technologies are becoming increasingly accessible and affordable, offering substantial benefits to farmers in terms of increased productivity, sustainable practices, and higher yield.

The integration of robotics technologies in agriculture brings forth a multitude of advantages that address key challenges faced by the farming industry. One of the primary benefits is enhanced efficiency and productivity. With autonomous and precise operations, robotics minimize human errors and reduce time-consuming manual labor, resulting in optimized farming processes. Moreover, robotics technologies enable data-driven decision-making, empowering farmers to make informed choices regarding crop management, resource allocation, and pest control. This data-centric approach fosters precision agriculture, where farmers can tailor treatments and interventions to specific areas of their fields, minimizing chemical usage and environmental impact. Robotics also play a pivotal role in reducing the dependency on labor, particularly in regions facing workforce shortages or high labor costs. As robotic systems become more sophisticated and user-friendly, even small-scale farmers can leverage these technologies to improve their agricultural practices. Additionally, robotics contributes to sustainable farming by minimizing soil compaction, preventing overfertilization, and conserving water resources through precise irrigation techniques. By promoting resource efficiency and reducing wastage, robotics technologies facilitate the transition toward more environmentally conscious and resilient farming practices, ensuring a greener future for agriculture (Horng et al., 2020).

8.4.1 Types of Agricultural Robots

Agricultural robots have emerged in various forms, catering to a multitude of tasks and challenges in modern farming practices. These versatile machines exist in many types, ranging from ground-based autonomous vehicles that handle planting, weeding, and harvesting, to aerial drones conducting aerial surveys, crop monitoring, and spraying operations from above. Moreover, underwater robots play a crucial role in aquaculture by monitoring water quality and assisting in fish farming practices. Each type of agricultural robot is equipped with specialized sensors, navigation systems, and intelligent algorithms tailored to the specific tasks they perform. With advancements in technology and the continuous development of robotics, the diversity and capabilities of agricultural robots continue to expand, revolutionizing the agricultural landscape and providing farmers with valuable tools to enhance efficiency, sustainability, and overall productivity. A taxonomy for classifying different types of agricultural robots (Figure 8.1) can be organized based on their design, mobility, and primary tasks (Muthusinghe et al., 2019; Wang et al., 2022; Xiong et al., 2020).

8.4.1.1 Design

The design category of taxonomy classifies agricultural robots based on their physical structure and form factor.

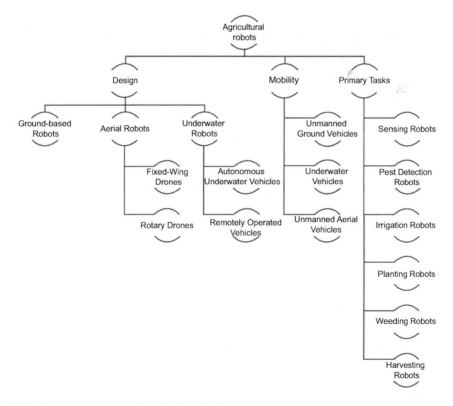

FIGURE 8.1 Taxonomy of Agricultural Robots.

8.4.1.1.1 Ground-Based Robots

Tracked robots: Tracked robots in agriculture have emerged as versatile and resilient workhorses, navigating challenging terrains with ease and precision. Their distinctive design, featuring continuous tracks akin to tank treads, grants them exceptional stability and traction, making them suitable for traversing rough and uneven surfaces commonly found in agricultural fields. They excel in tasks such as plowing, planting, and harvesting, where their robust mobility allows them to maintain steady progress, even in adverse weather conditions. These robots are equipped with advanced sensors and intelligent navigation systems, enabling them to autonomously adapt to changing environments and avoid obstacles efficiently. The versatility and reliability of tracked robots empower farmers to optimize resource utilization, reduce soil compaction, and improve overall farming efficiency. Through offering a practical solution for various agricultural applications, tracked robots continue to play a pivotal role in modernizing farming practices and promoting sustainable agriculture (Horng et al., 2020).

Wheeled robots: Wheeled robots have become integral components of the agricultural landscape, revolutionizing how farmers manage their crops and resources. These robots employ wheel-based locomotion, enabling them to navigate smoothly across flat terrains, making them well suited for large-scale farming operations. Equipped with precision control systems and advanced technologies, wheeled robots conduct a diverse range of tasks, including planting, weeding, and data collection. Their efficient mobility allows them to cover extensive areas effectively, reducing operational time and labor costs. Furthermore, wheeled robots often come in various sizes and configurations, making them accessible and adaptable to different farm sizes and crop types. With the integration of AI and ML, wheeled robots are becoming increasingly autonomous and capable of real-time decision-making, providing farmers with valuable insights into crop health, growth patterns, and resource management. As they continue to evolve, wheeled robots are instrumental in promoting precision agriculture and empowering farmers with data-driven strategies for sustainable and productive farming practices.

Legged robots: Legged robots have ushered in a new era of adaptability and dexterity in agriculture, offering unique solutions for navigating challenging terrains and precise interactions with crops. Inspired by the versatility of biological organisms, legged robots emulate the locomotion of animals to maneuver through uneven, sloped, or densely planted fields with remarkable agility. With their ability to traverse rough terrain, legged robots are ideal for tasks like monitoring orchards, inspecting crops, and performing delicate actions such as picking fruits. These robots excel in environments where wheeled or tracked vehicles face limitations, allowing farmers to optimize crop management and improve yield. Advanced sensor technologies and feedback control systems enable legged robots to maintain stability and avoid collisions, enhancing their safety and effectiveness on the farm. Although still at the forefront of agricultural robotics, legged robots hold immense promise in transforming agriculture by unlocking new possibilities for precision farming, environmental monitoring, and sustainable practices.

Swarm robots: Swarm robots represent a pioneering approach to agricultural automation, leveraging the power of collective intelligence and distributed systems to optimize farming operations. These robots, inspired by the behavior of social insect colonies, operate collaboratively as a swarm, coordinating their actions through communication and decentralized decision-making. Swarm robots are typically small, agile, and cost-effective, allowing them to work in unison across large areas of farmland. Their collaborative nature enables them to accomplish tasks more efficiently and rapidly than traditional single-unit robots. Swarm robots excel in precision tasks such as planting seeds, pollination, and pest control, where their collective efforts lead to more even coverage and targeted interventions. Furthermore, swarm robots can share information in real-time, enhancing their ability to respond to changing conditions and adapt their strategies accordingly. As agricultural robotics advances, swarm robots hold tremendous potential in revolutionizing farming practices, reducing resource waste, and maximizing crop yield while minimizing the environmental impact.

8.4.1.1.2   Aerial Robots (Drones)

Fixed-wing drones: Fixed-wing drones have become indispensable tools in modern agriculture, offering unparalleled capabilities for aerial surveys, crop monitoring, and precision agriculture. Shaped like traditional aircrafts, these drones are designed for efficient forward flight, covering large areas of farmland with speed and endurance. Equipped with high-resolution cameras and multispectral sensors, fixed-wing drones capture valuable data from above, providing farmers with detailed information on crop health, soil moisture, and field conditions. The long flight endurance of fixed-wing drones allows for extended missions, enabling them to survey vast agricultural landscapes in a single flight. These drones play a critical role in supporting data-driven decision-making, allowing farmers to identify crop stress, detect pest infestations, and optimize irrigation strategies. Additionally, fixed-wing drones aid in generating precise 3D maps and digital elevation models, assisting in land planning and yield prediction. Their ability to swiftly cover large areas, combined with the versatility of collected data, makes fixed-wing drones valuable assets in promoting sustainable farming practices, resource-efficient crop management, and informed decision-making for improved agricultural productivity.

   Rotary drones: Rotary drones, also known as quadcopters or multirotor drones, have revolutionized precision agriculture by providing close-range aerial capabilities and versatility for a wide range of farming tasks. Characterized by multiple rotating propellers, these drones offer vertical takeoff and landing, making them well suited for maneuvering in confined spaces and conducting precise inspections at low altitudes. Rotary drones are equipped with high-resolution cameras, sensors, and even spraying systems, allowing them to perform tasks such as crop monitoring, pest scouting, and targeted application of inputs. Their agility and ease of use enable farmers to quickly deploy them for real-time assessments and quick interventions, minimizing crop damage and enhancing overall farm efficiency. Rotary drones also play a pivotal role in detecting early signs of crop stress, facilitating timely responses to potential issues before they escalate. With advancements in technology, rotary drones are becoming increasingly autonomous, with features such as obstacle detection, intelligent flight planning, and automated data collection. As cost-effective and accessible tools, rotary drones have democratized precision agriculture, empowering farmers of all scales to benefit from data-driven insights, sustainable practices, and optimized crop management (Mohamed, 2023).

8.4.1.1.3   Underwater Robots

Autonomous underwater vehicles (AUVs): AUVs have revolutionized the field of underwater exploration and data collection in agriculture, offering unparalleled capabilities for monitoring aquatic environments and optimizing aquaculture practices. Shaped like streamlined submarines, AUVs operate independently, navigating through water without the need for direct human control. These robots are equipped with a range of sensors, including sonar, cameras, and water quality detectors, enabling them to collect valuable data on marine ecosystems, underwater structures, and aquaculture facilities. AUVs play a critical role in monitoring water quality parameters, detecting changes in temperature, salinity, and nutrient levels, which are essential for maintaining healthy aquatic environments. In aquaculture, AUVs aid in fish farm management by inspecting underwater cages, monitoring fish behavior, and detecting any signs of stress or disease outbreaks. Their ability to operate autonomously and cover large areas underwater enhances the efficiency of data collection and reduces the need for human divers, making underwater exploration and aquaculture management more cost-effective and environmentally sustainable. As the AUV technology continues to advance, their potential to support aquatic research and promote responsible aquaculture practices becomes increasingly significant.

Remotely operated vehicles (ROVs): ROVs have emerged as indispensable tools for underwater inspection and intervention in agriculture, providing valuable support for various marine-related tasks. ROVs are tethered underwater robots that are remotely controlled by human operators on the surface, enabling precise maneuvering and real-time supervision of underwater operations. These versatile robots are equipped with advanced cameras, lights, and manipulator arms, allowing them to conduct detailed inspections, perform maintenance tasks, and retrieve samples from underwater environments. In aquaculture, ROVs play a crucial role in inspecting submerged infrastructure, such as fish cages and nets, to identify damages or biofouling. They can also assist in feeding fish and performing other routine tasks, reducing the need for human divers and promoting safer practices in underwater environments. Moreover, ROVs are valuable tools for scientific research, enabling marine biologists to study marine life, coral reefs, and underwater habitats in intricate detail. With their precise control and human-operated supervision, ROVs offer a high degree of flexibility and accuracy, making them indispensable assets for ensuring the health and sustainability of marine ecosystems and aquaculture facilities. As the technology advances, ROVs continue to improve and diversify their applications, contributing to safer and more efficient underwater interventions and exploration.

8.4.1.2   Mobility

The mobility category of the taxonomy highlights the level of autonomy and control that agricultural robots possess.

8.4.1.2.1   Unmanned Ground Vehicles

Autonomous unmanned ground vehicles (UGVs): Autonomous UGVs have revolutionized the agricultural landscape by providing a new level of automation and efficiency in farming operations. These robots operate without direct human intervention, relying on advanced sensors, AI, and onboard navigation systems to navigate through fields and perform designated tasks. Equipped with cameras, LiDAR, GPS, and other sensors, autonomous UGVs can accurately map and survey farmland, identify crop health, and monitor environmental conditions. By leveraging ML algorithms, they can learn from data and adapt their behavior to changing field conditions. Autonomous UGVs excel in various tasks, such as precision planting, targeted spraying, and soil sampling. Their ability to operate autonomously leads to reduced labor requirements and more precise and consistent actions, optimizing resource usage and minimizing waste. Furthermore, autonomous UGVs operate around the clock, allowing farmers to maximize productivity and make data-driven decisions for improved crop management. As the technology continues to advance, the integration of autonomous UGVs in agriculture holds the promise of increased agricultural productivity, sustainability, and food security.

Teleoperated UGVs: Teleoperated UGVs are a crucial component of modern agricultural robotics, providing human operators with remote control over agricultural tasks and operations. These robots are equipped with a wide range of sensors and actuators, and their movements are controlled by human operators from a distance, often through a dedicated control station. Teleoperated UGVs offer a high degree of precision and flexibility, making them ideal for delicate tasks that require human intuition and real-time decision-making. They can be used for activities like fruit harvesting, selective pruning, or handling fragile crops. The teleoperation aspect allows for human supervision, enabling operators to respond quickly to unexpected situations and ensuring safety during operations. Teleoperated UGVs work in tandem with autonomous systems, providing a hybrid approach that combines the efficiency of automation with the adaptability of human control. This human–robot collaboration not only improves agricultural productivity but also enhances the potential for remote farming, allowing farmers to manage multiple tasks across large areas without the need for physical presence. As teleoperation technology continues to evolve, these robots are expected to play an increasingly integral role in modernizing agriculture, addressing labor challenges, and fostering sustainable and resource-efficient farming practices.

8.4.1.2.2   Unmanned Aerial Vehicles

Fully autonomous unmanned aerial vehicles (UAVs): They have revolutionized precision agriculture by providing efficient and independent aerial data collection and analysis. These drones are equipped with advanced sensors, GPS, and intelligent flight control systems, allowing them to autonomously execute predefined missions with little to no human intervention. Fully autonomous UAVs can follow predetermined flight paths, capture high-resolution imagery, and collect multispectral data, providing valuable insights into crop health, soil conditions, and irrigation needs. With their ability to cover large areas quickly and efficiently, these drones play a critical role in monitoring crop growth, detecting pest infestations, and assessing the effectiveness of agricultural practices. The data collected by fully autonomous UAVs is processed through sophisticated algorithms and ML models, enabling precise analysis and actionable recommendations for farmers. By automating data acquisition and analysis, fully autonomous UAVs streamline decision-making processes and empower farmers with real-time information for optimal resource management, leading to improved crop yields and sustainable agricultural practices.

Semiautonomous UAVs: They offer a unique balance between human control and automation, providing flexibility and adaptability in precision agriculture. These drones are equipped with advanced navigation systems, sensors, and flight planning software, enabling them to perform specific tasks autonomously while still allowing human operators to intervene and make real-time adjustments when necessary. Semiautonomous UAVs can execute predefined flight plans, follow waypoints, and maintain stable flight patterns independently. However, human operators have the ability to take manual control during critical phases, such as takeoff, landing, or when encountering unforeseen obstacles. This level of human supervision ensures safety, especially in complex or unpredictable environments. Semiautonomous UAVs excel in situations that require human judgment and intervention, such as close-range inspection, precise spraying, or monitoring sensitive areas. Their versatility makes them valuable tools in agriculture, enabling farmers to tailor their missions and adjust flight parameters to specific field conditions and requirements. With the integration of the advantages of automation with human expertise, semiautonomous UAVs empower farmers with enhanced situational awareness and decision-making capabilities, fostering efficient and responsive farming practices that leverage the best of both worlds.

8.4.1.3   Primary Tasks

The primary tasks category emphasizes the diverse range of functions agricultural robots fulfill in modern farming practices.

8.4.1.3.1   Harvesting Robots

Fruit harvesting robots: Fruit harvesting robots have revolutionized the agricultural industry by offering efficient and reliable solutions for the harvesting of fruits. These specialized robots are designed to delicately and accurately pick ripe fruits from trees or vines, reducing the reliance on manual labor and addressing labor shortages. Fruit harvesting robots are equipped with advanced vision systems and sensors that allow them to identify and differentiate between ripe and unripe fruits, ensuring that only the mature ones are harvested. These robots use gentle gripping mechanisms and specialized end-effectors to handle the fruits with care, minimizing bruising or damage during the harvesting process. The automation of fruit harvesting not only increases productivity and reduces labor costs but also improves the overall quality of harvested fruits, leading to higher market value and increased customer satisfaction. By streamlining the harvesting process and optimizing fruit yield, fruit harvesting robots play a significant role in enhancing the efficiency and sustainability of fruit production in modern agriculture.

Vegetable harvesting robots: Vegetable harvesting robots have emerged as transformative tools in the agriculture industry, providing effective solutions for the labor-intensive task of harvesting vegetables. These specialized robots are designed to handle a variety of vegetables, such as tomatoes, lettuce, cucumbers, and bell peppers, with precision and speed. These robots are equipped with advanced vision systems and sensors that can identify the location, size, and ripeness of the vegetables, ensuring optimal harvesting. They use specialized grippers and harvesting tools to delicately pick or cut the vegetables from the plants, minimizing damage and maintaining the produce's quality. By automating the vegetable harvesting process, these robots reduce the dependency on human labor, mitigate labor shortages, and improve the overall efficiency of vegetable production. Additionally, vegetable harvesting robots contribute to reducing food waste by ensuring that only fully ripe and mature vegetables are harvested, optimizing the use of resources and minimizing postharvest losses. With the ability to work in various weather conditions and adapt to different vegetable varieties, these robots play a critical role in modernizing vegetable farming, enhancing food supply chain logistics, and fostering sustainable agricultural practices (Horng et al., 2020).

8.4.1.3.2   Weeding Robots

Herbicide-spraying robots: Herbicide-spraying robots have emerged as essential tools in modern agriculture, providing targeted and efficient solutions for weed control. These specialized robots are equipped with precision spraying systems and advanced sensors, allowing them to identify and selectively target weeds while minimizing herbicide usage. These robots utilize ML algorithms and computer vision to distinguish between crops and weeds, ensuring that herbicides are applied only where necessary, reducing chemical drift and environmental impact. The automation of herbicide spraying minimizes human exposure to harmful chemicals and reduces the reliance on manual labor, making weed management safer and more cost-effective. Additionally, these robots can operate in various terrains and crop layouts, adapting to diverse farming environments. By providing a more controlled and precise approach to weed control, herbicide-spraying robots contribute to sustainable agriculture practices, optimizing crop yield, and minimizing the ecological footprint associated with weed management.

Mechanical weeding robots: Mechanical weeding robots have revolutionized weed control in agriculture by offering an alternative to chemical herbicides. These robots are equipped with specialized tools, such as mechanical arms, blades, or brushes, designed to remove weeds from the soil mechanically. Mechanical weeding robots can navigate between crop rows and precisely target weeds, uprooting or cutting them while leaving the crops undisturbed. Unlike herbicide spraying, mechanical weeding is a nonchemical and environmentally friendly approach to weed control, reducing chemical residues in crops and soil. These robots can be programmed to identify and handle various weed species, allowing farmers to customize their weed control strategies based on specific field conditions. Mechanical weeding robots are particularly effective in organic farming or regions where chemical herbicides are restricted, providing an eco-friendly solution to weed management. By minimizing the competition for nutrients and resources between weeds and crops, mechanical weeding robots promote healthy crop growth, optimize resource utilization, and contribute to sustainable farming practices that prioritize environmental conservation and reduced reliance on synthetic chemicals.

8.4.1.3.3 Planting Robots

Seed-planting robots: Seed-planting robots have revolutionized the process of sowing seeds in agriculture, providing accurate and efficient solutions for precision planting. These specialized robots are designed to handle a wide variety of seeds and can navigate through fields with precision, ensuring optimal seed placement and spacing. Seed-planting robots are equipped with advanced sensors and vision systems, enabling them to identify suitable planting locations and adjust their planting depth based on soil conditions. The automation of seed planting not only increases planting speed and reduces labor costs but also enhances planting accuracy, leading to improved crop uniformity and higher yields. These robots can be programmed to plant seeds in specific patterns or configurations, allowing farmers to implement various planting strategies tailored to different crop types and field layouts. By optimizing seed placement and reducing seed wastage, seed-planting robots contribute to resource-efficient farming practices and help to achieve more sustainable agricultural production. Furthermore, their ability to operate continuously and under various weather conditions allows for timely planting, ensuring that crops are sown at the optimal time for optimal growth and development. Overall, seed planting robots play a pivotal role in modernizing agriculture, improving planting efficiency, and supporting the advancement of precision farming techniques.

8.4.1.3.4 Irrigation Robots

Irrigation robots have emerged as innovative and efficient tools in precision agriculture, transforming the way water resources are managed and utilized. These specialized robots are designed to automate the process of irrigation, ensuring that crops receive the right amount of water at the right time and in the right place. Irrigation robots are equipped with sensors, such as soil moisture sensors and weather monitoring devices, which allow them to assess real-time conditions and determine the irrigation needs of the crops. Based on this data, the robots can autonomously adjust water flow, timing, and distribution, optimizing water usage and preventing over- or under-irrigation. By implementing precise irrigation techniques, these robots contribute to water conservation, minimizing water waste, and reducing the environmental impact of farming practices.

Moreover, irrigation robots can operate in different terrains and field configurations, adapting to various crop types and layouts. They can navigate through rows of crops, avoiding obstacles and minimizing soil compaction, ensuring that irrigation is evenly distributed across the entire field. The automation of irrigation not only saves labor and reduces operational costs but also enhances the efficiency of water distribution, leading to improved crop health, higher yields, and increased farm productivity.

Additionally, irrigation robots can be integrated with irrigation management systems and other smart agriculture technologies, allowing farmers to remotely monitor and control irrigation operations. With the aid of real-time data and analytics, farmers can make data-driven decisions to optimize irrigation schedules and strategies, responding to changing weather patterns and crop needs. As water scarcity and sustainable agriculture become critical concerns, irrigation robots play a pivotal role in promoting water-use efficiency, conserving natural resources, and ensuring the long-term viability of agricultural production. Their contribution to precision irrigation supports environmentally friendly farming practices and helps to create a more resilient and sustainable future for agriculture (Wang et al., 2022; Xiong et al., 2020; Bac et al., 2014).

8.4.1.3.5   Pest Detection Robots

Aerial pest detection drones: They have emerged as invaluable tools in agriculture, providing efficient and comprehensive solutions for monitoring and detecting pest infestations. These specialized drones are equipped with high-resolution cameras, multispectral sensors, and thermal imaging capabilities, allowing them to survey large agricultural areas from the air. Aerial pest detection drones can quickly identify signs of pest activity, such as crop damage, insect swarms, or disease symptoms, enabling farmers to take timely and targeted actions. By providing a bird's-eye view of the fields, these drones offer a unique perspective, allowing for the early detection of potential threats that may not be immediately visible from the ground. The ability of aerial pest detection drones to cover extensive areas rapidly helps in swift and efficient pest monitoring, reducing the risk of significant crop damage and losses. The data collected by these drones can be analyzed using advanced algorithms and ML techniques, enabling automated pest identification and quantification, further enhancing their effectiveness in detecting pest outbreaks and assessing their severity. By facilitating proactive pest management strategies, aerial pest detection drones support sustainable agriculture practices, minimizing the use of pesticides and promoting targeted interventions, which in turn contributes to reduced environmental impact and improved crop health.

  Ground-based pest detection robots: They offer a close-range and detailed approach to pest monitoring and identification, making them highly effective tools in precision agriculture. These robots are equipped with advanced sensors, cameras, and image recognition technology, allowing them to navigate through the fields and inspect crops at ground level. Ground-based pest detection robots can autonomously patrol the fields, scouting for signs of pests, diseases, or abnormalities on individual plants. They can also collect soil samples or plant tissues for further analysis to detect hidden pests or pathogens. By focusing on specific areas of interest and providing a granular view, these robots allow for precise and targeted pest monitoring, which is especially beneficial for early detection and localized intervention. The data collected by ground-based pest detection robots can be integrated into farming management systems, providing farmers with real-time updates on pest activity and trends, and facilitating prompt decision-making for pest control measures. Additionally, the use of ground-based robots minimizes human exposure to potentially harmful pesticides, enhancing safety for farmers and promoting environmentally friendly pest management practices. With their adaptability and ability to work closely with crops, ground-based pest detection robots play a critical role in promoting sustainable and integrated pest management approaches, contributing to improved crop productivity and minimizing the reliance on chemical pesticides (Kurita et al., 2017).

8.4.1.3.6   Sensing and Data Collection Robots

Soil-sampling robots: Soil-sampling robots have revolutionized soil analysis in agriculture, offering accurate and efficient solutions for gathering soil samples.

These specialized robots are equipped with precision drilling mechanisms or soil probes that can collect soil samples from specific depths and locations in the field. Soil-sampling robots are designed to navigate through various terrains and soil types, ensuring that representative samples are collected for comprehensive soil analysis. By automating the soil-sampling process, these robots reduce the labor and time required for manual soil sampling, making soil testing more accessible and cost-effective for farmers. The collected soil samples can be analyzed for nutrient levels, pH, organic matter content, and other important soil properties. By providing precise soil data, soil-sampling robots empower farmers to make informed decisions about nutrient management, fertilizer application, and irrigation strategies. Additionally, the data collected by these robots can be integrated with precision agriculture technologies, enabling farmers to create variable rate application maps and implement site-specific soil management practices. With their ability to provide valuable insights into soil health and fertility, soil-sampling robots contribute to sustainable agriculture practices, optimizing crop yields, and reducing the environmental impact associated with nutrient management.

Environmental-sensing drones: Environmental-sensing drones have become indispensable tools in agriculture, offering real-time data collection on various environmental factors crucial for crop health and farm management. These specialized drones are equipped with a wide array of sensors, such as cameras, multispectral sensors, infrared sensors, and weather monitoring devices, allowing them to measure and analyze various environmental parameters. Environmental-sensing drones can collect data on soil moisture levels, temperature, humidity, crop health, and other atmospheric conditions, providing farmers with a comprehensive view of their fields. By capturing data from above, these drones offer a unique perspective that enables early detection of potential issues, such as water stress, pest infestations, or nutrient deficiencies. The ability of environmental sensing drones to cover large areas quickly and efficiently facilitates timely decision-making for irrigation scheduling, pest control, and nutrient management. The data collected by these drones can be processed using advanced algorithms and integrated with agricultural management software, allowing farmers to create precise prescriptions for water and fertilizer application, leading to optimized resource utilization and improved crop performance. As environmental concerns and climate variability continue to impact agriculture, environmental-sensing drones play a vital role in promoting climate-smart farming practices, reducing resource waste, and enhancing the resilience of agricultural systems (Kang et al., 2020).

8.4.2 ROBOTIC PATH PLANNING AND NAVIGATION

The implementation of ML algorithms for path planning and navigation is a transformative advancement in agricultural robotics. ML techniques, such as supervised learning, unsupervised learning, and deep learning, empower agricultural robots to learn from vast amounts of data and make informed decisions about their movement in the field. By analyzing historical data on crop layouts, terrain characteristics, and environmental conditions, ML-enabled robots can devise optimal paths for planting, harvesting, and other tasks. These algorithms take into account factors like proximity to obstacles, soil types, and the location of crops, ensuring precise and efficient navigation. ML-driven path planning also enhances resource efficiency by minimizing unnecessary movement, reducing fuel consumption, and optimizing time management. As the algorithms continuously learn from new data and experiences, the robots improve their path-planning capabilities, leading to enhanced performance, adaptability, and overall productivity in agricultural operations.

Robotic path planning and navigation in agriculture involve confronting diverse challenges, such as navigating around obstacles, traversing uneven terrains, and adapting to dynamic environments. To address these complexities, robots are equipped with various sensors, such as LiDAR, cameras, and GPS, to perceive their surroundings accurately. Advanced obstacle detection algorithms enable robots to detect and avoid obstacles in real time, preventing collisions with plants, farm equipment, or other obstacles in the field. Uneven terrains are handled through sophisticated motion planning algorithms that consider the robot's kinematics and adjust its movements accordingly to maintain stability and traction. Additionally, dynamic environments, including changing weather conditions and the presence of moving objects like animals, demand real-time decision-making capabilities. Through the integration of ML techniques, robots can adapt their paths on the fly, responding to dynamic factors and ensuring safe and efficient navigation. By effectively handling obstacles, uneven terrain, and dynamic environments, agricultural robots enhance field accessibility, reduce the risk of damage, and ensure the safety of crops and equipment during their operations.

Reinforcement learning (RL) has emerged as a powerful approach for optimizing robot trajectories and minimizing collision risks in agricultural settings. RL algorithms enable robots to learn by interacting with the environment, receiving feedback in the form of rewards or penalties based on their actions. In the context of agricultural path planning and navigation, RL allows robots to explore different trajectories and learn from their outcomes, optimizing their movements to achieve specific objectives while avoiding collisions. For example, robots can learn to select paths that maximize crop coverage while minimizing the risk of damaging crops or farm infrastructure. RL also enables robots to adapt to changing field conditions, such as new obstacles or alterations in crop layouts, by continuously refining their path-planning strategies. By leveraging RL techniques, agricultural robots can navigate more intelligently, reducing the likelihood of accidents and improving the overall efficiency and safety of their operations. The ability to learn from experience and optimize trajectories in real time positions RL as a promising approach for the future of path planning and navigation in smart farming, ensuring robots become increasingly adept at adapting to evolution. In agricultural settings, multiple robots often work together to cover large areas or perform complex tasks collaboratively. Multi-agent coordination and swarm intelligence techniques play a crucial role in orchestrating the movements of multiple robots to optimize their collective performance. Through communication and coordination, the robots can efficiently divide tasks, share information, and work in harmony to achieve common goals. For instance, in tasks like crop monitoring or pest control, a swarm of robots can cover the entire field simultaneously, ensuring comprehensive data collection or targeted intervention. Swarm intelligence also allows the robots to adapt to changes in the environment or dynamic field conditions by adjusting their behavior collectively. This decentralized and self-organizing approach enhances the scalability and flexibility of agricultural robotic systems, enabling them to efficiently manage large farms and address agricultural challenges on a broader scale.

In agricultural environments, conditions can rapidly change due to factors such as weather variations, crop growth patterns, and unexpected obstacles. To address these dynamic challenges, agricultural robots need to be equipped with real-time path adaptation and dynamic replanning capabilities. Real-time path adaptation allows robots to adjust their trajectories on the fly based on live sensor data, ensuring that they navigate around newly detected obstacles or avoid areas of excessive soil compaction. Dynamic replanning involves recalculating paths in response to sudden changes in environmental conditions or the emergence of new priorities. For instance, if a robot detects signs of pest infestation in a particular area, it can dynamically adjust its path to prioritize targeted spraying in that region. Real-time path adaptation and dynamic replanning not only enhance the safety and efficiency of agricultural robots but also contribute to reducing resource wastage and improving the overall responsiveness of agricultural operations.

While agricultural robots are designed to operate autonomously, human–robot interaction remains crucial for ensuring safety, providing oversight, and addressing unexpected situations. Human operators can remotely monitor robot operations and intervene when necessary, especially in critical phases such as start-up, shutdown, or when handling delicate tasks. Additionally, human operators can define high-level objectives and constraints for the robots, allowing them to adapt their path planning and navigation strategies based on human preferences and domain-specific knowledge. Safety protocols are essential in agricultural robotic systems to prevent accidents and ensure the well-being of both humans and crops. Collaborative efforts between humans and robots create a symbiotic relationship where robots provide efficiency and automation, while humans contribute expertise and decision-making capabilities. By establishing effective human–robot interaction and safety protocols, agricultural robots can safely navigate fields, respond to unforeseen challenges, and maintain a harmonious coexistence with farm operators in the pursuit of sustainable and productive farming practices in agricultural landscapes.

8.4.3 Automated Harvesting Robotics and Robotics Control

Integrating ML techniques with robotic arms and grippers has revolutionized automated harvesting in agriculture. ML algorithms enable robots to learn from vast datasets, including images and sensor data, to identify and precisely handle ripe crops during harvesting. By training the robots on diverse crop varieties and different stages of ripeness, they can accurately determine the optimal moment for harvesting to maximize crop yield and quality. ML-driven robotic arms and grippers can adapt to the varying shapes and sizes of different crops, ensuring gentle and efficient harvesting without damaging the produce. These algorithms also consider environmental factors, such as lighting conditions and humidity, to optimize harvesting decisions. The integration of ML with robotic arms and grippers not only enhances the accuracy and productivity of automated harvesting but also reduces the reliance on manual labor, addressing labor shortages in the agricultural sector. Furthermore, ML algorithms continuously improve with more data, leading to adaptive and increasingly efficient harvesting strategies, which play a critical role in supporting sustainable agriculture practices and ensuring the consistent supply of high-quality crops to the market.

One of the significant challenges in automated harvesting is handling delicate crops without causing damage or bruising. Learning-based control strategies leverage ML algorithms to teach robots how to interact with fragile crops gently. These strategies employ RL or supervised learning approaches to learn optimal force and motion profiles for picking and handling delicate crops. Through trial and error, the robots learn to adjust their movements and gripping force, minimizing the risk of crop damage while still ensuring successful harvests. Learning-based control strategies allow robots to adapt to different crop types and conditions, enhancing their ability to handle a wide variety of delicate crops with precision and care. By reducing postharvest losses and preserving the quality of harvested crops, these strategies contribute to improved market value and reduced food waste. The use of learning-based control strategies exemplifies the potential of ML-driven robotics in addressing unique challenges in agriculture, ultimately leading to more sustainable and efficient automated harvesting processes (Šlajpah et al., 2023).

Both supervised and unsupervised learning approaches have found applications in robotics control for automated harvesting tasks. Supervised learning involves training robots with labeled datasets, where they learn from human-provided examples to perform specific harvesting actions. For instance, robots can be trained to identify ripe fruits or vegetables through labeled images and then perform picking actions accordingly. Unsupervised learning, on the other hand, allows robots to learn from unlabeled data, enabling them to discover patterns and structures in the data themselves. In the context of automated harvesting, unsupervised learning can be applied to identify crop ripeness patterns from sensor data or learn optimal trajectories for efficient harvesting without the need for explicit human guidance. The combination of supervised and unsupervised learning approaches in robotics control offers a comprehensive and versatile solution for automated harvesting tasks. As robots gather more data from their interactions with crops and the environment, unsupervised learning can help uncover underlying patterns, while supervised learning refines specific harvesting actions. The synergy of these approaches leads to more intelligent and adaptive robots, advancing the capabilities and reliability of automated harvesting robotics (Wakchaure et al., 2023).

Transfer learning is a powerful technique that enables robots to leverage knowledge gained from one task or domain and apply it to another. In the context of robotic harvesting, transfer learning allows robots to use knowledge acquired from harvesting one crop to improve efficiency and performance when harvesting a different crop. By learning common features and representations from multiple crops, robots can adapt more quickly to new harvesting tasks, reducing the need for extensive retraining from scratch. For example, a robot that has been trained to harvest apples can transfer its knowledge of grasping and handling techniques to harvest pears with minimal adjustments. This process accelerates the learning curve for new crops, leading to faster adoption of robotic harvesting across different agricultural settings. Transfer learning also optimizes resource utilization and reduces data collection efforts, making automated harvesting more accessible to farmers with diverse crop portfolios.

RL is a dynamic approach in which robots learn through interaction with their environment, receiving feedback in the form of rewards or penalties based on their actions. In the context of automated harvesting, RL enables robots to learn optimal trajectories and strategies for harvesting different crops. By experimenting with various harvesting movements and receiving feedback on the quality of harvested produce, robots can iteratively improve their harvesting strategies. RL algorithms enable robots to adapt to changes in crop conditions and variations in crop maturity, ensuring that they select the most efficient and effective harvesting trajectories. For instance, in dense crops with intertwined branches or vineyards with complex arrangements, RL can help robots identify the most advantageous paths to avoid damage and ensure thorough harvesting. With RL, robots can also learn to handle uncertainties and unpredictabilities, such as varying weather conditions, adapting their harvesting strategies accordingly. By optimizing harvesting trajectories through RL, robots become more capable of managing diverse crop layouts and field conditions, resulting in increased yield and minimized postharvest losses (Mohamed, 2023; Šlajpah et al., 2023).

Collaborative and swarm harvesting robotics represent a collaborative approach to automated harvesting, where multiple robots work together in a coordinated manner to accomplish harvesting tasks efficiently. In this approach, robots collaborate to divide the workload, share information, and collectively achieve harvesting objectives. For example, in orchards or vineyards, a swarm of robots can work in unison to harvest fruits from different areas simultaneously, significantly reducing harvesting time. Collaborative robotics leverages real-time communication and coordination algorithms to ensure that robots do not interfere with each other's operations and maintain an optimal working pace. This approach increases the scalability and productivity of automated harvesting, as the number of robots can be easily adjusted based on the size of the agricultural area or the complexity of the harvesting task. Collaborative and swarm harvesting robotics also offer redundancy, ensuring that harvesting continues smoothly even if some robots experience technical issues. By fostering teamwork and synergy among robots, collaborative and swarm harvesting robotics enhance the overall efficiency of agricultural operations, reduce the reliance on manual labor, and open possibilities for even more sophisticated and large-scale automated harvesting endeavors.

8.4.4 HUMAN–ROBOT INTERACTION AND SAFETY CONSIDERATIONS

As autonomous harvesting robots become an integral part of modern agriculture, ensuring safe collaboration between robots and human workers is paramount. Safety considerations are crucial to prevent accidents and promote a harmonious working environment. To achieve safe collaboration, robots are equipped with advanced sensor systems, including cameras, LiDAR, and proximity sensors, to detect the presence of human workers in their vicinity. These sensors enable robots to slow down, stop, or adjust their trajectories when they sense human presence, avoiding collisions and potential hazards. Additionally, the design of autonomous harvesting robots incorporates safety features such as soft, deformable materials and rounded edges to minimize the risk of injuries during interactions with human workers. Furthermore, the implementation of safety standards and guidelines for human–robot interaction in agriculture helps create a framework that prioritizes worker safety while maximizing the benefits of robotic automation. Effective training and education for farm operators and workers on how to interact safely with autonomous robots are also essential to promote a culture of safety and awareness. By ensuring safe collaboration between autonomous harvesting robots and human workers, the agricultural industry can harness the full potential of automation while prioritizing the well-being and safety of its workforce (Mohamed, 2023).

ML plays a vital role in enhancing human–robot interaction, communication, and user interfaces in agricultural robotics. ML algorithms enable robots to understand and respond to human commands, gestures, or voice instructions, facilitating intuitive communication with farm operators and workers. Natural language processing techniques empower robots to interpret and process verbal commands, making it easier for humans to interact with the machines without the need for complex programming interfaces. ML-based user-friendly interfaces allow farm operators to set tasks, define objectives, and monitor robot operations through intuitive control panels or mobile applications. Moreover, ML enables robots to learn from human feedback, making them more adaptable to individual preferences and farm-specific requirements. By continuously improving their responsiveness and understanding of human intent, ML-driven human–robot interaction promotes seamless collaboration and streamlines the integration of robots into agricultural workflows. Additionally, ML can aid in generating informative and intuitive visualizations of robot activities and data, enhancing situational awareness and facilitating decision-making for farm operators. The use of ML for human–robot interaction and user-friendly interfaces fosters an environment of effective communication and trust between humans and robots, contributing to the successful adoption of autonomous harvesting technology in agriculture.

With the increasing deployment of automated machinery in agriculture, addressing safety protocols and mitigating potential risks becomes paramount. Comprehensive safety protocols are established to ensure that the operation and behavior of autonomous harvesting robots comply with strict safety standards. Regular maintenance, safety inspections, and software updates are conducted to keep the robots in optimal condition and reduce the chances of technical failures that could lead to accidents. Safety sensors and interlocks are integrated into the robots to monitor and respond to anomalies in real time. For example, emergency stop mechanisms are in place to halt robot movements immediately in critical situations. Moreover, robots are programmed to navigate cautiously around sensitive areas or obstacles, avoiding potential dangers and minimizing the risk of crop damage or farm equipment collisions. To address potential risks associated with automated machinery, comprehensive risk assessments and hazard analysis are performed during the deployment of robots on farms. This includes identifying potential pinch points, entanglement hazards, and safety zones that human workers should avoid during robot operations. By rigorously addressing safety protocols and potential risks, the agricultural industry can embrace automation confidently, reaping the benefits of increased productivity and efficiency while ensuring the well-being and security of everyone involved in the farming process.

REFERENCES

Astanakulov, K., Abdillaev, T., Umirov, A., Fozilov, G., & Hatamov, B. (2021). Monitoring of the combine with smart devices in soybean harvesting. *E3S Web of Conferences*, *227*, 07003. https://doi.org/10.1051/E3SCONF/202122707003

Bac, C. W., Van Henten, E. J., Hemming, J., & Edan, Y. (2014). Harvesting robots for high-value crops: State-of-the-art review and challenges ahead. *Journal of Field Robotics*, *31*(6), 888–911. https://doi.org/10.1002/ROB.21525

Horng, G. J., Liu, M. X., & Chen, C. C. (2020). The smart image recognition mechanism for crop harvesting system in intelligent agriculture. *IEEE Sensors Journal*, *20*(5), 2766–2781. https://doi.org/10.1109/JSEN.2019.2954287

Kang, H., Zhou, H., & Chen, C. (2020). Visual perception and modeling for autonomous apple harvesting. *IEEE Access*, *8*, 62151–62163. https://doi.org/10.1109/ACCESS.2020.2984556

Kurita, H., Iida, M., Cho, W., & Suguri, M. (2017). Rice autonomous harvesting: Operation framework. *Journal of Field Robotics*, *34*(6), 1084–1099. https://doi.org/10.1002/ROB.21705

Mohamed, M. (2023). Agricultural sustainability in the age of deep learning: Current trends, challenges, and future trajectories. *Sustainable Machine Intelligence Journal*, *4*(4), 1–20. https://doi.org/10.61185/SMIJ.2023.44102

Muthusinghe, M. R. S., Palliyaguru, S. T., Weerakkody, W. A. N. D., Saranga, H. A. M., & Rankothge, W. H. (2019). Towards smart farming: Accurate prediction of paddy harvest and rice demand. In *IEEE Region 10 Humanitarian Technology Conference, R10-HTC, 2018-December*. https://doi.org/10.1109/R10-HTC.2018.8629843

Šlajpah, S., Munih, M., & Mihelj, M. (2023). Mobile robot system for selective asparagus harvesting. *Agronomy*, *13*(7), 1766.

Thangavel, S. K., & Murthi, M. (2017). A semi automated system for smart harvesting of tea leaves. In *2017 4th International Conference on Advanced Computing and Communication Systems, ICACCS 2017*. https://doi.org/10.1109/ICACCS.2017.8014724

Wakchaure, M., Patle, B. K., & Mahindrakar, A. K. (2023). Application of AI techniques and robotics in agriculture: A review. *Artificial Intelligence in the Life Sciences*, 100057.

Wang, D., Dong, Y., Lian, J., & Gu, D. (2022). Adaptive end-effector pose control for tomato harvesting robots. *Journal of Field Robotics*. https://doi.org/10.1002/ROB.22146

Xiong, Y., Ge, Y., Grimstad, L., & From, P. J. (2020). An autonomous strawberry-harvesting robot: Design, development, integration, and field evaluation. *Journal of Field Robotics*, *37*(2), 202–224. https://doi.org/10.1002/ROB.21889

9 The Convergence of AI and IoT in Smart Farming

9.1 INTRODUCTION

The agricultural industry stands at the cusp of a transformative era, where cutting-edge technologies are reshaping traditional farming practices into a dynamic and efficient landscape known as smart farming. At the heart of this revolution lies the convergence of two groundbreaking technologies: AI and the IoT. The seamless integration of AI and IoT has unlocked unparalleled potential for precision agriculture, creating a symbiotic relationship that empowers farmers with data-driven insights and real-time decision-making capabilities. This chapter delves into the compelling synergy between AI and IoT in smart farming, exploring their individual roles and the remarkable impact they have when harnessed together.

In recent years, the proliferation of IoT devices and sensors has woven a vast network across agricultural fields, gathering an abundance of real-time data on various environmental factors and crop conditions. Weather stations, soil moisture sensors, and drones, among other IoT-enabled devices, have revolutionized data acquisition, allowing farmers to monitor their land with unprecedented precision. However, the true potential of this data lies in the intelligent analysis and interpretation, which is where AI steps in. By harnessing the power of machine learning algorithms, AI transforms the data deluge into valuable insights, unraveling patterns, predicting trends, and identifying potential threats to crops. This symbiotic relationship enables smart farming to transcend traditional methods, unlocking new levels of efficiency and productivity.

The convergence of AI and IoT is driving a paradigm shift in agricultural practices. With AI-driven analytics, farmers can proactively address challenges such as crop diseases, water scarcity, and climate uncertainties. Real-time data analysis facilitates timely interventions, optimizing resource allocation and minimizing waste. Moreover, the emergence of AI-driven autonomous machinery has redefined precision agriculture. Smart tractors, robotic harvesters, and drones are now capable of executing tasks with unparalleled accuracy, ensuring that each action is tailored to specific requirements, resulting in a more sustainable and resource-efficient approach to farming.

This chapter explores and investigates ML solutions' integration into the IoT to develop a sustainable smart farming system. The IoT refers to the networked linking of physical objects such as sensors. Each sensor in a network can talk to every other sensor and, in turn, to the command center. The advantages of a wireless sensor network in IoT are numerous, including improved production efficiency, higher quality yields, the identification and avoidance of plant-eating dogs, and the detection of fires on farms. Smart irrigation, animal husbandry, and farming have all benefited

DOI: 10.1201/9781003400103-9

from the IoT. In agriculture, sensors are a crucial aspect of the IoT infrastructure. To put it simply, a sensor is a transducer that produces an electrical signal proportional to the physical quantity being sensed. Sensors can be categorized as either analog or digital, depending on the type of output signal they produce. Any IoT system would require a digital-to-analog conversion of an analog sensor's output before it could be fed into or processed by the system. The chapter also uncovers the promise of the recent IoT technologies, such as fifth-generation networks, blockchain, and digital twining, to improve the sustainability and productivity of smart farming systems.

9.2   THE ROLE OF IOT IN SMART FARMING

The IoT plays a pivotal role in propelling smart farming into the realm of precision agriculture. By deploying a network of interconnected devices and sensors throughout agricultural landscapes, farmers gain real-time access to a wealth of critical data. Weather stations stationed strategically across the fields constantly monitor atmospheric conditions, while soil moisture sensors provide precise measurements of hydration levels. Drones take to the skies, capturing aerial imagery and assessing crop health from above. All this data is seamlessly transmitted to central cloud-based platforms, allowing farmers to access crucial information at their fingertips. With IoT's data acquisition capabilities, smart farming transcends traditional methods, empowering farmers with a holistic view of their fields and facilitating data-driven decision-making.

One of the key advantages of IoT in smart farming is its ability to enable precise and resource-efficient agricultural practices. Armed with real-time data from IoT devices, farmers can optimize irrigation schedules based on actual soil moisture levels, mitigating water wastage and ensuring crops receive the necessary hydration. Moreover, IoT devices can monitor microclimates within greenhouses, allowing growers to fine-tune environmental conditions and create tailored habitats for different crops. The data from these devices can also be used to establish predictive models for crop behavior, helping farmers anticipate potential issues and proactively address them. IoT's role in collecting data from remote locations and providing insights on demand revolutionizes how farmers manage their land, promoting sustainability and fostering responsible resource usage.

The integration of IoT in smart farming extends beyond crop management, encompassing livestock monitoring and management as well. IoT-powered sensors are utilized in livestock farming to keep track of animal health, behavior, and welfare. Wearable devices on animals provide continuous data on vital signs and activity levels, enabling early detection of health issues and allowing farmers to administer timely medical attention. Additionally, IoT-driven automated feeding systems ensure livestock receive optimal nutrition, optimizing weight gain and overall herd health. By applying IoT technology in livestock farming, farmers can enhance animal welfare, reduce labor-intensive tasks, and maximize productivity, creating a more efficient and humane environment for raising livestock. The versatility of IoT in smart farming makes it an indispensable tool, facilitating data-driven practices that revolutionize every facet of modern agriculture.

AI and ML in agriculture are gaining traction and are on track to become a key component of all present and future agricultural activities. Its data- and algorithm-driven strategy efficiently optimizes and automates nearly all agricultural activities, and is fully capable of preparing the modern farmer for the ever-increasing complexity of this old art. "Can AI eventually remove humans out of the equation?" is a relevant question. Of course not, because all of the hard labor is eventually done by dedicated field workers. Yet, AI can significantly simplify many of their everyday duties and become an all-seeing, all-sensing adviser that can provide smart advice for making educated judgments. In the future, ML and AI will be at the heart of intelligent farms, connecting drone fleets in the sky and on the ground, fields of soil sensors, smart greenhouses, and connected farming business management systems, placing orders and posting offers in a fully automated fashion (Ajmani and Saigal, 2023). If you own or manage an agricultural business, now is the moment to embrace tomorrow's technology and begin reaping its numerous benefits before your competitors do. Similarly, to how the introduction of self-driving cars is sure to transform driving as we know it, the adoption of AI-driven autonomous equipment will redefine agriculture and farming within a decade. While AI and predictive analytics are now used to inform farmers' decision-making processes, robots will be able to work independently in the not-too-distant future. Autonomous devices in agriculture will consider more than just crop requirements. They will have the "intelligence" to analyze elements like as crop quality and financial concerns related to energy prices, among other things. While irrigation and water consumption are key places to start, this technology will also provide a foundation for other agronomic operations such as fertilization and crop protection (Alanazi and Alrashdi, 2023).

9.2.1 What Advantages Does Smart Farming Have over Traditional Farming Methods?

Smart farming is undoubtedly a key facilitator in generating more nourishment with less for a growing global population. Smart farming, for example, allows for greater output through more effective utilization of natural resources and inputs, as well as enhanced land and environmental management. While this is critical for feeding the world's rising population, smart farming also offers farmers and communities all over the world other benefits. Farmers have frequently had less leverage in traditional supply chains because they have had less knowledge about how their product performs in relation to client requirements. Smart farming connects all actors in the supply chain by promoting the effective and equitably distributed flow of information and, as a result, better decision-making. This has the ability to realign power and more equally disperse revenues along the production chain. If a farmer, for example, receives timely feedback on their product from multiple areas of the supply chain (such as processors and consumers), they might find chances to adjust their production system to match the demands of their customers, therefore enhancing the value of their product. Addressing the changing consumer wants is critical to agricultural enterprises being sustainable in the future, and smart farming may give insights to help this happen. Smart farming also aids in verification efforts by integrating information across the supply chain, allowing production claims to be verified. They may pertain to the safety of the food produced (such as ensuring that no dangerous chemical residues are present), where it was grown, animal welfare on-farm, or sustainability methods that aid in environmental protection (such as reducing greenhouse gas emissions).

Smart farming enables farmers to have a better understanding of critical aspects such as water, terrain, aspect, vegetation, and soil types. This enables farmers to identify the most efficient use of scarce resources in their production area and manage them in an ecologically and economically sustainable manner. It also allows farmers to track the amount and quality of their crops in real time and change their production strategies as needed. For instance, using the "normalized difference vegetation index," satellite images may be used to estimate crop and pasture health, or to detect pests and illnesses sooner than human monitoring approaches. With more data, the farmer in both scenarios may deploy timely and targeted tactics to avoid output losses and higher expenditures. This safeguards their livelihood, allows them to continue supplying food and other natural goods to the general public, and enhances environmental management.

9.2.2 How Is Automation Impacting Agriculture?

On-farm decision-making is evolving as a result of automation. They have a better understanding of prospective possibilities, difficulties, and restrictions. Farmers may also be more efficient and imaginative in their approaches, allowing them to grow more with less. From an economic standpoint, automation enables farmers to minimize costs, time, and waste, resulting in higher profit margins and more efficient resource usage. Also, automation is affecting the sorts of jobs available and how they are performed on farms. Understanding and employing smart agricultural technologies necessitates a unique set of skills. Acquiring new skills empowers industry members more broadly and attracts new people who would not have explored a career in agriculture previously. Smart farming, on the other hand, has the potential to lessen the complexity of skills necessary.

Variable-rate sowing and fertilizer application using smart agricultural technology is a prime example. It entails using software tools to alter sowing or fertilizer rates as a tractor moves along, based on mapped soil types that indicate soil fertility, salinity, soil moisture, and other characteristics. Rate adjustments can be "live" in certain situations, depending on real-time satellite images, or based on historical distributions observed on digital maps. With the exact adjustment of macro- and micronutrients to fulfill the unique demands of plants growing in varied settings, variable rate fertilizer treatment has the ability to drastically alter input utilization and output quality. In this situation, the tractor operator must comprehend the software and how the machinery works, as well as be able to read and analyze information, monitor the application as the tractor moves over the field, and make modifications as needed. Of course, the controller may or may not be on the tractor at all, which means they may be able to do other things while monitoring.

Similarly, smart farming solutions may connect variable water rate delivery systems with soil moisture monitors so that crops are only watered when and where they need it, yielding significant improvements for both water consumption and production. Similar technologies may be utilized in dryland farming systems to help operators understand the soil moisture profile and make better decisions about sowing, yield potential, and fertilizer use. Operators must comprehend the results of the soil moisture probes, as well as the implications for water supply and other factors. They must also be able to monitor and test the system, evaluate what is being reported or happening, and make any modifications or changes. Some farmers may face difficulties adapting to new technologies as a result of automation. To obtain widespread acceptance, technology companies must make their system simple to use and intuitive.

9.2.3 How Could Smart Farming Benefit the Vast Majority of Farmers Worldwide?

Accessing smart farming solutions always comes at a cost, although the cost is usually determined by the breadth and scale of the smart farming technology being used. If you view data and data exchange as "smart farming," in addition to hardware, there are cost-effective and accessible software that might be quite valuable for small holdings. Weather forecasting using smartphone applications is not something that most people identify with smart farming, yet it may have a significant impact on farmer decision-making. Weather radars and extreme event alerts, such as flood or storm forecasts, can provide smallholders enough time to transfer animals to higher ground or to safeguard or harvest their crops.

Farmers may also be warned of biosecurity issues via smartphones. Suppose a tiny goat owner receives a smartphone message about a probable disease epidemic in her region: she can choose to cease grazing in a common area rather than risk exposing her herd. This technique can also be utilized to expand the trade alternatives available to the same tiny holder. Assume she has to sell 6 liters of goat's milk today. If she can notify three potential purchasers of this milk, they will be able to bid on her goods, and she will be able to sell to the highest bidder. Increased market access can have a big transformative impact on small holdings.

Responding to forecasting, marketing products, or responding to a disease epidemic are all examples of smart farming solutions that benefit smallholder farmers. Another way for smallholders to have access to smart farming is through collective investment in technological solutions, maybe with government assistance. Vendors of smart agricultural solutions may also provide alternate payment plans or equipment leasing to make technology more accessible.

9.2.4 What Are the Most Noticeable Smart Farming Uses in Agriculture?

To be honest, customers will not always "see" the implementation of smart farming. What will become clear to them is the connection between what they are buying and where and how it was created. Smart farming plays an important role in validating consumer-facing production and provenance claims. Consumers are increasingly making purchase decisions based on their preferences for items that make claims about food safety, sustainability, animal welfare, and place of origin. All of these claims require traceability as the foundation, and most traceability solutions rely on smart agricultural technology. Other smart agricultural applications also help to validate these assertions. There are other examples of refrigerators that play movies communicating the "farm to fork" tale at the point of sale for items such as meat and milk, where consumers are able to observe and hear from the farmer.

9.2.5 WHAT ROLE CAN STANDARDS PLAY IN PROMOTING CLIMATE-SMART AGRICULTURE?

Agriculture is under growing pressure to provide food in a more environmentally responsible manner and for a greater number of people worldwide. This implies that agriculture is under intense pressure to increase productivity and grow more with fewer resources. Smart agricultural technology has the ability to help farmers with this challenge by:

- Allowing for resource optimization and efficient farming growth.
- Connecting the whole supply chain, from farm to fork and all in among both.
- Assisting in the implementation, monitoring, and reporting of political strategies.

The fundamental reason this promise has yet to be fulfilled is not a lack of technology or ideas, but rather a lack of organization and cohesiveness in how different technologies connect to ease data flow. To realize the promise of smart farming, digital technologies must be standardized, from data collecting, formats, and interfaces to optimization and interconnection across the whole supply chain. To address this issue, ISO established the Strategic Advisory Group on Smart Farming (SAG-SF). The SAG's first aim is to develop a standardization roadmap that will set the course for International Standards in smart farming for many years to come, allowing smart farming to realize its enormous potential (Lewis, 2022).

9.3 SYNERGIES AND APPLICATIONS OF AI AND IOT IN SMART FARMING

9.3.1 FIFTH-GENERATION NETWORKS

Fifth-Generation networks (5G) are the latest generation of wireless communication technology, offering unprecedented data transfer speeds, ultra-low latency, and high network capacity. 5G utilizes a combination of advanced technologies, such as millimeter-wave frequencies, massive multiple-input and multiple-output systems, and network slicing, to provide faster and more reliable connectivity. These improvements are expected to open up new possibilities in various industries, and smart farming is one of the domains set to benefit significantly from this technology.

In the context of smart farming, 5G has the potential to revolutionize agriculture by enabling a range of transformative applications. One of the key areas where 5G can make a significant impact is precision agriculture. With the low latency and high bandwidth of 5G, farmers can deploy advanced sensors and IoT devices throughout their fields to gather real-time data on soil moisture levels, temperature, humidity, and crop health. This data can be transmitted instantly to cloud-based analytics platforms, where it can be processed and analyzed. By leveraging 5G-powered smart devices and analytics, farmers can make data-driven decisions, optimize irrigation schedules, apply fertilizers more efficiently, and predict potential crop diseases, leading to higher yields and reduced resource wastage. Additionally, 5G's network slicing capability can be instrumental in providing reliable and dedicated connections to support critical agricultural applications. For instance, autonomous farming machinery like drones and robotic tractors require constant and uninterrupted connectivity. 5G's network slicing allows operators to allocate dedicated portions of the network with specific performance characteristics, ensuring that these mission-critical applications always receive the necessary bandwidth and low latency.

The adoption of 5G in smart farming offers several advantages, including increased productivity, resource optimization, and cost reduction. By leveraging real-time data and advanced analytics, farmers can optimize their operations, minimize waste, and enhance overall efficiency. Moreover, 5G-powered applications can also help reduce the environmental impact of agriculture by promoting sustainable practices and precise resource management. However, there are challenges that need to be addressed for successful implementation. The first challenge is the deployment of 5G infrastructure in rural areas where farms are often located. Extending 5G coverage to remote regions might require significant investments in infrastructure, including base stations and fiber optic cables. Additionally, there might be concerns about the cost of 5G-enabled devices and services, especially for small-scale farmers with limited budgets.

With over 9 billion people on the planet and counting, the demand for digital transformation in agriculture is fast increasing. To feed the world's population, we must use cutting-edge technology to optimize and speed farming operations. Using the correct technology, as in most businesses, may help us minimize water usage, streamline resource distribution, and boost production. Regrettably, agriculture appears to be resistant to change and innovation. Nevertheless, 5G technology might be the solution (Hsu et al., 2019; Tang et al., 2021). Sensors connected to 5G monitor field conditions and notify farmers when crops require care, such as water, herbicides, or fertilizer. Despite the fact that many farmers currently use sensors to collect data, devices in rural regions are still largely connected to public 4G or Wi-Fi networks. Since these farmers in rural regions lack access to even steady 4G, and Wi-Fi does not cover the necessary areas, private 5G networks offer a considerable boost. How will this increased speed benefit agriculture, and what technology may be employed to optimize farming processes? Let's look at 5G agriculture application cases and the technology's perks.

9.3.1.1 Drone Utilization

Drones can be employed by farmers to monitor crops, livestock, and the field itself, as well as to spray water and agrichemicals. They enable restricted and accurate spraying while avoiding overuse of chemicals and crop damage. It's also a lot less expensive than driving tractors around the fields and doing everything by hand.

Higher speed, which gives higher quality video data, is one of the advantages of a private 5G network for agriculture. Drones may use 5G's high-speed and ultra-reliable connectivity to automatically send HD videos and photographs, including thermal and topographical imagery, follow and identify items like cattle, weeds, and pests using AI, and act on instructions managed from hundreds of kilometers away. Agribusinesses will be able to better assess field conditions, spread seeds and sprays, and monitor crops and livestock in real time as a result of this.

9.3.1.2   Autonomous Agricultural Machinery

To manage fields and correctly utilize available resources, smart farming or smart agriculture employs sensors that monitor soil, water, humidity, light, and temperature. Farmers may enhance data collecting and communication while increasing output by implementing current agricultural technologies. 5G in agriculture may significantly speed up operations and provide more accurate and timely results. In addition, precision irrigation can result in higher-quality yield and less water use, which lowers expenses. The 5G farms can track the crops and fields and analyze the soil to determine water usage. Farmers may create exact predictions and schedule irrigation cycles to maximize profitability by using data on the composition of the soil and the salinity of the water.

The next big thing in smart farming is autonomous agricultural equipment. These will be linked through 5G to expedite agricultural operations and help with labor shortages, which have become an issue for some farmers. Farmers will be able to autonomously handle a range of autonomous gear, such as tractors and harvesters, as well as "field robots" that might manage activities such as weeding, using 5G's dependable and fast connectivity. 5G will also allow autonomous agricultural equipment to interact with one another in real time, allowing farmers to oversee crop management operations from start to finish and boost efficiency.

For example, John Deere revealed a conceptual fully unmanned tractor and "See & Spray," an AI-powered weed sprayer, as examples of how it plans to leverage 5G to make autonomous agricultural equipment smarter. Because both devices run in the cloud, they require an ultra-low latency 5G connection to be effective and grow more common on farms. A second smart tractor is the Monarch Tractor, an electric, self-driving tractor with 360-degree cameras and sensors that can gather field data. This tractor can be operated from a farmer's phone, and using 5G, farmers may remotely manage fleets of these tractors to manage whole farms.

9.3.1.3   Livestock Observation

To manage livestock cost-effectively, it is essential to keep track of their health, fertility, and food intake. The majority of animal monitoring equipment still uses Wi-Fi or Bluetooth rather than 5G sensors, which reduces the signal's stability and dependability. The robust signal in smart 5G collars and ear tags, which precisely locate animals and check their health, is one of the technology's key benefits for farming. Precision livestock farming (PLF) technology that uses real-time animal monitoring will spread more widely with 5G. For better livestock management, 5G-enabled technologies, such as animal tags, sensors, and cameras, will communicate precise and reliable data on an animal's health and whereabouts more quickly.

Farmers can supervise animal eating and sleeping habits, feed availability, both indoor and outdoor environments, and behavioral patterns through 5G's dependable connectivity to determine whether an animal is ill or even pregnant. This monitoring allows farmers to improve animal welfare by making better decisions for their livestock. Projects for 5G animal monitoring are currently being tested on farms. Farmers will be able to proactively target sick cows and remove them from the herd to stop the spread of illnesses thanks to 5G RuralFirst in the UK, which is deploying 5G-connected collars and biometric ear tags on cows for better surveillance and health monitoring over broad, distant regions. A 5G Innovation Initiative grant was obtained by TPG Telecom in Australia to test the use of its 5G network, along with AI-enabled image processing, computer vision, and edge computing technologies, to enable multiple high-quality 4K video streams to count sheep at a regional livestock exchange, automating the procedure and obviating human error.

9.3.1.4   Food Administration

Increasing food supply will require better food management. Food manufacturers will be able to link various IoT devices and sensors to track and monitor food along the supply chain, from production to storage and delivery, using high-speed and high-capacity 5G networks. This will enhance food safety, minimize the danger of contamination and food poisoning, and reduce food waste. It will also improve traceability and storage conditions. While sensors and video feeds are not new in the field of food management, 5G will offer faster and more accurate data and vision analysis.

For instance, the Australian Meat Processor Corporation is utilizing 5G-enabled video technology as part of the Australian 5G Innovation Initiative to enhance the quality assurance process of meat production. This initiative aims to lower compliance costs while also improving the efficiency of compliance auditing for farmers in regional and rural Australia. The capacity to check storage conditions in real-time would substantially aid other experiments in food storage, such as Simplot Australia's study of sensors in seed potato storage bins to detect CO_2 levels to identify the best storage conditions and prevent seed loss.

9.3.1.5   Weather Forecasts

Farmers set up weather stations that continually monitor temperature, UV light exposure, wind speed, humidity, and soil texture to attain high levels of weather precision. Real-time weather data can aid farmers in making timely decisions and preventing crop losses. High connection speeds and immediate report production using the most recent data are two benefits of 5G in agriculture. To assist farmers in increasing crop yields, 5G can detect weather variables including rainfall, temperature, wind speed and direction, air pressure, and humidity in real-time across many and huge estates.

The first 5G weather stations are already starting to appear on the market. One such station is called Origo, which was created in Perth, Western Australia, and employs a mesh network and 5G IoT services to offer continuous coverage across farms. A huge possibility exists with regionally networked weather stations in addition to this. To provide farmers in the area with a hyper-local weather data and forecast system to support better management decisions on crop production, labor, and the supply chain, mobile network operator Telstra is currently deploying 55 reliable, high-quality IoT-enabled weather stations around Toowoomba, Queensland. These weather stations are using existing mobile network sites. With the continuous roll-out of IoT 5G networks, which are complementary to public 5G networks, the project will evaluate the sustainability of a weather network service to deliver more localized weather for farmers and might become more extensively utilized throughout Australia.

9.3.2 BLOCKCHAIN

To increase food safety, blockchain agriculture makes it possible to trace information across the food supply chain. Traceability, which is utilized to simplify the creation and deployment of innovations for smart farming agriculture insurance, is created by the blockchain's ability to store and manage data (Vangala et al., 2021). It represents a significant advance in contemporary agriculture. With the rise in popularity of Bitcoin and other cryptocurrencies, you've probably heard a lot about blockchain technology, so it might come as a surprise to learn that it also has applications in agriculture. To track data and keep the flow of information going, we have traditionally employed databases and information and communication technology (ICT). An innovative technique to power these databases is via blockchain technology. They grant privileges to every member of the network as opposed to just one server and administrator. The database's new entries may then be accessed and verified by a number of parties, increasing security and reducing the possibility of corruption. Also, it is more secure than conventional technologies since everyone involved must agree to add security restrictions on top of encryption. Every system becomes very tough to manipulate.

Blockchain technology has the ability to track a variety of information about plants, including the quality of the seed, how crops develop, and even the path a plant takes after leaving the farm. This information can improve supply chain openness and lessen problems with unethical and illegal production. Also, they can make it simpler, in the case of a recall, to identify the source of any contamination or other issues. With these technologies, sustainability and food security come first. Customers can make wise selections regarding their purchases when there is this level of openness. They frequently make use of this data to honor farmers and other producers that follow ethical standards. From a projected $41.2 million in 2017 to roughly $430 million by 2023, the market for agricultural blockchain is expected to develop at an incredible 47.8% compound annual growth rate. The blockchain is already revolutionizing the way commerce is conducted in the sector by reducing the likelihood of fraud, accelerating transaction times, helping farmers manage and analyze their crops, and doing much more.

In particular, blockchain, usually referred to as a blockchain ledger, is a distributed record of transactions and accounts that is kept up to date by all stakeholders. Because of its focus on accountability and transparency, blockchain technology is increasingly being used in contemporary agriculture. The adoption of blockchain technology in the agricultural sector increases the amount of trustworthy information that is available regarding inventories, the agricultural industry, and the general health of the farms. Data storage used to be an expensive procedure, but blockchain has the potential to change that soon. With the use of blockchain in the agricultural sector, it is now possible to improve the quality of the management of the food supply chain and maintain trust between consumers and farmers. As it is a reliable and trustworthy method of storing data, it enables the facilitation of multiple data-driven technologies to usher in the era of the smart agricultural sector. Accelerating the whole process helps to smooth out the nature of transactions between various parties when used in conjunction with the idea of smart contracts. We will examine significant blockchain application cases in the agricultural sector. The agriculture industry already has a number of blockchain applications, and more are being developed as a result of recent technology developments. The blockchain in agriculture business is emerging in developing nations in a few key areas.

9.3.2.1   More Effective Smart Farming with Blockchain

The primary blockchain use case in the agriculture sector is smart farming, commonly referred to as smart agriculture. To improve its effectiveness and dependability, precision farming makes use of a number of recent technical developments. It makes use of sensors, ML technology, information and communications technology, as well as a variety of data-gathering and analysis tools. Although farming has had access to smart technology for some time, creating a strong and complete security system to manage and utilize the data obtained is a significant challenge in its deployment.

The centralization of the classical smart technology management system processes leads to a variety of errors and distortions in data collection. Additionally, it raises the possibility that the entire system will be the target of a cyberattack. Yet with today's blockchain technology, it is possible to store data securely. The several parties involved in the whole process can at any time produce the necessary environmental monitoring data, from the seed to the sale of various agricultural products. Blockchain specialists may use the technology in ways that promote data openness and guarantee the immutability of all statistics.

The decentralization of blockchain is by far its biggest strength in smart agriculture. This functionality makes it easier to provide data to various users' screens while decreasing data loss and distortion. All transactions in a blockchain are accurately documented for the sake of transparency. So far, several smart farming models have been developed based on the value and promise of blockchain in the agriculture business. These models aid in the integration of blockchain technology with IoT characteristics. One such system was developed specifically for greenhouses, which necessitates the use of IoT sensors to function as a private local blockchain that the farmer can simply maintain.

Another alternative, using IoT and blockchain technology, has been created for widespread use. The primary idea behind this structure is to help build trust among the different blockchain actors. Smartphones may be used by a variety of users to access data recorded at every stage of the farming process, from seed to product sales. Some companies are also investing significantly in the rural development of the smart agriculture sector and supply chain. "Filament," for example, is a brand that offers goods that connect many networks to actual objects using smart farming technology. The company developed a coin-sized technology to assist customers in executing secure blockchain transactions.

9.3.2.2 The Agri-Food Supply Chain and Blockchain

Due to the globalization process, the food supply chain in the agriculture sector has grown longer and more intensive than it has ever been. Yet, there are various issues in the current food supply chain transparency, including concerns about food security, quality, traceability, trust, and supply chain inefficiencies. This stresses the economy and society while putting customers' health at risk. Several of these issues are addressed by blockchain technology, which establishes trust between producers (or the supply chain) and buyers. Providing precise product data within the blockchain can increase transparency significantly in this process. This has far-reaching implications for companies as well as farmers. It helps firms to increase the value of their products and hence their market competitiveness. It would also make it extremely difficult for low-quality or phony product producers to remain in the system if they maintained their negative behaviors.

9.3.2.2.1 Product Quality Assurance

According to surveys, around of fruits and vegetables are thrown in the trash in developed countries owing to poor storage and transportation circumstances, with 34% of these commodities becoming unfit before reaching the pitch. This is mostly due to the fact that neither the farmer, goods transporter, nor supplier has control over the indicators of humidity, temperature, CO_2, and so on. Dedicated sensors may collect important information and record it in real time in a blockchain-based decentralized distribution book to track the storage and movement of agricultural products. As a consequence, stakeholders (farmers, distributors, and consumers) can pinpoint the point at which the product decayed and prevent it from happening again.

9.3.2.2.2 Improving Supply Chains

The agricultural product market is international. Supermarkets stock food from Africa, South America, Europe, and Alaska. The delivery is handled by a convoluted logistic structure that channels products via hundreds of middlemen; to put it mildly, the efficacy of the connection between them left something to be desired (Krasteva et al., 2021). According to World Economic Forum research, reducing bureaucratic barriers in logistics and supply chains with new technology will increase global commerce by 15% and global GDP by 5%. Experts think that blockchain is the only solution capable of overcoming these constraints.

9.3.2.2.3 Value for Money

Weather, inelastic demand and supply, and global market circumstances all contribute to the majority of agricultural commodity sales revenues ending up in the wallets of middlemen and merchants. But the wages of farmers and raw material producers remain extremely low. Farmers may directly participate in transactions with merchants on more favorable terms since blockchain reduces the number of intermediaries. Blockchain improves market transparency, which may be used to exert societal pressure on parties that make excessive profits. This strategy has been demonstrated to be effective in the practice of eco-organizations.

Farmers may utilize blockchain-based platforms to organize global trade unions to protect their rights. All of this will increase farmers' earnings. This is one of the most significant advantages of blockchain agriculture for poor nations, where agriculture employs a large section of the population and saves many people from famine. Uganda, for example, had nine out of ten people living in the countryside in the 1990s. According to research, a 10% rise in the price of coffee beans results in a 6% drop in the number of poor families (2 million people).

9.3.2.3 How Does Blockchain Technology Help Food Production?

Blockchain technology provides transparency, security, and decentralization in food production. Blockchain has the feature of immutability. Every update is tracked, logged, and made available to the whole network of persons who have access to the information, ensuring that transactions cannot be modified or concealed. It also stores information in a distributed manner. This means that data is not kept on a single server. Instead, many copies of the data are kept on other networks, which all members may access and view. Because blockchain offers such a transparent environment, there is no need for trust and no need for a central authority to arbitrate between the parties.

The properties of blockchain technology that are especially useful in food tampering, fraud, and deceptive advertising must all be avoided. Helping with large-scale hazardous product recalls. Food waste detection in supply chain networks. Lowering the possibility of food deterioration. Moreover, firms will be able to certify organic or fair-food sources. Yet, there are a few challenges that must be solved with blockchain. The first challenge for novices in the sector is overcoming the complexity of the food ecology. For a typical agricultural food production facility, blockchain technology needs a customized system and enhanced data entry techniques. Agricultural commodities are available in a variety of forms, sizes, storage systems, handling operations, and data recording methods.

Different platforms and non-synchronized language might make transitioning to the food system challenging. The food ecosystem involves several players and infrastructural levels. Scaling blockchain requires deep customization, from farm operations to working around existing ERP systems and modifying the data collection technique. Numerous platforms and non-synchronized language might make it difficult to acclimatize to the food system. The food ecosystem involves several players and infrastructural levels. Deploying blockchain at scale demands deep customization, from farm operations to working around existing ERP systems and modifying the data-collection technique.

Opponents of blockchain for food have also expressed concerns about data transparency. On the one hand, data openness would hold inclusive commerce and agriculture sector processes accountable, boosting organic, freshness, and higher-quality claims. On the other hand, if something goes wrong, exact information may be reviewed, resulting in a reaction against firms.

Asking for voluntary information exchange is difficult, especially when the information is critical and might have an impact on businesses. If a pesticide is used to cure plant disease during manufacturing in agricultural food production, buyers may diminish the product's value or reject it entirely. Farmers may be hesitant to utilize smart contracts and blockchain if their competitors get a competitive edge by hiding specific items or processing data.

Another source of worry is blockchain's capacity to manage massive volumes of data, particularly trading data. Thus far, the application of blockchain in transactions, where more significant economic ramifications may arise, has garnered the least attention. Secondly, huge corporations are exhibiting interest in blockchain because they already have the infrastructure, both technical systems and data, to enable farm-level data processing automation. Additionally, because one of the blockchain's limitations is that each transaction added to it raises the size of the database, the structure and scaling must be carefully considered. Either a smaller ledger or more centralized control is required for the network. As a result, firms are asking large trials to evaluate the limits of blockchain before using it.

9.3.3 DIGITAL TWINNING

Digital twinning is a cutting-edge concept that has gained immense popularity in various industries. At its core, digital twinning involves creating a virtual counterpart of a physical object, system, or process. This digital representation, known as a digital twin, mirrors the real-world entity in a highly dynamic and accurate manner. The idea behind digital twinning is to bridge the gap between the physical and digital worlds, allowing real-time monitoring, analysis, and optimization of physical assets through their virtual counterparts. This transformative technology holds the potential to revolutionize industries, including manufacturing, healthcare, and transportation, by offering unprecedented insights, predictive capabilities, and enhanced efficiency. In recent years, digital twinning has emerged as a promising paradigm for modernizing and optimizing agriculture.

In its essence, digital twinning can be described as a virtual doppelgänger of a physical entity, system, or process. The creation of a digital twin involves constructing a sophisticated and dynamic digital model that accurately replicates the physical attributes, behavior, and characteristics of the corresponding real-world asset. This digital representation extends beyond mere static 3D models, as it integrates real-time data streams from IoT sensors embedded in the physical entity. By fusing real-time data with the digital model, the digital twin becomes a living, evolving simulation that closely mirrors the changes and fluctuations occurring in its physical counterpart. This virtual-physical interconnection empowers decision-makers with actionable insights, enabling them to monitor, analyze, and optimize performance, identify potential issues, and make informed choices based on the real-time behavior of the physical asset.

The creation of a digital twin relies on the seamless integration of real-time data from sensors with the digital model through advanced technologies such as the IoT and cloud computing. IoT sensors strategically deployed on the physical asset gather a wealth of data related to its operational parameters, environmental conditions, and performance metrics. This data is then transmitted to cloud-based platforms, where it undergoes processing, analysis, and integration with the digital model. Through advanced algorithms and simulations, the digital model assimilates the incoming data, continuously updating and fine-tuning its representation to maintain a high degree of fidelity with the physical asset. As a result, decision-makers can access real-time information, visualize the state of the physical asset in a virtual environment, and leverage predictive capabilities to forecast future behavior. This symbiotic relationship between real-time data and digital models forms the backbone of digital twinning, making it a powerful tool for achieving precision, efficiency, and optimization in a wide range of industries, including smart farming (Pylianidis et al., 2021).

The application of digital twinning in the agricultural sector represents a groundbreaking shift in the way farmers approach modern farming practices. By adopting digital twins, farmers can create virtual replicas of various agricultural assets, including crops, livestock, and farm equipment. These virtual counterparts offer an unprecedented level of insight into their real-world counterparts, facilitating data-driven decision-making and precision agriculture. Digital twins serve as a bridge between the physical and digital realms of farming, enabling real-time monitoring and analysis of agricultural assets, thereby empowering farmers to optimize resource allocation, predict outcomes, and enhance overall efficiency. One of the primary applications of digital twinning in agriculture is the creation of virtual replicas of crops, livestock, and farm equipment. For crops, digital twins provide a comprehensive understanding of their growth patterns, development stages, and response to changing environmental conditions. By simulating crop behavior, farmers can predict yields, identify potential stress factors, and tailor cultivation practices for optimum results. Likewise, digital twins of livestock offer insights into animal health, behavior, and well-being. By continuously monitoring real-time data from IoT sensors attached to the livestock, farmers can ensure timely medical attention, balanced nutrition, and improved breeding strategies. Furthermore, creating digital twins of farm equipment allows for predictive maintenance, reducing downtime, and enhancing operational efficiency, as well as facilitating automated tasks through AI-driven control systems.

Real-time data collection through IoT sensors plays a pivotal role in enabling the creation of accurate and dynamic digital twins in smart farming. These IoT sensors are strategically deployed throughout the agricultural landscape, collecting a wide array of data related to environmental factors, crop health parameters, livestock behavior, and machinery performance. The data collected is then transmitted to cloud-based platforms, where it is analyzed and integrated with the digital models of the corresponding agricultural assets. This constant flow of real-time data ensures that the digital twins remain highly synchronized with their physical counterparts, enabling farmers to gain timely insights, respond to emerging challenges, and adjust farming practices to optimize outcomes.

The types of data collected through IoT sensors for digital twinning in smart farming cover a diverse range of parameters critical for agricultural operations. Environmental factors, such as temperature, humidity, rainfall, and sunlight intensity, provide crucial insights into the growing conditions for crops. Crop health parameters, including soil moisture levels, nutrient content, and disease presence, enable farmers to fine-tune irrigation and fertilization practices, as well as implement targeted pest management strategies. In the case of livestock, data on animal behavior, vital signs, and feeding patterns contribute to a comprehensive understanding of their health and well-being. Moreover, data related to machinery performance, such as fuel consumption, engine temperature, and equipment usage, supports predictive maintenance, reducing downtime, and optimizing farming operations. The integration of these diverse datasets forms the foundation for creating accurate, dynamic, and effective digital twins that empower farmers to navigate the complexities of modern agriculture with greater precision and efficiency.

As a result, farmers may manage operations remotely based on (near) real-time digital data rather than relying on direct observation and manual duties on-site. This enables them to intervene quickly in the event of (anticipated) deviations and to model the impact of actions based on real-world data. In particular, digital twin is a sufficiently accurate digital replica of a physical object. These may be used to remotely monitor the "object." A digital twin of a cow, for example, may notify the farmer of bad health without the farmer having to check the animal. More specifically, a digital twin has to be:

1. **Individual:** It must symbolize something particular, such as "Daisy the cow," rather than a generic cow.
2. **Near real-time**: This implies that the digital twin should be "always on," or available for as long as its physical counterpart is.
3. **Data-informed:** It must be kept up to date by a digital measurement of the real-world item, such as a soil moisture meter or a frequent satellite observation.
4. **Realistic:** The twin has to be a convincing substitute for the genuine thing.
5. **Actionable:** Input from the real-world twin must be capable of leading to an action.

Digital twins are made feasible by a convergence of technical breakthroughs, including enhanced monitoring via sensors and devices, ubiquitous connection and processing, and increased system understanding and modeling via ML. Consider a field's digital twin. Sensing systems such as satellites, drones, weather stations, tractor-mounted sensors, and soil probes may provide us with field status updates (Neethirajan and Kemp, 2021). We can also collect information on past soil conditions, slope, and aspect. Management data, such as what crops were planted when and when they were fertilized, is another important source of information; they are frequently kept digitally on systems such as Gatekeeper and Muddy Boots. All of these data sources give a diverse set of signals, but they are not exhaustive. Gaps will arise owing to a lack of accessible data or because that metric cannot be directly monitored. It would be impossible, for example, to directly estimate the total digestible dry matter provided in a field of grass.

Several industries' smart factories are beginning to use digital twins. This has permitted the growth of predictive maintenance, among other things. Nonetheless, these metrics are frequently inferable from other data. As a result, digital twins often feature a computer modeling system to address these gaps. These systems must go further than generic models, such as grass growth, and accurately represent all relevant processes occurring in the field, including chemical, physical, and biological processes (Verdouw et al., 2021). The model must accurately represent the field's grass species mix. And it must be capable of learning. They must also make access to extremely complicated information easier for decision-makers. A digital twin does not have to be complex. They might represent a very specific feature of reality, such as the fluid content in a milk tank. The key is that they are realistic enough.

9.3.3.1 What Distinguishes Digital Twin from Models?

Algorithms are used in models to simulate and occasionally forecast systems. This is comparable to the procedures used by digital twins to patch informational gaps. Digital twins, on the other hand, do much more than only include such models. Individual models often help us get a more basic knowledge of a system or make broad predictions. They are rarely utilized to correctly depict the current state of anything. These are frequently incorrect. Several models are occasionally mixed to show how incorrect they are. This can be accomplished, for example, by examining how different model predictions differ to comprehend how predictions are impacted by their formulation.

Models in a digital twin are intended to simulate real-world unpredictability. They serve very particular functions, and their output is perceived in the context of hundreds, if not millions, of other data points and outputs. This raises the chance that the model is correct. Moreover, digital twins are intended to protect the user from unwanted technological complications. They are designed to disclose information about the actual world in a way that allows actions to be made quickly. They are also designed to be "always on" and "real time": regardless of when you consult it, the state of the twin should always properly represent the current status of the actual object. None of these characteristics is expected of models in general.

9.3.3.2 How Can You Communicate with a Digital Twin?

Digital twins are often accessed via a virtual interface that shows information about the "thing's" state. Interacting with a digital twin is often done via a visual interface on a phone, tablet, or computer. This would allow you to view information about the thing's current, past (e.g., an ewe's health history), or expected future (e.g., a crop growth forecast). You may also be able to interact with the physical system via the digital twin, such as turning on an irrigation system. In the future, you may be able to execute what-if scenario tests, such as "What would happen if I injected plant growth regulator now?" A significant characteristic is that a user is concealed from practically all of the complexity. The digital twin's inner workings remain hidden. The user is only shown properties that they would ordinarily see when working with a real-world equivalent. Yet, they had the extra benefit of being able to accomplish things with the digital twin that they couldn't do in the actual world.

9.3.3.3 Where Will I Most Likely Find Digital Twins in Agriculture?

The first digital twins are surfacing. Livestock monitors provide monitoring systems and modeling of animal health issues. Field information systems provide data on the state of fields and crops to help managers make management decisions. Remote monitoring of farm machinery, such as tractors, allows for issue identification and even prevention. With these, a subset of the real-world object is monitored and represented realistically enough that the live update has genuine significance regarding the system's condition. Unfortunately, the breadth of these digital twins is limited: you may only consult the digital twin for a cow about particular elements of its health, not, for example, its antibody levels.

In other sectors, such as engineering, digital twins can cover a larger set of attributes since the monitoring is more thorough (more sensors) and the system's operation is better known (physics-based models). In agriculture, we are still waiting for sufficient understanding and monitoring capability to allow comprehensive digital surrogates. digital twins are most likely to be found when necessity and practicality meet. Supply chain twins are being built in other industries, and agri-food will undoubtedly follow. The disruption created by Covid-19 is a big motivation, but even before the outbreak, there were strong calls for enhanced traceability and waste reduction. Farm and agricultural landscape digital twins might possibly be in the future.

9.3.3.4 What Are the Applications of Digital Twins in Agriculture?

9.3.3.4.1 Livestock Administration

Herd management is a common use for digital twins. A constant stream of data is collected by sensors on or in the cow (e.g., accelerometers and boluses), at feeding and milking stations, and elsewhere (e.g., weighbridge). This data is analyzed to offer an indicator of milk or meat production efficiency and animal health. The farmer can then take appropriate action. While the approach conducted is not innovative, the data gathered from the digital twin will allow for earlier—and probably more effective—intervention, thereby improving animal outcomes.

9.3.3.4.2 Cultivation of Arable Crops

Farm managers on arable land would often review digital twins of their fields. This would provide information about the existing soil, water, crop, and other features. These would also help future property forecasts. These data would be used to advise management measures such as dealing with production deficits, the danger of lodging, projected over- or underproduction, and crop rotation plans.

9.3.3.4.3 Indoor Agriculture

Controlled growth conditions, such as indoor farming, aquaculture, and under glass, are among the most promising landscapes for Digital Twins. Capturing enough data and determining what is going on is easier analytically in these circumstances. A producer would consult the digital twin on a frequent basis to maintain track of production, issue interventions (likely remotely), and build a future management schedule. Because of the regulated atmosphere and the relatively high value of their output, indoor farming is a viable option for early digital twins.

9.3.3.4.4 Enhancing Sustainability

Digital twins might be utilized to give guarantees about an agricultural landscape's natural capital. Sensors that provide proof would need to be broadly spread, which is why satellite data is so appealing. Digital twins in agriculture would allow for the tracking of carbon, biodiversity, pollination, and water catchment services. It would inform us if they were altering and, more crucially, whether such changes are the result of our actions. Each of these use cases may be satisfied at some level now, with the correct investment in sensors, models, and interfaces.

Nevertheless, because they rely on generic agricultural, livestock, and other models, these would not necessarily fulfill the definition of a digital twin. These models must learn through observation and evolve to become customized models for the twinned entity to be considered true Digital Twins.

9.3.3.5   Integration of AI and IoT with Digital Twinning

The synergy among AI, IoT, and digital twinning forms the backbone of advanced smart farming practices. AI and IoT technologies complement digital twinning by providing the necessary tools for collecting, processing, and analyzing vast amounts of real-time data from agricultural assets. While digital twins create virtual replicas of crops, livestock, and farm equipment, IoT sensors act as the eyes and ears of the system, continuously feeding data to the digital models. This seamless integration ensures that the digital twins remain accurate, dynamic, and up to date, while AI-driven analytics extract valuable insights from the data stream, empowering farmers with actionable information to optimize farm management.

AI-driven analytics plays a pivotal role in making sense of the massive amount of data collected from IoT sensors in smart farming. The sheer volume and complexity of data generated can overwhelm traditional data processing methods. However, AI algorithms excel in handling such big data, enabling efficient data mining, pattern recognition, and trend analysis. By leveraging ML techniques, AI can identify correlations between different variables, predict potential outcomes, and detect anomalies or early signs of issues in crop health or livestock behavior. The integration of AI-driven analytics with the real-time data flow from IoT sensors equips farmers with valuable insights that aid in proactive decision-making and resource optimization.

The integration of AI algorithms into digital twins unlocks the potential for predictive and prescriptive recommendations in farm management. By assimilating historical data, real-time sensor inputs, and external factors like weather forecasts, AI-driven digital twins can simulate future scenarios. This predictive capability allows farmers to anticipate challenges, forecast crop yields, and plan for potential resource constraints. Moreover, AI-driven digital twins can prescribe optimized action plans, suggesting precise irrigation schedules, customized fertilization strategies, or even livestock breeding recommendations. These predictive and prescriptive functionalities elevate farm management to a new level of precision, empowering farmers with actionable strategies to maximize yields, minimize risks, and operate sustainably.

IoT sensors play a crucial role in continuously updating the data used to refine and improve digital twin simulations. The real-time data collected by IoT sensors provides the most accurate representation of the physical assets, capturing the dynamic nature of agricultural processes. This constant flow of real-time data ensures that the digital twins remain synchronized with their physical counterparts, allowing farmers to monitor changes in environmental conditions, crop health, or livestock behavior in real time. The continuous feedback loop between IoT sensors and digital twins ensures that the simulations remain accurate and responsive, providing reliable insights for decision-making.

The seamless integration of AI, IoT, and digital twinning in smart farming is further enhanced by the advent of 5G networks. 5G's real-time connectivity and low-latency data transmission capabilities provide the essential infrastructure for seamless data exchange between physical assets and their digital twins. The ultra-fast data transfer speeds of 5G enable near-instantaneous communication between IoT sensors and cloud-based platforms, ensuring that data is available for analysis and decision-making without delay. The low-latency nature of 5G networks ensures that AI-driven analytics can process data in real time, enabling rapid responses to changing agricultural conditions. This seamless integration of 5G with AI, IoT, and digital twinning unleashes the full potential of smart farming, revolutionizing the agricultural industry with precision, efficiency, and sustainable practices.

REFERENCES

Ajmani, P., & Saigal, P. (2023). *5G and IoT for smart farming* (pp. 124–139). https://doi.org/10.4018/978-1-6684-6413-7.CH008

Alanazi, B., & Alrashdi, I. (2023). Anomaly detection in smart agriculture systems on network edge using deep learning technique. *Sustainable Machine Intelligence Journal, 3*, 1–31. https://doi.org/10.61185/SMIJ.2023.33104

Hsu, C. K., Chiu, Y. H., Wu, K. R., Liang, J. M., Chen, J. J., & Tseng, Y. C. (2019). Design and implementation of image electronic fence with 5G technology for smart farms. In *Proceedings—2019 IEEE VTS Asia Pacific Wireless Communications Symposium, APWCS 2019*. https://doi.org/10.1109/VTS-APWCS.2019.8851659

Krasteva, I., Glushkova, T., Stoyanova-Doycheva, A., Moralivska, N., Doukovska, L., & Radeva, I. (2021). Blockchain-based approach to supply chain modeling in a smart farming system. In *Big Data, Knowledge and Control Systems Engineering—Proceedings of the 7th International Conference, BdKCSE 2021*. https://doi.org/10.1109/BDKCSE53180.2021.9627309

Lewis, B. (2022). *ISO—how smart farming is changing the future of food*. Retrieved March 27, 2023, from www.iso.org/news/ref2799.html

Neethirajan, S., & Kemp, B. (2021). Digital twins in livestock farming. *Animals, 11*(4), 1008. https://doi.org/10.3390/ANI11041008

Pylianidis, C., Osinga, S., & Athanasiadis, I. N. (2021). Introducing digital twins to agriculture. *Computers and Electronics in Agriculture, 184*, 105942. https://doi.org/10.1016/J.COMPAG.2020.105942

Tang, Y., Dananjayan, S., Hou, C., Guo, Q., Luo, S., & He, Y. (2021). A survey on the 5G network and its impact on agriculture: Challenges and opportunities. *Computers and Electronics in Agriculture, 180*, 105895. https://doi.org/10.1016/J.COMPAG.2020.105895

Vangala, A., Sutrala, A. K., Das, A. K., & Jo, M. (2021). Smart contract-based blockchain-envisioned authentication scheme for smart farming. *IEEE Internet of Things Journal, 8*(13), 10792–10806. https://doi.org/10.1109/JIOT.2021.3050676

Verdouw, C., Tekinerdogan, B., Beulens, A., & Wolfert, S. (2021). Digital twins in smart farming. *Agricultural Systems, 189*, 103046. https://doi.org/10.1016/J.AGSY.2020.103046

10 Toward Agriculture 5.0
The Convergence of Machine Learning and Nanotechnology for Next-Generation Farming

10.1 INTRODUCTION

In today's rapidly evolving world, the intersection of technology and agriculture has ushered in a new era of farming practices. As the global population continues to grow, ensuring sustainable food production becomes an increasingly pressing challenge. Fortunately, cutting-edge advancements in machine learning (ML) and nanotechnology offer a promising solution, revolutionizing traditional farming methods and paving the way for a more efficient, productive, and environmentally conscious approach: Agriculture 5.0. Agriculture 5.0 represents the seamless integration of ML and nanotechnology into the agricultural landscape, harnessing their combined power to address the complex challenges faced by modern farmers. By leveraging the potential of these innovative technologies, we can optimize crop production, conserve resources, enhance food quality, and promote sustainable farming practices.

In this chapter, we embark on an exploration of the convergence of ML and nanotechnology in smart farming. We delve into the foundations, applications, and potential of this transformative alliance, highlighting the remarkable strides made in the field and the profound impact it has on shaping the future of agriculture. We begin by providing a brief overview of precision agriculture, setting the stage for understanding the significance of incorporating advanced technologies into farming practices. From there, we dive into the realm of nanotechnology, exploring its applications in smart farming, including nanosensors and imaging techniques, nanomaterials for soil and crop enhancement, and nanoscale delivery systems for targeted agrochemical delivery.

Next, we shift our focus and discuss the progress made in the field of nanotechnology for agricultural applications, as well as the obstacles that have prevented the full potential of nanomaterials as sensors, soil enhancers, and plant growth stimulators, from being exploited. These obstacles include a lack of understanding of plant–nanomaterial interactions, an absence of efficient methods for delivering nanomaterials to plants and soil, and the risk of potentially hazardous effects of nanomaterials on human health due to their accumulation. The chapter then delves into the function of AI techniques in accelerating the development of nano-enabled

DOI: 10.1201/9781003400103-10

agriculture, thereby facilitating safe-by-design nanomaterials for various consumer products and medical applications.

While discussing these innovative technologies, we remain mindful of the importance of inclusivity in agricultural advancements. We explore how accessibility and equitable adoption of ML and nanotechnology can benefit farmers across diverse backgrounds, regions, and scales of operation. Furthermore, we consider the ethical and regulatory considerations surrounding the use of these technologies, ensuring responsible and sustainable integration into farming practices. Finally, we contemplate the challenges and future directions of this dynamic field, highlighting the need for continued research, collaboration, and knowledge sharing to unlock the full potential of Agriculture 5.0. As we conclude this chapter, we envision a future where the convergence of ML and nanotechnology propels agriculture to new heights, fostering a resilient, productive, and inclusive food system for generations to come.

10.2   NANOTECHNOLOGY IN SMART FARMING

Nanotechnology refers to the fields of science and engineering in which phenomena occurring at nanometer scales are used in the design, characterization, manufacture, and application of materials, structures, devices, and systems. Although there are many examples of structures with nanometer dimensions (hereafter referred to as the nanoscale) in the natural world, such as essential molecules in the human body and food components, and although many technologies have inadvertently involved nanoscale structures for many years, it has only been in the last quarter-century that it has been possible to actively and intentionally alter molecules and structures within this size range (Alishah et al., 2023). Nanotechnology is distinguished from other fields of technology by its ability to regulate at the nanometer scale.

In particular, understanding and controlling matter at the nanoscale scale is the goal of nanotechnology. The nanoscale is concerned with dimensions ranging from 1 to 100 nanometers. A nanometer is a unit of length that is one billionth ($10-9$) of a meter. What exactly is a nanometer (nm)? A single human hair measures between 80,000 and 100,000 nm in width. Materials with unexpected characteristics can be found at the nanoscale scale. As the size of a particle changes, it can change color, for example. Because the arrangement of atoms in nanometer-scale particles reflects light differently. Silver might seem yellowish or amber-colored, whereas gold can appear dark red or purple. Nanotechnology may enhance the surface area of a substance. This permits extra atoms to interact with other materials. One of the main motives nanometer-scale materials can be tougher, more robust, and more sensitive than their larger-scale (referred to as bulk) counterparts is their higher surface area.

Obviously, different types of nanotechnology have the potential to have a big influence on society. In general, it is reasonable to expect that the deployment of nanotechnology will benefit both individuals and organizations. Several of these applications include novel materials that give dramatically different qualities by operating at the nanoscale, where new phenomena are connected with the extremely huge surface area to volume ratios seen at these dimensions, as well as quantum effects not observed at larger scales (Puolamaa, 2006). Materials in the form of extremely thin films are employed in catalysis and electronics, two-dimensional nanotubes and nanowires are utilized in optical and magnetic systems, and nanoparticles are used in cosmetics, medicines, and coatings. The telecommunications and information sector, including electronic and optoelectronic fields, food technology, energy technology, and the medical products sector, which includes many different facets of pharmaceuticals and drug delivery systems, diagnostics, and medical technology, are the industrial sectors most readily embracing nanotechnology. Nanotechnology goods may potentially present fresh challenges for environmental pollution mitigation.

However, just as phenomena occurring at the nanoscale may be quite different from those happening at larger dimensions and may be exploitable for the benefit of mankind, these newly identified processes and their products may expose the same humans, as well as the environment in general, to new health risks, potentially involving quite various mechanisms of interaction with the physiology of human and environmental species. These possibilities might be focused on the destiny of free nanoparticles created in nanotechnology operations and either purposely or mistakenly discharged into the environment or supplied directly to persons through the operation of a nanotechnology-based product. Those whose jobs expose them to free nanoparticles on a regular and persistent basis should be especially concerned. The fact that progression has defined that the human species has evolved methodologies of protection against environmental agents, either living or dead, is central to these health risk concerns. This process is determined by the nature of the agents commonly encountered, with size being an important factor. Exposure to nanoparticles with novel properties may test the typical immune defenses associated with, for example, the immunological and inflammatory systems. It is also likely that nanotechnology goods will have an environmental impact due to mechanisms of dispersion and persistence of nanoparticles in the environment.

10.2.1   Descriptions and Purpose of Nanotechnologies

The terms "nanotechnology" and "nanotechnology products," which are frequently developed for particular uses, have a variety of meanings. The linguistics of a definition are not as crucial in this viewpoint as the underlying scientific principles of nanotechnology; thus, they are taken into account first. The following definitions are provided for the key generic terms:

- **Nanoscale**: It means having 1 or more dimensions of 100 nm or less.
- **Nanoscience**: It is the study and manipulation of events and materials at atomic, molecular, and macromolecular sizes, where characteristics change considerably from those at higher scales.
- **Nanotechnology**: It is the design, characterization, manufacture, and use of structures, devices, and systems at the nanoscale by regulating form and size.
- **Nanomaterial**: It is a material with one or more exterior dimensions or an interior structure that exhibits unique properties when compared to the identical material without nanoscale features.
- **Nanoparticle**: It is a molecule with one or more nanoscale dimensions.

- **Nanocomposite**: It is a composite with at least one dimension on the nanoscale.
- **Nanostructured:** It is having a nanoscale structure.

There have been and continue to be significant challenges in precisely measuring nanoscale characteristics, such that it is not always feasible to have complete trust in the data and conclusions reached concerning specific phenomena linked to specific aspects of nanostructures and nanomaterials. In addition, when it comes to nanoparticles, keep in mind that a sample of a substance containing nanoparticles will not be monodisperse, but will often comprise a variety of particle sizes. This makes assessing the nanoscale characteristics more challenging, especially when considering dosages for toxicological investigations. Moreover, nanoparticles will have a tendency to agglomerate in specific settings. It may be believed that an aggregation of nanoparticles, with dimensions measured in microns rather than nanometers, would act differently than individual nanoparticles, but there is no reason to anticipate the aggregate to behave like one huge particle. Similarly, it is reasonable to predict that the behavior of nanoparticles will be determined by their solubility and susceptibility to degradation, and that neither the chemical composition nor particle size are assured to remain constant throughout time. With the aforementioned definitions and limitations in mind, it is evident that there are two sorts of Nanomaterials to examine in terms of both intrinsic features and health hazards. Next, both classifications will be discussed.

10.2.2 CLASSIFICATION OF NANOMATERIALS

There are several types of nanomaterials and various ways to categorize them.

10.2.2.1 Natural versus Man-Made Nanomaterials

Natural nanomaterials are those that exist naturally in the world, as the name implies. They include volcanic ash particles, smoke, and even molecules in our bodies, such as hemoglobin in our blood. The vibrant hues of a peacock's feathers are caused by the spacing of nanometer-scale structures on its surface. Man-made nanomaterials are those that develop because of human-created items or processes. Exhaust from fossil-fuel-burning engines and various kinds of pollution are examples. While some of them are just by chance nanomaterials (car exhaust, for example), scientists and engineers are striving to produce them for application in sectors ranging from manufacturing to medical. They are known as purposely created nanomaterials.

10.2.2.2 Fullerenes versus Nanoparticles Nanomaterials

Fullerenes are carbon allotropes. Diverse molecular structures of an identical element are referred to as allotropes. Diamond and graphite, a form of coal, are arguably the most well-known carbon allotropes. Fullerenes are spheres or tubes made from atom-thick sheets of graphene, another carbon allotrope. Buckminsterfullerene, often known as the buckyball, is the most well-known kind of spherical fullerene. Buckyballs are nanometer-sized carbon molecules formed like soccer balls, with hexagons and pentagons that are securely linked. Buckyballs are extremely stable, withstanding severe temperatures and pressure. Buckyballs may therefore live in highly hostile conditions such as deep space. Buckyballs, the biggest molecules yet observed in space, were discovered in 2010 near a planetary nebula.

Buckyballs' cage-like structure appears to safeguard any confined atom or molecule. Numerous scientists are attempting to "impregnate" buckyballs with elements such as helium. These impregnated buckyballs might serve as effective chemical "tracers," allowing scientists to track them as they move through a system. Water contamination, for example, might be tracked kilometers distant from where it reached a stream, lake, or sea. Nanotubes are tubular fullerenes. Carbon nanotubes are incredibly strong and flexible because of the manner in which carbon atoms link to one another. Carbon nanotubes are more flexible than rubber and tougher than diamond. Carbon nanotubes have enormous scientific and technological promise. NASA, for instance, is experimenting with carbon nanotubes to create "blacker than black" satellite colors. This reduces reflection, ensuring that data acquired by the satellite is not "polluted" by light.

Carbon, like fullerenes, may be found in nanoparticles, as can nanometer-scale equivalents of many other elements, such as gold, silicon, and titanium. Quantum dots, a form of nanoparticle, are semiconductors composed of several elements such as cadmium and sulfur. Quantum dots offer extraordinary fluorescence properties. Quantum dots have been employed in anything from photovoltaic cells (used for solar power) to fabric dye by scientists and engineers. Nanoparticle characteristics have proven crucial in the research of nanomedicine. The utilization of gold nanoparticles to treat lymphoma, a kind of cancer that assaults cholesterol cells, is one hopeful advancement in nanomedicine. Researchers created a nanoparticle that resembles a cholesterol cell but contains gold at its center. When this nanoparticle binds to a lymphoma cell, it inhibits the cancer from "feeding" on genuine cholesterol cells, thereby starving the lymphoma to death.

10.2.3 NANOMANUFACTURING

Nanometer-scale scientists and engineers require specialized microscopes. The atomic force microscope (AFM) and scanning tunneling microscope (STM) are crucial tools in nanotechnology research. These sophisticated instruments allow scientists and engineers to view and control individual atoms. AFMs and Ms enable researchers to construct a topographic map-like picture of a particular atom or molecule. Researchers can grab and move atoms and molecules like small building bricks using the sensitive tip of an AFM or STM.

Materials on the nanoscale scale can be built in two ways: top-down or bottom-up. Top-down nanomanufacturing entails cutting bulk materials to generate nanometer-scale features (Malik et al., 2023). Top-down manufacturing has been used to make computer chips for decades. Manufacturers strive to improve the quickness and effectiveness of each "generation" of microchips. The production of graphene-based (rather than silicon-based) microchips has the potential to transform the industry. Bottom-up nanomanufacturing creates things one atom at a time or molecule by molecule. Tech companies are experimenting with quantum dots and other nanomaterials to create transistors and other electrical devices using individual molecules. These atom-thick transistors might herald the future of the microchip industry.

Note: AFMs scan a nanostructure with a very small probe—a cantilever with a very small tip. The diameter of the tip is barely a few nanometers. The cantilever moves when the tip approaches the sample being studied due to atomic forces between the tip and the sample's surface. On the other hand, Ms work by sending an electrical signal between the microscope's tip (which is made up of a single atom) and the surface of the sample being scanned. The tip travels up and down to maintain a steady signal and distance from the sample.

10.3　NANOSENSORS AND DATA COLLECTION

Nanosensors play a pivotal role in modern smart farming, revolutionizing the way we monitor and understand agricultural systems at a microscale level. These miniature devices are designed to detect and quantify various parameters and conditions within the farming environment, offering real-time data for informed decision-making (Figure 10.1). Built with nanoscale components and materials, nanosensors possess unique properties that enable them to provide highly sensitive, selective, and accurate measurements. Their compact size and versatility make them suitable for integration into diverse agricultural applications, ranging from soil analysis to plant health monitoring and beyond.

The main idea behind nanosensors is to capture and translate the complex biological and environmental signals in agriculture into measurable data. By utilizing nanosensors, farmers and researchers gain precise insights into soil fertility, nutrient levels, moisture content, temperature fluctuations, and other vital factors influencing crop growth and health. These sensors operate based on a variety of sensing mechanisms, such as optical, electrical, or chemical principles, tailored to specific target analytes or environmental parameters. The data collected by nanosensors can be wirelessly transmitted to centralized systems for analysis and interpretation. Integrating ML algorithms with nanosensor data enables the development of predictive models and decision support systems, empowering farmers to optimize resource allocation, minimize waste, and enhance overall agricultural productivity.

The taxonomy of nanosensors plays a crucial role in organizing and categorizing these miniature devices based on their underlying principles and functionalities. By establishing a systematic classification, researchers and practitioners gain a clearer understanding of the different types of nanosensors available for application in smart farming. This taxonomy is essential for several reasons. First, the taxonomy provides a structured framework for classifying nanosensors according to their sensing mechanisms and properties. It enables researchers to identify and differentiate between various types of nanosensors, such as optical, electrical, chemical, mechanical, magnetic, biosensors, and gas/environmental sensors. This categorization helps in comprehending the unique advantages, limitations, and operational principles associated with each type of nanosensor. Second, the taxonomy aids in comparing and selecting nanosensors for specific agricultural applications. Each category within the taxonomy represents a distinct set of nanosensors with specific characteristics and

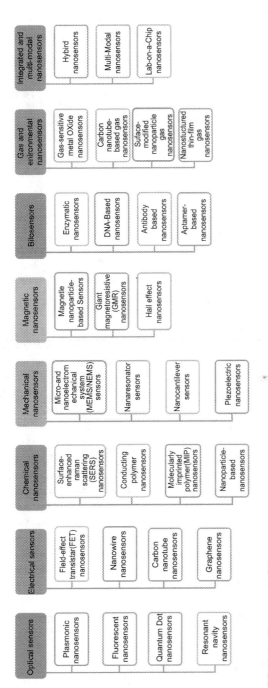

FIGURE 10.1 Taxonomy of Nanosensors.

performance metrics. Researchers and practitioners can refer to taxonomy to identify the most suitable nanosensors based on the parameters they wish to measure, such as soil fertility, moisture content, temperature, gas concentrations, or biomolecular interactions. This systematic approach facilitates informed decision-making regarding sensor selection and deployment in smart farming systems. Further, the taxonomy of nanosensors fosters knowledge sharing and collaboration within the scientific community. By using a standardized classification system, researchers can communicate their findings, methodologies, and advancements more effectively. It promotes the exchange of information, facilitates benchmarking, and enables researchers to build upon existing work in a structured manner. Additionally, a shared taxonomy enhances interdisciplinary collaboration among experts from diverse fields, such as nanotechnology, agriculture, and data science, fostering innovation and the development of novel sensor designs and applications.

To sum up, the taxonomy of nanosensors serves as a vital organizational tool for understanding, comparing, and selecting the most appropriate sensors for smart farming applications. By providing a systematic framework, it enables researchers to navigate through the diverse landscape of nanosensors, facilitating knowledge sharing, collaboration, and advancements in the field.

10.3.1 Optical Nanosensors

Optical nanosensors represent cutting-edge technology with significant potential in various fields, including smart farming. These miniature devices harness the unique optical properties of nanomaterials to detect, quantify, and monitor a wide range of analytes and parameters in agricultural systems. By leveraging principles such as plasmon resonance, fluorescence, quantum effects, and optical interference, optical nanosensors offer exceptional sensitivity, selectivity, and real-time monitoring capabilities. They can be engineered to target specific analytes, including nutrients, pollutants, pathogens, and environmental factors, enabling precise data collection for informed decision-making in agriculture. Whether integrated into soil monitoring systems, water quality assessments, or plant health monitoring setups, optical nanosensors empower farmers to optimize resource management, enhance crop productivity, and foster sustainable farming practices. With their versatility and potential for integration with data analytics platforms, optical nanosensors pave the way for data-driven precision agriculture, enabling farmers to make data-informed choices and cultivate resilient and efficient agricultural systems.

10.3.1.1 Plasmonic Nanosensors

Plasmonic nanosensors utilize the unique properties of plasmon resonance to detect and analyze target analytes. They employ noble metal nanoparticles, such as gold or silver, which exhibit strong localized surface plasmon resonance (LSPR) effects. The interaction between the plasmonic nanoparticles and the analyte leads to measurable changes in their optical properties, such as absorbance or scattering spectra. Plasmonic nanosensors are highly sensitive and can be used for various applications, including detecting biomolecules, monitoring chemical reactions, and analyzing environmental pollutants.

Plasmonic nanosensors have shown great potential in data collection and monitoring in smart farming. By leveraging their ability to interact with analytes and produce measurable changes in optical properties, plasmonic nanosensors enable real-time monitoring of key parameters in agricultural systems. These sensors can be integrated into smart farming setups to measure analytes such as nutrients, pesticides, or heavy metals in soil, water, or plant samples. The collected data can be transmitted wirelessly to a central monitoring system, providing valuable insights into the quality of soil, water, and overall environmental conditions. The ability of plasmonic nanosensors to provide rapid, sensitive, and selective measurements makes them a promising tool for precision agriculture, allowing farmers to make informed decisions about resource allocation, crop health, and environmental sustainability.

10.3.1.2 Fluorescent Nanosensors

Fluorescent nanosensors rely on the emission and detection of fluorescent signals to quantify target analytes. They typically consist of fluorescent dyes or quantum dots that undergo changes in their emission characteristics upon interacting with the analyte of interest. This change can be due to fluorescence quenching, enhancement, or a shift in emission wavelength. Fluorescent nanosensors are widely used in bioimaging, environmental monitoring, and food safety applications due to their high sensitivity, specificity, and imaging capabilities.

Fluorescent nanosensors offer exceptional capabilities for data collection and monitoring in smart farming applications. These sensors can be engineered to specifically target and detect analytes of interest, including biological indicators or environmental pollutants. By incorporating fluorescent dyes or quantum dots, they enable the sensitive and real-time monitoring of various parameters in agricultural systems. Fluorescent nanosensors can be deployed in soil, water, or plant samples to measure parameters like pH, temperature, nutrient levels, or the presence of specific pathogens. The emitted fluorescent signals can be captured using specialized detectors or imaging systems, providing valuable data for decision-making in precision agriculture. The ability to collect and analyze data from fluorescent nanosensors helps optimize resource utilization, detect disease outbreaks, and monitor the effectiveness of agricultural interventions.

10.3.1.3 Quantum Dot Nanosensors

Quantum dot (QD) nanosensors are a specific type of fluorescent nanosensor that utilizes semiconductor nanoparticles called quantum dots. These nanoscale crystals possess unique optical properties, including size-dependent tunable emission wavelengths and high quantum yield. QD nanosensors offer advantages such as high brightness, photostability, and multiplexing capabilities, enabling simultaneous detection of multiple analytes. They find applications in cellular imaging, disease diagnosis, and DNA detection.

QD nanosensors offer significant advantages for data collection and monitoring in smart farming. Their unique optical properties, such as tunable emission wavelengths and high quantum yield, enable precise and sensitive measurements of target analytes. QD nanosensors can be utilized to detect and monitor parameters like pH, temperature, or the presence of specific biomarkers in agricultural samples. The emitted fluorescence from the quantum dots can be quantified using spectroscopic techniques or imaging systems. By integrating QD nanosensors into smart farming platforms, farmers can continuously collect data on soil conditions, crop health, and environmental factors. This data can be used to optimize irrigation schedules, nutrient management, and disease control strategies, leading to improved crop productivity and resource efficiency.

10.3.1.4   Resonant Cavity Nanosensors

Resonant cavity nanosensors exploit the principle of optical interference within a resonant cavity structure to detect changes in the refractive index or thickness of the surrounding medium. These sensors typically consist of a micro- or nanoscale cavity with high-quality factor (Q-factor) optical modes. When the analyte interacts with the resonant cavity, it alters the cavity's optical path length, leading to changes in the resonant wavelengths or intensities. Resonant cavity nanosensors are used in label-free biosensing, environmental monitoring, and chemical detection applications.

Resonant cavity nanosensors offer unique opportunities for data collection and monitoring in smart farming applications. These sensors rely on optical interference within a resonant cavity structure, enabling precise detection and quantification of changes in the surrounding medium. Resonant cavity nanosensors can be designed to monitor parameters like refractive index, analyte concentration, or temperature in agricultural systems. By tracking the shifts in resonant wavelengths or intensities, these sensors provide valuable data on soil moisture levels, nutrient concentrations, or the presence of specific molecules. The collected data can be wirelessly transmitted to a central monitoring system, allowing farmers to gain real-time insights into the environmental conditions and make informed decisions about irrigation, fertilization, or pest control. Resonant cavity nanosensors contribute to data-driven agriculture by enabling continuous and non-destructive monitoring of key parameters, promoting sustainable farming practices and efficient resource utilization.

10.3.2   Electrical Nanosensors

Electrical nanosensors represent a remarkable technological advancement with wide-ranging applications, including in the field of smart farming. These nanoscale devices leverage the unique electrical properties of materials such as nanowires, carbon nanotubes, and graphene to detect and monitor various parameters in agricultural systems. Electrical nanosensors can measure factors such as pH, temperature, humidity, and the presence of specific analytes or pathogens with remarkable sensitivity and specificity. By integrating these nanosensors into smart farming platforms, farmers can gain real-time insights into soil conditions, plant health, and environmental factors crucial for optimal crop growth. The small size and high surface-to-volume ratio of electrical nanosensors enable their integration into wearable devices, wireless sensor networks, and precision agriculture systems. With their ability to collect accurate and continuous data, electrical nanosensors empower farmers to make data-driven decisions, enhance resource efficiency, and implement targeted interventions to maximize crop yield while minimizing environmental impact. By combining the principles of nanotechnology and electrical engineering, electrical nanosensors pave the way for transformative advancements in smart farming, facilitating sustainable and intelligent agricultural practices.

10.3.2.1 Field-Effect Transistor Nanosensors

Field-effect transistor (FET) nanosensors are nanoscale devices that utilize the field-effect principle to detect and quantify various analytes in smart farming applications. These sensors consist of a nanoscale transistor structure, typically based on materials such as nanowires, graphene, or other two-dimensional materials. The FET nanosensor operates by modulating the conductivity or charge carrier density in response to the presence of the target analyte. This modulation can be achieved through the interaction between the analyte and the nanoscale transistor's active sensing region, which can be functionalized with specific receptors or sensing elements. By measuring the changes in electrical properties, such as current or voltage, FET nanosensors can provide sensitive and selective detection of analytes, including gases, biomolecules, or environmental parameters.

FET nanosensors play a crucial role in data collection and monitoring in smart farming. By integrating these nanosensors into agricultural systems, farmers can continuously monitor and collect real-time data on key parameters. For example, FET nanosensors can be employed to measure soil moisture levels, temperature, or nutrient concentrations. The changes in electrical properties detected by the FET nanosensors are converted into measurable signals, which can be wirelessly transmitted to a central monitoring system. This enables farmers to remotely access and analyze the collected data, gaining insights into the dynamic conditions of the farm. The continuous monitoring capability of FET nanosensors allows for timely interventions, precise irrigation scheduling, and optimal resource allocation. By leveraging FET nanosensors for data collection and monitoring, smart farming systems can achieve enhanced efficiency, improved crop health, and sustainable agricultural practices.

10.3.2.2 Nanowire Nanosensors

Nanowire nanosensors are nanoscale devices composed of semiconductor nanowires that enable the detection and quantification of analytes in smart farming. These nanosensors leverage the unique electrical properties of nanowires, such as their high surface-to-volume ratio and quantum confinement effects, to provide highly sensitive and selective measurements. Nanowire nanosensors can be functionalized with receptors or probes specific to the target analytes of interest. When the analyte interacts with the functionalized nanowire surface, it induces changes in the electrical conductance or other electrical properties, enabling the detection and measurement of the analyte.

In smart farming, nanowire nanosensors play a crucial role in data collection and monitoring. These nanosensors can be utilized for a wide range of applications, such as detecting pollutants, monitoring soil pH, or measuring the presence of specific pathogens. The high sensitivity of nanowire nanosensors allows for precise detection, even at low concentrations. The collected data from these nanosensors can be integrated into smart farming systems, providing farmers with real-time information about soil quality, environmental conditions, and the presence of harmful agents. With their small size and compatibility with wireless sensor networks, nanowire nanosensors offer the advantage of distributed sensing, enabling the monitoring of multiple locations simultaneously. By leveraging nanowire nanosensors for data collection and monitoring, farmers can make informed decisions regarding fertilization, disease control, and resource management, leading to improved crop productivity, reduced environmental impact, and sustainable farming practices.

10.3.3 Chemical Nanosensors

Chemical nanosensors are at the forefront of technological advancements in various fields, including the realm of smart farming. These nanoscale devices harness the unique chemical properties of nanoparticles, molecularly imprinted polymers (MIPs), and conducting polymers to detect and analyze a wide range of analytes in agricultural systems. Chemical nanosensors can selectively and sensitively monitor parameters such as nutrient levels, pesticide residues, soil fertility, and water quality. They operate on principles such as surface plasmon resonance, molecular recognition, or conductance changes to capture and quantify target analytes. By integrating chemical nanosensors into smart farming technologies, farmers can obtain real-time data on crucial chemical parameters, enabling precise monitoring and informed decision-making. These nanosensors provide valuable insights into environmental conditions, assist in optimizing resource utilization, and aid in the detection of contaminants or disease outbreaks. Chemical nanosensors hold great promise for sustainable agriculture, promoting efficient resource management, and facilitating the production of high-quality, safe food with minimized environmental impact.

10.3.3.1 Nanoparticle-Based Nanosensors

Nanoparticle-based nanosensors are a category of chemical nanosensors that utilize nanoparticles as the sensing elements. These nanosensors are designed to detect and quantify specific analytes or environmental parameters in smart farming applications. Nanoparticles, such as metal oxides, quantum dots, or surface-modified nanoparticles, can be functionalized with receptors or probes that selectively bind to the target analytes. When the analyte interacts with the functionalized nanoparticles, it induces changes in the optical, electrical, or magnetic properties of the nanoparticles, enabling the detection and measurement of the analyte. Nanoparticle-based nanosensors offer high sensitivity, specificity, and rapid response times, making them suitable for various applications, including detecting pollutants, monitoring nutrient levels, or assessing soil health in smart farming.

Nanoparticle-based nanosensors play a vital role in data collection and monitoring in smart farming. By integrating these nanosensors into agricultural systems, farmers can obtain real-time information on key chemical parameters. For instance, nanoparticle-based nanosensors can be employed to monitor soil fertility, detect the presence of harmful contaminants, or assess water quality. The interactions between the target analytes and the functionalized nanoparticles generate measurable signals that can be captured and quantified. The collected data can be transmitted wirelessly to a central database or monitoring system, allowing farmers to analyze and interpret the information in real time. This enables data-driven decision-making for optimizing fertilizer application, managing soil health, and implementing timely interventions. By leveraging nanoparticle-based nanosensors for data collection and monitoring, smart farming systems can achieve improved resource management, reduced environmental impact, and enhanced crop productivity.

10.3.3.2   Molecularly Imprinted Polymer Nanosensors

MIP nanosensors are a class of chemical nanosensors that utilize synthetic polymer materials with specific molecular recognition capabilities. MIPs are designed to mimic the binding sites of target molecules, allowing them to selectively capture and detect specific analytes in complex samples. MIP nanosensors are created through a process known as molecular imprinting, where the target analyte is used as a template during the polymer synthesis, resulting in the formation of cavities or binding sites that are complementary to the target analyte's shape, size, and functional groups. When the target analyte comes into contact with the MIP nanosensor, it selectively binds to the imprinted sites, leading to detectable changes in electrical, optical, or mechanical properties that can be measured and quantified. MIP nanosensors offer high selectivity, stability, and reusability, making them valuable tools for detecting and monitoring specific analytes in smart farming.

In smart farming, MIP nanosensors play a significant role in data collection and monitoring. These nanosensors can be tailored to target various analytes of agricultural importance, such as pesticides, mycotoxins, or specific plant pathogens. By integrating MIP nanosensors into agricultural systems, farmers can obtain real-time data on the presence and concentration of target analytes in their crops, soils, or water sources. The selective binding between the analyte and the MIP nanosensor generates measurable signals that can be translated into quantitative information about the analyte's concentration. This data enables farmers to make informed decisions about pesticide application, disease management, and food safety. The high selectivity and stability of MIP nanosensors contribute to accurate and reliable monitoring, reducing the risk of false positives or false negatives. By leveraging MIP nanosensors for data collection and monitoring, smart farming systems can improve crop quality, minimize environmental contamination, and promote sustainable agricultural practices.

10.3.4   Mechanical Nanosensors

Mechanical nanosensors are paving the way for transformative advancements in smart farming. These nanoscale devices utilize mechanical properties, such as deflection, resonance, and vibration, to detect and monitor a range of parameters in agricultural systems. Nanocantilevers, nanoresonators, and micro- and nanoelectromechanical systems (MEMS/NEMS) are examples of mechanical nanosensors that enable precise measurements of factors such as soil compaction, moisture levels, plant growth, and environmental conditions. The inherent sensitivity of mechanical nanosensors allows for the detection of minute changes in these parameters. By integrating mechanical nanosensors into smart farming applications, farmers gain access to real-time data on soil health, irrigation needs, and plant stress, enabling them to make data-driven decisions for optimized crop growth and resource management. These nanosensors provide valuable insights into the physical dynamics of agricultural systems, empowering farmers to maximize yields, reduce waste, and promote sustainable farming practices. With their ability to capture nanoscale mechanical changes, mechanical nanosensors hold tremendous potential for revolutionizing precision agriculture and creating more efficient, resilient, and environmentally friendly food production systems.

10.3.4.1 Nanocantilever Sensors

Nanocantilever sensors are mechanical nanosensors that utilize the bending or deflection of nanoscale cantilevers to detect and quantify analytes in smart farming. These sensors consist of thin and flexible cantilever beams, typically made of materials such as silicon or polymers. When the target analyte interacts with the functionalized surface of the nanocantilever, it induces a mechanical stress or adsorption that causes the cantilever to bend. The bending can be measured as a change in electrical resistance, capacitance, or optical signal, allowing for the detection and measurement of the analyte. Nanocantilever sensors offer high sensitivity, fast response times, and the ability to detect a wide range of analytes. They can be functionalized with specific receptors or probes to target analytes such as pathogens, toxins, or environmental parameters.

Nanocantilever sensors play a vital role in data collection and monitoring in smart farming. By integrating these nanosensors into agricultural systems, farmers can obtain real-time information on various parameters. For example, nanocantilever sensors can be utilized to monitor soil compaction, moisture levels, or the presence of specific pathogens. The deflection of the nanocantilevers due to the interaction with the analyte generates measurable signals that can be converted into quantitative data. This data can be wirelessly transmitted to a central monitoring system, allowing farmers to remotely access and analyze the information. The continuous monitoring capability of nanocantilever sensors enables farmers to make data-driven decisions regarding irrigation scheduling, soil management, and disease control. By leveraging nanocantilever sensors for data collection and monitoring, smart farming systems can achieve optimized resource utilization, enhanced crop health, and improved agricultural productivity.

10.3.4.2 Nanoresonator Sensors

Nanoresonator sensors are mechanical nanosensors that rely on the resonant frequency or vibration of nanoscale resonators to detect and quantify analytes in smart farming. These sensors consist of tiny structures, such as beams, cantilevers, or strings, with specific dimensions and mechanical properties. When the target analyte interacts with the resonator, it changes the mass or stiffness, resulting in a shift in the resonant frequency or amplitude of vibration. This change can be detected and measured, allowing for the identification and quantification of the analyte. Nanoresonator sensors offer high sensitivity, fast response times, and the ability to detect minute changes in the surrounding environment. They can be engineered to target specific analytes, including gases, pollutants, or environmental parameters.

In smart farming, nanoresonator sensors play a significant role in data collection and monitoring. These sensors can be deployed to monitor air quality, greenhouse gas emissions, or the presence of specific gases in agricultural systems. The changes in resonant frequency or vibration amplitude provide real-time data on the concentration and variations of the target analytes. This data can be integrated into smart farming systems, enabling farmers to monitor and analyze environmental conditions and make informed decisions. Nanoresonator sensors can be used for precision agriculture, facilitating targeted interventions for improving crop health, optimizing irrigation, and minimizing environmental impact. With their small size, high sensitivity, and compatibility with wireless sensor networks, nanoresonator sensors offer the advantage of distributed sensing, enabling the monitoring of multiple locations simultaneously. By leveraging nanoresonator sensors for data collection and monitoring, farmers can implement data-driven strategies for resource management, crop protection, and sustainable farming practices.

10.3.5 MAGNETIC NANOSENSORS

Magnetic nanosensors are at the forefront of technological advancements in smart farming, offering unique capabilities for monitoring and detecting various parameters in agricultural systems. These nanoscale devices utilize magnetic properties and phenomena, such as magnetic nanoparticles and magnetoresistive effects, to sense and quantify factors such as soil moisture, temperature, magnetic fields, and the presence of contaminants. Magnetic nanosensors provide high sensitivity, fast response times, and the ability to operate in complex environments. By integrating magnetic nanosensors into smart farming applications, farmers can gain real-time data on soil conditions, environmental factors, and the presence of specific analytes. This information enables precise monitoring of crop health, resource management, and the implementation of targeted interventions. Magnetic nanosensors offer the potential for noninvasive, label-free detection, allowing for cost-effective and efficient monitoring of agricultural systems. Their versatility and compatibility with wireless sensor networks make them valuable tools for enhancing crop productivity, optimizing irrigation, and ensuring the overall sustainability of farming practices. Through the integration of magnetic nanosensors, smart farming is poised to enter a new era of precision agriculture, where data-driven decision-making and optimized resource utilization can contribute to increased yields and reduced environmental impact.

10.3.5.1 Magnetic Nanoparticle-Based Sensors

Magnetic nanoparticle-based sensors are a category of magnetic nanosensors that utilize nanoparticles with magnetic properties to detect and quantify analytes in smart farming. These sensors consist of magnetic nanoparticles, typically made of materials such as iron oxide, coated with specific receptors or probes that selectively bind to the target analytes. When the target analyte interacts with the functionalized magnetic nanoparticles, it induces changes in the magnetic properties, such as magnetization or magnetic susceptibility. These changes can be detected and measured using techniques like magnetoresistance or magnetic relaxation, enabling the detection and quantification of the analyte. Magnetic nanoparticle-based sensors offer high sensitivity, selectivity, and the ability to detect a wide range of analytes. They can be applied in various smart farming applications, such as detecting contaminants, monitoring water quality, or assessing soil health.

Magnetic nanoparticle-based sensors play a crucial role in data collection and monitoring in smart farming. By integrating these nanosensors into agricultural systems, farmers can obtain real-time data on key parameters and analytes. For instance, magnetic nanoparticle-based sensors can be employed to monitor heavy metal concentrations in soil, detect the presence of pesticides or toxins, or assess the quality of irrigation water. The interactions between the target analytes and the functionalized magnetic nanoparticles generate measurable changes in the magnetic properties that can be quantified. The collected data from these nanosensors can be wirelessly transmitted to a central monitoring system, allowing farmers to analyze and interpret the information. This enables data-driven decision-making for optimizing agricultural practices, reducing environmental impact, and ensuring food safety. By leveraging magnetic nanoparticle-based sensors for data collection and monitoring, smart farming systems can achieve improved resource management, enhanced crop productivity, and sustainable agricultural practices.

10.3.5.2 Giant Magnetoresistive Nanosensors

Giant magnetoresistive (GMR) nanosensors are another category of magnetic nanosensors that utilize the magnetoresistive effect to detect and quantify analytes in smart farming. GMR nanosensors consist of thin layers of ferromagnetic or ferrimagnetic materials separated by nonmagnetic spacer layers. When the target analyte interacts with the GMR nanosensor, it induces changes in the electrical resistance due to the magnetoresistive effect. These changes in resistance can be measured and correlated with the concentration or presence of the analyte. GMR nanosensors offer high sensitivity, rapid response times, and compatibility with miniaturization, making them suitable for various smart farming applications, such as detecting gases, monitoring environmental parameters, or assessing soil health.

GMR nanosensors play a significant role in data collection and monitoring in smart farming. These nanosensors can be utilized to monitor and quantify key parameters in agricultural systems, such as gas concentrations or variations in environmental conditions. The changes in electrical resistance induced by the interaction of the target analyte with the GMR nanosensor provide real-time data on the presence and concentration of the analyte. This data can be integrated into smart farming systems, allowing farmers to monitor and analyze environmental conditions, optimize resource management, and make informed decisions. GMR nanosensors contribute to data-driven precision agriculture by enabling real-time monitoring and remote sensing capabilities. With their high sensitivity and compatibility with wireless sensor networks, GMR nanosensors enable distributed sensing and continuous data collection in multiple locations simultaneously. By leveraging GMR nanosensors for data collection and monitoring, farmers can improve crop health, optimize irrigation, and promote sustainable farming practices.

10.3.6 BIOSENSORS

Biosensors have emerged as powerful tools revolutionizing the field of smart farming. These sensing devices combine the principles of biology and nanotechnology to detect and analyze biological components or processes in agricultural systems. Biosensors can be designed to target specific biomarkers, enzymes, DNA sequences, or antibodies, enabling the detection of pathogens, pests, diseases, or nutrient deficiencies. By leveraging biological interactions, biosensors provide high specificity and sensitivity in real-time monitoring. They offer rapid and accurate results, allowing farmers to make informed decisions promptly. Biosensors can be integrated into wearable devices, handheld devices, or automated systems for on-site analysis or remote monitoring. With the ability to rapidly identify and quantify biological targets, biosensors contribute to early detection of plant diseases, precise nutrient management, and timely intervention strategies. The integration of biosensors in smart farming holds immense potential for optimizing agricultural practices, improving crop yield, and ensuring the sustainability of agricultural systems while reducing the use of chemical inputs and promoting environmentally friendly farming practices.

10.3.6.1 Enzymatic Nanosensors

Enzymatic nanosensors are a category of biosensors that utilize enzymes as the recognition element to detect and quantify analytes in smart farming. These nanosensors consist of nanoscale structures, such as nanoparticles or nanowires, functionalized with specific enzymes that selectively interact with the target analytes. When the target analyte is present, it undergoes a specific enzymatic reaction that produces a measurable signal, such as a change in electrical, optical, or electrochemical properties. Enzymatic nanosensors offer high specificity, sensitivity, and the ability to detect a wide range of analytes. They can be tailored to detect various parameters in smart farming, including nutrients, pesticides, or pathogens. Enzymatic nanosensors play a crucial role in data collection and monitoring by providing real-time information on the presence and concentration of analytes in agricultural systems. These nanosensors can be integrated into smart farming setups to continuously monitor soil conditions, water quality, or plant health. The interactions between the target analytes and the enzymes on the nanosensor surface generate measurable signals that can be converted into quantitative data. By wirelessly transmitting this data to a central monitoring system, farmers can gain insights into the dynamic conditions of their farms. Enzymatic nanosensors enable data-driven decision-making, allowing farmers to optimize resource allocation, implement targeted interventions, and ensure the overall health and productivity of their crops.

10.3.6.2 DNA-Based Nanosensors

DNA-based nanosensors are biosensors that utilize DNA molecules as the recognition element to detect and quantify analytes in smart farming. These nanosensors employ DNA sequences or aptamers that are specifically designed to bind with the target analytes of interest. When the analyte interacts with the DNA-based nanosensor, it triggers a conformational change or binding event that generates a detectable signal, such as fluorescence, electrochemical response, or colorimetric change.

DNA-based nanosensors offer high selectivity, sensitivity, and the ability to detect various analytes, including pathogens, genetic markers, or environmental parameters. In smart farming, DNA-based nanosensors play a crucial role in data collection and monitoring by providing real-time information on key biological factors. These nanosensors can be employed to monitor plant diseases, detect specific pathogens or genetically modified organisms, or assess soil microbial diversity. The interactions between the target analytes and the DNA-based nanosensors generate measurable signals that can be quantified. The collected data can be wirelessly transmitted to a central monitoring system, allowing farmers to remotely access and analyze the information. This enables data-driven decision-making, facilitating prompt interventions, disease management, and the implementation of appropriate agricultural practices. By leveraging DNA-based nanosensors for data collection and monitoring, smart farming systems can optimize crop health, minimize risks, and ensure sustainable agricultural practices.

10.3.7 Gas and Environmental Nanosensors

Gas and environmental nanosensors are revolutionizing the monitoring and assessment of air quality and environmental conditions in smart farming. These nanoscale devices utilize nanomaterials, such as metal oxides, carbon nanotubes, or surface-modified nanoparticles, to detect and quantify various gases, pollutants, and environmental parameters. Gas nanosensors can rapidly detect and identify gases such as carbon dioxide, methane, nitrogen dioxide, or volatile organic compounds that are crucial for assessing soil health, crop growth, and environmental impact. Environmental nanosensors enable the monitoring of parameters like temperature, humidity, and atmospheric pressure. These nanosensors offer high sensitivity, selectivity, and fast response times, making them ideal for real-time monitoring in agricultural settings. By integrating gas and environmental nanosensors into smart farming systems, farmers gain valuable insights into air quality, greenhouse gas emissions, and microclimate conditions. This data allows for the implementation of precise and targeted interventions to optimize crop growth, minimize environmental impact, and promote sustainable farming practices. Gas and environmental nanosensors play a critical role in advancing data-driven smart farming, enabling farmers to make informed decisions for efficient resource management and environmental stewardship.

10.3.7.1 Gas Nanosensors

Gas nanosensors are a category of nanosensors that are specifically designed to detect and quantify gases in the environment. These nanosensors utilize various nanomaterials, such as metal oxides, carbon nanotubes, or quantum dots, to detect specific gases or variations in environmental parameters. Gas nanosensors operate based on the principle that the interaction between the target gas and the nanosensor surface induces changes in electrical, optical, or chemical properties, resulting in a measurable signal. These nanosensors offer high sensitivity, selectivity, and rapid response times, making them suitable for monitoring air quality, detecting emissions, or assessing environmental conditions. In smart farming, gas nanosensors play a crucial role in data collection and monitoring by providing real-time information on air quality, greenhouse gas emissions, or volatile compounds in agricultural systems. These nanosensors can be integrated into smart farming setups to continuously monitor gas concentrations, identify pollutant sources, or detect the presence of harmful gases. The interactions between the target gases and the nanosensor surface generate measurable signals that can be converted into quantitative data. By wirelessly transmitting this data to a central monitoring system, farmers can gain insights into the quality of the air surrounding their crops, identify potential risks, and implement appropriate mitigation strategies. Gas nanosensors enable data-driven decision-making, allowing farmers to optimize crop growth, ensure environmental sustainability, and promote the health and well-being of their agricultural systems.

10.3.7.2   Environmental Nanosensors

Environmental nanosensors encompass a wide range of nanosensors designed to monitor various environmental parameters in smart farming. These nanosensors can detect and quantify factors such as temperature, humidity, light intensity, soil moisture, or water quality. They utilize nanomaterials with specific properties, such as nanoparticles, nanowires, or thin films, to sense and measure environmental conditions. Environmental nanosensors operate by translating changes in the target parameters into measurable signals, such as electrical resistance, optical properties, or capacitance. They offer high sensitivity, accuracy, and the ability to operate in diverse environmental conditions. In smart farming, environmental nanosensors play a significant role in data collection and monitoring by providing real-time information on crucial environmental factors. These nanosensors can be deployed in agricultural systems to continuously monitor microclimate conditions, soil moisture levels, or water quality parameters. The measurable signals generated by the interactions between the environmental factors and the nanosensor surface can be wirelessly transmitted to a central monitoring system. This enables farmers to gain insights into the dynamic conditions of their farms and make data-driven decisions. By leveraging environmental nanosensors for data collection and monitoring, smart farming systems can optimize irrigation, implement targeted interventions, and ensure the overall health and productivity of crops. Environmental nanosensors contribute to resource-efficient and sustainable farming practices by providing precise monitoring of key environmental parameters.

10.4   WIRELESS COMMUNICATION AND NETWORKING OF NANOSENSORS IN AGRICULTURE

Wireless communication and networking play a pivotal role in the integration and operation of nanosensors in agriculture. The deployment of nanosensors throughout agricultural systems generates vast amounts of data that need to be efficiently collected, transmitted, and analyzed. Wireless communication enables seamless connectivity between nanosensors and the central monitoring system, facilitating real-time data collection and monitoring. Nanosensors equipped with wireless communication capabilities can transmit data wirelessly, eliminating the need for physical connections and enabling flexible placement in the field. Wireless networking allows nanosensors to form a distributed network, enabling simultaneous data collection from multiple locations within the agricultural system. This network can be established through protocols such as Wi-Fi, Zigbee, or LoRaWAN, ensuring reliable and secure communication between nanosensors and the central monitoring system.

The wireless communication and networking of nanosensors in agriculture provide numerous benefits. First, it enables remote data access, allowing farmers to monitor and analyze agricultural parameters without being physically present in the field. This remote access facilitates timely decision-making, as farmers can promptly respond to changes in environmental conditions or crop health. Second, wireless communication allows for real-time monitoring and feedback, enabling rapid intervention in the case of abnormalities or critical events. Farmers can receive instant alerts or notifications regarding potential issues, allowing them to take immediate action. Moreover, wireless networking enables data aggregation and integration from multiple nanosensors, providing a comprehensive view of the agricultural system. This collective data can be analyzed to identify patterns, trends, and correlations, assisting farmers in making informed decisions and optimizing resource management.

10.5   NANOBOTS AND PRECISION AGRICULTURE

Nanobots, also known as nanorobots or nanomachines, are tiny robots at the nanoscale level with immense potential to revolutionize precision agriculture. These minuscule machines are typically a few nanometers to a few micrometers in size and can be designed to perform specific tasks with exceptional precision. In precision agriculture, nanobots offer a range of applications, from autonomous navigation and targeted delivery of inputs to real-time monitoring and analysis. These nanoscale wonders hold promise for optimizing resource utilization, enhancing crop productivity, and implementing sustainable farming practices. By harnessing the power of nanobots in precision agriculture, farmers can embark on a new era of data-driven, efficient, and environmentally friendly farming.

One of the most compelling aspects of nanobots in precision agriculture is their ability to autonomously navigate through complex environments and deliver inputs precisely where needed. ML algorithms play a pivotal role in empowering nanobots with intelligent decision-making capabilities. By integrating ML algorithms with onboard sensors and imaging systems, nanobots can identify key areas within the field requiring specific treatments, such as fertilization or pesticide application. These algorithms enable nanobots to adapt and optimize their navigation routes, avoiding obstacles and efficiently reaching their target destinations. Through ML-driven decision-making, nanobots can reduce input wastage, minimize environmental impact, and improve the overall efficiency of agricultural operations.

Soil health is a critical factor in precision agriculture, and nanobots offer a groundbreaking solution for accurate soil sampling and analysis. Equipped with specialized sensors, nanobots can collect soil samples at various locations with high precision and minimal disruption to the soil structure. These nanobots can analyze soil properties, such as nutrient levels, pH, and organic matter content, providing real-time data to farmers. By accessing comprehensive soil data, farmers can fine-tune their nutrient management strategies and implement tailored solutions for each specific area of their fields. The integration of nanobots for soil sampling and analysis offers a proactive approach to soil health management, contributing to improved crop yield, reduced fertilizer usage, and enhanced soil fertility.

Nanobots' miniature size and versatility enable them to continuously monitor a wide range of parameters within the agricultural environment. These nanoscale agents can gather real-time data on factors such as temperature, humidity, soil moisture, and plant health. By transmitting this data wirelessly to a central monitoring system, farmers gain valuable insights into the dynamic conditions of their fields. The real-time monitoring and feedback provided by nanobots enable farmers to promptly respond to changes, identify potential issues, and implement precise interventions. This proactive approach to data-driven farming ensures timely decision-making, promoting optimal resource utilization and increased resilience to environmental fluctuations.

Nanobots, in conjunction with ML algorithms, hold immense potential in transforming traditional irrigation systems into intelligent and efficient smart irrigation networks. By monitoring soil moisture levels, nanobots can provide real-time data on plant water needs. ML algorithms can analyze this data, along with weather forecasts and historical trends, to optimize irrigation schedules and deliver water precisely when and where needed. The integration of nanobots and ML in smart irrigation systems empowers farmers to practice deficit irrigation, minimizing water wastage while ensuring optimal plant hydration. Moreover, this intelligent irrigation approach contributes to water conservation, reduced energy consumption, and improved crop water-use efficiency, ultimately fostering sustainable agricultural practices.

10.6   NANOMATERIALS FOR ENHANCED CROP PERFORMANCE

Nano-enhanced fertilizers have emerged as a promising solution to improve nutrient efficiency and enhance crop performance. These fertilizers are designed to deliver nutrients more effectively to plants, thereby reducing nutrient losses and optimizing nutrient uptake. The nanoscale properties of these fertilizers, such as high surface area and reactivity, allow for enhanced nutrient solubility and controlled release. Additionally, nano-enhanced fertilizers can be functionalized with specific coatings or ligands to target nutrient delivery to plant roots. By employing nanotechnology, these fertilizers can significantly increase nutrient use efficiency and promote sustainable agricultural practices.

Nano fertilizers come in various forms, each designed to address specific agricultural needs. One common type is nanocomposite fertilizers, where nanoparticles are incorporated into conventional fertilizers to enhance their performance. Another type is nano-coated fertilizers, where nutrients are encapsulated within nanoscale coatings, enabling slow and controlled nutrient release. Furthermore, nanoparticle-based fertilizers, such as nanoscale nutrient carriers, deliver nutrients directly to plant roots or foliage. The characteristics of nano fertilizers, including their particle size, surface charge, and nutrient-loading capacity, can be tailored to optimize nutrient delivery and plant response. These versatile nano fertilizers hold great potential for targeted nutrient application, leading to improved crop yields and reduced environmental impact.

Nano fertilizers employ various mechanisms to enhance nutrient delivery to plants. In the case of nanocomposite fertilizers, the nanoparticles facilitate improved nutrient solubility and prevent nutrient leaching, ensuring efficient nutrient uptake by plants. Nano-coated fertilizers use nanoscale coatings to control nutrient release rates, matching the nutrient demand of plants over time. Nanoparticle-based fertilizers offer targeted delivery, as nanoparticles can be functionalized to interact with specific plant receptors or root exudates, ensuring nutrient uptake at critical growth stages. The unique properties of nanomaterials, combined with their controlled release mechanisms, make nano fertilizers a cutting-edge solution to address nutrient inefficiencies in agriculture.

ML algorithms have a significant role to play in optimizing the dosing and application strategies for nano fertilizers. ML models can analyze vast datasets, including soil properties, weather conditions, and crop requirements, to determine the ideal dosage and timing of nano fertilizers for each specific field. By employing ML-based dosing and application strategies, farmers can ensure precise and targeted nutrient delivery, reducing wastage and environmental contamination. Additionally, ML can aid in the optimization of nano fertilizer compositions by identifying the most effective combination of nanomaterials and nutrients for specific crop types and environmental conditions. This data-driven approach maximizes the efficiency of nano fertilizers and promotes sustainable agricultural practices.

In addition to enhancing nutrient delivery, nanomaterials offer innovative solutions for pest and disease management in agriculture. Nanopesticides are engineered to deliver active ingredients, such as pesticides or fungicides, with enhanced efficiency and reduced environmental impact. The nanoscale formulations allow for controlled release and targeted delivery of the active compounds, resulting in improved efficacy against pests and pathogens. Furthermore, nanopesticides can overcome issues of pesticide resistance and reduce the need for frequent applications. These smart nanomaterials open new avenues for sustainable pest management practices, safeguarding crop health while minimizing chemical residues in the environment.

Smart nanomaterials have the ability to release nutrients in response to specific triggers, such as soil moisture levels or plant root exudates. These nanomaterials offer controlled release mechanisms that match the nutrient demand of plants over time. For instance, nanoscale hydrogels can respond to soil moisture conditions and gradually release nutrients during dry periods, ensuring sustained plant nutrition. Similarly, stimuli-responsive nanomaterials can release nutrients in response to changes in pH or temperature, optimizing nutrient availability for plants. The controlled release capabilities of smart nanomaterials contribute to efficient nutrient utilization and minimize nutrient losses, thereby promoting resource-efficient and sustainable crop production.

While nanomaterials offer significant benefits in enhancing crop performance, it is crucial to consider their potential environmental and safety implications. The use of nanomaterials in agriculture requires careful assessment of their behavior in the environment, including their potential for mobility, persistence, and bioaccumulation. Furthermore, the safety of nanomaterial exposure to humans and nontarget organisms should be thoroughly evaluated. Implementing appropriate risk assessments and regulatory measures will ensure the responsible and sustainable use of nanomaterials in agriculture. By prioritizing environmental considerations and safety aspects, farmers can confidently embrace nanotechnology as a valuable tool in precision agriculture, leading to improved crop yields and environmental stewardship.

10.7 MACHINE LEARNING MEETS NANOTECHNOLOGY

The integration of ML and nanotechnology in agriculture holds immense potential to revolutionize farming practices. ML algorithms can analyze vast amounts of data collected from nanosensors and nanomaterials, enabling data-driven decision-making and precise control over agricultural processes. By combining the high sensitivity and real-time data capabilities of nanosensors with ML's predictive power, farmers can gain valuable insights into crop health, environmental conditions, and nutrient requirements. This synergistic approach empowers farmers to implement precision agriculture strategies, optimize resource utilization, and achieve sustainable and efficient crop production.

Nanosensors equipped with ML algorithms offer real-time monitoring and prediction capabilities, providing farmers with a continuous stream of data on various parameters such as soil moisture, nutrient levels, and pest infestations. ML algorithms analyze the sensor data and identify patterns and trends, enabling the prediction of potential challenges or opportunities in crop growth. This real-time monitoring and prediction empower farmers to take proactive measures, such as adjusting irrigation schedules or implementing pest management strategies, to optimize crop performance. By leveraging the combined power of ML and nanosensors, farmers can make data-driven decisions with speed and precision, maximizing yields and minimizing risks.

Nanotechnology offers a wide array of nanomaterials with diverse properties that can be applied in agriculture for various purposes, including nutrient delivery, pest management, and environmental monitoring. ML algorithms can analyze the performance of different nanomaterials in specific agricultural contexts, optimizing their dosages, application methods, and timing for each crop type and growth stage. This ML-driven optimization ensures that nanomaterials are used efficiently, reducing waste and environmental impact. By harnessing the potential of ML to fine-tune nanomaterial applications, farmers can enhance crop performance, improve resource efficiency, and promote sustainable agricultural practices.

The integration of ML and nanotechnology paves the way for autonomous decision-making and control systems in smart farming. Autonomous robots and nanobots equipped with ML algorithms can navigate through fields, collect data from nanosensors, and analyze the information in real time. These intelligent systems can autonomously adjust irrigation levels, nutrient applications, and pest control measures based on ML predictions and environmental conditions. The result is a self-regulating and responsive farming ecosystem that optimizes agricultural inputs, minimizes labor requirements, and maximizes yields. This autonomous decision-making and control systems enable farmers to manage large-scale operations efficiently and adopt sustainable practices that ensure the health of crops and the environment.

Several case studies have demonstrated the successful integration of ML and nanotechnology in agriculture, showcasing the transformative impact of this combination.

From ML-guided dosing and application of nanofertilizers to nanobots performing real-time soil analysis and precise nutrient delivery, these case studies highlight the potential of ML-driven nanotechnology in promoting sustainable farming practices. Furthermore, ML algorithms have been employed to analyze data from nanosensors and nanopesticides to optimize pest management strategies, leading to reduced chemical use and enhanced crop protection. These case studies serve as valuable examples of how ML and nanotechnology can work together to address agricultural challenges, improve crop performance, and foster environmental stewardship.

10.8   AGRICULTURAL NANOTECHNOLOGY

The agricultural industry is facing huge issues such as fast climate change, decreased soil fertility, macro and micronutrient insufficiency, excessive use of chemical fertilizers and pesticides, and heavy metal presence in the soil (Moulick et al., 2020). But, as the world's population has grown, so has food consumption. Nanotechnology has made significant contributions to sustainable agriculture by increasing crop yield and recovering and improving soil quality. Apart from these domains, the impact of nanotechnology may be observed in the food and agriculture industries, whether it's about decreasing the negative environmental consequences of agricultural techniques, assuring food supply, or inventing nanotech-based tools and equipment to improve production. Let's take a look at the numerous ways in which nanotechnology is supporting agriculture.

10.8.1   AGRICULTURE'S SUSTAINABLE INTENSIFICATION

Sustainable Intensification is the notion of improving output while minimizing environmental impact. The strategy is to choose a combination of methods while keeping the biophysical, social, economic, and cultural circumstances in mind. Novel nanomaterials for boosting productivity, such as inorganic, lipid, and polymeric nanoparticles, have been produced for this aim. They can be used in intelligent nano-systems developed for nutrient immobilization and release into the soil. Also, it may aid in lowering eutrophication by limiting the quantity of nitrogen transferred to groundwater (Mukhopadhyay, 2014). In addition, the use of nanoherbicides and nanopesticides to control weeds and pests has considerably enhanced agricultural output. Nanoparticles of various sorts, such as polymeric nanoparticles and inorganic nanoparticles, are used in nanoherbicide compositions. Herbicide distribution channels have been devised by scientists in a variety of ways. Poly(epsilon-caprolactone) nanoparticles, for example, contain the pesticide atrazine. This nanocapsule demonstrated strong control of the targeted species, decreased genotoxicity, and had the potential to greatly reduce atrazine mobility in the soil.

10.8.2   EXPERIMENTS ON A LONGER TIME SCALE

Long-term experiments are required to demonstrate the influence of various techniques on soil properties necessary for sustainability and to provide substantial information on this goal. Nanochemical development has become a potential pest control and plant growth agent in the United States. Plant development needs the use of fertilizers. Nanomaterials work as fertilizers and may have properties such as crop improvement and lower eco-toxicity. Plants can provide a significant pathway for bioaccumulation into the food chain. The most recent agricultural innovations encompass nanoparticle uses, which allow pesticides to be employed safely and effectively on plants.

Several researchers documented the effects of various nanoparticles on phytotoxicity and plant growth, including plant growth, magnetite (Fe_3O_4) nanoparticles, zinc, alumina, and zinc oxide on the seed germination and root growth of the five higher plant species, cucumber, corn, lettuce, rape, and radish; silver nanoparticles and seedling growth in wheat; and nanoparticles of ZnO, NiO, MnO, FeO, and AlO. The silver nanoparticles can promote wheat growth and yield. The 25 ppm soluble nitrogen phosphorus given to the soil had significant impacts on wheat production and growth.

10.8.3 Pesticides and Herbicides at the Nanoscale

Each year, microbiological (virus, fungus, and bacterium) illnesses cause significant losses in the agriculture sector. Certain antibacterial nanomaterials aid in preventing microbial infestations. *Colletotrichum gloeosporioides*, *Fusarium oxysporum*, *F. solani*, and *Dematophora necatrix* are a few of the typical pathogenic fungi that cause infections. Several nanoparticles, including copper and nickel ferrite nanoparticles, have potent antifungal properties and are utilized to control illness. Chitosan nanoparticles, zinc oxide nanoparticles, and silica nanoparticles are beneficial in the treatment of viral infections, including the mosaic virus for tobacco, potatoes, and alfalfa.

Due to its severe production losses, the fungus' longer survival in the soil, and the emergence of resistant strains, fusarium wilt is regarded as the most damaging disease of lettuce and tomatoes in numerous nations (Prasad et al., 2017). The use of resistant cultivars and pesticides can help to reduce the illness to some extent. Nonetheless, the creation and prevalence of the most recent pathogenic races continue to be a problem, and the chemicals utilized are frequently both pricy and ineffective. In recent years, using nanomaterials as a control method for plant diseases has become an option. Ghidan et al. (2019) have created Nanoparticles of magnesium oxide (MgO). In a greenhouse setting, he also examined how various doses affected the green peach aphid. MgO is an important inorganic substance used in a variety of applications, including photo electronic materials, the removal of hazardous waste, improved ceramics, fire retardants, and adsorbents. As a result, many methods and pathways for making magnesium oxide nanoparticles (MgONPs) have been reported. Using nontoxic neem leaf extract, acacia gum, and citrus limon leaf extract, green techniques were employed to create Magnesium hydroxide (MgOH).

The spherical virus in particular contains naturally occurring nanomaterials, as do other plant viruses. The tiniest plant viruses currently understood are the 18 nanometer-diameter satellite tobacco necrosis viruses. Plant viruses are made up of double- or single-stranded DNA/RNA as the genome is enclosed in a protein sheath. They must be used in nanotechnology because of their capacity to infect, transmit the host cell's nucleic acid genome to a specific spot, replicate, package the nucleic acid, and exit the host cell precisely and in an organized fashion. Recent research by Sleem

(2022) reviewed the use of plant viruses as bio templates for nanomaterials and their applications.

10.8.4 SOIL QUALITY, IRRIGATION, AND NANOFERTILIZERS

To identify soil diseases, scientists can quantitatively compare how much oxygen "good microorganisms" and "bad microorganisms" in the soil take in during respiration. Two sensors are submerged in a suspension of soil sample in a buffer solution, one impregnated with "good microorganisms" and the other with "pathogenic organisms," and the oxygen consumption data by the two bacteria is recorded (Bala et al., 2023). It has been claimed that hydrogels, nano-clays, and nano-zeolites improve soil water-holding capacity and allow for delayed water release. As a result, the hydric scarcity is reduced, especially during the agricultural season. Similar approaches are also beneficial in reforesting degraded regions that have lost soil fertility. Moreover, organic materials such as polymers and carbon nanotubes, as well as inorganic components such as nanometals and metal oxides, can be employed to absorb pollutants, boosting soil remediation capability while decreasing time and cost.

Automation of irrigation systems is critical for sensible agricultural operations, particularly in locations where water is scarce. Sensor technology has the potential to significantly increase the efficiency of water consumption (Kalita et al., 2021). When coupled with autonomous irrigation controls, they can determine soil water tension in real time. Those characteristics contribute to sustainable irrigation, which involves evaluating climatic and agricultural growth elements, which is otherwise fairly difficult to do.

To combat nutrient insufficiency in plants, scientists employed nanotechnology to build a smart delivery system that would distribute nutrients in a gradual and regulated manner to the targeted spot. Nanofertilizers boost crop output by increasing the plant's availability of vital nutrients. The use of nanophosphorus fertilizers in dry environments resulted in a considerable improvement in millet and cluster bean yields. Crop output has also been boosted by chitosan nanoparticle suspensions containing nitrogen, phosphorus, and salt.

10.8.5 MONITORING AND GROWTH STIMULATION OF PLANTS

Nanosensors, as opposed to analytical biosensors, are a potent instrument with enhanced capabilities. These are analytical instruments having at least one dimension of less than 100 nm that are meant to monitor physiochemical parameters in difficult-to-reach locations. Nanotubes, nanowires, nanoparticles, and nanocrystals are utilized to improve the signal transduction elicited by sensing components in response to similar-sized biological and chemical analytes.

Carbon nanotubes and nanoparticles of silver, zinc oxide, and other metals can be quite beneficial in rehabilitating plant development by ensuring that nutrients are used properly by the plants. Nevertheless, success is dependent on a variety of variables, including plant species susceptibility and other criteria such as nanomaterial concentration, composition, size, and chemical qualities (Indira et al., 2021). Furthermore, understanding the interaction between plants and nanomaterials is critical in determining how much influence is made in the operation. New methodologies can be devised for this aim, and various analytical techniques including microscopy, magnetic resonance imaging, and fluorescence spectroscopy can be employed.

10.8.6 NANOTECHNOLOGY IN THE PRODUCTION OF SEEDS

Crop production depends on several factors, one of which is seed quality. Carbon nanotubes have been seen to penetrate the tough tomato seed coat and dramatically increase the germination index and plant development. Similar to this, spraying maize and soybean seeds with a multiwall carbon nanotube resulted in a higher germination rate. To improve the germination index of plants, many nano treatments are available.

The process of producing seeds is challenging, especially for crops that are pollinated by the wind since pollen can travel great distances (Pandey, 2018). Humidity, wind speed, and temperature are a few variables that affect pollen burden. A particularly efficient method of guaranteeing genetic purity is to identify pollen loads that induce contamination. To lessen contamination, bionanosensors can also be employed to identify particularly contaminated pollen.

10.8.7 FOOD SUPPLY CHAIN USING NANOTECHNOLOGY

The management of the many stages of the food supply chain, such as crop growth, harvesting, food processing, transportation, packaging, and distribution, can benefit from the use of nanosensors. To promote sustainable agricultural practices, they are employed as instruments to evaluate soil characteristics to detect pathogens or anticipate the absorption of nitrogen. Moreover, these may be used to track and adjust the amount of pesticides used on crops.

The food industry has taken the lead in producing foods with high nutritional value. For example, they use highly impermeable packaging nanomaterials to shield foods from UV rays and provide additional strength to keep the food shielded from the environment, enhancing and extending their shelf life (Neme et al., 2021). Pathogens, gases, and chemicals may all be found in food thanks to the use of nanosensors. In contemporary jargon, this form of packaging is frequently referred to as smart packaging. Several studies claim that individuals do not accept nanoparticles' direct participation in food because of some of the dangerous aspects. As a result, various safety precautions have to be offered to reduce risk and ensure human security.

REFERENCES

Alishah Aratboni, H., Rafiei, N., Mehdizadeh Allaf, M., Abedini, S., Naseema Rasheed, R., Seif, A., Barati, B., Wang, S., & Morones-Ramírez, J. R. (2023). Nanotechnology: An outstanding tool for increasing and better exploitation of microalgae valuable compounds. *Algal Research, 71,* 103019. https://doi.org/10.1016/J.ALGAL.2023.103019

Bala, M., Kumar Bansal, S., & Fatima, F. (2023). Nanotechnology: A boon for agriculture. *Materials Today: Proceedings, 73,* 267–270. https://doi.org/10.1016/J.MATPR.2022.09.498

Ghidan, A. Y., Antary, T. M. A., Ghidan, A. Y., & Antary, T. M. A. (2019). Applications of nanotechnology in agriculture. *Applications of Nanobiotechnology.* https://doi.org/10.5772/INTECHOPEN.88390

Indira, M., Krupanidhi, S., Venkateswarulu, T. C., Pallavi, G., & Peele, K. A. (2021). Current aspects of nanotechnology: Applications in agriculture. *Nanotechnology in the Life Sciences*, 73–99. https://doi.org/10.1007/978-3-030-61985-5_3/TABLES/5

Kalita, R., Saha, O., Rahman, N., Tiwari, S., & Phukon, M. (2021). Nanotechnology in Agriculture. *Nanobiotechnology*, 101–116. https://doi.org/10.1007/978-3-030-73606-4_5

Malik, S., Muhammad, K., & Waheed, Y. (2023). Nanotechnology: A revolution in modern industry. *Molecules*, *28*(2), 661. https://doi.org/10.3390/MOLECULES28020661

Moulick, R. G., Das, S., Debnath, N., & Bandyopadhyay, K. (2020). Potential use of nanotechnology in sustainable and 'smart' agriculture: Advancements made in the last decade. *Plant Biotechnology Reports*, *14*(5), 505–513. https://doi.org/10.1007/S11816-020-00636-3/FIGURES/4

Mukhopadhyay, S. S. (2014). Nanotechnology in agriculture: Prospects and constraints. *Nanotechnology, Science and Applications*, *7*(2), 63–71. https://doi.org/10.2147/NSA.S39409

Neme, K., Nafady, A., Uddin, S., & Tola, Y. B. (2021). Application of nanotechnology in agriculture, postharvest loss reduction and food processing: Food security implication and challenges. *Heliyon*, *7*(12), e08539. https://doi.org/10.1016/J.HELIYON.2021.E08539

Pandey, G. (2018). Challenges and future prospects of agri-nanotechnology for sustainable agriculture in India. *Environmental Technology & Innovation*, *11*, 299–307. https://doi.org/10.1016/J.ETI.2018.06.012

Prasad, R., Bhattacharyya, A., & Nguyen, Q. D. (2017). Nanotechnology in sustainable agriculture: Recent developments, challenges, and perspectives. *Frontiers in Microbiology*, *8*. https://doi.org/10.3389/FMICB.2017.01014

Puolamaa, M. (2006). *The appropriateness of existing methodologies to assess the potential risks associated with engineered and adventitious products of nanotechnologies*. EUAA: European Union Agency for Asylum.

Sleem, A. (2022). Empowering smart farming with machine intelligence: An approach for plant leaf disease recognition. *Sustainable Machine Intelligence Journal*, *1*(1), 1–11. https://doi.org/10.61185/SMIJ.2022.1013

Index

A

abnormal, 22, 82–84, 182, 187

abnormalities, 26, 105, 114, 189, 225, 272

accelerometers, 114, 120, 121, 250

accessibility, 16, 51, 227, 254

accessible, 5, 16, 21, 100, 142, 148, 149, 181, 194, 213, 216, 218, 219, 226, 230, 237, 248

accountability, 44, 97, 242

accuracy, 6, 16, 19, 21, 29, 48, 50, 51, 54, 63, 71, 73, 81, 100, 127, 130, 141, 142, 149, 151, 152, 170, 174–176, 180, 183, 186, 187, 189, 193, 195, 197, 198, 203, 212, 214, 215, 220, 224, 228, 233, 271

accurate, 15, 16, 27, 50, 52, 77, 78, 88, 92, 94, 96, 99–104, 108, 112–116, 118, 121, 123, 128–130, 132–134, 140–142, 145, 180, 183, 186–188, 191, 196, 211, 214, 224, 225, 232, 239–241, 246–248, 251, 258, 262, 265, 269, 272

activation, 92–95, 198, 200

activities, 2, 4, 5, 8, 15, 23, 26, 32, 41, 44, 47, 89–91, 103, 129, 210, 211, 213, 221, 231, 235, 240

activity, 12, 18, 19, 22, 106, 114, 125, 180, 181, 185, 192, 210, 225, 234

adaptive, 12, 14, 64, 65, 149, 182, 188, 194, 229, 232

additionally, 3–5, 11, 13, 15, 16, 18, 23, 51, 67, 71, 77, 95, 100, 103, 108, 113, 116, 125–127, 129–132, 140, 141, 143, 148, 154, 170, 180–182, 184, 187, 189, 209, 213–216, 219, 223–228, 231, 234, 239, 243, 246, 260, 273, 274

adjustments, 12, 67, 94, 125, 139, 188, 222, 229, 236

administration, 19, 28, 41, 42, 44, 110, 241, 250

advanced, 7, 10, 21, 51, 57, 63, 67, 70, 94–97, 99, 101, 107, 111–114, 117, 118, 120, 121, 123, 128, 129, 131, 133, 135–137, 141, 143, 148, 149, 182, 184, 194, 197, 209, 211, 215, 216, 218, 220–227, 230, 232, 238, 239, 246, 251, 253

advancements, 6, 41, 44, 94, 95, 113, 179, 181, 195, 209, 210, 212, 217, 219, 253, 254, 260, 263, 264, 265, 267, 280

advantages, 8, 21, 22, 26, 28, 35, 37, 42, 64–66, 68–70, 79, 90, 96, 99, 124, 128, 141, 181, 186–189, 209, 215, 216, 222, 233–235, 239, 240, 245, 258, 261, 264, 267

adverse, 10, 82, 129, 143, 150, 188, 211, 216, 218

aerial, 9, 18, 20, 21, 23, 112, 116, 118, 124, 145, 188, 195, 196, 216, 217, 219, 221, 225, 234

affecting, 4, 10, 13, 57, 77, 111, 140, 151, 236

agent, 48, 90, 91, 276

agribusinesses, 8, 18, 37, 215, 216, 240

agricultural, 3–27, 29, 37, 38, 40–43, 45–47, 51, 52, 57, 61, 68, 69, 71, 75, 77, 92, 96, 97, 99–105, 107, 109–112, 115–125, 128–136, 138–143, 145, 147–149, 179, 180, 183, 186, 191–194, 196, 197, 207, 209–214, 216–240, 242–245, 247, 250–254, 258–279

agriculture, 3–8, 12, 13, 15–25, 27, 37, 40, 42, 43, 47, 68, 69, 75, 77, 95–102, 108–113, 117–125, 129, 131, 133–136, 138–140, 142–145, 147–150, 178, 183, 190–192, 195–197, 207, 209–250, 252–255, 257–264, 265–272, 273–277, 279

agronomists, 11, 13, 130, 148, 149

agronomy, 20, 23, 24, 136, 208, 232

AI, 6, 8, 18, 24, 26, 27, 37, 38, 42, 48, 49, 89, 95–97, 138, 139, 144, 145, 149, 179, 180, 182–186, 189, 192–196, 207, 209–212, 218, 221, 232, 233, 235, 237–241, 243, 245, 247, 249, 251–253

AI-based, 18, 139, 144, 145, 179, 186, 194, 207

AI-driven, 182, 193, 233, 235, 247, 251, 252

air, 15, 102, 103, 115, 122, 141, 151, 187, 188, 225, 241, 267, 270, 271

algorithms, 6, 10, 18, 21, 36, 40, 41, 47–53, 48–51, 57, 62, 71, 74, 78–80, 79–81, 82–88, 90, 91, 93, 94, 95, 98, 100, 127, 128, 130, 131, 133, 139, 144, 148, 149, 151, 152, 174, 175, 176, 179–189, 184, 186, 193, 196, 197, 209, 211–215, 217, 221–223, 225–231, 233, 246, 249, 251, 258, 272–276

all, 2, 7, 8, 17, 18, 21, 23, 26, 27, 29, 31, 33–35, 38, 41, 43–45, 47, 48, 79, 81, 83, 87, 89, 90, 93, 117, 126, 142, 146, 148, 168, 174, 179, 183, 185, 192, 199, 210, 211, 220, 233–238, 242–245, 248, 249, 279

allocation, 14, 16, 44, 99, 112, 113, 116, 123, 124, 129, 131, 134, 135, 139, 143, 149, 182, 185, 212, 215, 216, 233, 247, 258, 261, 263, 268

allowing, 6, 9, 11, 13, 14, 16, 18, 21, 22, 27, 33, 35, 38, 45, 49, 76, 79, 94, 95, 99, 103, 105, 107, 108, 110, 117, 119–123, 125, 128–131, 139, 141, 144, 148, 173, 180, 182, 184–187, 189, 196, 205, 211, 212, 214, 215, 218–226, 228, 233–236, 238, 240, 246, 251, 257, 261, 262, 265–272